Studies in Emotion and Social Interaction

Paul Ekman
University of California, San Francisco

Klaus R. Scherer
Justus-Liebig-Universität Giessen

General Editors

Structures of Social Action

Studies in Emotion and Social Interaction

This series is jointly published by the Cambridge University Press and the Editions de la Maison des Sciences de l'Homme, as part of the joint publishing agreement established in 1977 between the Fondation de la Maison des Sciences de l'Homme and the Syndics of the Cambridge University Press.

Cette collection est publiée en co-édition par Cambridge University Press et les Editions de la Maison des Sciences de l'Homme. Elle s'intègre dans le programme de co-édition établi en 1977 par la Fondation de la Maison des Sciences de l'Homme et les Syndics de Cambridge University Press.

Other books in the series:

Klaus R. Scherer and Paul Ekman (eds.) *Handbook of Methods in Nonverbal Behavior Research*
Paul Ekman (ed.) *Emotion in the Human Face*

Structures of Social Action

Studies in Conversation Analysis

Edited by J. Maxwell Atkinson *and* John Heritage

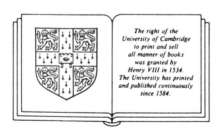

The right of the
University of Cambridge
to print and sell
all manner of books
was granted by
Henry VIII in 1534.
The University has printed
and published continuously
since 1584.

Cambridge University Press

Cambridge

London   New York   New Rochelle

Melbourne   Sydney

Editions de la Maison des Sciences de l'Homme

Paris

Published by the Press Syndicate of the University of Cambridge
The Pitt Building, Trumpington Street, Cambridge CB2 1RP
32 East 57th Street, New York, NY 10022, USA
10 Stamford Road, Oakleigh, Melbourne 3166, Australia
and
Editions de la Maison des Sciences de l'Homme
54 Boulevard Raspail, 75270 Paris Cedex 06

First published 1984
Reprinted 1986

Printed in Great Britain at the University Press, Cambridge

Library of Congress Cataloging in Publication Data
Main entry under title:
Structures of social action.
(Studies in emotion and social interaction)
Includes index.
1. Conversation. 2. Oral communication.
I. Atkinson, J. Maxwell (John Maxwell) II. Heritage,
John. III. Series.
P95.45.S86 1984 001.54'2 84–12169

ISBN 0 521 24815 9 hard covers
ISBN 0 521 31862 9 paperback

Contents

vi   Contents

Preface

This book is the result of a collaboration that began when, as co-convenors of the Sociology of Language Study Group of the British Sociological Association, we organized the Social Science Research Council/British Sociological Association International Conference on Practical Reasoning and Discourse Processes, which was held 2–6 July 1979 at St. Hugh's College, Oxford. All the contributors to the present book, with the exception of the late Harvey Sacks, were among those who participated at the conference, and earlier versions of Chapters 5, 8 and 14 were originally presented there. Although the book is not a full collection of the proceedings, it is the result of a cooperative endeavor that began at the Oxford conference.

In acknowledging our debt to all those who helped to make the conference a memorable intellectual experience, we would like to record our thanks to the Sociology and Social Administration Committee of the (British) Social Science Research Council (SSRC) for the award of a grant that made it possible. Our gratitude to SSRC also extends beyond this grant to a longer-term appreciation of the active and constructive part it has played in facilitating the development of conversation analytic research in Britain. For it may be noted that no fewer than eight of the twelve contributors to this book have, at one time or another, had the benefit of financial support from SSRC, as research students, as recipients of project grants, or as members of its research staff. It is never easy to establish new approaches to social science research, especially if the concerns of those approaches are perceived as being "pure" or "fundamental," rather than "applied" or "policy-oriented." Where the number of active researchers is relatively small, funding even on quite a modest scale can have a major impact on the extent to which it is possible to develop such work. Conversation analysis in Britain has benefited greatly from the flexibility and responsiveness of SSRC funding policies,

vii

and we hope very much that this book will add to the growing evidence that such investments are beginning to pay dividends.

Of the many colleagues whose assistance made this book possible, we are grateful to Emanuel Schegloff, who, in his capacity as literary executor, gave us the necessary permissions to include two previously unpublished pieces by Harvey Sacks. We also thank Gail Jefferson, who selected and edited the original transcripts of his lectures. Her comments, together with those of Anita Pomerantz, on earlier drafts of our introduction were also much appreciated, though we have probably taken less notice of them than we should have done. The fact that Gail Jefferson contributed two original papers is only the most visible evidence of a commitment to the present project that was undertaken more seriously and generously than editors can reasonably expect.

Neither the original Oxford conference nor this book would have become a reality without the help of Noël Blatchford of the Centre for Socio-Legal Studies, who, among other things, carried out the onerous task of preparing camera-ready copy of the transcripts. We are also grateful to Sue Allen-Mills of Cambridge University Press for her patience, advice, and general support during the various stages leading up to publication.

J. Maxwell Atkinson
John Heritage

Transcript notation

The transcript notation used in this book, and in conversation analytic research more generally, has been developed by Gail Jefferson. It is a system that continues to evolve in response to current research interests, and for some of the chapters included in the present collection it has been necessary to incorporate symbols for representing various non-vocal activities, such as gaze, gestures, and applause.

Previous experience suggests that it is useful to group symbols with reference to the phenomena they represent.

1. Simultaneous utterances

Utterances starting simultaneously are linked together with either double or single left-hand brackets:

```
[[      Tom:      [[I used to smoke a lot when I was young
        Bob:      [[I used to smoke Camels
```

2. Overlapping utterances

When overlapping utterances do not start simultaneously, the point at which an ongoing utterance is joined by another is marked with a single left-hand bracket, linking an ongoing with an overlapping utterance at the point where overlap begins:

```
[       Tom:      I used to smoke [a lot
        Bob:                      [He thinks he's real tough
```

The point where overlapping utterances stop overlapping is marked with a single right-hand bracket:

```
]       Tom:      I used to smoke [a lot] more than this
        Bob:                      [I see]
```

3. Contiguous utterances

When there is no interval between adjacent utterances, the second being latched immediately to the first (without overlapping it), the utterances are linked together with equal signs:

```
=        Tom:    I used to smoke a lot=
         Bob:    =He thinks he's real tough
```

The equal signs are also used to link different parts of a single speaker's utterance when those parts constitute a continuous flow of speech that has been carried over to another line, by transcript design, to accommodate an intervening interruption:

```
Tom:    I used to smoke ⌜a lot more than this=
Bob:                    ⌊You used to smoke
Tom:    =but I never inhaled the smoke
```

Sometimes more than one speaker latches directly onto a just-completed utterance, and a case of this sort is marked with a combination of equal signs and double left-hand brackets:

```
          Tom:    I used to smoke a lot=
=[ [      Bob:    =[ [He thinks he's tough
          Ann:       [ [So did I
```

When overlapping utterances end simultaneously and are latched onto by a subsequent utterance, the link is marked by a single right-handed bracket and equal signs:

```
          Tom:    I used to smoke ⌜a lot⌝=
] =       Bob:                    ⌊I see⌋
          Ann:    =So did I
```

4. Intervals within and between utterances

When intervals in the stream of talk occur, they are timed in tenths of a second and inserted within parentheses, either within an utterance:

```
(0.0)  Lil:    When I was (0.6) oh nine or ten
```

or between utterances:

```
Hal:    Step right up
        (1.3)
```

```
Hal:   I said step right up
       (0.8)
Joe:   Are you talking to me
```

A short untimed pause within an utterance is indicated by a dash:

```
-      Dee:   Umm - my mother will be right in
```

Untimed intervals heard between utterances are described within double parentheses and inserted where they occur:

```
((pause)) Rex: Are you ready to order
                 ((pause))
          Pam: Yes thank you we are
```

5. Characteristics of speech delivery

In these transcripts, punctuation is used to mark not conventional grammatical units but, rather, attempts to capture characteristics of speech delivery. For example, a colon indicates an extension of the sound or syllable it follows:

```
co:lon     Ron:   What ha:ppened to you
```

and more colons prolong the stretch:

```
co::lons   Mae:   I ju::ss can't come
           Tim:   I'm so::: sorry re:::ally I am
```

The other punctuation marks are used as follows:

```
.          A period indicates a stopping fall in tone,
           not necessarily the end of a sentence.

,          A comma indicates a continuing intonation,
           not necessarily between clauses of sentences.

?          A question mark indicates a rising inflection,
           not necessarily a question.

?          A combined question mark/comma indicates a rising
,          intonation weaker than that indicated by a
           question mark.

!          An exclamation point indicates an animated
           tone, not necessarily an exclamation.
```

–   A single dash indicates a halting, abrupt
cutoff, or, when multiple dashes hyphenate
the syllables of a word or connect strings
of words, the stream of talk so marked has
a stammering quality.

Marked rising and falling shifts in intonation are indicated by upward
and downward pointing arrows immediately prior to the rise or fall:

↓ ↑   Thatcher: I am however (0.2) very ↓fortunate
                     (0.4) in having (0.6) a ↑mar:vlous
                     dep↓uty

Emphasis is indicated by underlining:

Ann: It happens to be <u>mine</u>

Capital letters are used to indicate an utterance, or part thereof, that is
spoken much louder than the surrounding talk:

Announcer: an the winner: ↓iz:s (1.4) RACHEL ROBERTS
               for Y↑ANKS

A degree sign is used to indicate a passage of talk which is quieter than
the surrounding talk:

o o   M: ·hhhh (.)°Um::°'Ow is yih <u>mother</u>
             by: th'<u>wa:y</u>.h

Audible aspirations (hhh) and inhalations (·hhh) are inserted in the
speech where they occur:

hhh   Pam: An thi(hh)s is for you hhh
·hhh   Don: ·hhhh O(hh) tha(h)nk you rea(hh)lly

A 'gh' placed within a word indicates gutturalness:

gh   J: Ohgh(h)h hhuh <u>huh</u> <u>huh</u> ·huh

A subscribed dot is used as a "hardener." In this capacity it can indicate,
for example, an especially dentalized "t":

dot   J: Was it ↑la:s' night.

Double parentheses are used to enclose a description of some phenomenon with which the transcriptionist does not want to wrestle.

These can be vocalizations that are not, for example, spelled gracefully or recognizably:

```
((   ))          Tom:    I used to ((cough)) smoke a lot
                 Bob:    ((sniff)) He thinks he's tough
                 Ann:    ((snorts))
```

or other details of the conversational scene:

```
                 Jan:    This is just delicious
                         ((telephone rings))
                 Kim:    I'll get it
```

or various characterizations of the talk:

```
                 Ron:    ((in falsetto)) I can do it now
                 Max:    ((whispered)) He'll never do it
```

When part of an utterance is delivered at a pace quicker than the surrounding talk, it is indicated by being enclosed between "less than " signs:

```
>< Steel:        the Guar:dian newspaper looked through >the
                 manifestoes< la:st ↑week
```

6. Transcriptionist doubt

In addition to the timings of intervals and inserted aspirations and inhalations, items enclosed within single parentheses are in doubt, as in:

```
(     )          Ted:    I ('spose I'm not)
                 (Ben):  We all (t-              )
```

Here "spose I'm not," the identity of the second speaker, and "t-" represent different varieties of transcriptionist doubt.

Sometimes multiple possibilities are indicated:

```
                 Ted:    I⌈(spoke to Mark)
                          ⌊('spose I'm not)
                 Ben:    We all try to figure a (tough angle   ) for it
                                                (stuffing girl)
```

When single parentheses are empty, no hearing could be achieved for the string of talk or item in question:

```
   Todd:    My (           ) catching
( ):    In the highest (              )
```

Here the middle of Todd's utterance, the speaker of the subsequent utterance, and the end of the subsequent utterance could not be recovered.

7. Gaze direction

The gaze of the speaker is marked above an utterance, and that of the addressee below it. A line indicates that the party marked is gazing toward the other. The absence of a line indicates lack of gaze. Dots mark the transition movement from nongaze to gaze, and the point where the gaze reaches the other is marked with an X:

```
Beth:    . . . .┌X_____
         Terry- └Jerry's fa┌scinated with elephants
Don:              . . . . .└X_____
```

Here Beth moves her gaze toward Don while saying "Terry"; Don's gaze shifts toward and reaches hers just after she starts to say "fascinated."

If gaze arrives within a pause each tenth of a second within the pause is marked with a dash:

```
Ann:                        . . .┌X_____
         Well (--- ┌-) We coulda used └a liddle, marijuana.=
Beth:              └X_____
```

Here Beth's gaze reaches Ann three-tenths of a second after she has said "Well-," and one-tenth of a second before she continues with "We coulda used. . . ."

Commas are used to indicate the dropping of gaze:

```
Ann:     _____
         Karen has this new hou:se. en it's got all this
Beth:    _____ , , ,
```

Here Beth's gaze starts to drop away as Ann begins to say "new."

Movements like head nodding are marked at points in the talk where they occur:

Ann:
```
        Karen has this new hou:se. en it's got all this
Beth:   _____  , , ,              ((Nod))
```

Here Beth, who is no longer gazing at Ann, nods as the latter says "got."

Asterisks are used in a more ad hoc fashion to indicate particular phenomena discussed in the text. In the following fragment, for example, Goodwin uses them to indicate the position where Beth puts food in her mouth:

Ann:
```
        =like- (0.2) ssilvery:: g-go:ld wwa: ⌈llpaper.
Beth:                            *******  . . ⌊x_____
```

8. Applause

Strings of X's are used to indicate applause, with lower- and uppercase letters marking quiet and loud applause respectively:

```
Audience:   xxXXXXXXXXXXXXxxx
```

Here applause amplitude increases and then decreases.

An isolated single clap is indicated by dashes on each side of the x:

```
Audience:   -x-
```

Spasmodic or hesitant clapping is indicated by a chain punctuated by dashes:

```
Audience:   -x-x-x
```

A line broken by numbers in parentheses indicates the duration of applause from the point of onset (or prior object) to the nearest tenth of a second. The number of X's does *not* indicate applause duration except where it overlaps with talk, as in the second of the following examples:

```
Speaker:    I beg >to support the m↓otion<=
            ⊦-----------(8.0)-------------⊦
Audience:   =x-xxXXXXXXXXXXXXXXXXXXXXXxxxx-x
```

```
Speaker:    THIS ↓WEEK  ⌐SO > THAT YOU CAN STILL MAKE⌐
Audience:              ⌊xx–XXXXXXXXXXXXXXXXXXXXXXXXX⌋ =

Speaker:        ⌐⌐YER MINDS UP<
Audience:     = ⌊⌊XXXXXXXXXXXXXXXXXXX ((edited cut))
```

9. Other transcript symbols

The left-hand margin of the transcript is sometimes used to point to a
feature of interest to the analyst at the time the fragment is introduced in
the text. Lines in the transcript where the phenomenon of interest occurs are frequently indicated by arrows in the left-hand margin. For
example, if the analyst had been involved in a discussion of continuations and introduced the following fragment:

```
     Don:    I like that blue one very much
  →  Sam:    And I'll bet your wife would like it
     Don:    If I had the money I'd get one for her
  →  Sam:    And one for your mother too I'll bet
```

the arrows in the margin would call attention to Sam's utterances as
instances of continuations.

Horizontal ellipses indicate that an utterance is being reported only in
part, with additional speech coming before, in the middle of, or after the
reported fragment, depending on the location of the ellipses. Thus, in
the following example, the parts of Don's utterance between "said" and
"y'know" are omitted:

```
Don:  But I said . . . y'know
```

Vertical ellipses indicate that intervening turns at talking have been
omitted from the fragment:

```
Bob:   Well I always say give it your all

         .

         .

Bob:   And I always say give it everything
```

Codes that identify fragments being quoted designate parts of the
chapter authors' own tape collections.

1. Introduction

JOHN HERITAGE   J. MAXWELL ATKINSON
University of Warwick   *University of Oxford*

The present collection adds to a growing range of studies that report on recent research into naturally occurring social action and interaction undertaken from a conversation analytic perspective. Foreshadowed by the investigative initiatives of Harold Garfinkel and Erving Goffman into the organization of everyday conduct, this perspective was extensively articulated in Harvey Sacks's privately circulated lectures and developed into a distinctive research literature in association with his collaborators, Emanuel Schegloff and Gail Jefferson.

The central goal of conversation analytic research is the description and explication of the competences that ordinary speakers use and rely on in participating in intelligible, socially organized interaction. At its most basic, this objective is one of describing the procedures by which conversationalists produce their own behavior and understand and deal with the behavior of others. A basic assumption throughout is Garfinkel's (1967:1) proposal that these activities – producing conduct and understanding and dealing with it – are accomplished as the accountable products of common sets of procedures.

This objective and its underlying assumption provide a basic means of analysis. Specifically, analysis can be generated out of matters observable in the data of interaction. The analyst is thus not required to speculate upon what the interactants hypothetically or imaginably understood, or the procedures or constraints to which they could conceivably have been oriented. Instead, analysis can emerge from observation of the conduct of the participants. Schegloff and Sacks have summarized the assumptions that guide this form of research, and the analytic resource thus provided:

> We have proceeded under the assumption (an assumption borne out by our research) that in so far as the materials we worked with exhibited orderliness, they did so not only to us, indeed not in the first place for us, but for the co-participants who had produced

them. If the materials (records of natural conversation) were orderly, they were so because they had been methodically produced
by members of the society for one another, and it was a feature of
the conversations we treated as data that they were produced so as
to allow the display by the co-participants to each other of their
orderliness, and to allow the participants to display to each other
their analysis, appreciation and use of that orderliness. Accordingly, our analysis has sought to explicate the ways in which the
materials are produced by members in orderly ways that exhibit
their orderliness and have their orderliness appreciated and used,
and have that appreciation displayed and treated as the basis for
subsequent action. (1973:290)

Conversation analysts have tended to present their findings by showing regular forms of organization in a large variety of materials produced
by a range of speakers. However, the explication of such forms is only
part of the analytic process. Generally, the analyst will also take steps to
demonstrate that the regularities are methodically produced and oriented to by the participants as normatively oriented-to grounds for inference and action. As part of this latter objective, the analysis of "deviant cases" – in which some proposed regular conversational procedure or form is *not* implemented or realized – is regularly undertaken.
Integral to this analysis is the task of describing the role that particular
conversational procedures play in relation to specific interactional activities. Beyond this task lie the wider objectives of describing, wherever
possible given the current state of knowledge, the role that particular
conversational procedures play in relation to one another and to other
orders of conversational and social organization. The pursuit of these
various aims has involved the formulation of a distinctive approach to
data collection and of new attitudes toward its analysis.

1. The collection and analysis of data

Within conversation analysis there is an insistence on the use of materials collected from *naturally occurring* occasions of everyday interaction
by means of audio- and video-recording equipment or film. This policy
contrasts markedly with many of the traditional methods of data collection prominent in the social and behavioral sciences. Most obviously, it
represents a departure both from the use of interviewing techniques in
which the verbal reports of interview subjects are treated as acceptable
surrogates for the observation of actual behavior and from the use of
experimental methodologies in which the social scientist must neces-

sarily manipulate, direct, or otherwise intervene in the subjects' behavior. It also contrasts with observational studies in which data are recorded in field notes or with the use of precoded schedules. Finally, the empirical emphasis of the research program also breaks with those theoretical traditions in which native intuitions, expressed as idealized or invented examples, are treated as an adequate basis for making and debating analytic claims.

A number of factors inform the insistence on the use of recording technologies as a means of data collection over subjects' reports, observers' notes, or unaided intuitions. Anyone who is familiar with conversational materials or who examines the transcripts of talk used in this book will be vividly aware of the limitations of recollection or intuition in generating data by comparison with the richness and diversity of empirically occurring interaction. Virtually none of the data of this volume could conceivably be the product of recollection or intuitive invention, nor, as Sacks points out in Chapter 2, would such invented "data" prove persuasive as *evidence* relevant to the analysis of interaction. Data of this sort can always be viewed as the implausible products of selective processes involving recollection, attention, or imagination.

A parallel range of considerations emerges in connection with the use of experimentally produced data. Experimental procedures are generally successful to the extent that, through experimental manipulation, behavioral variation is limited to those aspects selected for investigation under controlled conditions. In this context, it is the experimenter who must determine the relevant dependent and independent variables, and the experimenter's formulation of these variables will tend to be restricted by what he or she can anticipate on an intuitive basis. Yet without previous exposure to a range of naturally occurring interactional data, the experimenter is unlikely to anticipate the range, scope, and variety of behavioral variation that might be responsive to experimental manipulation, nor will he or she be in a position to extrapolate from experimental findings to real situations of conduct. By the same token, while certain of the experimenter's data may or may not be artifacts of the more general experimental situation in which the data were produced, such influences (if any) can be determined only by systematic comparison with a large corpus of naturally occurring data. The most economical procedure, therefore, has been to work on naturally occurring materials from the outset. Naturally occurring interaction presents an immense range of circumstances – effectively amounting to a "natural laboratory" – for the pursuit of hunches and the investigation of the limits of particular formulations by systematic comparison.

A further, more general issue is raised by the previous observations. Conversation analytic researchers have come to an awareness that only the smallest fraction of what is used and relied on in interaction is available to unaided intuition. Conversation analytic studies are thus designed to achieve systematic analyses of what, at best, is intuitively known and, more commonly, is tacitly oriented to in ordinary conduct. In this context, nothing that occurs in interaction can be ruled out, a priori, as random, insignificant, or irrelevant. The pursuit of systematic analysis thus requires that recorded data be available, not only for repeated observation, analysis, and reanalysis, but also for the public evaluation of observations and findings that is an essential precondition for analytic advance. Therefore in both the original work and its collective assessment, the analytic intuitions of research workers are developed, elaborated, and supported by reference to bodies of data and collections of instances of phenomena. In this process, an analytic culture has gradually developed that is firmly based in naturally occurring empirical materials.

In sum, the use of recorded data serves as a control on the limitations and fallibilities of intuition and recollection; it exposes the observer to a wide range of interactional materials and circumstances and also provides some guarantee that analytic conclusions will not arise as artifacts of intuitive idiosyncrasy, selective attention or recollection, or experimental design. The availability of a taped record enables *repeated* and *detailed* examination of particular events in interaction and hence greatly enhances the range and precision of the observations that can be made. The use of such materials has the additional advantage of providing hearers and, to a lesser extent, readers of research reports with *direct* access to the data about which analytic claims are being made, thereby making them available for public scrutiny in a way that further minimizes the influence of individual preconceptions. Finally, because the data are available in raw form, they are cumulatively reusable in a variety of investigations and can be reexamined in the light of new observations or findings. Each recording necessarily preserves a very substantial range of interactional phenomena, and an initial noticing of any one of these can motivate a search through other data for similar occurrences which were previously overlooked or the significance of which had remained unrecognized. Such a research process is possible only by virtue of the fact that the data-collection procedure is not constrained by a specific research design or by reference to some particular hypothesis.

This approach to data collection and use is closely associated with significant innovations in the way everyday behavior is researched.[1]

Rather than studying single utterances or actions as the isolated products of individuals having particular goals or communicative intents, the analyses presented in this book, without exception, focus on uncovering the *socially organized features of talk in context*, with a major focus on action sequences. Although the central research topic of these essays – conversational interaction – might seem to render this focus on sequence self-recommending, it represents a sufficiently substantial departure from accepted practices, both within linguistics and sociology, to require some further comment.

2. The focus on sequential analysis

The development of speech act theory (Austin 1962; Searle 1969) in linguistics has greatly forwarded the view that utterances can be usefully analyzed as conventionally grounded social actions. However, this viewpoint has developed within a disciplinary matrix which gives analytic primacy to the isolated sentence, and in which sentence analysis is conducted in terms of syntactic and semantic features that are themselves treated as independent of discursive considerations.[2] The net result is an approach to speech acts that in the first place seeks to establish the act accomplished by an utterance considered in isolation – the "literal meaning" of the utterance – and then proceeds to account for variations in the meaning or uptake of the utterance according to variations of the circumstances in which it is uttered (Gordon and Lakoff 1971; Searle 1975).[3] This mode of analysis has been the object of sustained criticism within the literature of conversation analysis from Sacks's earliest lectures onward.[4] Its many difficulties (Levinson 1979, 1981a, 1981b) ultimately derive, as Schegloff (Chapter 3) points out, from the failure of its proponents to grasp that utterances are *in the first instance* contextually understood by reference to their placement and participation within sequences of actions. For conversation analysts, therefore, it is sequences and turns within sequences, rather than isolated sentences or utterances, that have become the primary units of analysis. This focus on participant orientation to the turn-within-sequence character of utterances in conversational interaction has significant substantive and methodological consequences.

At the substantive level, conversation analytic research into sequence is based on the recognition that, in a variety of ways, the production of some current conversational action proposes a here-and-now definition of the situation to which subsequent talk will be oriented. Comparatively straightforward instances of this process occur when a current turn projects a relevant next action, or range of actions, to be accomplished by another speaker in the next turn – a phenomenon generically referenced as the "sequential implicativeness" of a turn's talk (Schegloff and Sacks 1973:296). In its strongest form, this projection of a relevant next action may be accomplished by the production of the first-pair part of an "adjacency-pair" structure (ibid.), such as "greeting–greeting," "question–answer," or "invitation–acceptance/rejection."

Once it is recognized that some current or "first" action projects some appropriate "second," it becomes relevant to examine the various ways in which a second speaker may accomplish such a second, or analyzably withhold its accomplishment, or avoid its accomplishment by undertaking some other activity. If it can then be shown that the producers of the first action deal in systematically organized ways with a variety of alternative seconds (or a noticeably absent second), then it will also be demonstrated that the object of investigation is an institutionalized organization for the activity in question that is systematically oriented to by speakers.

These observations can be generalized outward from the comparatively simple adjacency-pair organization by remarking that virtually every utterance (excluding "response cries" [Goffman 1981] but including initial utterances) occurs at some structurally defined place in talk (see Schegloff, Chapter 3). Thus the vast majority of utterances occur as selections from a field of possibilities made relevant by some prior utterance, and in their turn project a range of possible "nexts." Most utterances, therefore, can be analyzed as dealing with a prior in some way and, among other things, as indicating their producers' preparedness to forward, acquiesce in, or resist the course of action aimed at by an earlier speaker. Self-evidently, considerations concerning the regulation of social relationships are raised by these issues (Goffman 1955, 1963, 1964, 1971). It follows, then, that just as the "literal meaning" of a sentence cannot be determined by reference to a "null context" (Garfinkel 1967; Garfinkel and Sacks 1970; Searle 1979, 1980), so too no empirically occurring utterance ever occurs outside, or external to, some specific sequence. Whatever is said will be said in some sequential context, and its illocutionary force will be determined by reference to what it accomplishes in relation to some sequentially prior utterance or set of utterances. As long as a state of talk prevails, there will be no escape or time-out from these considerations. And, insofar as unfolding sequences and their constituent turns are unavoidable analytic concerns for interactants, they provide a powerful and readily accessible point of entry into the unavoidable contextedness of actual talk.

All of the chapters in the present book deal with the systematically organized workings of interaction sequences. The particular activities studied vary widely from the organization of gaze and bodily comportment in relation to turns at talk (described in the chapters by Schegloff, Goodwin, and Heath); through the sequencing of laughter (Jefferson), particle use (Heritage), the structuring of sequences involving assessments (Pomerantz), proposals (Davidson), invitations (Drew), sequences in which topics are initiated (Button and Casey) or shifted (Jefferson); to the rhetorical techniques of public speakers (Atkinson). In all cases, however, basic structural forms for the activities in question are outlined, their logic is described and variations or more complex cases are discussed. Throughout, the authors show the normative organization of and orientation to the standard sequences as structures of activity and how particular sequential variations can be understood with reference to the ways in which they display a sensitivity to their interactional contexts (e.g., by being specifically designed for some particular recipient [Sacks, Schegloff, and Jefferson 1974:727]). And, although a shorthand "intentionalist" language is employed in these chapters, the perspective focuses on the underlying structures informing the interpretation and treatment of a speaker's action by a recipient and maintains, except in specific cases, a relatively agnostic stance on the question of how far the speaker consciously aimed at some particular interpretation. This agnosticism is consistent with the proposal that the objects of study are institutionalized structures of talk that are oriented to by speakers with varying degrees of reflexive awareness.

3. Sequential organization: methodological aspects

At the methodological level, that speakers understand an utterance by reference to its turn-within-sequence character provides a central resource for both the participants and the overhearing analyst to make sense of the talk. A number of points can be made in this connection.

First, it is a general finding within conversation analytic studies that talk analyzably proceeds on a turn-by-turn basis and that "generally, a turn's talk will be heard as directed to a prior turn's talk, unless special techniques are used to locate some other talk to which it is directed" (Sacks, Schegloff, and Jefferson 1974:728). Moreover, given that each next turn at talk is heard as directed to the prior, its producer will generally be heard to display an analysis, understanding, or appreciation of the prior turn's talk that is exhibited in his or her responsive treatment of it (see Schegloff, Chapter 3).

Thus in the following two sequences the same individual (J) is the recipient of information from different coparticipants about the recent arrival of furniture:

(1) [Rah:B:1:(11):3:(R)]

      A: the two beds'v come this mo:rning. the new
              be:ds. ·ĥhhh An:d uh b't o⌐nly one
      J: →   [↑Ih b't that wz ↓quick
              that wz °quick them coming.°
      A: Not too ba:d. B't thez only one ma:tress ↓with it.

(2) [Rah:B:1:(12):1:(R)]

      I: the things 'ev arrived from Ba:rker:'n
              Stone'ou⌐:se,
      J: [Oh::::.
              (.)
      J: → O⌐h c'n a⌐h c'm rou:nd,h⌐h
      I: [A n '   [Ye⌐s: ⌐please⌐ that's⌐w't=
                                    [ha [h a] ·a : h]
      I: =I wantche tih come rou:nd.

Here it can be noticed that while the two "informings" are rather similar in character, J's subsequent treatment of them evidences quite different analyses of their implicativeness. Whereas she treats the first as the occasion for a comment about the speed with which an order was delivered, she treats the second as implicating that her informant wants her to come and inspect/admire the new furniture by preempting a (possibly) forthcoming invitation (see Drew, Chapter 6, for a discussion of this and related examples).

The point here, and it is a crucial one, is that however a recipient analyzes these informings and whatever the interpretative conclusions of such an analysis, *some conclusion will be displayed in the recipient's next turn at talk.* Thus whereas J's assessment of the events reported in the first informing treats the latter as plain news, her self-invitation in response to the second treats it as implicating her informant's desire to have her come round. And these treatments of the prior turn are available and publicly visible as the means by which first speakers can determine how they were understood. Thus the sequential next-positioned linkage between any two actions is a critical resource by which a first speaker can determine the sense that a second made of his or her utterance. Schegloff and Sacks's observations concerning paired utterances can thus be generalized to next-positioned utterances as well:

By an adjacently produced second, a speaker can show that he understood what a prior aimed at, and that he is willing to go along with that. Also, by virtue of the occurrence of an adjacently produced second, the doer of a first can see that what he intended was indeed understood, and that it was or was not accepted. Also, of course, a second can assert his failure to understand, or disagreement, and, inspection of a second by a first can allow the first speaker to see that while the second thought he understood, indeed he misunderstood. It is then through the use of adjacent positioning that appreciations, failures, correctings, et cetera can themselves be understandably attempted. (Schegloff and Sacks 1973:297–8)[5]

It needs only to be added that, just as a second speaker's analysis and treatment of the prior is available to the first speaker, so it is also available to overhearers of the talk, including social scientists. The latter may thus proceed to analyze turns at talk, together with the analyses and treatments of them that are produced by the parties to the talk, and employ methodologies that fully take account of these analyses and treatments. Students of talk are thus provided with a considerable advantage that is unavailable to analysts of isolated sentences or other "text" materials that cannot be analyzed without hypothesizing or speculating about the possible ways in which utterances, sentences, or texts might be interpreted.

This discussion can now be further generalized by the observation that the second speaker can subsequently, by looking to the next turn in the sequence, determine the adequacy of the understanding and treatment of a prior displayed in his or her own turn. This observation can be pursued by noticing, firstly, that one option pervasively open to the first speaker after any second turn is explicitly to correct or repair any misunderstanding displayed in the second speaker's turn. A rather clear instance of this kind of "third position repair" (Schegloff 1979c) is the following:

(3) |CDHQ:I:52|

```
   A:     Which on::s are closed, an' which ones are open.
   Z:     Most of 'em. This, this ⌈this, this ((pointing))
   A:  →                          ⌊I 'on't mean on the
          shelters, I mean on the roads.
```

In this case, Z's analysis of the prior question as referring to the shelters (as displayed in what he says and the direction pointed to) is explicitly corrected by the first speaker in an overlapping next turn. This example illustrates a general phenomenon, namely, that after any second action the producer of the first action has an opportunity to repair any misunderstanding of the first that may have been displayed in the second. Given the generic availability of this procedure, any second speaker may look to a third action to see whether this opportunity was taken and, if it was not, to conclude that the analysis and treatment displayed in his or her own second turn was adequate. Any third action, therefore, that implements some normal onward development of a sequence confirms the adequacy of the displayed understandings in the sequence so far.[6] By means of this framework, speakers are released from what would otherwise be the endless task of explicitly confirming and reconfirming their understandings of one another's actions.

Viewed in these terms, it can be seen that J's treatments of the informings instanced in (1) and (2) were confirmed as adequate. Thus in (1), her assessment is briefly (and downgradedly [see Pomerantz, Chapter 4]) corroborated by A, who subsequently goes on to detail a misadventure with the delivery of the beds (which was initiated, and then abandoned, in A's first turn). Although, as it turns out in the light of the subsequent detailing, J's assessment was produced a little prematurely, its treatment of the prior informing as plain news is nonetheless confirmed as adequate in the subsequent talk. Similarly, in (2), I's treatment of J's self-invitation confirms that J's "coming round" was indeed what was desired.

It may be added here that these observations concerning the maintenance of intersubjective understanding in talk do not simply apply to occasions in which a second speaker evidences an understanding of the activity (e.g., an invitation, complaint, accusation, etc.) accomplished with a prior turn at talk. They also apply to other aspects or dimensions of speakers' activities that also, in a variety of ways, display some analysis of the state of the talk. For example, when a speaker initiates a new topic or direction for talk that is disjoined from what precedes it, the speaker exhibits an analysis that "then and there" is an appropriate place for something new to be raised, something that may, once again, be confirmed or resisted in the next turn. And studies of such initiations will reveal systematic features to which they are oriented, alternative means of initiation, ways in which such initiations are worked at, and so on (cf. Button and Casey, Chapter 8; Jefferson, Chapter 9).

Although we have focused on the methodological value of sequential considerations in relation to the analysis of responsive utterances, the examination of sequences can also prove a valuable resource in investigating the design features of utterances that are initiatory of (or even premonitory of) sequences rather than responsive within them (cf. Jefferson 1980b, Pomerantz 1980a, Schegloff 1980). At the minimum, examination of the talk that is produced in response to initiating utterances may have utility for confirming (or undermining) the analyst's intuition that utterances designed in a particular way are characteristically produced to accomplish a particular task. Such confirmation can be valuable in encouraging investigation into the operative design features of an utterance type and, once isolated, the role of such design features can once again be checked with the comparative use of sequential data.

In sum, in examining talk the analyst is immediately confronted with an organization which is implemented on a turn-by-turn basis, and through which a context of publicly displayed and continuously updated intersubjective understandings is systematically sustained. It is through this turn-by-turn character of talk that the participants display their understandings of the state of the talk for one another, and because these understandings are publicly produced, they are available for analytic treatment by social scientists. Analysts may thus proceed to study with some assurance the factual exhibits of understandings that are displayed and ratified at the conversational surface.

Before we leave this topic, one final caveat is in order. Although the value of sequential analysis in getting at the participants' understandings of the talk has been stressed in this section, it should not be concluded that the way in which a speaker responds to a prior utterance can, in every case, be treated as criterial in determining how the utterance should be viewed analytically. Obviously, speakers may respond to earlier talk so as to avoid taking up and dealing with what they perfectly well know it accomplishes or implicates and, by these means, may negotiate the direction of the talk away from an undesired outcome or toward a desired one. Such occasions are common in talk, and they may be varyingly transparent to analytic inspection. The characteristics of these events can themselves be documented by means of comparative sequential analysis, but their existence serves to emphasize that official treatments of talk occurring at the conversational surface are the *starting point* for interpretative and analytic work and cannot be treated simply as unproblematic representations of what the speakers' understandings or intentions in the talk consisted of.

4. The presentation of data in the book

The progressive accumulation of studies in conversation analysis has been accompanied by a growing appreciation of the extraordinarily detailed ways in which conversationalists produce and orient to actions.

This appreciation has engendered an increasing awareness of the fundamental organizational importance of details that might seem, on a cursory inspection, to be random or insignificant.[7] The growing attention to detail is evident in, and has been facilitated by, the continuing refinement of the transcription system evolved by Gail Jefferson. However, the widespread inclusion in research reports of extracts transcribed according to these conventions occasionally gives rise to misunderstandings about the ways in which the transcripts are viewed and used in relation to the recorded data from which they were derived.

At the risk of stating the obvious, conversation analysts do *not* claim that the transcription system captures the details of a tape recording in all its particularities, *or* that a transcript should (or ever could) be viewed as a literal representation of, or observationally adequate substitute for, the data under analysis.[8] Like all transcription systems, the one used in this book is necessarily selective (Ochs 1979), and indeed this system is particularly concerned with capturing sequential features of talk. It is therefore important to stress that, although the transcripts serve as an extremely convenient research tool, they are produced and designed for use in *close conjunction with* the tape-recorded materials that constitute the data base. The fact that publication conventions allow for the inclusion only of data extracts in written form should therefore not lead readers to the conclusion that the analyses are based exclusively on an inspection of transcripts conducted independently of direct reference to the original recordings.

The transcription system uses standard English orthographic symbols, together with some additional symbols and some modifications of English spelling. The system is sometimes objected to as a form of "comic book" orthography that can be interpreted as being somewhat derogatory to the speakers whose talk is thus represented (Sacks, Schegloff, and Jefferson 1974:734). In this context, it should be noted that the transcripts result from and represent an attempt to get as much as possible of the actual sound and sequential positioning of talk onto the page, while at the same time making this material accessible to readers unfamiliar with systems further removed from standard orthography.

5. Concluding remarks

Studies of ordinary conversation have been developed on the premise, first suggested by Sacks, Schegloff, and Jefferson (1974), that conversational interaction has a "bedrock" status in relation to other institutionalized forms of interpersonal conduct. Not only is conversation the most pervasively used mode of interaction in social life and the form within which, with whatever modifications (Ervin-Tripp and Mitchell-Kernan 1977, Ochs and Schieffelin 1979, Snow and Ferguson 1977), language is first acquired, but also it consists of the fullest matrix of socially organized communicative practices and procedures. A parallel body of studies involves the implementation of conversation analytic techniques in a range of specialized or institutional interactional settings such as courts, classrooms, news interviews, and medical encounters.[9] A recurrent theme in these studies concerns the ways in which such specialized interactions exhibit varyingly detailed and systematic differences from what is found in ordinary conversation. The practices involved in such settings appear to involve a clustering of particular subsets of those found in conversation, and their use commonly involves a reshaping of the relevances associated with their use in everyday interaction. These characteristics may eventually be shown to contribute to what Garfinkel (forthcoming) has referred to as the special "quiddities" and "identifying details" of institutional conduct.

In conclusion, it will be apparent to readers, both of the contributions to this book and of papers published elsewhere, that conversation analytic research has involved an extended and continuing reappraisal of foundational issues in the theory of social action. The results of this reappraisal, which is far from complete, cannot be anticipated here. However, the detailed study of actual, particular social actions and interactions has revealed the immense variety of the phenomena of action, and it is this variety which has informed our pluralization of Talcott Parsons's famous title – *The Structure of Social Action* (1937). This pluralization represents one aspect of an evolving framework of assumptions that is current in the field to which the following essays contribute.

Notes

1. For a sophisticated discussion of the relation between the use of filmed data and the development of social psychological perspectives on interaction that run parallel to those outlined here, see Kendon (1979a).
2. Some relationships between syntactic phenomena and discourse processes are discussed in Schegloff (1979b) and C. Goodwin (1979a, 1981a).
3. Sociologists may see in the linguistic distinction between the literal and the contextual meanings of an utterance a modern variant of the classical Weberian distinction (Weber 1968:8–9) between "direct observational understanding" and "motivational understanding." The notion of "literal meaning" has had a checkered career in linguistics. Applied to word meaning, the idea has attracted criticism from the Prague School onward (Karcevskij 1964). It is not supported by studies of translation (Nida 1964) or by current research under-

taken from a psycholinguistic perspective (e.g., Rosch 1977; Rosch and Mervis 1975; Rosch, Mervis, Gray, Johnson, and Boyes-Braem 1976; Rosch, Simpson, and Miller 1976). In application to sentences or locutions, the notion of literal meaning has been extensively criticized by Searle (1979, 1980), and the conclusion that the interpretation of a sentence arises from an interaction between practical and lexical knowledge appears quite unavoidable (Miller 1978). In the context of analyses of discourses or texts, the idea of literal meaning tends to engender one of two alternative forms of skepticism. Those who believe that access to literal meaning is both possible and necessary for their analysis exhibit dismay at the number of contextual rules required to provide for the indefinitely large range of contextual determinations for any locution (van Dijk 1977). Alternatively, those who view analyses that purport to establish the literal meanings of locutions more skeptically (Harris 1979) conclude that the quest for literal meaning is hopeless and that the analysis of discourse is therefore impossible. This latter conclusion, however, is equally premised on a model of meaning for locutions that demands a "literal meaning" as the basis for the analysis of subsequent "contextual variation." The affinities between the search for literal meaning and a research program taking the isolated sentence as its central object have been raised by Goffman (1976). For variously programmatic objections to decontextualized approaches to meaning from the sociological literature, see Garfinkel (1967); Garfinkel and Sacks (1970); Coulter (1971, 1973); and Heritage (1978).
4. In his unpublished transcribed lectures, Sacks notes (lecture 1, winter 1965) the insufficiency of studies based on isolated sentences for the analysis of natural activities. Elsewhere he stresses the crucial significance of an utterance's placement for the analysis of its illocutionary force. For example, he proposes (lecture 1, fall 1966) that "what it is that a given object is doing may well require analysis of its locus in conversation . . . The specification of the uses of sets of objects requires a formulation of the structure of conversational possibilities."
5. In his spring 1972 lectures, Sacks proposes that the "adjacency relationship between utterances is the most powerful device for relating utterances" and that "adjacency pairs constitute the institutionalized (i.e., formal) means for exploiting the relating power of adjacency" (lecture 4).
6. However, it should be borne in mind that first speakers may, and do, go along with a second speaker's mis-hearing or mistreatment of their prior utterances. A clear case is the following:

```
[NB:II:1:R:10]

E:      she gets ↓awful depressed over these things↓ yihknow
        she's rea:l (0.2) p'litical mi:nded'n,
        (0.3)
L:      Ye:ah:
E:      wo┌r k -┐
L:  →      └She a┘ Democra:t?
E:  →   ·t·hhhh I vote eether wa:y.h
        (.)
L:  →   Yeah,
E:      ·hmhh·t·h I didn' git tuh vote I decline'tuh
        state this ti:me when I registered so: . . .
```

Here L makes no attempt in third turn to correct E's mis-hearing, or mistreatment, of her prior utterance.

7. Jefferson (forthcoming c) has elegantly described how a change in the approach to transcribing laughter made it possible to describe organized features of sequences that would otherwise have been overlooked.

8. If it is the case that, in the light of Wittgenstein's discussions, the notion of a "literal" transcript is an illusion, then it is impossible to accept Harris's (1979) contention that, in the absence of such transcriptions, the analysis of discourse is impossible. The programmatic relevance of the provision of a literal transcript appears to derive from presuppositions of linguistic method that insist that "each linguistic form has a constant and specific meaning" (Bloomfield 1933:145) and that, ipso facto, each linguistic form is itself constant and specific. Talbot Taylor has recently published (1981) a subtle discussion of this issue from a Wittgensteinian perspective.

9. Institutional conduct analyzed with the use of conversation analytic techniques embraces a wide variety of domains and substantive phenomena. Several investigators, taking up Sacks, Schegloff, and Jefferson's (1974:729–30) distinction between locally allocated and preallocated turn-taking systems, have described the forms of turn taking that are characteristic in classroom (McHoul 1978, Mehan 1979), courtroom (Atkinson and Drew 1979), and news interview interaction (Greatbatch 1982), respectively. A considerable corpus of research has been occupied with the variety of tasks that are accomplished through the activities of questioning and answering in different institutional settings. This research has involved attempts to describe the ways in which particular institutional contexts are being reproduced in the talk of the interactants (Drew forthcoming; Heritage 1980, forthcoming; Heritage and Atkinson 1983). Detailed studies maintain this focus while analyzing the accomplishment of specific activities, such as the management of accusations and defenses in criminal courts (Atkinson and Drew 1979, Dunstan 1980), conflict (Pomerantz and Atkinson forthcoming) and arbitrator neutrality (Atkinson 1979b) in small claims courts, plea bargaining (Maynard 1982, 1983, forthcoming), and pretrial conferences (Lynch forthcoming). D. R. Watson (forthcoming a, forthcoming b) has examined some aspects of police-suspect interaction (see also Eglin and Wideman 1983) and has also followed Sacks (1972a) in examining interactions with suicide-prevention agency officials (D. Watson 1978, 1981). A variety of aspects of classroom interaction have been discussed by Mehan (see especially Mehan 1979). Finally Heath (1981, 1982b, in prep.), Frankel (1980, forthcoming), Anderson and Sharrock (forthcoming), Bergmann (1979), and Davidson (1978b), among others, have examined aspects of doctor–patient interaction from a conversation analytic perspective.

PART I
Orientations

The first of the two chapters in this section – "Notes on Methodology" by the late Harvey Sacks – consists of a series of programmatic and methodological observations taken largely from Sacks's transcribed lectures given between 1965 and 1971 and edited into a continuous discussion by Gail Jefferson. These observations vividly convey the pioneering quality of his work, some of his motives for undertaking it, and the "lateral thinking" that was such a characteristic feature of his lectures. They also outline some revolutionary methodological orientations that have since become standard both within the field of conversation analysis and beyond it. In particular, Sacks insists (1) that ordinary talk is systematically and strongly organized; (2) that its analysis should be based upon naturally occurring data; and (3) that analytic interests should not be constrained by external considerations. These three recommendations are closely interconnected.

Sacks's initial remarks tackle head on what has arguably been the major factor inhibiting studies of interaction: the assumption that talk is not sufficiently orderly to bear formal description. This assumption is shared by those linguists who have treated empirically occurring talk as a degenerate realization of linguistic competence and by sociologists (including anthropologists) who, doubting that social organization reaches "downward" to the details of interaction, have tended to regard the data of talk as idiosyncratic or random. One consequence of this assumption is that many linguists and social scientists have been content to develop idealized models of language and action, respectively. Chomsky's (1965) conception of "competence" and Parsons's (1937) treatment of the "unit act" are merely prominent theoretical expressions of this belief. Such an attitude is paralleled at the empirical level by the use of data – whether invented or glossed by a variety of methodological techniques including, most commonly, observer coding – that are essentially idealized. The net result is that theories are developed with the use of data that themselves bear an unknown relationship to what is used and acted upon in actual occasions of interaction.

If, by contrast, research begins from the assumption that actual talk is strongly organized, it becomes essential to develop analyses that deal with the specific events of interaction, including, as Sacks notes, singular instances and, it may be added, deviant cases. This practice represents a strong constraint on analysis, but it has the particular virtue of connecting model building with actually occurring data. And, as Sacks shrewdly notes, it can be difficult to advance claims about the events of interaction with the use of imagined examples.

To develop a "natural observational science" of interaction demands an openness to empirical phenomena. Here Sacks insists that observation should proceed without preconceptions concerning what is there to be found, the intrinsic importance of the talk, or its significance for the "big issues" of the social sciences. Openness to fact is of course a hallmark of scientific endeavor and a precondition of genuine discovery, and its urging is particularly appropriate for a fledgling discipline approaching the relatively uncharted domain of interaction. Nonetheless, since interaction is the matrix both within which language is learned and used and through which institutional activity is conducted, it is unlikely that the study of talk will fail to turn up results of major significance for the parent social science disciplines. If Sacks's suggestion that the "detailed study of small phenomena may give an enormous understanding of the way humans do things" seemed an act of faith when it was uttered in 1964, it no longer seems so today. And the independent adoption of the methodological orientations here recommended by Sacks in a range of domains where interaction is the focus of interest – child language development, nonverbal behavior, psychotherapy studies, and human ethology – speaks to a general recognition of their validity.

If Sacks's contribution takes the form of general methodological recommendations, Schegloff (Chapter 3) takes up a number of more specific issues that arise from the study of naturally occurring sequences of talk. In particular, Schegloff focuses on a central issue arising at the interface of linguistics and sociology when speech is analyzed as social action, namely, the extent to which the linguistic form of an utterance can be relied upon as an indicator of the activity that an utterance is accomplishing. In addressing this issue, he explores the methodological implications of a fundamental feature of ordinary conversation: the fact that speakers design their utterances with regard to their specific placement in the talk and that hearers routinely attend to such placements as a means of determining what was intended or attempted with the utterance.

Schegloff begins by noting a range of ways in which the linguistic form of an utterance may fail to square with its interpretation even though hearers may experience no corresponding sense of ambiguity in the utterance. Question-formed utterances that do not accomplish questioning and statement-formed questions are cases in point. Though these kinds of observations have motivated considerable work on indirect speech acts, Schegloff uses these cases to question the central assumption of this approach, namely, that linguistic form is to be treated as the hearer's central interpretative resource unless it is overridden by other factors. He develops this issue by noting that for a variety of cases hearers may orient to the *structural location* of an utterance (rather than its linguistic form) as a primary means of interpreting it.

In the main body of the chapter, conversationalists' orientations to the structural locations of utterances are exemplified through a detailed description of an empirically occurring case of ambiguity, in which a question-formed utterance is interpreted initially as a question and subsequently as an instance of showing agreement. Two important features of this discussion can be noted. First, Schegloff takes care to demonstrate that the ambiguity in question is not a theoretically possible ambiguity but rather one that is encountered and dealt with by both speakers. Second, he shows that the ambiguity is potentiated by two alternative and equiprobable *structural* analyses of the sequence that precedes and informs it. Thus the structural positioning of an utterance is a critical resource for determining what it is accomplishing. It is used, for example, to determine when a question-formed utterance is questioning and when it is not. Similarly, when, as in Schegloff's central datum, the positioning of a question-formed utterance is structurally ambiguous, the resolution of the resulting ambiguity may invade the talk as a task for the speakers. The analysis of the positioning of utterances within a sequence thus goes some considerable way toward answering the sets of questions that arise if one abandons the notion that linguistic form is an interpretive resource of first resort for conversationalists, "not only about how a question does something other than questioning, but about how it does questioning; not only about how questioning is done by nonquestion forms, but about how it gets accomplished by question forms."

Schegloff's concluding remarks stand as a valuable corrective to prevailing misconceptions about indexicality and ambiguity in natural languages. Noting that much of the logical and linguistic work on indexicality and ambiguity has arisen from the study of statements stripped of local context, he points out that talk is produced so as to *exploit* the context dependencies that formal languages are designed to exclude. The indexicality of natural language is thus to be viewed as a powerful resource for participants' understandings rather than as an obstacle to their achievement.

2. Notes on methodology

HARVEY SACKS

Late of the University of California, Irvine

I want to propose that a domain of research exists that is not part of any other established science. The domain is one that those who are pursuing it have come to call ethnomethodology/conversation analysis. That domain seeks to describe methods persons use in doing social life. It is our claim that, although the range of activities this domain describes may be as yet unknown, the mode of description, the way it is cast, is intrinsically stable.[1]

Following are some central findings of the researches in which I am engaged.

> The detailed ways in which actual, naturally occurring social activities occur are subjectable to formal description.
>
> Social activities – actual, singular sequences of them – are methodical occurrences. That is, their description consists of the description of sets of formal procedures persons employ.
>
> The methods persons employ to produce their activities permit formal description of singular occurrences that are generalizable in intuitively nonapparent ways and are highly reproducibly usable.

Such findings have significance for what it is that sociology can aim to do, and for how it can proceed. In brief, sociology can be a natural observational science.[2]

The important theories in the social sciences have tended to view a society as a piece of machinery with relatively few orderly products, where, then, much of what else takes place is more or less random. Such a view suggests that there are a few places where, if we can find them, we will be able to attack the problem of order. If we do not find them, we will not. So we can have an image of a machine with a couple of holes in

This chapter consists of a series of programmatic/methodological considerations by the late Harvey Sacks, culled primarily from his lectures transcribed by Gail Jefferson. Jefferson writes: "I have occasionally edited the selected segments, and that procedure has undoubtedly resulted in some distortion." The publisher has imposed some further editing.

the front. It spews out some nice stuff from those holes, and at the back it spews out garbage. There is, then, a concern among social scientists for finding "good problems," that is, those data generated by the machine which *are* orderly, and then attempt to construct the apparatus necessary to give those results.

Now such a view tends to be heavily controlled by an overriding interest in what are in the first instance known to be "big issues," and not those which are terribly mundane, occasional, local, and the like. It is perfectly possible, at least theoretically, to treat such a view as historically adventitious; a mere fact; an accident of the history of the way persons came to think about social problems, and to suppose, or discover, or propose to discover, that no such thing is the case, but that wherever we happen to attack the phenomenon we are going to find (some would say "impose") detailed order.

That possibility would have enormous consequences for what we intend to build. The search for good problems by reference to known big issues will have large-scale, massive institutions as the apparatus by which order is generated and by a study of which order will be found. If, on the other hand, we figure or guess or decide that whatever humans do, they are just another animal after all, maybe more complicated than others but perhaps not noticeably so, then whatever humans do can be examined to discover some way they do it, and that way will be stably describable. That is, we may alternatively take it that there is order at all points.

That sort of order would be an important resource of a culture, such that, for example, any members of the culture, encountering from their infancy a very small portion of it, and a random portion in a way (the parents they happen to have, the experiences they happen to have, the vocabulary that happens to be thrown at them in whatever utterances they happen to encounter), would come out in many ways much like everybody else and able to deal with just about anyone else. Were it important for nature to ensure that if persons are to be workable things in a society they have an adequate sampling setup, then a culture might well be so arranged. And then, of course, research might employ the same resources: Tap into whomsoever, wheresoever, and we get much the same things.

Furthermore, the fact of order at all points could be used to explain what are otherwise fairly strange facts – for example, that conventional sociological survey research, though it recurrently fails to satisfy constraints on proper statistical procedures, nevertheless gets orderly results; or, for example, that the anthropologists' procedures, which tend to involve an occasional tapping into a society, asking one or two people more or less extended questions, turn out to be often extremely generalizable. Now the orderly results and the generalizability could be treated as a warrant for such procedures, or as a tremendous puzzle. Or they could be seen as a consequence of the fact that, given the possibility that there is overwhelming order, it would be extremely hard *not* to find it, no matter how or where we looked.

If a culture and its members are constructed in that way, then the fact that orderly results are obtained from one informant, or from some sampling procedure, would be not necessarily a warrant for those things being good procedures on their own terms but evidence for an arrangement of the world that could be seen to be usable. We may well find that we get an enormous generalizability because things are so arranged that we *can* get orderly results, given that for members encountering a limited environment they have to be able to do that, and things are so arranged as to permit them to. And if we figure that that is the way things are to some extent, then it really would not matter very much what it is we look at, if we look at it carefully enough (lecture 33, spring 1966).

A couple of possibly relevant passages from some authorities follow. The first is from *Language*, by Edward Sapir:

> We're not in ordinary life so much concerned with concepts as such. . . . When I say, for instance, "I had a good breakfast this morning," it is clear that I am not in the throes of laborious thought; that what I have to transmit is hardly more than a pleasurable memory symbolically rendered in the grooves of habitual expression . . . the sentence as a whole has no conceptual significance whatsoever.
>
> It is somewhat as though a generator capable of generating enough power to run an elevator were operated almost exclusively to feed an electric doorbell. The parallel is more suggestive than it at first sight appears. Language may be looked upon as an instrument capable of running a gamut of psychic uses. (1921:13)

In the first instance, consider what, for Sapir, is obvious: that what could be said to be being done by use of language specifically is transparently obvious; statable by stating the sentence itself, and then to be seen to be using little of what language really could do. The import for researchers of a statement like Sapir's could be small or large.

The second passage refers to this earlier one and draws some consequences from it. Weinreich comments:

> In a remarkable passage, Sapir likens language to a dynamo capable of powering an elevator but ordinarily operating to feed an electric doorbell. Language is used more often than not in ways that do not draw upon its full semantic capacity. In its "phatic"

functions, when speech is used merely to signify the presence of a sympathetic interlocutor, it easily becomes "desematicized" to a formidable extent. In its various ceremonial functions, language may come to be desemanticized by still another mechanism . . .

. . . The more pressing task for linguistics, it seems to me, is to explain the elevator, not the doorbell; avoiding samples of excessively casual or ceremonial speech; to examine language under conditions of its full fledged utilization. (1963:147)

Now one thing being proposed here is that we know, right off, where language is deep and interesting, that we can know that without an analysis of what it is that it might be doing. And we want to see that the set of ways the statement "I had a good breakfast this morning" can be talked about – for example, "phatic," "nonconceptual," "desemanticized," and so on – are given as a set of alternatives without its, or anything else's, being studied very much. But a program is laid out. And among the important things about that program is what is *not* to be studied. And what is not to be studied is proposed by virtue of presumed results. Those are really quite extraordinary arguments. And if they don't proceed quite strictly from a notion that we can or must know what the aims of a discipline are before we begin, at least a good deal of that notion is involved in such formulations.

I mention these matters to notice that it is perhaps not incidental that people have not devoted their lives to studying sentences like "I had a good breakfast this morning" or "How are you?" There are more or less defensible reasons for not studying such sentences. Not studying such sentences, however, may have real consequences. The question of what language can do, what people can do with language, what the results of an analysis of "I had a good breakfast this morning" would involve, what kind of program it poses for a field – all these things remain absolutely open (lecture 6, fall 1966).

It is possible that detailed study of small phenomena may give an enormous understanding of the way humans do things and the kinds of objects they use to construct and order their affairs.

It may well be that things are very finely ordered; that there are collections of social objects (including "I had a good breakfast this morning" and "How are you?") that persons assemble to do their activities; that the way they assemble them is describable with respect to any one of the activities they happen to do, and has to be seen by attempting to analyze particular objects.

We would want to name those objects and see how they work, as we know how verbs and adjectives and sentences work. Thereby we can come to see how an activity is assembled, as we see a sentence assembled with a verb, a predicate, and so on. Ideally, of course, we would have a formally describable method, as the assembling of a sentence is formally describable. The description not only would handle sentences in general, but particular sentences. What we would be doing, then, is developing another grammar. And grammar, of course, is the model of routinely observable, closely ordered social activities (lecture, fall 1964, tape 3).

In that the kinds of observations I make involve catching some details of actual occurrences, then we can come to find a difference between the way I proceed and one characteristic way social science proceeds, which is to use hypotheticalized, proposedly typicalized versions of the world as a base for theorizing about it. Often enough in sociological reports, somebody will say, "Let us suppose that such and such happened," or, "Typical things that happen are . . ." Now a reader finds himself perfectly willing to grant that such things happen. On the basis of assertions, suppositions, proposals about what is typical, some explanation about the world is built.

I want to argue that, however rich our imaginations are, if we use hypothetical, or hypothetical-typical versions of the world we are constrained by reference to what an audience, an audience of professionals, can accept as reasonable. That might not appear to be a terrible constraint until we come to look at the kinds of things that actually occur. Were I to say about many of the objects we work with "Let us suppose that this happened; now I am going to consider it," then an audience might feel hesistant about what I would make of it by reference to whether such things happen. That is to say, under such a constraint many things that actually occur are debarred from use as a basis for theorizing about conversation. I take it that this debarring affects the character of social sciences strongly.

Our business will be to proceed somewhat differently. We will be using observation as a basis for theorizing. Thus we can start with things that are not currently imaginable, by showing that they happened. We can then come to see that a base for using close looking at the world for theorizing about it is that from close looking at the world we can find things that we could not, by imagination, assert were there. We would not know that they were "typical" (lecture 1, fall 1971). Indeed, we might not have noticed that they happen.

Therefore, the kind of phenomena I deal with are always transcriptions of actual occurrences in their actual sequence. But my research is about conversation only in this incidental way: that conversation is something that we can get the actual happenings of on tape and that we can get more or less transcribed; that is, conversation is simply something to begin with (lecture 2, fall 1968).

When I started to do research in sociology I figured that sociology could not be an actual science unless it was able to handle the details of actual events, handle them formally, and in the first instance be informative about them in the direct ways in which primitive sciences tend to be informative – that is, that anyone else can go and see whether what was said is so. And that is a tremendous control on seeing whether one is learning anything.

So the question was, could there be some way that sociology could hope to deal with the details of actual events, formally and informatively? One might figure that it had already been shown that it was perfectly possible given the vast literature, or alternatively that it was obviously impossible given the literature. For a variety of reasons I figured that it had not been shown either way, and I wanted to locate some set of materials that would permit a test; materials that would have the virtue of permitting us to see whether it was possible, and if so, whether it was interesting. The results might be positive or negative.

I started to work with tape-recorded conversations. Such materials had a single virtue, that I could replay them. I could transcribe them somewhat and study them extendedly – however long it might take. The tape-recorded materials constituted a "good enough" record of what happened. Other things, to be sure, happened, but at least what was on the tape had happened. It was not from any large interest in language or from some theoretical formulation of what should be studied that I started with tape-recorded conversations, but simply because I could get my hands on it and I could study it again and again, and also, consequentially, because others could look at what I had studied and make of it what they could, if, for example, they wanted to be able to disagree with me.

So the work I am doing is about talk. It is about the details of talk. In some sense it is about how conversation works. The specific aim is, in the first instance, to see whether actual single events are studiable and how they might be studiable, and then what an explanation of them would look like (lecture, fall 1967, Intro.).

Thus is it not any particular conversation, as an object, that we are primarily interested in. Our aim is to get into a position to transform, in an almost literal, physical sense, our view of "what happened," from a matter of a particular interaction done by particular people, to a matter of interactions as products of a machinery. We are trying to find the machinery. In order to do so we have to get access to its products. At this point, it is conversation that provides us such access (lecture 1, winter 1970).

Now people often ask me why I choose the particular data I choose. Is it some problem that I have in mind that caused me to pick this corpus or this segment? And I am insistent that I just happened to have it, it became fascinating, and I spent some time at it. Furthermore, it is not that I attack any piece of data I happen to have according to some problems I bring to it (lecture 7, spring 1967). When we start out with a piece of data, the question of what we are going to end up with, what kind of findings it will give, should not be a consideration. We sit down with a piece of data, make a bunch of observations, and see where they will go (lecture 5, fall 1967).

Treating some actual conversation in an unmotivated way, that is, giving some consideration to whatever can be found in any particular conversation we happen to have our hands on, subjecting it to investigation in any direction that can be produced from it, can have strong payoffs (lecture 2, winter 1970). Recurrently, what stands as a solution to some problem emerges from unmotivated examination of some piece of data, where, had we started out with a specific interest in the problem, it would not have been supposed in the first instance that this piece of data was a resource with which to consider, and come up with a solution for, that particular problem.

Thus there can be some real gains in trying to fit what we can hope to do to anything that happens to come up. I mean not merely that if we pick any data we will find something, but that if we pick any data, without bringing any problems to it, we will find something. And how interesting what we may come up with will be is something we cannot in the first instance say (lecture 7, spring 1967).

Notes

1. H. Sacks, "A foundation for sociology," MS, Department of Sociology, UCLA.
2. H. Sacks, introduction to untitled MS, Department of Sociology, UCLA, first line starts with "For sociology . . ."

3. On some questions and ambiguities in conversation

EMANUEL A. SCHEGLOFF
University of California, Los Angeles

The datum I am concerned with is the following, in particular the last two exchanges:

(1)

```
1    B:    An's- an (   ) we were discussing, it tur-
2          it comes down, he s- he says, I-I-you've talked
3          with thi- si- i- about this many times. I said,
4          it come down t'this:=
5    B:    =Our main difference: I feel that a government,
6          i- the main thing, is- th-the purpose a'the
7          government, is, what is best for the country.
8    A:    Mmhmm
9    B:    He says, governments, an' you know he keeps- he
10         talks about governments, they sh- the thing that
11         they sh'd do is what's right or wrong.
12   A:    For whom.
13   B:    Well he says- ┌he-
14   A:               └By what standard
15   B:    That's what- that's exactly what I mean. he s-
16         but he says ...
```

B has been describing to A the differences he (B) has been having with his high school history teacher over the morality of American foreign

This lecture was delivered to a conference on Linguistics and Language Teaching at Rutgers University, April 1972. I am grateful to Dr. J. Barone for inviting me to address the conference. Some of the themes and analyses presented herein were developed in lectures at Columbia University between 1966 and 1972. At the time of writing I was a visitor in the Department of Psychology at Rockefeller University. My appreciation goes to Professor Michael Cole for the opportunity and for his hospitality. The lecture is reproduced here essentially unchanged. Several mechanical errors have been set right; several obscurities clarified, though others certainly remain; the effects of certain psychological and stylistic peculiarities of the time repaired. Some bibliographic references, many of which were unavailable in 1972, have been supplied. A fuller version of the essay was published in *Pragmatics Microfiche*, 1976, 2.2, D8-G1.

Ways of working change over time, and in many respects this lecture and the statement of many of its themes are now a bit archaic to me. But it may still be of some use; some friends specially liked it, and I still like parts of it.

policy since the time of George Washington. I suppose I should say now that the excerpt is taken from a conversation in a radio call-in show (A being the radio personality), although that will not matter at all to the analysis except in one distant way, in which a formal structural characteristic of the conversation is in this case supplied by that fact; but it is the structural feature that counts, not the fact that in this case it is supplied by the radio setting, the feature being supplied in other conversations by other circumstances of setting.

My initial concern with the sequence 12–15 focused on the interruption in 14. Early work on the sequential organization of turn taking in conversation (especially that of my colleague Harvey Sacks) made occurrences of interruptions and interutterance gaps of special interest, as possible violations of the normative organization of the transition from one to a next. Given the recurrent management of that transition with no (or minimal) gap and overlap, and a regular respect for the rights of a speaker, having begun an utterance, to bring it to a point of possible completion (cf. the later statement in Sacks, Schegloff, and Jefferson 1974), interruptions seemed to warrant examination to find what was involved in departures from that normative practice. In particular, I was attracted by the possibility that interruptions, or some interruptions, might be – so to speak – finely tuned, that is, quite precisely placed by an interrupter (a similar interest animates Jefferson 1973a). An adequate analysis of what was otherwise going on in the sequence might then yield an understanding of the occurrence, and the precise placement, of the interruption; and some degree of confidence in an analysis of what a sequence was occupied with might be derived if, by reference to it, an otherwise not particularly ordered interruption could get seen as "placed."

1

Before turning directly to this datum, let me address a few remarks to the notion "question" in a more or less unlocated way. It is a strong candidate for popularity in a time when some concessions are thought necessary to the "uses of language," or sentences of a language; when, for example, it is argued that some notion of a performative or some type of speech act or some kind of presupposition is involved in the production, and presumably in the comprehension, of a sentence or an utterance. If the mere presence of lexical items such as "I promise," "I bet," "I guarantee" can be taken as invoking the possible membership of the sentence in which they appropriately appear in a class such as "promises" or "bets," with an attached presuppositional structure underlying them, how much more powerful is the appeal of syntactic forms such as "question" or "injunction." A ready bridge is apparently before us to cross from language to social behavior, in which, it might appear, the syntax will bear the load. Though it might be conceded that no complete or neat linguistic account of questions is yet available, the relevant attributes being variously apportioned among syntax, prosody, and other resources, still it might appear that linguistic resources will allow the construction and recognition of utterances as questions, and thus as actions of a certain type. Now I think such a view is, or would be, as misleading with regard to questions as a way of bridging language and social action as it is in the case of promises. The general point is that it is misleading to start to account for such categories of action as questions, promises, and so on as the analytic objects of interest. They are commonsense, not technical, categories and should be treated accordingly. I cannot pursue that general point here, so let me address it with regard to some particular categories.

Most of the problems derive from treating the categories (such as questions or promises), rather than particular data, as problematic. For example, Sacks has noted that for a great many cases (I should hazard a "most" here) of utterances like "I promise" or "I bet," it is not "promising" or "betting" at all that is going on, but rather an attempt at unit closure, such as topic or argument or "making arrangements" closure. The use of the sheer occurrence of the lexical items, without regard to the placement of the utterances in which they occur in the sequential organization of conversation, can be badly misleading, though not implausible.

The same thing is true where syntax is so used. Consider "injunction." The following is taken from a recent paper on the closing of conversation:

(2)

((B has called to invite C, but has been told that C
  is going out to dinner))

    B: Yeah. Well get on your clothes and get out and
         collect some of that free food and we'll make
         it some other time Judy then.
    C: Okay then Jack.
    B: Bye bye
    C: Bye bye

While B's initial utterance in this excerpt might be grammatically characterized as an imperative or a command, and C's "Okay" then appears to be a submission or accession to it, in no sense but a narrowly syntactic one would those be anything but whimsical characterizations. While B's utterance has certain imperative aspects in its language form, those are not ones that count; his utterance is a closing initiation; and C's utterance agrees not to a command to get dressed (nor would she be inconsistent if she failed to get dressed after the conversation), but to an invitation to close the conversation. The point is that no analysis, grammatical, semantic, pragmatic, etc., of these utterances taken singly and out of sequence, will yield their import in use, will show what co-participants might make of them and do about them. That B's utterance here accomplishes a form of closing initiation, and C's accepts the closing form and not what seems to be proposed in it, turns on the placement of these utterances in the conversation. (Schegloff and Sacks 1973:313)

And so also with regard to questions. Consider the following (from Schegloff 1972:107):

(3)

B_1: Why don't you <u>come</u> and see me some⌜times
A_1:   ⌊I would
     like to
B_2: I would like you to. Lemme ⌜just
A_2:   ⌊I don't know just
     where the-us-this address <u>is</u>.

Where are the questions here? Is there a question here? For a participant whose next utterance or action may be contingent on finding about a current utterance whether it is a "question," because, if it is, an "answer" may be a relevant next thing for him to do, does syntax, or linguistic form, solve his problem? Not only does our intuition suggest that, although no syntactic question (nor question intonation, for that matter) occurs in A's second utterance of the excerpt, a question–answer (Q–A) sequence pair has been initiated, a request for directions if you like; more important, it is so heard by B, who proceeds to give directions. And although B's first utterance in the excerpt looks syntactically like a question, it is not a "question" that A "answers," but an "invitation" (in question form) that she "accepts."

Now it might do to play with this last point a bit. It might be argued that there is an easy way to provide for not analyzing B_1 as a question. To wit: consider that the utterance contains in it a component of imperative or injunctive form, "Come and see me sometime." Let us name a construction in English, or American English, an "injunction mitigator."

Instances of injunction mitigators are "why don't you," "would you like to," and undoubtedly others. A rule for its use might be that it can front or precede any injunctive form. It might, I suppose, be made a "sociolinguistic" rule, in the narrow sense of that term, if its use is made contingent on certain relative statuses between speaker and recipient(s), and so on. The rule might be said to transform the syntactic form from "injunctive" to "question," and the action, accordingly, from "command" to "request," "invitation," or "suggestion." And certainly, in a wide range of cases that we can imagine or invent, that transformation seems to be what is involved. In such cases, we would have provided for a recipient not hearing in the utterance a question, but a mitigated injunction, or an invitation, and so on, though, interestingly enough, a question would still be available to a literal analysis, and so declining the invitation might be done by treating the utterance for the question which it could be proposed to contain. But then we might note that in the present case, B_1, the utterance would be an invitation without the mitigator. And other injunctions do not seem to allow the use of a mitigator, so that if one is used, it does not mitigate an injunction, but rather makes it sarcastic, as in "Why don't you go away and leave me alone." In short, whereas the forms I have for now named "injunction mitigators" may be operators or particles of a sort, what one of them is doing in any particular case will depend on what it is attached to, and where that is placed. It will not, therefore, serve as a generalized means, or even as a restricted one, for depriving nonquestion question forms of a question interpretation.

In insisting that the B_1–A_1 sequence involves accepting an invitation rather than answering a question, I may seem to be niggling over details. Still, from the point of view of a recipient of the B_1 utterance, whereas a response of some sort is relevant, important differences turn on whether an answer or an acceptance/rejection is in point. Underlying this theme is the comembership of question–answer and invitation–acceptance/rejection sequences in the class of sequential units elsewhere called "adjacency pairs."

> Adjacency pairs consist of sequences which properly have the following features: (1) Two utterance length; (2) Adjacent positioning of component utterances; (3) Different speakers producing each utterance.
>
> The component utterances of such sequences have an achieved relatedness beyond that which may otherwise obtain between adjacent utterances. That relatedness is partially the product of the operation of a typology in the speakers' production of the se-

quences. The typology operates in two ways: it partitions utterance types into "first pair parts" (i.e., first parts of pairs) and second pair parts; and it affiliates a first pair part and a second pair part to form a "pair type." Question-answer," "greeting-greeting," "offer-acceptance/refusal" are instances of pair types. A given sequence will thus be composed of an utterance that is a first pair produced by one speaker directly followed by the production by a different speaker of an utterance which is a) a second pair part, and b) is from the same pair type as the first utterance in the sequence is a member of. Adjacency pair sequences, then, exhibit the further features (4) relative ordering of parts (i.e., first pair parts precede second pair parts), and (5) discriminative relations (i.e., the pair type of which a first pair part is a member is relevant to the selection among second pair parts).

A basic rule of adjacency pair operation is: given the recognizable production of a first pair part, on its first possible completion its speaker should stop and a next speaker should start and produce a second pair part from the pair type of which the first is recognizably a member. (Schegloff and Sacks 1973:295–6; cf. also Sacks, Schegloff, and Jefferson 1974:716–8)

It is by virtue of the pair organization that a "response" is relevant for either a question or an invitation; it is by virtue of the differing pair types that different second pair parts will be required, depending on which first pair part is found to have been just finished.

Consider, in a similar vein, the following, in which a husband and wife are discussing arrangements for visiting another couple, with whom the previous night's scheduled visit had been canceled, while their 1½-year-old daughter plays on the floor:

(4)

```
W:   Why is it that we have to go there.
H:   Because she ((head-motioning to daughter)) can go
     out more easily than their kids can.
```

Note that H hears and treats W's utterance as a question, and answers it by giving a reason. But also note, as H and W subsequently did, that W's utterance can be heard as a complaint, and a complaint on the part of "us" against "them." In terms of that possible hearing, H's response comes off as a "defense" of them against W's complaint, and some troublesome issues about lines of solidarity might be seen to be raised. Were W's utterance heard and treated as a complaint in the first place, then a quite different response to it might be in order, such as joining the complaint, with possibly quite different consequences for the location, and indeed the occurrence, of the visiting. Again, in either case adjacency pairs are involved; in one case question–answer, in the other complaint–echo complaint, or agreement.

One consequence of this discussion, to my mind, is that not only is the path from linguistic questions to interactional ones not a straight line, but not much may lie at its end. For a substantial part of what we might expect to be available to us as understanding of questions as a category of action is best and most parsimoniously subsumed under the category "adjacency pairs"; much of what is so about questions is so by virtue of the adjacency-pair format. And what distinguishes questions from first pair parts of other sorts does not seem in any straightforward way to be sought from linguistic resources.

Is there, then, no import at all of linguistic form, such as question form, for the action interpretation of an utterance? Could not one say that linguistic form supplies a prima facie basis for the analysis of an utterance, which will hold unless superseded by other features; in other words, that it provides a presumption, an "unmarked" interpretation if you will, such that the burden falls elsewhere to make an utterance something else? A likely unparsimoniousness aside, one trouble with such a view is that it treats an utterance's syntactic form as a "first" feature about it, hence prima facie. And in the traditional practice of linguists, as well as of ordinary language philosophers, in which single sentences are (the) normal units of analysis, this may well be the case. But in the real world of conversation, it is not. Most centrally, an utterance will occur someplace sequentially. Most obviously, except for initial utterances, it will occur after some other utterance or sequence of utterances with which it will have, in some fashion, to deal and which will be relevant to its analysis for coparticipants. Less obviously, but more importantly, it (and here initial utterances are not excepted) may occur in a structurally defined place in conversation, in which case its structural location can have attached to its slot a set of features that may overwhelm its syntactic or prosodic structure in primacy. "Well, get on your clothes and get out and collect some of that free food" occurs in such a structurally defined place. Second slots in adjacency pairs are such a structural place.

Even where an utterance is in the linguistic form of a question, and seems to be doing questioning, the latter will not be adequately accounted for by the former. For if the question form can be used for actions other than questioning, and questioning can be accomplished by linguistic forms other than questions, then a relevant problem can be posed not only about how a question does something other than questioning, but about how it does questioning; not only about how questioning is done by nonquestion forms, but about how it gets accomplished by question forms.

Let me now try one more line on the theme I have been trying to develop. One thing one might mean by an utterance being interactionally or conversationally a question is that it lays constraints on the next slot in the conversation of a sort special to the Q–A pair type of adjacency pairs. Leaving aside an explication of what those special constraints might be, we can consider how some of the materials already mentioned and some additional ones look in terms of this notion. There is what I suppose might be called "the clear case"; for example:

(5)

A: What time is it?
B: It's noon.

in which an adjacency pair is initiated making a second pair part relevant, and the second pair part seems to satisfy whatever formulation of the notion "answer" one uses. There is an earlier considered fragment:

(6)

B: Why don't you come and see me sometimes.
A: I would like to.

in which an adjacency pair is initiated, but one whose constraints are not of a Q–A sort, or whose treatment as of a Q–A sort, that is, giving reasons why not, will likely get a hearing as rudeness or teasing rather than answering, as in the similar case of requests, like "Do you have a cigarette?" "Yes (pause) would you like one?" There is yet another interesting case that merits extended treatment, though it cannot be given here. It is the case in which a Q–A format is used to package a sequence, such that the initial utterance is indeed used to set answer-relevant constraints on the next slot, but where the sequence is not used to do questioning or answering at all. Here, the format is determined by the linguistic forms, but what is done in that format has nothing to do with questioning. A relevant example is drawn from an earlier point in the conversation from which the initially cited datum comes.

(7)

1   B: Because– an'he did the same thing, in
2   War of– The War of Eighteen Twelve, he said

```
3              the fact that we were interested in expansion,
4              t'carrying farther, was ( ) something against.
5              Y'know a-argument t'use against.  But see the
6              whole thing is he's against, he's⌐very- he's ( )
7   A:                                         ⌊Is he teaching
8              history or Divinity
9   B:    I don'kno(h)w. But he's very anti-imperialistic.
```

Now whatever its appearance when excerpted from the conversation, these last two turns (at lines 7–9) are not respectively a question as to someone's subject matter, and a confession of ignorance, which is the interpretation required if we see them as a Q–A sequence. The conversation contains early on:

(8)

```
B:    ... I'm taking 'merican history this term, I'm
      a junior.  Well I- now the new term began I
      gotta new teacher, so, we're starting from
      about you know, Washington's foreign policy
      ((interpolations by A omitted))
```

"Is he teaching history or divinity" is not asking subject matter, and "I don't know" is not a confession of ignorance. This is not questioning and answering, though a question–answer format is used to "package" the sequence. The distinction is critical to what will be placed in the second slot of the pair, and how what is placed there will be understood.

Though in many of these cases, alternative analyses of the first utterance in the sequence are theoretically, or heuristically, conceivable (e.g., the analysis of "why don't you come visit," etc.), they do not appear to be in practice confounded in an ambiguity. The "distinctions" I have been pointing out are quite academic, in the sense that their proper, perhaps only, place is here in the lecture hall. They are not distinctions drawn by the participants, for whom rather it appears that what is being done is quite straightforwardly available or analyzable. Because the constraints on a next utterance for a next speaker can be quite sharply different if a last utterance is seen to be a question or something else, we might do well to examine in some detail a case in which both possibilities, with their attendant constraints, are entertained by the participants – a case, that is, of *empirical* ambiguity as to whether an utterance is a question or some determinate alternative. And in examining such an ambiguity, we shall encounter some sequential features of conversation, of the sort I suggested before, that overshadow the contribution made by its linguistic form to what an utterance is doing.

2

I now turn to the sequence I put before you at the beginning. My intention is to try to locate the sources of the ambiguity of "for whom" in the sequential structures of the conversation. I further want this to be explication of a real ambiguity rather than a theoretical one, that is, not one where only one sense is actually operative for the participants, though an analyst can conjure up other senses it might have, under some other circumstances. Therefore, I shall want to support the claim that both analyses of the utterance, which I argue compose the ambiguity, are available to, and are employed by, the participants, that is, both analyses will have been dealt with by both parties. Then we can turn to the utterance itself and attempt to explicate the sequential basis for the ambiguity.

The tool I shall use initially is one based on, and fundamental to, a great deal of prior work in conversational analysis. It is that coparticipants in conversation operate under the constraint that their utterances be so constructed and so placed as to show attention to, and understanding of, their placement. That means that utterances, or larger units, are constructed to display to coparticipants that their speaker has attended a last utterance, or sequence of utterances, or other unit, and that this current utterance, in its construction, is placed with due regard for where it is occurring.

Now that constraint, and what is required to meet it, can vary in power and in detail. Adjacency pairs are especially strong constraints, a first pair part making relevant a particular action, or a restricted set of actions, to be done next. When next speakers do such an action, they not only comply with the requirements of the particular adjacency pair initiated; they show in their utterance their understanding of what the prior utterance was doing – a first pair part of that pair type (cf. Sacks, Schegloff, and Jefferson 1974:728–9). At the other end of the scale, the constraint of showing attention to sequential context may be satisfied by speakers' showing that although they may know what is relevant next, what they are about to do is something else. Thus, there is a form we have elsewhere termed "misplacement markers" (Schegloff and Sacks 1973:319–20) – "by the way" is a familiar one – which speakers may use at the beginning of an utterance. This form can show, among other things, that they know that something other than what they are about to do is in order, or that what they are about to do is "out of place." Although they may then go on to do it, they will have had their utterance display their attention to, and understanding of, the preceding utterance or sequence at least enough to know that what they are doing is not "naturally" or "properly" placed there. There are other such forms, such as starting an utterance with an "oh" (sometimes combined with using it to interrupt), when it is not topically coherent with what precedes, a show of unplannedness if you like, the way "free association" is accomplished conversationally, a display that what follows has been "touched off," a disjunction marker. Or, the use of "anyway" as a right-hand parenthesis, to show that what it precedes is fitted not to the immediately preceding, but to what preceded that.

Across the range of power and detail, utterances are built to display speakers' understanding; they are thereby made available for coparticipants' inspection to see if they display an adequate understanding of that which they claim to understand. This resource we will come back to later. For now, we want to notice that they also thereby make available to the *analyst* a basis in the data for claiming what the coparticipants' understanding is of prior utterances, for as they display it to one another, we can see it too (cf. Sacks, Schegloff, and Jefferson 1974:728–9). It is this resource that will be used in an initial run-through of the sequence that engages us.

Since the turn at line 12 in this sequence is the one we shall want to focus on, we shall be returning to it in considerable detail. Let it then suffice for now that it appears to be a question. It is, furthermore, a question specifically designed for the place in which it is used. Now the phrase "place in which it is used" is critical, and how we formulate "place" will be central to the later analysis. For now we can note that the turn at line 12 is not a fully formed question, but shows its attention to what preceded it, at least in part, by requiring of its hearer attention to what preceded it for its very understanding: it is, so to speak, built off of, or on to, the preceding turn, uses it as a resource for its construction, and requires its use as a resource for its understanding. One thing further needs to be said at this point about its relation to what precedes it, and that is that what it is appended to is a statement of someone else's views; you will note the prior turn starts "*He* says." So a preliminary characterization of 12 might be that it is a question, requesting clarification by B of someone else's views, of which he (B) has just given a (summary) version.

Now "for whom" will sustain a quite different analysis. That is, it can stand as a way for A to show agreement with B. I say "show agreement" to differentiate it from agreeing, or more particularly from claiming or asserting agreement, for agreement, like understanding, is subject to incorrect or manipulative treatment. That is, there can be extrinsic reasons for claiming understanding or agreement, for example, in the case of agreement, to achieve closure of a topic or argument, a theme to which we will return. In any case, for both understanding and agreement, "claiming" them and "showing" them are different sorts of things, and impose different requirements. In the present case, "for whom" can be seen as an attempt to show understanding of, and agreement with, B. It does this by complaining about, or challenging, a position with which B has just asserted himself to be in disagreement, proferring a possible argument of B's. Under that analysis, it is not an answer to a question that is a relevant next utterance or action, for a question has not been asked (though a question form has been used); rather, an acknowledgment of agreement is relevant.

It should be noted that neither of these putative "analyses" of "for whom" has yet been provided a basis. They are proposed now as observations, I hope with some cogency. I intend next to show that the sequel in the conversation is consistent with first one, and then the other, of these analyses being taken up. But the basis of these understandings of "for whom," either by the parties to the conversation, or for the analyst, remains to be analyzed. Certainly, "for whom" is not a question by virtue of its linguistic form, its inclusion of a "wh-word," alone, for not all utterances with wh-words are questions. And it is not a complaint/agreement in any self-evident way, for no basis has been provided for hearing "for whom" as in some way B's position (which is central to that analysis) rather than A's.

If 12 is a question, then it is a first pair part of an adjacency pair, a pair of the type question–answer, and the one to whom it is addressed should do the second pair part for that pair type, that is, here he (B) should do an answer. Further, if the question is doing a request for clarification, the answer should do a clarification. And, finally if the clarification requested is of another's view, as was suggested by appending the question that requests it to a statement of those views, then the answer should assign the clarification, that is, the extension of the views, to their holder. As much of an utterance as B gets to produce at 13 is consistent with all of this. In seeming to undertake a clarification, or further explication, and starting with "he says" where the "he" finds as its referent the same referent as the "he"'s in lines 9–11, B can be seen to display his understanding of 12 as a question he is now answering, a request he is now satisfying. Let me emphasize that while for us now he is displaying it too, in the first place he is displaying it to A. And as B is engaged in an analysis of 12 to find what it was doing and what he might then do next, so A is engaged in an analysis of 13. And from the amount of 13 that gets out before A interrupts, what has been suggested above about it is available. "Well he says" is all that is needed to see that B heard 12 as a question, a request for clarification of the other's position, and is starting to do what he should on that analysis, namely, answer the question by giving clarification of the other's position. When enough of the utterance is out to display that, and no more, A interrupts.

It appears that the understanding of 12 "for whom" that B displays himself in 13 to have, is for A, the speaker of that utterance, incorrect. That is, it appears that while B understood that to be a question, requesting clarification of the teacher's position, A did not produce it to be that.

That one party can see that, and how, an utterance of his has been misanalyzed by another from that other's subsequent utterance we have found on quite other materials. For example, someone doing an intendedly terminal greeting who gets back a "yes?" can find that it was heard incorrectly, and, in particular, what wrong thing it was heard as; that is, the greeting was heard as a summons (cf. Schegloff 1968:1082). In particular, parties can detect such errors by seeing an interlocutor's utterance as a second pair part, finding the first pair part it would be a proper sequel for, and seeing how the utterance it follows, in many cases their own prior utterance, could have been heard as such a first pair part. Here, I am proposing, A can hear 13 as a possible answer, can locate a question as a prior form of utterance that would have elicited an answer as its proper sequel, and can see how 12, his own prior utterance, while not produced to be a question, could be so analyzed. That much is available from 13, B: "Well he says." By interrupting at that point with an utterance of the type involved, A in effect disallows B's proceeding on that analysis of 12 in this slot.

The utterance with which A interrupts at line 14 is exquisitely designed for its place. While we do not have any equivalence rules for utterances in conversation that I know of, this utterance – "By what *standard*" – is as close to an equivalent for 12 – "for *whom*" – as I can imagine. In its syntactic form, in its intonational contour, in its stress placement, the two are isomorphic. And, importantly, it is built on to, or off of, attaches itself in exactly the same way as did 12, to line 11. It is more a duplicate of 12 than a repetition of 12 would have been. It is, it appears, *the* way of repeating the turn at line 12.

Its use here is that it invites a reanalysis with a different outcome of the utterance it repeats. It seems to invoke a procedure I will call a "redo invitation": that is, it invites the last speaker to repeat some last operation and come up with a different output. One way the procedure may be invoked is by repeating the element on which the operation is to be redone. Let me cite two quite different sorts of data (in both of which, however, the repetition is done by the recipient of the repeated element, not its speaker):

(9)

```
S:    Do you need any help up there.
D:    All we can get.
S:    All you can get.
D:    Yes, you have a station wagon or anything
      that can haul injured?
```

in which a reanalysis of what would be an adequate answer is elicited, more specifics then being produced; and the following which I take from a paper by Gail Jefferson (1972:295):

(10)

```
St:   One two three ((pause)) four five six
      ((pause)) eleven eight nine ten.
Su:   "Eleven"? – eight nine ten?
St:   Eleven eight nine ten
Na:   "Eleven?"
St:   Seven eight nine ten.
```

As this last citation suggests, one way of invoking the procedure involves paralinguistically marked repetition – a special upward intonation pattern, and a special stress placement. Note that neither of these is possible at 14 in the data we are concerned with. An upward intonation on an utterance of question form with a wh-word makes it into a recipient's repeat of another's question; and the initial version of A's utterance, at 12, already had a heavy stress at the point where the stress would go to invite redoing. And so A does as close to an equivalent utterance as is perhaps possible, and thereby invites reanalysis of what his utterance was doing. It is worth noting that by building his utterance at 14 to attach to 11 in just the way 12 did, A brings off that the reanalysis he is inviting is what he "intended all along," that is, it was the correct analysis of 12 too, rather than being only what he is doing now, leaving open what a correct understanding of 12 would have been.[1] That is, the form of his construction here provides for the retroactive, or retrospective, relevance of the understanding it is intended to elicit, namely, the alternative we suggested earlier for 12, agreement with B via complaint about B's opponent.

That all of this is effective is shown by 15. It was suggested earlier that the alternative analysis of "for whom," under which it is seen as showing agreement with B, makes relevant as a next utterance an acknowledgment of agreement. B, in starting his utterance at 15 with an acknowledgment of agreement, then, displays his understanding of what A has been about as a show of agreement.

This point bears a bit of elaboration, for the form of the utterance at 15 is noteworthy. There is a range of forms through the use of which conversationalists can do the work of bringing off collaboratively that they are in agreement. Some are nearly prepackaged, for example, "I agree," "I know," "Right," and the like, which are assertions of agreement; others, unlistable because they are in particulars fitted to the matter being agreed on, show agreement by a variety of techniques, for example, showing one knows what the other has in mind by saying it for him, as in completing his sentence or his argument. Both of these, concerned with claiming or showing agreement, should be distinguished from a quite different action, namely, "acknowledging agreement." The issue of who agrees with whom can be a real one, with sequential consequences, and not, as might be thought, one of vanity, in the face of the raw fact of agreement. That issue is: whose "position" is the point of departure, is the thing to be agreed with, and, therefore, who is in a position to be doing "agreeing": the one who does the "base statement" is not one who can do agreement with it (he can do reassertion of it). Thus if X takes a position, Y may claim or assert agreement. But if X takes a position, and Y then states a position intended to show, rather than claim, agreement with X's position, then X should *acknowledge* agreement to show his appreciation that Y was *showing* agreement. If X should, in that position, agree with Y (rather than acknowledge agreement), it may not be clear to Y that X has understood that he (Y) was showing *his* agreement with X. That is: a first agreement may not take a second, it should get an agreement–acknowledgment. If a second agreement is produced, it may be seen as displaying that the first agreement was not heard or not correctly analyzed.[2] A bit of data to illustrate some of this is taken from a later point in this same conversation:

(11)

```
B:    ... the only difference which is made between
      Mexico 'r United States or Canada or any other
      countries.
A:    Mm/hmm
B:    is that if the country has different interest.
      Because of their background, and their al-an'
      history / an'
A:    and different statures of power. Quite ⌈correct.
B:                                          ⌊right
```

in which A shows agreement by adding a piece of B's argument, then asserts his intention, in doing so, of agreeing – "quite correct" – (relevant here because the stress on the "and" could be taken as modifying it), and B acknowledges the agreement.

Now some forms, like "right," seem to be used both for agreeing and for acknowledgment of agreement. But the one that B uses at 15 is clearly not an agreement, but an understanding not only of A's position, but of A's action. For since shows of agreement (as compared to assertions or claims) are overtly addressed to the matter being agreed on and not to the fact of agreement, which is left to be analyzed by a coparticipant, for *them* acknowledgments are specially relevant to show understanding.

Let me note at this point that one of the aims in explicating this sequence may now perhaps be claimed, namely, that the ambiguity I want to address is an empirical one, in that both parties deal with both possible analyses: A both gets his show of agreement understood and recognizes the "question" analysis that the utterance at 13 displays B to have made, so *he* deals with both; 13 displays B to have attended the question analysis of "for whom," and his acknowledgment of agreement at 15 shows him to have employed *that* analysis as well. We have here, then, not merely a theoretically imaginable ambiguity, but an empirically encountered one.

3

At the beginning of the preceding discussion of the sequence from 12–15, I offered initial accounts of two alternative analyses of "for whom," one as a question, requesting clarification of the teacher's position, the other as a show of agreement by A with B by producing a possible piece of B's argument against the teacher. No basis for either analysis was offered, and it is now time to seek them. By that I mean that no basis for analyzing "for whom" as a question has been established, no procedure whereby B could have come to hear it that way. I clearly am not suggesting that he did not, or could not, hear it that way, having just finished trying to show that he did; only that *how* he could come to hear it that way has not been shown.

Let me start with the analysis of "for whom" as a question or a request for clarification. I shall need some resources developed on quite different material by Sacks (1973a, 1974).

Sacks speaks of a story recipient's slot after story completion as a structural, or a structurally defined, "place" in conversation. One line of reasoning that provides for it is this: the basic turn-taking organization of conversation operates on an utterance to utterance basis, an over-simplified version of a transition rule being that any next possible utter-ance completion point is a point at which a possible next speaker may seek to effect transition. The first application of this rule, clearly, will come at the first possible completion point, which, for now only, let us treat as a first possible sentence completion point (cf. Sacks, Schegloff, and Jefferson 1974, for details). A sequential problem for prospective storytellers, insofar as stories require more than a sentence/utterance to tell, is how to get potential next speakers, who may use a first possible completion point to start talking, to not start talking. There is a variety of techniques for so doing, which I cannot describe here, all of which have the consequence of depriving the sentence/utterance of its transition-to-next-speaker relevance. Extended utterance completion, or speaker turn completion, will then have to be detected by hearers by finding story completion. One reason for the story recipient's slot upon story comple-tion being a structural place is, then, that in it recipients must display appreciation of story completion. Another is that, not being afforded over the course of a story occasion for displaying their understanding of the story, there is an issue, upon story completion, of story recipients displaying their understanding of the story, and there is a range of ways of doing so. Showing appreciation of completion, and showing under-standing of the story are, or can be, linked tasks, one way of showing one sees the completion being to display one's understanding. Since, as long as the story is ongoing, other speakers properly hold off, story completion is central to the sequential organization of conversation, and the story recipient's slot after story completion is a specially marked place.

I have gone into all of this because the utterance at 12 "for whom" is, or can be seen by participants as, a story recipient's utterance upon possible story completion. Without going through the whole of the pre-ceding conversation, in which with three exceptions, A does only what we call "continuers" (versions of "mmhmm") which is, among other things, a form for hearers showing they see an extended unit, like a story, is in progress and not yet completed, two features of 1–11 suggest that story completion can be found here: (1) B announces it to be a summary ("it came down to this") and summaries or reviews are com-pletion-relevant or closing-relevant (as also in conversational closure [Schegloff and Sacks 1973], "I just called to find out . . ."); and (2) the teller has the characters in the story do a closing relevant action, in this case *in the story* summing their positions, that being a way of agreeing to disagree, and agreeing being a way arguments are brought to a close (and thus the use of "I agree" to mean no more than "let's end it," no one believing agreement has been reached). A way of ending stories, as Sacks (1972b) has nicely shown holds even for children's stories, is by having the characters do a terminal action in a behavior stream, like going to sleep. If I am allowed to omit further elaboration of this claim, then story completion being findable in 1–11, A is talking at 12 in recipient's slot upon story completion, and his utterance is to be scrutinized for its display of appreciation of completion, and for its understanding of the story.

I want now to introduce a small modification in our understanding of this structural place in conversation. It is intended to take account of the fact that in conversation little if anything can be done assuredly unilaterally. Even for utterances, we speak of their *"possible* completion points" because, in part, the speaker may continue or another speaker may build something onto an otherwise seemingly completed utterance, so that its initiator turns out not to control fully what his utterance turns out to be. So also for larger units, like "topics," and so I propose for stories. Rather than speaking of story completion, then, I shall speak of story-completion proposal. Tellers of a story can at some point *propose* story completion, but they cannot by themselves *guarantee* it. A story is complete when, its completion having been proposed by the teller, it is accepted by the recipient by recognition of completion and display of understanding.

But allowing completion and (or by) showing understanding is only one of the tacks recipients can take upon a completion proposal. Another thing they can do is disallow completion. They can do this in effect, but unintentionally, by being wrong when they try to show understanding; that is, by producing as their understanding an understanding of the story that is unacceptable to the teller. The story may then be kept open for correction. Recipients can do this intentionally also; that is, they can produce an intentional misunderstanding of the story: for example, B has just reported to A that "Sibbi's sister had a baby boy"; she continues

(12)

```
B:   but uh she was long overdue
A:   Mm
B:   And she-she had gained about forty pounds
     anyway.  They said she was tremendous.  So
     I'm sure they're happy about that.
A:   Yeah that she's tremendous hh.
```

But the most regularly used form by which a recipient can keep a story open, one designed in a sense to do that job, is a question about the story. A question about the story, in requiring an answer from the teller about the story, may keep the story open. Thus, just as that recipient slot is specially inspected for the possible appreciation of completion and the understanding of the story it may contain, so it is inspected for the other relevant possibility it may contain, namely, a question about the story to keep the story open. That is a thing for the teller to look for, since if it is there he or she will have to deal with it. And if an utterance in question form appears there, it should be heard, on this account, as a question. It should be heard that way not by virtue of the question form, but by virtue of the relevance of finding a question there if one can, that last condition being satisfiable by a question form. With that, I hope to have shown a basis for the first possible analysis of "for whom," that is, hearing it as a question, requesting clarification. It is through and through provided by the sequential structure in which it is implicated, and the place it occupies in it. And I hope to have suggested one sort of power linguistic form may have, other than the "action-determining" power rejected in the beginning of this paper. We may call it "constraint-meeting power"; that is, given an independent sequential basis for finding an utterance to be a question "if one can" (the last being the constraint), that constraint can be met by the linguistic form of the utterance – its interrogative form.

Let me now try to provide a basis for the other analysis, according to which A is in the utterance at 12 showing agreement with B by disagreeing with B's announced opponent, or more specifically, by showing he can produce a piece of B's possible argument, and thereby that he understands and is sympathetic. Insofar as this initial gloss is a bit richer than the initial statement of the first alternative, less may be required in the explication. The major point needing development here is the basis for hearing "for whom" as proposedly B's position, or part of it. Certainly we don't want to rely on intuitions about what that position would be if we extrapolated from what is given in the conversation, in order to find "for whom" consistent with it. Let me propose instead that A relies (unsuccessfully at first, as it turns out) on a sequential structure that is operative *within the conversation being reported in the story*, and that is the alternation formula for two-party conversation that is conventionally described as "ababab" but ought, for clarity's sake here be referred to as BCBCBC, in which C is the teacher.

What I am suggesting is that A produces his utterance not only by reference to the position of his slot as after proposed story completion, but that in constructing an utterance he employs another positioning of that slot, fitted not merely to the fact that he is following *a* story, but fitted to the particular story type and the particular instance of it that his utterance is following. That is, he employs that this is an "opposition-type" story; that it is about a conversation; that it reports the conversation using the BCBC format; that the positions that are in opposition are mapped into that format (that is, that BCBC tracks not only the alternation of turns but also the alternation of positions), and finally that all of this is presented in the proposed story completion, with the BCBC formula turning out to have C's position be the one occupying the last turn. His utterance at 12 – "for whom" – is then, by an extension, produced in a slot *in that conversation* (i.e., the one being reported on) that the formula assigns to B, or if you like B's side, and there is a basis then for hearing it as a contribution to, and thereby an understanding of and agreement with, that side, or with B. It is thus that it can come off as a proposed piece of B's argument, for B eventually to appreciate as "exactly what I mean." In support of this device, which requires for its accomplishment seeing that A is extending the story one slot as his way of showing his appreciation of its completion and his understanding (not to mention his siding with B to which we shall return), and thus that his utterance be seen in terms of the sequencing structure internal to the conversation the story reports, in support of this device A builds his utterance, as we noted before, so that it requires reference to the last utterance in *that* sequence for its understanding. It seeks to make his utterance analyzable as a possible next utterance in the conversation in which the utterance it is appended to occurred. But to no avail, it turns out, the first time around.

If we can appreciate that, on this analysis of "for whom," A is agreeing with B by "siding" with him, joining his side in an oppositional story in which sides are represented by alternating conversational slots, and we can appreciate the relevance, for recipients and tellers, of recipients choosing sides in oppositional stories in which the teller is one of the characters, then perhaps we can briefly reexamine "for whom" under the first analysis – the question analysis – to see how *it* might be understood in terms of A's siding.

Consider: B is presenting an oppositional story in which he is one of the protagonists. One thing A can do is side with one or the other, teller/protagonist or his opponent. Regularly recipients side with tellers, I suppose because that is in part how tellers choose recipients for stories. But recipients don't invariably side with tellers. Is there a way that "for whom" as a question might appear relevant to A's siding with B's opponent? To be sure, a request for clarification can be doing a show of nonunderstanding, and especially in that structural place; but it can also be examined, when siding is an issue as it may be here, for evidence of siding with an opponent.

Let me suggest that "for whom" can be heard in a way that makes it relevant to siding with "the teacher." That involves hearing "for whom" as a presequence question. "Presequence" is a global term for utterances (typically questions) whose relevance is treated by participants as given not so much by what preceded but by what they are foreshadowing. That is, they are treated as specifically preplaced utterances. Dealing with them can then be sensitive to the sequences they are seen to foreshadow. Thus, for example, pre-invitations, such as "Are you doing anything," are heard for their prefatory character. And seeing them as pre-invitations, or prerequests, can involve that their answers are selected not only, if at all, with an eye to their descriptive adequacy, but with an eye to what is to be done with the anticipatable utterance they preface. And, indeed, a next utterance can inquire for the specifics being prefaced. Thus "Are you doing anything" "Why?" or "What did you have in mind?"

Now the presequence character of an utterance is not linguistically marked; it is a sequential feature. The utterance following A_2 in data excerpt (3) above, following, that is, "I don't know just where the – uh – this address *is*," which we earlier suggested is a request for directions, is "Well, what part of town do *you* live," which is here treated as a presequence to direction giving; in other sequential contexts it could be a straightforward question.

I am suggesting that, in the excerpt with which we are concerned, "for whom" can be heard as a presequence to agreement with the teacher and disagreement with B, speculatively proconstructing the putative sequence as A: For whom, B: Well he says . . . A: What's wrong with that. On that hearing, the question complains not about the position to which it is appended, but about the presentation the position has been given by another, the "not having done it justice," and that is a complaint of one who has a possible interest in its being done justice, one such interest being that it is the complainer's position. In the present case, that would be, then, a disagreement, or a presequence to disagreement, with B.

Now I want to note that this view of "for whom" places it differently from the initial analysis as a matter of "strategy" if you will; at a minimum, it locates it strategically. Nonetheless, it falls within the earlier analysis, and is but one kind of extension of it, in that it keeps the story open.

. . . . *

*About five pages of the original typescript have been omitted here [Eds.].

This matter can be approached in a different way, and one that may elucidate the trouble with using a participant's putative "role," for example, one established at the beginning of the conversation, as of definitive import at any given place in it, or as governing the production and analysis of utterances rather than being controlled by them. While those encountering this form of analysis for the first time regularly feel that the fact this datum occurred on a radio talk show is of massive and pervasive relevance, the critical fact being the relevance of "performer" role; or feel the status of the caller as teenager vis-à-vis an adult is crucial; or any other of a range of "roles" or identifications of the parties, none of these are critical here. What seems to be critical to the conversational phenomenon of telling a story in which the teller is a protagonist is the respective relevance of teller versus protagonist. In the present data the analysis of "for whom" as a request for clarification is linked to an identification of B as protagonist in the story, that is, the particular protagonist he is, vis-à-vis whom A can align himself.

The "derived" action – showing agreement – is linked to an identification of B as protagonist, which is how a derived action is possible here, for via B's status as protagonist the teacher is relevantly available as the target for the "primary" action of the utterance on that analysis. And the primary action as clarification – request is linked to B's identification as storyteller, that is, what he is doing in the this-conversation.

Let me only note that A eventually allows B to deal with "for whom" and "by what standard" under both analyses, as long as the "agreement" analysis is dealt with first.

4

Let me conclude by refocusing on three themes that run through the preceding, in order of increasing generality.

First, *question:* whatever defines the class "questions" as a linguistic form will not do for questions as conversational objects, or interactional objects, or social actions. If by "question" we want to mean anything like a sequentially relevant or implicative object, so that in some way it would adumbrate the notion "answer," if, therefore, something like adjacency-pair organization is involved, with special constraints on the second pair part of a sort not yet analytically explicated; if, finally, we intend "question" to be able to serve as a form of account of *conversationalists'* behavior, rather than idealized speakers and hearers, or "subjects," then it will not do, for a variety of reasons, to use features of linguistic form as sole, or even invariant though not exhaustive, indicators or embodiments of such objects. Sequential organization is critical. That much given, whether it is useful to discriminate such a class "question" as a special object of interest, rather than assimilating it to the class "adjacency pairs" seems to me less clear. But that matter cannot be pursued here.

Second, *ambiguity:* to whatever received accounts we have of sources of ambiguity of utterances, we should add the basis for ambiguity provided by the sequencing structures of conversation. The ambiguity discussed here, concerning the possible question status of an utterance, is certainly not the only sequentially based ambiguity; nor are the sequential organizations implicated in it, and cases like it, the only such ambiguity-generating combination. When we get further along in explicating the various sequential organizations of conversation, and interaction, and importantly, their integration, we shall first get a sense of the range of this phenomenon. And then, perhaps, we will be in a position to see not only how surviving ambiguities of the sort here examined may be yielded by sequential organization, but how a range of potential ones are produced and solved before surfacing.

That last clause is produced by an analytic strategy that ought to be made explicit, and perhaps questioned. Most theoretically or heuristically conjurable ambiguities never actually arise. That could be so because of the operations of a so-called disambiguator, as a component of the brain, as a service of context to syntax, and so on. Or it could be that the theoretically depictable ambiguities are derived by procedures that are not relevant to naturally occurring interaction, and therefore in natural contexts the ambiguities are not there to disambiguate.

The problem of ambiguity can be seen as an "overhearer's problem." That is, an overhearer, getting a snatch of conversation, or even all of it without knowing the "what-is-being-talked-about" independently of the talk he is hearing about it, can hear ambiguities in the talk that are not there for the ratified participants (to use Goffman's term) in the conversation. Talk being designed by conversationalists for what the other does and does not know (Sacks and Schegloff 1979; Sacks, Schegloff, and Jefferson 1974; and Schegloff 1972), such design can be expected to avoid in advance much of the potential ambiguity for the coparticipants. Hearers for whom it has not been designed will find ambiguities at points at which their knowledge is not isomorphic with that of the party for whom the talk was designed. Of course, an important part of what a coparticipant knows is what has already been said in the conversation, and so one getting a snatch of it is almost guaranteed to be able to find an ambiguity.

It is expectable that the problems of ambiguity and indexicality should have had their origin and most pointed interest for logic and science, whose interest is in the evaluation of statements stripped from local context, an evaluation that would hold for any man, anywhere, anytime, and not turning on what anyone in particular knows. That almost defines the conditions in their most extreme form for the discovery of ambiguity empirically. Paradoxically, then, ambiguity as a topic of interest, and the discovery of ambiguities empirically in practice, is a natural consequence of the search for "rational" discourse, under one major sense of rational in this context, that is, "universalistic." Nor is it, on this view, odd that ambiguity should be treasured by intellectual traditions that are, on the whole, counterposed to rationalism, for example, the so-called New Criticism.

A great deal of the ambiguity that has troubled philosophers, logicians, linguists, and some sociologists seems to me characterizable in terms of the overhearer's problem, though the disciplines have not relied on being overhearers in fact. A ready procedure is at hand for generating ambiguities of the appropriate form: One starts with a single sentence, sometimes putting into it a classical source of ambiguity (e.g., an indexical expression like a pronoun), sometimes not, and one imagines a range of settings or scenarios in each of which the sentence, or some component of it would have, or be said to have, a "different meaning" or "different sense." In the finding that the "same sentence" or "same component" can have "different meanings" across the imagined range of scenarios is the kernel of the problem of ambiguity. It is because actual participants in actual conversations do not encounter utterances as isolated sentences, and because they do not encounter them in a range of scenarios, but in actual detailed single scenarios embedded in fine-grained context, that I began this discussion with the observation that most theoretically or heuristically depictable ambiguities do not ever arise.

Again, then, a great deal of the ambiguity with which our disciplines have concerned themselves seems to me to be the product of such a procedure. I do not mean to denigrate its status as a problem. I mean only to suggest that the study of such theoretical ambiguity needs to be distinguished from the sort of ambiguity that actual conversationalists actually, empirically encounter as ambiguities in the natural course of conversation. There are such empirical ambiguities, and I am proposing that they are a different sort of thing analytically, and should be considered separately.

When we look for the basis of such ambiguities, I think we must recognize a (major) source for them in the sequential organizations of conversation. And that will necessarily differentiate their investigation from that of the more traditional ambiguities, which are precipitated in the first place by depriving them of their sequential placement.

If, finally, these are different classes of ambiguities, with different bases, and different forms of investigation appropriate to them, it is not clear to what, in natural interaction, findings about theoretical or heuristic ambiguities and their disambiguation apply. For they are findings about objects that may not, or may not much, appear in the world naturalistically observed or findings that are models from which natural objects in the world to one degree or another depart. And if this argument turns on the consideration that the sentences are divorced from the contexts in which they might in the "real world" appear, then it goes not only to ambiguities, but to findings such as the claimed greater complexity, syntactically and psychologically, of negatives, passives, questions, and so on. The point here is that taking sentences in isolation is not just a matter of taking such sentences that might appear *in* a context *out* of the context; but that the very composition, construction, assemblage of the sentences is predicated by their speakers on the place in which it is being produced, and it is through *that* that a sentence is context-bound, rather than possibly independent sentences being different intact objects in or out of context. The latter is what artificial languages, such as mathematics, are designed to achieve. To treat natural languages in that way is to treat them as *having* the very properties whose absence has motivated the search for artificial formal languages. But it is also to continue to disattend, and indeed to deprecate, the very features that make language, and in particular, its everyday interactional use, the powerful natural object that it is.

Notes

1. An observation for which I am indebted to Katherine Campbell.
2. An illuminating, and more empirically worked through, treatment of many of the issues (concerning agreement) may be found in Pomerantz (1975). (See also Chapter 4 herein.)

PART II
Preference organization

The concept of "preference" has developed in conversation analytic research to characterize conversational events in which alternative, but nonequivalent, courses of action are available to the participants (Sacks 1973c). Such alternatives may arise at the level of lexical selection, utterance design, and action or sequence choice – to name only the most prominent areas of investigation in this field. The term "preference" refers to a range of phenomena associated with the fact that choices among nonequivalent courses of action are routinely implemented in ways that reflect an institutionalized ranking of alternatives. Despite its connotations, the term is *not* intended to reference personal, subjective, or "psychological" desires or dispositions.

That selections among activities are shaped by institutionalized rankings is evidenced in a range of ways. First, there is the primary distributional evidence that, in situations of choice, particular actions are avoided, withheld, or delayed across large numbers of occasions involving a variety of speakers in a range of contexts.

Second, across a similarly varied range of occasions, preferred/dispreferred alternatives are routinely performed in distinctive ways. Preferred activities are normally performed directly and with little delay. Dispreferred activities, by contrast, are usually performed with delay between turns, are commonly delayed within turns, and are variously softened and made indirect. The evidence here is of double significance. Not only is the routine use of alternative turn designs for preferred/dispreferred activities evidence for the institutionalized status of these preferences, but it also evidences that these alternative "packagings" – which are general to a variety of action types – are themselves institutionalized as features of the organization of talk.

Finally, the distinction (and often disjunction) between a personal desire or disposition to choose a particular course of action and the institutionalized preferences bearing on that choice is a matter of com-

53

mon experience. For example, most speakers will have refused a thoroughly undesired invitation with appropriate delay and expressions of regret at a competing engagement. Here the separation between a disposition and its expression is oriented to by the speaker, who avoids producing an outright and unvarnished rejection. A similar separation is oriented to by hearers who must interpret the action. Thus a delayed refusal of an invitation because of a competing obligation may, as the standard form for such refusals, be treated as opaque concerning the refuser's real dispositions. By contrast, an early and unvarnished refusal may be treated as disclosing these dispositions and, indeed, as designed to do so. Thus it is often in *departures* from institutionalized designs for actions that real dispositions are found to be displayed. Hence the communication of personal dispositions is itself accomplished by reference to basic institutionalized forms. And by the same token, a desire to avoid the inferences that such departures can inherit may motivate the routine use of the relevant preference packagings for actions.

In the first contribution to this part, Pomerantz shows that a first speaker's assessment of someone or something known to the recipient routinely invites a subsequent (second) assessment, with which the recipient can (nonequivalently) agree or disagree with the first speaker. She then shows that second speakers orient to the nonequivalence of these alternatives by designing turns and sequences that embody agreement differently from those embodying disagreement. In a majority of contexts and cases, agreement turns are fully occupied with turn components that assert or implicate agreement. Moreover, agreement turns are commonly explicitly stated and performed with a minimum of gap between the completion of the prior turn and the initiation of the agreement turn. By contrast, disagreements are less commonly stated explicitly, are often prefaced with agreement components, and are often delayed within a turn and/or over a series of turns. Thus "agreement turns/sequences are structured so as to maximize occurrences of stated agreements, and disagreement turns/sequences so as to minimize occurrences of stated disagreements."

In some cases – for example, when a first assessment is a self-deprecation and agreement with it would constitute a criticism of its producer – Pomerantz demonstrates that the packaging of agreements and disagreements is the reverse of the normal case. Here it is disagreements that are overtly stated and occupy whole turns, whereas agreements are in various ways muted or downgraded. Thus the preferred/dispreferred design of second assessments is sensitive to the activities being accomplished through first assessments (see Pomerantz 1978a for a discussion of the more complicated considerations bearing on compliment responses).

Toward the end of Chapter 4, Pomerantz indicates that recipient silence after a first assessment may be analyzed as implicating an unstated or as-yet-unstated dispreferred action. In Chapter 5, Davidson develops this suggestive conclusion by analyzing a range of sequences involving invitations, offers, requests, and proposals. She demonstrates that the producers of these actions, analyzing recipient silence as implicating an as-yet-unstated dispreferred action (rejection), may seek to preempt its occurrence with a subsequent version of the initial invitation, offer, or whatever. Common to these subsequent versions, she notes, is (1) some attempt to make the initial version more acceptable and (2) the provision of a further opportunity for a favorable response.

Davidson also demonstrates that the basic features of preference design can invade the fine details of turn and sequence structure. For whereas the producer of a first version may wait out the production of a rejection before developing a subsequent version, a rejection can be anticipated from initial turn components (such as "uh" and "well") that are routinely used to delay rejection components within the turn, and a preemptive subsequent version can be produced there and then. Moreover, given that preferred actions (e.g., acceptances) should properly be produced with a minimum of gap, producers of first versions can build a series of possible response points into their utterances, or stretch an existing response point, so as to monitor for an early accepting response. Here, Davidson shows, speakers can react to the absence of response at these points by developing a subsequent version that is continuous with the first and, once again, preemptive of rejection.

It will be apparent from these chapters that the institutionalized design features of preferred/dispreferred actions are both inherently structured and actively used so as to maximize cooperation and affiliation and to minimize conflict in conversational activities. A further conversational procedure that contributes to these outcomes is described in the third chapter of this part by Drew, who focuses on the ways in which speakers' reportings of circumstances or events can be used to accomplish dispreferred activities inexplicitly and, in a variety of ways, cautiously. He similarly shows that such reportings can be used to hint at invitations and to check indirectly on recipients' availability for joint activities. By these means, speakers can avoid both on-the-record proposals and stereotypically overt presequence objects (such as "Are you doing anything tomorrow") that could encounter on-the-record rejection. These reportings thus constitute extremely embedded or indirect presequence objects.

In the final chapter of this part, we return to the phenomenon of recipient silence in the face of an utterance that solicits response. Here, as Pomerantz shows, there are a variety of ways in which a response may be pursued and the silence dealt with. Moreover each of these ways will display a particular analysis or interpretation of the silence as a product, for example, of a co-interactant's not having heard the prior utterance, not understanding it, or tacitly disagreeing with it. Additionally, each form of pursuit will tend to imply a particular type and distribution of responsibility for the silence, and the production of pursuit objects may be sensitive to this consideration. Thus, although they are highly indirect, silences are nonetheless consequential social actions. Part of their effectiveness as actions may derive from the onus that they place on others about whether and how a pursuit is to be attempted.

Studies of preference organization have involved a wide range of conversational activities (Davidson forthcoming; Pomerantz 1975, 1978a; Sacks 1973c; Sacks and Schegloff 1979; Schegloff, Jefferson, and Sacks 1977; Wootton 1981a). Preference considerations are clearly implicated in the extensive use of presequence organizations (Sacks 1974; Schegloff 1977, 1980; Terasaki 1976), and given the close connections between presequence organization and conventionalized indirection in speech activity (Goffman 1976, Heringer 1977, Levinson 1983, Schegloff 1977), they are also implicated as factors influencing the design of conventionalized indirect speech acts. Finally, it may be suggested that the design features associated with the production of preferred/dispreferred activities may inform and be informed by a logic of "face" considerations (Brown and Levinson 1978, Goffman 1955) at the levels of both form and usage.

4. Agreeing and disagreeing with assessments: some features of preferred/dispreferred turn shapes

ANITA POMERANTZ
University of Oxford

1. Introduction

When persons partake in social activities, they routinely make assessments. Participating in an event and assessing that event are related enterprises, as the following excerpt illustrates:

(1) (VIYMC 1:4)

    J: Let's feel the water. Oh, it ...
    R: It's wonderful. It's just right. It's like
          bathtub water.

In response to J's suggestion to "feel the water," R proffers a series of assessments that are purportedly derived from her participation in feeling the water. The references within those assessments ("It's wonderful. It's just right. It's like bathtub water.") refer to the water that R claims, via the assessments, to have experienced. Assessments are produced as *products* of participation; with an assessment, a speaker claims knowledge of that which he or she is assessing.

The feature of the connectedness between (1) a speaker's proffering an assessment and (2) that speaker's presumed access to, and knowledge of, the assessed referent is visible in declinations to assess. In each of the following fragments, an assessment that is requested in a prior turn is not proffered. A declination is accomplished with a claim of no access to, or insufficient knowledge of, the particular referent in question:

(2) (SBL:2.2.–2)

    A: An how's the dresses coming along. How d'they look.
    →B: Well uh I haven't been uh by there- ...

The work presented in this chapter is deeply indebted to the research carried out by the late Harvey Sacks. An earlier version of some of the materials presented here was submitted as part of a Ph.D. thesis (University of California, Irvine, 1975). Emanuel Schegloff and Michael Moerman have given extensive comments and suggestions on various drafts.

(3)   (SBL:2.2.-1)

    A: How <u>is</u> Aunt Kallie.
    B: Well, I (suspect) she's <u>be</u>tter.
    A: Oh that's good.
    B: Las' time we talked tuh mother she was uh
           better
    B: Uh Allen, (she wants to know about   ),
           (2.0)
 → B: No, Allen doesn't know anything new out there
           either.[1]

The speakers' claiming insufficient knowledge serves as a warrant for their not giving assessments because assessments are properly based on the speakers' knowledge of what they assess. One of the ways of warranting a declination, then, is to deny the proper basis, that is, sufficient knowledge, for its production.[2]

Although assessments may be seen as products of participation in social activities, the proffering of them is part and parcel of participating in such activities. That is, they are occasioned conversational events with sequential constraints, where one major locus of their occurrences is on the occasions of participation. Recall excerpt (1), in which J suggests that he and R feel the temperature of the water. While participating in that activity R proffers the assessments "It's wonderful. It's just right. It's like bathtub water." Part of participating includes proffering assessments.

A second locus of assessments occurs within speakers' reports of their partaking in activities. The connection between participating and assessing may be seen in such reports. Each of the following excerpts has a sequence of two parts. In the first part, a speaker references an occasion in which he or she had direct experience, for example, "We saw Midnight Cowboy yesterday." The depiction of the event in question is not complete with the referencing alone. A conclusion or point is needed: a summary of the actor's sense or experience of the event. In the second part, then, the speaker indicates a sense of his or her experience by giving an assessment.

(4)   (JS:II:41)

    J: [1] I –n then I tasted it [2] it w'z really
           horrible ...

(5)   (SBL:2.1.7.-1)

    B: [1] I just saw Wengreen outside [2] an' she's an
           she's in <u>bad</u> shape.

(6) (JS:II:61) (J and L are husband and wife.)

    J: [1] We saw Midnight Cowboy yesterday –or
               ⌈suh–Friday
    E: ⌊Oh?
    L: Didju s- <u>you</u> saw that, [2] it's really good

(7) (NB:VIII.-3)

    A: [1] We're painting like mad in the kitchen and,
           [2] Oh ev'rything's workin' out so pretty here
           with our–

(8) (FD:1)

    C: Uh what's the condition of the building.
    D: Well, I haven't made an inspection of it.
           [1] but I've driven by it a few times, [2] and
           uh it doesn't appear to be too bad, ...

A third locus of assessments is in next turns to initial assessments. Recall that proffering an assessment is a way of participating in at least some activities; for example, assessing the water is a way of participating in "feeling the water." Persons also have ways of coparticipating in activities. One way of coparticipating with a co-conversant who has just proffered an assessment is by proffering a second assessment. It is a description of some features of second assessments that is the aim of this paper.

2. Second assessments

Second assessments are assessments produced by recipients of prior assessments in which the referents in the seconds are the same as those in the priors. A sample of a larger corpus of assessment pairs – initial assessments followed by second assessments – is presented here. Initial assessments are notated with A_1, second assessments with A_2.

(9)   (NB:IV.7.-44)

    A_1 A: Adeline's such a swell ⌈gal
    A_2 P: ⌊Oh God, <u>whadda</u> gal.
               You know it!

(10)   (JS:II:28)

    A_1 J: T's- tsuh beautiful day out isn't it?
    A_2 L: Yeh it's jus' gorgeous ...

(11)   (NB:1.6.-2)

A_1 A: ... Well, anyway, ihs-ihs not too co:ld,
A_2^1 C: Oh it's warm ...

(12)   (VIYMC: 1.-2) (J and R are in a rowboat on a lake.)

A_1 J: It's really a clear lake, isn't it?
A_2^1 R: It's wonderful.

(13)   (M.Y.)

A_1 A: That (heh) s(heh)sounded (hhh) g(hh)uh!
A_2^1 B: That soun' -- that sounded lovely ...

(14)   (SBL:2.2.4.-3)

A_1 A: Oh it was just beautiful.
A_2^1 B: Well thank you Uh I thought it was quite
                   nice,

(15)   (NB:VII.-2)

A_1 E: e-that Pa:t isn'she a do:[:ll?
A_2^1 M: [iYeh isn't she
                   pretty,

(16)   (NB:VII.-13)

A_1 E: ... yihknow he's a goodlooking fel'n eez got
                   a beautiful wi:fe.=
A_2 M: =Ye:s::. Go:rgeous girl- ...

(17)   (SBL:2.2.3.-46)

A_1 B: Well, it was fun Cla[ire,
A_2^1 A: [Yeah, I enjoyed every
                   minute of it.

(18)   (MC:1) ("He" refers to a neighborhood dog.)

A_1 B: Isn't he cute
A_2^1 A: O::h he::s a::DORable

(19)   (JK:3)

A_1 C: ... She was a nice lady--I liked her
A_2^1 G: I liked her too

(20)   (MC:1.-45)

A_1 L: ... I'm so dumb I don't even know it.
                   hhh! -- heh!
A_2 W: Y-no, y-you're not du:mb, ...

(21)   (NB:IV:1.-6)

A₁   A: ... ˙hhh Oh well it's me̲ too Portia,
               hh yihknow I'm no bott̲l̲e a' milk,
               (0.6)
A₂   P: Oh:: well yer̲ easy tuh get along with, ...

(22)   (NB:IV:11.-1)

A₁   A: God̲ izn it dreary̲.
               (0.6)
       A: ⌜Y'know I don't think-
A₂   P: ⌞˙hh- it's warm̲ though,

When a speaker assesses a referent that is expectably accessible to a
recipient, the initial assessment provides the relevance of the recipient's
second assessment. That relevance is particularly visible when initial
assessments have a format to invite/constrain subsequence, for example, as interrogatives:

(15)   (NB:VIII.-2)   (Pat is M's friend whom E
                           recently met.)

→E: e̲-that Pa̲:t i̲sn'she a do:⌜:ll?
 M: ⌞iYeh i̲sn't she
        pretty,

            •

(18)   (MC:1)   ("He" refers to a neighborhood dog.)

→B: Isn't he cute
 A: O::h he::s a::DORab̲le

or with interrogative tags:

(10)   (JS:II:28)

→J: T's- tsuh beautiful day out isn't it?
 R: Yeh it's jus' gorgeous ...

(12)   (VIYMC: 1.-2) (J and R are in a rowboat on a lake.)

→J: It's really a clear lake, isn't it?
 R: It's wonderful.

That relevance, however, does not rely for its operation upon an
interrogative format; initial assessments that are asserted also provide
for the relevance of, and engender, recipients' second assessments:

(13)   (M.Y.)

          (A and B both participated in the performance which
          is referred to.)

```
→A:    That (heh) s(heh) sounded (hhh) g(hh)uh!
 B:    That soun' -- that sounded lovely ...
```

(17)   (SBL:2.2.3.-46)

   (A and B both attended the bridge party which is
   referred to.)

```
→B:    Well, it was fun Cla⌐ire,
 A:                        ⌊Yeah, I enjoyed every
        minute of it.
```

The discussion thus far may be summarized as follows. One systematic environment in which assessments are proffered is in turns just subsequent to coparticipants' initial assessments. Just as the proffering of an initial assessment is the first speaker's claim of access to the assessed referent, the proffering of a second is the second speaker's claim of access to that referent.[3] The description of assessment pairs as serial claims of access, however, leaves unexplicated the procedures used to coordinate the assessments: the initial one with an anticipated next and a subsequent one with the just prior. This analysis now turns to some of the features of the coordination of second assessments with their priors.[4]

Second assessments have been described as subsequent assessments that refer to the same referents as in the prior assessments. This feature may be restated as a speaker's procedural rule: A recipient of an initial assessment turns his or her attention to that which was just assessed and proffers his or her own assessment of this referent.

Though speakers do coordinate their second assessments with the prior ones by assessing the same referents, there are finer ways in which they coordinate their talk. Consider the following sequence of assessments:

(10)   (JS.II.28)

```
   J:    T's- tsuh beautiful day out isn't it?
   L:    Yeh it's jus' gorgeous ...
```

J's initial assessment is an expression of approval, incorporating the positive descriptor "beautiful." In proffering a praise assessment, he invites the recipient to coparticipate in praising the referent, that is, to agree with him by proffering a subsequent praise assessment.

In a next turn to an assessment that invites agreement, a recipient may, and often does, elect to agree with the prior. In datum (10) above, L's second assessment is a second praise assessment; it is a second expression of approval, incorporating the positive descriptor "gorgeous." The initial assessment invites a subsequent agreement; the second assessment is proffered *as* an agreement.

While a recipient may elect to agree with a prior assessment that invites agreement, the recipient may alternatively elect to disagree. The following excerpt illustrates this option:

(22)   (NB:IV:11.-1)

A_1 A: <u>God</u> izn it <u>dreary</u>.
               (0.6)
       A: [Y'know I don't think-
A_2 B: [˙hh- It's <u>warm</u> though,

A's initial assessment is a complaint about the weather, incorporating the negative descriptor *"dreary."* In proffering the complaint, A invites the recipient, P, to coparticipate in complaining about the weather – to agree with her by proffering a subsequent complaint assessment.[5]

P's second assessment is proffered as a partial disagreement with A's prior complaint. The inclusion of "though" does the work of claiming to agree with the prior while marking, and accompanying, a shift in assessed parameters which partially contrasts with the prior. It contrasts insofar as it is not proffered as a subsequent complaint assessment.[6]

It was proposed earlier that the proffering of an initial assessment to a recipient who may expectably claim access to the referent assessed provides the relevance of the recipient's second assessment. It was also suggested that this proposal, as it stands, leaves unexplicated the ways in which the parts of the assessment pairs are coordinated one with the other. A refinement of the earlier proposal is now in order.

In proffering an initial assessment, a speaker formulates the assessment so as to accomplish an action or multiple actions, for example, praise, complain, compliment, insult, brag, self-deprecate. In the next turn to the initial proffering, an action by the recipient is relevant: to agree or disagree with the prior. Agreement/disagreement names alternative actions that become relevant upon the profferings of initial assessments. Such agreements and disagreements are performed, by and large, with second assessments.

The proffering of an initial assessment, though it provides for the relevance of a recipient's agreement *or* disagreement, may be so structured that it invites one next action over its alternative. A next action that is oriented to as invited will be called a *preferred next action;* its alternative, a *dispreferred next action.*

Agreement is a preferred next action across a large diversity of initial assessments.[7] Agreement is not *invariably* – across all initial assessments – a preferred next action. What is the preferred next action is structured, in part, by the action performed with the initial assessment. For example, subsequent to a self-deprecation, the usual preference for agreement is nonoperative: An agreement with a prior self-deprecation is dispreferred. (See Section 4).

An import of the preference status of actions is that it bears on how those actions are performed. Isolatable turn-and-sequence shapes provide for different kinds of actualizations of the actions being performed with and through them. Two types of shapes are of interest for this study: One type is a design that maximizes the occurrences of the actions being performed with them, utilizes minimization of gap between its initiation and prior turn's completion, and contains components that are explicitly stated instances of the action being performed. The other type minimizes the occurrences of the actions performed with them, in part utilizing the organization of delays and nonexplicitly stated action components, such as actions other than a conditionally relevant next. The respective turn shapes will be called *preferred-action turn shape* and *dispreferred-action turn shape*.

The thesis of this chapter is that an action, by virtue of how the participants orient to it, will be housed in and performed through a turn shape that reflects their orientation. That is, there is an association between an action's preference status and the turn shape in which it is produced.

This chapter describes the kinds of organizations that bear on the productions of second assessments. To show the relevance and operation of preference status on second-assessment productions, two environments with differing preferences are examined: (1) second assessments that are produced when agreements are preferred, and (2) second assessments produced when agreements are dispreferred.

3. Second-assessment productions: agreement preferred

Subsequent to initial assessments that invite agreement, recipients' agreements and disagreements, respectively, are performed in differently organized turns and sequences. In general, agreement turns/sequences are structured so as to maximize occurrences of stated agreements and disagreement turns/sequences so as to minimize occurrences of stated disagreements. Some overall features of the respective turn and sequence shapes are summarized in the points below:

1. Agreements have agreement components occupying the entire agreement turns; disagreements are often prefaced.
2. Agreements are accomplished with stated agreement components; disagreements may be accomplished with a variety of forms, ranging from unstated to stated disagreements. Frequently disagreements, when stated, are formed as partial agreements/partial disagreements; they are weak forms of disagreement.
3. In general, agreements are performed with a minimization of gap between the prior turn's completion and the agreement turn's initiation; disagreement components are frequently delayed within a turn or over a series of turns.
4. Absences of forthcoming agreements or disagreements by recipients with gaps, requests for clarification, and the like are interpretable as instances of unstated, or as-yet-unstated, disagreements.

Agreements (agreement preferred)

For a recipient to agree with a prior assessment, he or she should show that *his or her* assessment of the referent just assessed by the prior speaker stands in agreement with the prior speaker's assessment. Different types of agreements are produced with second assessments. As will be shown, the types are differentiated on sequential grounds, particularly with respect to their capacities to occur in disagreement turns and sequences.

One type of agreement is the *upgrade*. An upgraded agreement is an assessment of the referent assessed in the prior that incorporates upgraded evaluation terms relative to the prior.[8] Two common techniques for upgrading evaluations are:

(1) A stronger evaluative term than the prior, given graded sets of descriptors, is selected:

(10)　(JS:II:28)

```
      J:   T's- tsuh beautiful day out isn't it?
 → L:   Yeh it's just gorgeous ...
```

(13)　(M.Y.)

```
      A:   That (heh) s(heh) sounded (hhh)
           g(hh)uh!
 → B:   That sound' --- that sounded lovely ...
```

(18)　(MC:1)

```
      A:   Isn't he cute
 → B:   O::h he::s a::DORable
```

(2) An intensifier modifying the prior evaluative descriptor is included:

(23)   (CH:4.-14)
      M: You must admit it was fun the night we
           we ⌈nt down
  → J: ⌊It was great fun ...

(24)   (SBL:2.1.8.-5)
      B: She seems like a nice little ⌈lady
  → A: ⌊Awfully nice
           little person.

(25)   (JS:I:11)
      E: Hal couldn' get over what a good <u>buy</u> that
           was, ⌈(Jon),
  → J: ⌊Yeah That's a r- e (rerry good buy).

Upgrades following assessments may be considered strong agreements on sequential grounds. When they occur, they occur in agreement turns and sequences and not in combinations with disagreements.[9] Upgraded agreements often occur as parts of clusters of agreements, or agreement series, for example:

(25)   (JS:I:11)
      E: Hal couldn' get over what a good <u>buy</u> that was
           ⌈(Jon),
      J: ⌊Yeah That's a r- a (rerry ⌈good buy).
      E: ⌊Yea:h,   Great bu:y,

(18)   (MC:1)
      A: They keep 'im awful nice somehow
      B: Oh yeah I think she must wash 'im
           every ⌈week
      A: ⌊God-che must (h) wash 'im every day the
           way he looks ⌈to me
      B: ⌊I know it
      A: He don't get a chance to roll in the dirt
           ⌈even
      B: ⌊Right,
      B: (Yeah)

Another type of agreement is *same* evaluation. In this type, a recipient
asserts the same evaluation as the prior speaker's evaluation. To assert
the same evaluation, a recipient may repeat the prior evaluative terms,
marking it as a second in a like series with, for example, "too":

(19)   (JK:3)

    C: ... She was a nice lady--I liked her
→ G: I liked her too

(26)   (J & J)

    A: Yeah I like it (   )
→ B: I like it too ...

or include proterms indicating same as prior:

(27)   (GTS:4:6)

    R: Ohh man, that was bitchin.
→ J: That was.

(28)   (GTS:4:15)

    K: ... He's terrific!
→ J: He is.

(29)   (SBL:2.1.8.-5)

    B: I think everyone enjoyed just sitting around
           talking.
→ A :   I do too.

Same evaluations, of course, occur in agreement turns and agreement sequences. But they also, importantly, occur as components within disagreement turns and sequences. The following data show that same evaluations, indicated by (1), may preface disagreements, indicated by (2).

(26)   (J & J)

    A: Yeah I like it [(   )
    B: [[1] I like it too [2] but uhh
        hahheh it blows my mind.

(6)   (JS:II:61)   (E is L's mother. J and L are husband and wife.)

    E: ... 'n she said she f- depressed her terribly
    J: [1] Oh it's [terribly depressing.
    L: [[1] Oh it's depressing.
    E: Ve[ry
    L: [[2] But it's a fantastic [film.
    J: [[2] It's a
        beautiful movie

(30)   (NB:IV:4)

    P: I wish you were gunnuh <u>sta:y</u>
    A: [1] I do too. [2] But I <u>think</u> Oh I've got suh
        <u>damn</u> much tuh do. I really, I'<u>ve</u> gotta get
        <u>home</u> fer- hh <u>I</u> may stay next <u>week</u>.

In that at least some same evaluations are regularly selected as disagreement prefaces, they may be considered a kind of weak agreement.[10]

A third type of agreement is the *downgrade*. A downgraded agreement is an assessment of the same referent as had been assessed in the prior with scaled-down or weakened evaluation terms relative to the prior.

(31) (GJ:1)

    A: She's a fox!
→ L: Yeh, she's a pretty girl.

(15) (NB:VII:2)

    E: e-that <u>Pa:t</u> <u>isn'</u>she a do:[:ll?
→ M: [¡Yeh <u>isn't</u> she
    pretty,

(14) (SBL:2.2.4.-3)

    A: Oh it was just beautiful.
→ B: Well <u>thank</u> you uh I thought it was quite nice.

(32) (KC:4:10)

    F: That's beautiful
→ K: Is'n it pretty

Downgraded agreements frequently engender disagreement sequences. One response that conversants make when disagreed with is to reassert the positions that they have previously taken. In response to downgraded assessments, participants often reassert stronger assessments.

(31) (GJ:1)

    A: She's a fox.
    L: Yeh, she's a pretty girl.
→ A: Oh, she's gorgeous!

(15) (NB:VII:2)

    E: e-that <u>Pa</u>:t <u>isn</u>'she a do:⌈:11?
    M: ⌊iYeh <u>isn</u>'t she
         pretty,
         (.)
→ E: <u>Oh</u>: she's a beautiful girl.

(33) (AP:1)

    G: That's fantastic
→ B: Isn't that good
    G: That's marvelous

(14) (SBL:2.2.4.-3)

    B: An I thought thet uh (1.0) uhm Gene's (1.0)
        singing was --
    A: Oh, was lo⌈vely.
    B: ⌊pretty much like himse⌈lf
→A: ⌊Yes, uh huh,
        it's- Oh it was wonderful

On the basis that at least some downgraded agreements regularly engender disagreement sequences, they, like same evaluation agreements, may be considered a kind of weak agreement.

When an initial assessment is proffered, agreement/disagreement is relevant upon the completion, or more accurately, upon a possible completion point, of the proffering.[11] The temporal coordination of the recipient's second assessment relative to the prior assessment's possible completion is a feature that bears on the accomplishment of the agreement/disagreement. When agreements are invited, strong or upgraded agreements are performed with a minimization of gap (in fact, frequently in slight overlap):

(34) (NB:PT:19:r)

    L: God it's good.=
→ E: =<u>Isn</u>'t that exci:ting,

(35) (JS:I:17)

    B: Isn'at <u>good</u>?=
→ E: =It's <u>duh</u>::<u>licious.

(24) (SBL:2.1.8.-5)

    B: She seems like a nice little ⌈lady
→A: ⌊Awfully nice
        little person.

(25)   (JS:I:11)

    E: Hal couldn' get over what a good <u>buy</u> that was
            (Jon)
→ J: [Yeah That's a r- a (rerry [good buy).
→ E: [<u>Yea:h</u>,   Great bu:y,

(18)   (MC:1)

    A: They keep 'im awful nice somehow
    B: Oh yeah I think she must wash 'm [every week
→ A: [God-che must(h)
        wash 'im every <u>day</u> the way he looks [to me.
    B: [I know it

Disagreements (agreement preferred)

When conversants feel that they are being asked to agree with co-conversants' assessments, they may nonetheless find themselves in the position of disagreeing with them. A substantial number of such disagreements are produced with stated disagreement components delayed or withheld from early positioning within turns and sequences. When a conversant hears a coparticipant's assessment being completed and his or her own agreement/disagreement is relevant and due, he or she may produce delays, such as "no talk," requests for clarification, partial repeats, and other repair initiators, turn prefaces, and so on. Incorporating delay devices constitutes a typical turn shape for disagreements when agreements are invited.

One type of delay device is "no immediately forthcoming talk." Upon the completion of an assessment that invites agreement or confirmation, a conversant, in the course of producing a disagreement, may initially respond with silence. In the fragments below, gaps are notated with (→), disagreement turns with (D).

(22)   (NB:IV:11.-1)

    A: God izn it <u>dreary</u>.
(→)   (0.6)
    A: [Y'know I don't think-
(D) B: [·hh It's <u>warm</u> though,

(36)   (SBL:2.1.7.-14)

    A: (   ) cause those things take working at,
(→)   (2.0)
(D) B: (hhhhh) well, they [do, but
    A: [They aren't accidents,

```
    B:    No, they take working at, But on the other hand,
          some people are born with uhm (1.0) well a
          sense of humor, I think is something yer born
          with Bea.
    A:    Yes. Or it's c- I have the- eh yes, I think a
          lotta people are, but then I think it can be
          developed, too.
(→)       (1.0)
(D) B:    Yeah,  but  ┌there's-
    A:               └Any-
    A:    Any of those attributes can be developed.
```

(37) (TG:3)

```
    A:    ... You sound very far away.
(→)       (0.7)
    B:    I do?
    A:    Ymeahm.
(D) B:    mNo I'm no:t,
```

Another class of delay devices includes repair initiators. In the course of producing a disagreement, a recipient may request clarification with "what?" "Hm?" questioning repeats, and the like. In the following excerpts, clarification requests are marked with (*), disagreements/ disconfirmations with (D).

(38) (MC:1:30)

```
    L:    Maybe it's just ez well Wilbur,
(*) W:    Hm?
    L:    Maybe it's just ez well you don't know.
          (2.0)
(D) W:    Well ./ uh-I say it's suspicious it could be
          something good too.
```

(39) (TG:1)

```
    B:    Why whhat'sa mattuh with y-Yih sou┌nd=
    A:                                      └Nothing.
    B:    = HA:PPY, hh
(*) A:    I sound ha:p┌py?
    B:                └Ye:uh.
          (0.3)
(D) A:    No:,
```

(37) (TG:3)

```
    A:    ... You sound very far away.
          (0.7)
(*) B:    I do?
    A:    Meahm.
(D) B:    mNo? I'm no:t,
```

Disagreement components may also be delayed within turns. Conversants start the turns in which they will disagree in some systematic ways. One way consists of prefacing the disagreement with "uh's," "well's" and the like, thus displaying reluctancy or discomfort.[12] Another way is to preface the disagreement by agreeing with the prior speaker's position. Agreement prefaces are of particular interest because agreements and disagreements are, of course, contrastive components. When they are included within a same turn, the agreement component is conjoined with the disagreement component with a contrast conjunction like "but." An apparent puzzle regarding the agreement-plus-disagreement turn shape is *why* recipients agree with assessments when they will shortly disagree with them.

Agreement components that occur as disagreement prefaces regularly are weak agreements. They are primarily agreement tokens, asserted or claimed agreements, same evaluation agreements, and qualified or weakened agreements:

Tokens

(40) (JG: II.1.–15)

```
      C:    ... you've really both basically honestly
            gone your own ways.
    → D:    Essentially, except we've hadda good
            relationship et home.
    → C:    'hhhh Ye:s, but I mean it's a relationship
            where ...
```

(41) (MC:1.–13)

```
      W:    I sew by hand (    ), -- (uh huh), I'm
            fantastic (you never ⌐saw anything like it)
    → L:                         └I know but I, I-I still say
            thet the sewing machine's quicker,
```

(42) (JG: II:1.–27)

```
      C:    ... 'hh a:n' uh by god I can' even send my
            kid tuh public school b'cuz they're so god
            damn lousy.
      D:    We::ll, that's a generality.
      C:    'hhh
      D:    We've got sm pretty ⌐(good schools.)
    → C:                        └Well, yeah but where in
            the hell em I gonna live.
```

Asserted agreements

(43) (GTS 4:32)

    R: Butchu admit he is having fun and you think
           it's funny.
→K: I think it's funny, yeah. But it's a
           ridiculous funny.

(36) (SBL:2.1.7.-14)

    A: ... cause those things take working at,
           (2.0)
→ B: (hhhhh) well, they ⌐do, but–
    A: ⌊They aren't accidents,
→ B: No, they take working at but on the other
           hand, some people ...

(44) (SBL:2.1.7.-15)

    A: Well, oh uh I think Alice has uh:: i- may- and
           maybe as you say, slightly different, but I
           think she has a good sense ⌐ of humor
→ B: ⌊ Yeh, I think she
           does <u>too</u> but she has a different type.

Weakened and/or qualified agreement assertions

(45) (SBL:1.1.10.-9)

    B: I think I'll call her and ask her if she's
           interested because she's a good nurse, and I
           think they would like her don't you?
→A: Well, I'll tell you, I haven't seen Mary for
           <u>years</u>. I should- As I remember, yes.
    B: Well do you think she would fit in?
→A: Uhm, uh, I don't know, What I'm uh
           hesitating about is uh -- uhm maybe she would.
           (1.0)
    A: Uh but I would hesitate to uhm --

(41) (MC:1.-13)

    L: I know but I, I-I still say thet the sewing
           machine's quicker.
→W: Oh it c'n be quicker but it doesn' do the jo:b,

(36) (SBL:2.1.7.-14)

    B: ... well a sense of humor, I think is something
           yer <u>born</u> with Bea.

→ A: Yea. Or it's c- I have the- eh yes, I think a
          lotta people <u>are</u>, but then I think it can be
          de<u>ve</u>loped, too.

(46) (MC:1.-22)
    W: ... The-the way <u>I</u> feel about it i:s, that as
           long as she coo<u>pe</u>rates, an'-an'she belie:ves
           that she's running my li:fe, or, you know, or
           directing it one way or anothuh, and she feels
           <u>ha</u>ppy about it, I do whatever I please (h)any
           (h)wa(h) ·HHH! ⌜(   )
    L: ⌞Yeah.
→ L: We::ll - eh-that's true: - I mean eh-that's
           alright, -- uhb-ut uh, ez long ez you do::.
           But h-it's-eh-to me::, -- after anyone ...

    Just as the agreement components that preface disagreements are
characteristically weak, so are the disagreement components that follow.

    Disagreement types may be differentiated as strong or weak on se-
quential grounds: They differ in their relative capacities to co-occur with
agreement components.

    A strong disagreement is one in which a conversant utters an evalua-
tion which is directly contrastive with the prior evaluation. Such disagreements are strong inasmuch as they occur in turns containing exclusively disagreement components, and not in combination with
agreement components, for example:

(20) (MC:1.-45)
    L: ... I'm so dumb I don't even know it hhh! --
           heh!
→ W: Y-no, y-you're not du:mb, ...

(47) (SPC:144)
    R: ... well never mind. It's not important.
→ D: Well, it is important.

    The disagreements that occur in the agreement-plus-disagreement
turns are not the strong type, that is, same referent–contrastive evaluation construction. Co-occurring with agreements, the disagreement
components are formed as partial agreements/partial disagreements: as
qualifications, exceptions, additions, and the like.

(43) (GTS 4:32)

    R: Butchu admit he is having fun and you think
             it's funny.

→ K: I think it's funny, yeah. But it's a
             ridiculous funny.

K, after asserting an agreement ("I think it's funny, yeah"), produces a qualification of the agreement by specifying a kind of funny ("it's a ridiculous funny"). The disagreement component is formed as partial agreement/partial disagreement with the prior.

(40) (JG:II.1.–15)

    C: ... you've really both basically honestly gone
             your own ways.

→ D: Essentially, except we've hadda good
             relationship et home.

In response to C's initial critical assessment, D's turn is organized with an initial agreement token (" Essentially") followed by a favorable assessment ("we've hadda good relationship et home"). In shifting the class of evaluation from critical to favorable, D performs a disagreement. The specification of the referent ("relationship et home") in the favorable assessment permits D to claim agreement with the prior critical assessment while producing the favorable assessment/disagreement as a qualification of, or exception to, the prior. (See the material relating to note 6).

Although both agreement and disagreement components are present in the agreement-plus-disagreement turn organization, such turn shapes are used for disagreeing rather than agreeing. That is, disagreement, and not agreement, is centrally sequentially implicative in next turn.

To reiterate, when agreements are invited by initial assessments, disagreements that are proffered regularly are performed in turns and sequences that exhibit the following features: (1) the inclusion of delay devices prior to stated disagreements like silences, hesitating prefaces, requests for clarification, and/or (2) the inclusion of weakly stated disagreement components, that is, partial agreements/partial disagreements. These two features – delaying the stated components of an action being performed, and/or producing weakly stated components of that action – are partially constitutive of turn/sequence organizations associated with dispreferred actions.

These turn/sequence shapes not only house disagreements when agreements are invited, but constitute part of the apparatus for accomplishing disagreements *as* dispreferred. That the set of devices used in these turn/sequence shapes may be oriented to as disagreements in the course of production provides for the possibility and actualization of minimizing the occurrences of overtly stated disagreements in these environments.

When a speaker proffers an initial assessment that invites agreement, a recipient may elect to respond with actions that are neither stated agreements nor stated disagreements like silences. Inasmuch as such responses co-occur with disagreements they may be oriented to as instances of disagreements in the course of production, that is, unstated, or as yet unstated, disagreements.

Prior speakers may elect to resume talk in the emergent gap. In the resumption, they may orient to their coparticipants as disagreeing or probably disagreeing. That orientation can be seen in the modifications that they make. They assert new positions that lessen the differences between their own positions and presumed contrary positions.[13] In the following excerpts, prior speakers resume talk with reversals of and/or backdowns from, prior assessments:[14]

```
(48) (SBL:3.1.-8)
      B:    ...an' that's not an awful lotta fruitcake.
            (1.0)
  → B:     Course it is. A little piece goes a long way.


(49) (SBL:3.1.-6)
      A:    Un livers 'n- gizzards 'n stuff like that,
            makes it real yummy.
            (1.6)
  → A:     Makes it too rich fer me::, but--makes it
            yummy.


(50) (JS:II:48)
      L:    D'they have a good cook there?
            (1.7)
  → L:     Nothing special?
```

Backdowns, then, may be proffered when recipients *potentially* disagree. A disagreement is potential at such points because, though the participants seem headed toward a disagreement, there is still room to avert it. For example, a resumption which contains an appropriately modified assessment may elicit a recipient's agreement:

(48) (SBL:3.1.-8)

    B: ... an' that's not an awful lotta <u>fruitcake</u>
          (1.0)
    B: Course it is. A little piece goes a long way.
→ A: Well that's right

(50) (JS:II:48)

    L: D'they have a good cook there?
          (1.7)
    L: Nothing special?
→ J: No. -- Every- everybody takes their turns.

The combination of conversants' delaying or withholding their disagreements together with fellow conversants' modifying their positions permits stated disagreements to be minimized and stated agreements to be maximized. It is not only that what would be a disagreement might not get said, but that what comes to be said may be said as an agreement.

Just as silences may signal potential disagreement, so may hesitations, questioning repeats, requests for clarification, weakly stated agreements, and the like, do the same. In general, dispreferred-action turn organization serves as a resource to avoid or reduce the occurrences of overtly stated instances of an action.

The preference structure that has just been discussed – agreement preferred, disagreement dispreferred – is the one in effect and operative for the vast majority of assessment pairs. Put another way, across different situations, conversants orient to agreeing with one another as comfortable, supportive, reinforcing, perhaps as being sociable and as showing that they are like-minded. This phenomenon seems to hold whether persons are talking about the weather, a neighborhood dog, or a film that they just saw. Likewise, across a variety of situations conversants orient to their disagreeing with one another as uncomfortable, unpleasant, difficult, risking threat, insult, or offense.

Though sociability, support, and solidarity often involve the participants' agreeing or at least not overtly disagreeing with one another, there are nonetheless circumstances in which sociability and support are accomplished by disagreeing. After self-deprecations, conversants typically treat disagreements as preferred and agreements as dispreferred.

4. Second-assessment productions: agreement dispreferred

When a speaker produces a self-deprecating assessment, the recipient's agreement or disagreement is relevant in the next turn. An agreement with a prior speaker's self-critical assessment amounts to the second speaker's criticism of his or her coparticipant.

Criticisms of one's coparticipants are a class of actions that often are performed in dispreferred-action turn/sequence shapes. A brief summary of evidence to that effect is provided in the two points below:

(1) A substantial number of coparticipant criticisms are performed by speakers' delaying or withholding the criticisms from early positioning within turns and sequences.

In the following datum, D is asked to assess A's newly acquired print. (+) indicates favorable assessment, (−) indicates critical assessment.

```
(51) (JS:I.-1)
        A:    D'yuh li:ke it?
    (+)D:    ˙hhh Yes I do like it=
    (→)D:    =although I rreally::=
        C:    =Dju make it?
        A:    No We bought it, It's a ˙hh a Mary Kerrida
              print.
        D:    O:h (I k-)=
        A:    =Dz that make any sense to you?
        C:    Mm mh. I don' even know who she is.
        A:    She's that's, the Sister Kerrida, ┌who,
        D:                                       └˙hhh
        D:    Oh ┌that's the one you to:ld ┌me you bou:ght.=
        C:       └Oh-
        A:                                 └Ye:h
        D:    ┌Ya:h.
        A:    └Right.
              (1.0)
        A:    It's worth, something,
              (1.0)
        A:    There's only a hundred  of'm
              (0.5)
        D:    Hmm
        E:    Which picture is that.
        A:    The one thet says Life.
              (1.5)
        A:    (                  ).
    (-)D:    ˙hhh Well I don't- I'm not a great fan of this
              type of a:rt. There are certain- ones I see
              thet I like, But I like the w- =
        E:    =Is there ano┌thuh way of spelling Life?
    (-)D:                  └-more realistic-
        A:    hhmh!
        E:    That's all ┌I wd loo(hh)k fo(h),
        D:                └hh!
    (-)D:    Yih d-know why I don't go fer this type of uh::
              art,  Becuz it- it strikes me ez being the
              magazine adverti:sement ty:pe. Which some uh-uh
```

```
        some a' them are really great. But tuhm I-my,
        taste in art is for the more uh:: uh it-t-treh-
        it tends tuh be realistic.
```

A speaker's coparticipant criticism may be potential through a number of turns in which no stated criticism is produced. That is, a speaker may withhold a criticism in one sequential environment and come to state it in another. In the following datum, F asks N to evaluate the nail manicure that F did on N's nails. N's initial report is positive. Subsequently, F proffers a trouble ("·hh Well I was afraid . . .") that invites N to confirm, or alternatively to disconfirm, that trouble or similar ones. The trouble is confirmed by N, who then elaborates with critical descriptions:

(52) (JG:R5:6)

```
     F:     ·hh well how did the polish work otherwise.
  (+)N:     F-eh, fi:ne, fi:ne. In fact I didn' even
            touch em up this week at all
     F:     You didn't
  (+)N:     No
     F:     ·hh Well I was afraid maybe they might uhh uh
            bubble a little bit y'know they ⌈kinda
  (-)N:                                      ⌊Well they di:d.
            Tha-tha-that one thing it with the artificial
            nail bubbled some
     F:     Yeah. Well I was afraid it would
  (-)N:     (   ) the patch bubbled ...
```

Coparticipant criticisms may be withheld, that is, not said, over the course of entire sequences. Since what is not said is, obviously, unavailable in the record of what is said, instances of withholds cannot be directly pointed out. There are, however, reports of withholds. A class of talk routinely reported as withheld, or normatively withholdable, is coparticipant criticism:[15]

(53) (NB:IV.-30)

```
        ((What is reported as not said is a critical
        assessment of a restaurant which Kate, Frank's wife,
        apparently chose.))

   → P:     En I didn' wanna say-eh:: Kate said she always
            wanduh see it so, ·hhh I never said anything
            but- uh Frank said t'day he sez "wasn' that the
            dirtiest place?"
     A:     ⌈Yeh.
   → P:     ⌊En I said "Yihknow? I felt the same thing? But
```

```
            I didn' wanna say anything to yuh, but I jus'
            f elt- -dirty when I walked on the carpet."
    A:       └Yah.
```

(54) (JG:4.6.-20)

```
    C:    An I said now wait till you see me get all this
          stuff on. Well you know what I looked like. I
          looked like I was thirty-six old- years old
          tryin to look sixteen.
    J:    Ohhh Go: ┌d
  → C:            └An you know everybody just sorta
          stood there an nobody wanned to say well you
          look pretty stupid h-h-h mo:ther.
```

Withholdable talk like a coparticipant criticism provides for recipients' interpreting silences.

(2) When coparticipant criticisms are proffered, the criticism turns frequently have weak-type criticism components. This feature may be seen most clearly with criticisms that are delivered with contrastive prefaces:

(26) (J & J)

```
    ((B is assessing a coparticipant's change of hair
    color))

    B:    I like it too but uhh hahheh It blows my mind
```

(51) (JS:I.-1)

```
    E:    ˙hhh Yes I do like it=although I really::::
                   .
                   .
                   .
                   .
                   .
                   .
    E:    ˙hhh Well I don't- I'm not a great fan of this
          type of a:rt ...
```

With this type of construction, the prefacing favorable assessment is typically a moderately positive term (e.g. "like") and the prefaced unfavorable assessment is generally formed as an exception.

The contrastive-preface turn shape for coparticipant criticisms (favorable assessment plus critical assessment) is structurally similar to the turn shape for disagreements (agreement plus disagreement). In each case the contrastive prefacing component is a weak or token instance of the preferred action; the prefaced component is a weak instance of the sequentially implicative dispreferred action.

Subsequent to self-deprecations, the alternative actions of agreeing or disagreeing are nonequivalent. When conversants overtly agree, they of course endorse the prior criticisms as their own. Participants may be critical, and recognized as such, even when they do not overtly agree with the criticisms. If criticizing a co-conversant is viewed as impolite, hurtful, or wrong (as a dispreferred action), a conversant may hesitate, hedge, or even minimally disagree rather than agree with the criticism. When conversants disagree with prior self-deprecations, they show support of their co-conversants. If supporting co-conversants is viewed as natural, right, and/or desirable (as a preferred action), conversants would state their disagreements with prior self-deprecations overtly.

The constraints that bear on such disagreements are specific to prior self-deprecations and not critical assessments in general or of nonpresent parties. In the following fragments the coparticipants are collaboratively criticizing nonpresent parties. In the course of criticism sequences, self-critical assessments may be engendered. (SD) marks a turn in which the speaker criticizes both a nonpresent party and herself:

(55) (SBL:2.2.3.–15)

```
      A:    But she doubled uh Gladyses three hearts, and
            uhm -- Lil uh, -- uh mh mh gosh she led out a
            real small heart, a little three 'r somethin
            like that 'n hehh I th(hh)ink I th(hhh) think
            Elva took it wi(h)th a four.
      A:    ·hhh hehh heh heh ┌heh heh heh heh G(hh)od I=
      B:                      └Hhehh heh heh
      A:    =coulda died
      A:     ┌·hhh heh heh heh
      B:     └·hhh hhh hhh hhhh
      A:    ·hhh This's when she had the trump all th-
            well I only had two an' so on, but but an'
            she was tryina get- But it seem' tuh me
            li(hh)ke she had eh- she had ┌ace-king left
      B:                                 └heh heh heh=
      B:    =heh heh heh
      A:    heh heh heh ·heh heh ┌heh heh heh heh
      B:                         └An' then she lays down
            has the ace, a little ol' little you know,
            ┌An' here-
      A:    └·heh heh
      B:    An' she lets everybody take 'm
      A:     ┌·heh heh heh
      B:     └hhh ·hhh hh hh ·hhh ┌Well you know uh-
(SD)  A:                          └Well, at least I feel
```

```
                    be- I mean I feel good when I'm playin with
                    her because I feel like uh her and I play alike
                    hehh
            B:      No.  You play beautifully. But y- uh see, when
                    we get used to people we'll just realize with
                    Gladys she's gonna do this.
```

(21) (NB:IV:1.-6)

```
            A:      'hhhh I called las' ni- he sez "Don't call me
                    tuh come down fer the, Thanksgiving, deal" nah-
            P:      'hh Well HE DID THE SAME DAMN THING ET CHRISTMAS
                    TI:ME,
            A:      CHRISTMAS EVE 'E LEFT ME HERE ALONE.
            P:      YEAH
(SD)        A:      'hhh I can't say anything, I'm stupid, er uh 'f
                    I think uh- the-f-uh-sump'n about a ma:n er
                    the gover'ment yihknow, I uh- 'hhh Oh well it's
                    me too Portia, hh' yihknow I'm no bottle a'milk.
                    (0.6)
            P:      Oh:: well yer easy tuh get along with, but I
                    know he's that way. God, jist tuh go out fishin
                    with im w'd- drives me up a wa:ll,
```

In each instance, the two kinds of criticisms, self and nonpresent party, are treated separately in the next turn. The self-deprecation has priority; it is addressed first with a disagreement. That unit is followed by a contrast conjunction, and the criticism of the nonpresent party is subsequently agreed with.

(55) (SBL:2.2.3.-15)

```
        Disagreement:   No. You play beautifully.
        Transition:     But
        Agreement:      y' uh see, when we get used to
                        people we'll just realize with
                        Gladys she's gonna do this.
```

(21) (NB:IV:1.-6)

```
        Disagreement:   Oh well yer easy tuh get along with,
        Transition:     but
        Agreement:      I know he's that way. God, jist tuh
                        go out fishin with im w'd- drives me
                        up a wa:ll,
```

The units in the prior turns with which the disagreements disagree are the self-deprecatory components. Such disagreements are specifically and selectively responsive to the prior self-deprecations. They are locally engendered disagreements that are performed with stated disagreement components, that is, contrastively classed second assessments.

Subsequent to self-deprecations, disagreements and agreements, respectively, are performed with different turn organizations. In the next two sections, some features of disagreement and agreement turns subsequent to self-deprecations are described.

Disagreements with prior speakers' self-deprecations

When disagreements are performed, disagreement components generally occupy the entire self-deprecation response units. That is, there are routinely no contrastive components before or after the disagreements as part of the units. Some of the more prevalent disagreement components are briefly discussed below.

Partial repeats. Disagreements may include partial repeats that challenge and/or disagree with their priors.[16] They are often followed in the same turn or in a subsequent turn by other disagreement components. In the following fragments, responses to self-deprecations include partial repeats (PR) followed by stated disagreements (D):

```
(56) (AP:fn)
        L:     You're not bored (huh)?
 (PR)S:        Bored?=
  (D)S:        =No. We're fascinated.


(57) (SBL:1.6.-1)
        B:     ... I'm tryina get slim.
 (PR) A:       Ye:ah? ⌈You get slim, my heavens.
        B:            ⌊heh heh heh heh hh̄ h̄h
  (D) A:       You don't need to get any slimmah,


(58) (JG:II.2.14a)
        C:     ... c(h)ept in my old age I'm: slowin down
               considera⌈bly.˙⌉  ˙hhhhhh ⌉=
 (PR) D:                 ⌊He:ll⌋ Old age.⌋=
  (D) D:       =⌈What'r you thirdy fi:v⌉ve?
        C:        ⌊hheh – heh-heh-heh-heh⌋e-h⌋ hYhe(h)e(h)e(h)es
        D:       hh–hh hhh–hhh!                ˙
        C:       ˙t˙hhhhhhhh⌈hhh
  (D) D:                    ⌊But a young thirdy fi:ve.
```

(59) (JG:4.6.–6)

```
        C:   I have no dates.  I don't go:
             there ⌈is no sense in hanging onto the clothes.
        J:         ⌊(Are you-) ((high pitch))
  (PR)  J:   What do ya mean you don't have any
             da:tes ((low pitch))
        C:   Well: I just don't go out anymore that's all
   (D)  J:   Oh: that's ridiculous
```

Negations. Disagreements may include negations like "no," "hm-mh," "not." A "no" may occur as a first component in an answer to a self-deprecating question:

(60) (JG:2)

```
        R:   Did she get my card.
        C:   Yeah she gotcher card.
        R:   Did she t'ink it was terrible
      → C:   No she thought it was very adohrable.
```

(61) (SBL:2.1.8.–8)

```
        B:   I was wondering if I'd ruined yer- weekend
             ⌈by uh
      → A:   ⌊No.  No. Hm-mh.  No. I just loved to have- ...
```

(56) (AP:fn)

```
             ((L, the hostess, is showing slides.))

        L:   You're not bored (huh)?
        S:   Bored?=
      → S:   =No. We're fascinated
```

or as a first component in a response to a self-deprecating assertion:

(55) (SBL:2.2.3.–15)

```
        A:   ... I feel like uh her and I play alike hehh
      → B:   No.  You play beautifully.
```

(20) (MC:1.–45)

```
        L:   ... En I thought tuh myself- ((with a gravelly yodel))
             -gee whi:z when do I get smart.  I'm so dumb I don't
             even know it.  hhh! -- heh!
      → W:   Y-no, y-you're yer not du:mb, my God you- you hit it
             right on the head, ...
```

A disagreement may be an assertion that contains the prior deprecating term negated with a "not":

(20) (MC:1.-45)

    L: ... I'm so dumb I don't even know it. hhh! -- heh!
→ W: y-no, y-you're not du:mb, ...

(62) (JK:1)

    G: ... but it's not bad for an old lady.
→ C: You're not old, Grandma ...

Compliments. Disagreements with prior self-deprecations very frequently include evaluative terms. Such terms are contrastively classed relative to the prior self-deprecatory formulations; they are favorable, complimentary evaluative terms:

(55) (SBL:2.2.3.-15)

    A: I mean I feel good when I'm playing with her because
        I feel like uh her and I play alike hehh
→ B: No. You play beautifully.

(63) (SBL:2.2.3.-40)

    B: And I never was a grea(h)t Bri(h)dge plav(h)er
        Clai(h)re,
→ A: Well I think you've always been real good,

(64) (MC)

    C: ... 'ere Momma She talks better than I do
→ B: Aw you talk fine

(60) (JG:2)

    R: Did she get my card.
    C: Yeah she gotcher card.
    R: Did she t'ink it was terrible
→ C: No she thought it was very adohrable.

(21) (NB:IV:1.6)

    A: ... 'hhh Oh well it's me too Portia, hh yihknow
        I'm no bottle a' milk,
        (0.6)
→ P: Oh:: well yer easy tuh get along with, but I
        know he's that way.

(61) (SBL:2.1.8.-8)

    B: I was wondering if I'd ruined yer-weekend
        ⌈by uh
    A: ⌊No.
→ A: No. Hm-mh. No. I just loved to have- ...

(56) (AP:fn)

    L: You're not bored (huh)?
→ S: Bored? No. we're fascinated.

(65) (EB:1)

    S: ... I hope by next semester it'll be a bi(h)t
          b(h)edd(h)er heh heh heh heh ˙hh
          ˙hh⌈heh (prob'ly not)
→ B: ⌊(   ) You're doing very great no:w

Disagreements with prior self-deprecations are performed as stated disagreements. Even in a minimal disagreement, a stated disagreement component such as "no" is employed, followed by a shift in referent and/or topic:

(66) (SBL:2.2.3.–10)

    B: And uh that poor li'l Gladys she, know she
          never did get it right about where she played
    A: hh
    B: She was heh!
    A: She was almost as bad ⌈as I was.
    B: ⌊heheh
→ B: ⌈No, but she ⌉=
    A: ⌊heh heh hehheh⌋
→ B: =⌈even up to the last one, they practically=
    A: ⌊heh heh
    B: =hadtuh th(h)row her outta that ⌈first ta(hhh)ble
          ˙heh heh ...   ⌊
    A: ⌊˙heh ˙heh heh
          heh heh heh ...

(67) (fn)

    C: I'm talking nonsense now
→ A: No::
    A: but I think I'm ready for dinner anyway.

The preceding discussion of partial repeats, negations, and compliments focuses on some of the more common components used to disagree by recipients of prior self-deprecations. This description, of course, is not exhaustive of the disagreement procedures used in these environments. While some of the more prevalent disagreement components have been mentioned, self-deprecations are overtly disagreed with in quite a range of forms. Some illustrations of stated disagreements, undermines, disaffiliations, and the like follow:

    (1) A speaker may disagree by proffering an assessment that claims

access to the attribute critically assessed, that is by proffering a contrastive second assessment (compliment and/or negation).

(55) (SBL:2.2.3.-15)

```
    A:    ... I feel like uh her and I play alike hehh
 →  B:    No. You play beautifully.
```

(20) (MC:1.-45)

```
    L:    ... I'm so dumb I don't even know it. hhh!
          - heh!
 →  W:    Y-no, y-you're not du:mb, ...
```

(2) A speaker may disaffiliate with a prior critical assessment by proffering an assessment that makes no claim of access, that is, by proffering a critical assessment of the prior talk.

(59) (JG:4.6.-6)

```
    C:    I have no dates.  I don't go:
          there  is no sense in hanging onto the clothes.
    J:          (Are you-)  ((high pitch))
    J:    Wha do ya mean you don't have any da:tes.
          ((low pitch))
    C:    Well: I just don't go out anymore that's all.
 →  J:    Oh: that's ridiculous.
```

(3) A speaker may undermine a prior self-critical assessment by more favorably recategorizing or reformulating the self-deprecating attribute. Instances include:

(68) (JG:3C.-7)

```
    R:    'hh But I'm only getting a C on my report card
          in math.
 →  C:    Yeh but that's passing Ronald,
```

R's self-deprecatory formulation, "only . . . a C" is a member of the collection of letter grades that has other members ("A" and "B") ranked above it. C's formulation "*passing*" involves a shift to the collection of grades, "pass"–"fail," where the selection is the success member of the set.

(69) (MC:1.-38)

```
    W:    Yet I've got quite a distance tuh go yet.
 →  L:    Everybody has a distance.
```

In response to W's self-deprecation, L proposes that W's condition is a general condition ("Everybody has a distance"). By proposing that it is a common and normal condition L undermines the validity of W's self-deprecation.

```
(70)  (SBL:2.2.3.-4)
      B:    Well, do you remember that we could even hear the
            music.  I had the hi fi playing?
      A:    Mm hm, ·····
      B:    An' I had two table in the living room, an' you
            could almost hear a pin drop.
            .
            .
            .
            .
      A:    ... I don't remember being at yer house with Mercy,
            I was- only time I saw her was over at Jo's
            ⌜that night.
      B:    ⌊Oh well then you must not've come to this one.
(SD)  A:    Maybe that's why it was so quiet.
            (1.0)
  →   B:    Well, I-I was just remembering now, they did
            plenty a' talking, an everything, ...
```

A deprecates herself by proposing that the consequence of her absence at a bridge party was that it was a quiet occasion. In response to A's self-deprecating comment, B recharacterizes the event from "so *quiet*" to "plenty a' talking." With the new characterization, B suggests that the bridge party was like their other bridge parties, not special and not needing explanation. The new characterization works to invalidate the prior self-deprecation.

(4) A speaker may undermine a prior self-deprecation by proposing that it is a product of an improper activity.

```
(71)  (MC:1.-47)
      W:    And I'm being irritable right now by telling you
            so⌜,
  →   L:       ⌊Ah! ah! ˙HHHH No. hehhheh!  No but- but uh-yuh-
            Wilbur agai::n.  Again.  Stop trying to do this
            of your se:lf.  (1.2)-- leave it alone en you'll
            be shown the way to overcome it.
```

```
(72)  (JC:4.6.-26)
      C:    They'll take up a collection for my examination
      J:    Ha hu ⌜hu
      C:         ⌊with the taddered stockings
```

```
C:  ┌an the knees torn out an the whole schmere you=
J:  └ (      ha) ha
C:  =know. An the three inch underskirt
         ┌on
→ J:  └ Right you're a perf- (   perfectionis  )
```

(73) (GTS:1:19)

```
   R:  We're mentally ill, children, run ehhehhh
→ L:  ahh ha ha ha ha hehh What's wrong with you
        today?
```

This type of undermine typically occurs subsequent to an nth self-deprecation, that is, after a series of self-deprecations. For example, the fragment below has a series of disagreements with self-deprecations prior to L's formulating W's self-deprecating activity as improper:

(71) (MC:1.-47)

```
       W:  A:nd I'm-I'm, I'm eating the right foods
           'n the right balance of foods,
 (SD)  W:  but, I'm still, drinking coffee.
 (D)   L:  That's not (drinking).
       W:  You think so,
       L:  No::.
 (SD)  W:  It creates a nasty disposition.
 (D)   L:  I don't believe (that ┌at'all),
 (SD)  W:                         └it, makes you irritable
 (D)   L:  (It does not/)
       W:  It doe:s, ┌(It ca:n.)
       L:           └You- er you-yuh-that-s a (        )
           (           )! ┌heh heh! hah! hah! hah! hah!
 (SD)  W:                 └And I'm being irritable right
           now by telling you so┌,
→ L:                             └Ah!ah! ˙HHHH No, hehhheh!
           No but- but uh- yuh-Wilbur agai:n. Again. Stop
           trying to do this of your se:lf.
           (1.2)
       L:  leave it alone en you'll be shown the way to
           overcome it.
```

In the next turns to self-deprecations, the productions of overtly stated disagreements, disaffiliations, and undermines are understandable in the light of the constraints that have been previously described: that a recipient of a self-deprecation has as relevant alternative actions either to agree and endorse the prior critical assessment or to disagree and undermine its validity. Critically assessing one's coparticipant is quite regularly a dispreferred action and, as such, performed with delays, withholds, and weakly stated components. If participants exhibit hesitations, evasiveness, stalling, and the like in response to self-deprecations, they may be interpreted as agreeing with the prior comments. To disaffiliate, they need to state their disagreements forthrightly.

Agreements with prior speakers' self-deprecations

Agreements with prior self-deprecations may be performed with stated agreement components. When they are, they are accomplished, prevalently, with weak agreement types.

One kind of agreement that occurs in response to self-deprecations is formed by the recipient proffering a second self-deprecation, formulating it as second in an agreement sequence. The deprecating attribute that the prior speaker claimed may also be claimed by the recipient:

(74) (EB:1:2)

```
      B:   Not only that he gets everything done.
           (pause)
      B:   Everybody else- not everybody else,
           I have my desk full of trash.
 →  S:   Me too ...
```

or may be upgraded by the recipient:

(75) (SBL:2.2.3.-20)

```
      A:   And I shoulda went back tuh diamonds.
 →  B:   I think we were ⌜all so confused,
      A:                    ⌊So-
 →  B:   I know I wasn't bidding right, I wasn't --
           eh playing right, I wa'nt doing anything right.
```

With responses such as "Me too" and "I think we were *all* so confused" recipients implicitly agree with the prior self-deprecations by proposing themselves as "also" instances. The agreements are weak in that though they agree they simultaneously undermine the prior self-deprecations by proposing that the prior deprecating attributes are more generally shared (see also example [69]) and/or are less negative than prior speakers had proposed.

Another type of stated agreement with a prior self-deprecation is a confirmation of the prior. Confirmations, as well, tend to be done in weak forms. One way to weaken a confirmation is with a suppositional:

(76) (MC:1.-23)

```
      W:   ... Do you know what I was all that time?
      L:   (No).
```

```
    W:      Pavlov's dog.
            (2.0)
 → L:       (I suppose),
```

The productions of weak agreement components subsequent to self-deprecations may be seen to be an artifact of the dispreferred status of the action, criticizing one's coparticipants. Given the relevance of coparticipant criticism in the position of responding to self-deprecations and the norms constraining it, responses that exhibit dispreferred-action turn shape, like weakly stated agreements, constitute a way of performing coparticipant criticism and are interpretable as such (see Section 4).

A recipient of a prior self-deprecation may produce a response that is neither an agreement nor a disagreement. Two frequently occurring classes of such responses include (1) silences, that is, no immediate forthcoming talk, and (2) acknowledgments.

(1) When a speaker producing a self-deprecation reaches a possible turn completion point and stops talking, a recipient may respond with no immediate forthcoming talk. When both parties are silent, a gap emerges.

(76) (MC:1.–23)

```
    W:      ... Do you know what I was all that time?
    L:      (No).
    W:      Pavlov's dog.
 →          (2.0)
```

(77) (GTS:2.–15)

```
    K:      I couldn't, I'm a weak ling.
    ( ):                         hmh!
 →          (1.0)
    K:      I am.   I'm comin t'that conclusion.
            I'm a damn weakling.
 →          (1.0)
```

Recipients' silences after prior speakers' self-deprecations are responses that exhibit dispreferred-action turn shape. They constitute a turn shape associated with coparticipant criticism, that is, delaying (or withholding) potential agreements with prior self-deprecations.

After a gap, a potential agreement may be actualized by a recipient. That is, the recipient may terminate the emergent gap by producing an agreement [A].

(76) (MC:1.–23)

```
    W:      ... Do you know what I was all that time?
    L:      (no).
```

```
(SD) W:    Pavlov's dog.
  →        (2.0)
 (A) L:    (I suppose),
     W:    D'you remember that ⌈story?
     L:                        ⌊Yes, I do.
     W:    Yah.  She, was brainwashing me Lila,
     L:    Oh yes!
  →        (0.7)
 (A) L:    ⌈'N you were pickin' it up like mad.
     W:    ⌊And–
```

L's delayed weak agreement ("I suppose") is strengthened in a later turn ("N you were pickin' it [the ball] up like mad") which is also delivered after a gap.

Rather than wait out a recipient response, the prior speaker quite frequently will resume talk if a recipient silence (or gap) begins to emerge. These alternatives after a gap are contrasted:

Potential Agreement Is Actualized

```
    A:    [Self Deprecation]
          [Gap]
→ B:      [Agreement]
```

Potential Agreement Is Unactualized

```
    A:    [Self Deprecation]
          [Gap]
→ A:      [Resumption]
```

If a potential agreement by a recipient is delayed with silence, the prior speaker has an opportunity to talk in a turn that might otherwise contain an agreement. At the point of the prior speaker's resumption, no agreement has been stated. With the prior speaker's resumption, further negotiations are possible. A recipient's silence after a self-deprecation, then, is a response that makes an opportunity for minimizing stated coparticipant criticisms.

(2) When a speaker producing a self-deprecation reaches a turn completion point, a recipient may produce an acknowledgment in response such as "uh huh" "mm hm." Acknowledgments are different from agreements. With agreements – for example, assessments – recipients of prior assessments claim access to the referents assessed; with acknowledgments they acknowledge prior deliveries but make no claims of independent access (see material relating to note 3).

(78) (SBL:2.1.7.-4)

    B: Weh- Bea, uh it's just wuh- uh as I say
            uh I- sometimes feel I'm too critical of these
            people, an' I have to restrain myself, an'
            I-cause I think "How do I know. I-I dunno
            what their mind works like,"
  → A: Mn hm,

(79) (SBL:2.2.3.-27)

    B: ... I wasn't understanding anybody today.
  → A: Uh huh,

When a self-deprecation is neither overtly confirmed nor denied, as in recipient silence or acknowledgment, the self-deprecating party often will extend the sequence, the extensions providing subsequent turn spaces for recipient's disagreements/agreements:

(77) (GTS:2.15)

    K: <u>I</u> couldn't, I'm a weak₍ling.
    ():   ˡhmh!
            (1.0)
  → K: I am. I'm comin t'that conclusion.
            I'm a damn weakling.
            (1.0)
  → K: No damn good.
    R: Well we're not gonna stick up for ya, hehh hhh
            ₍hehh hhh
    A: ˡhehhh

(78) (SBL:2.1.7.-4)

    B: Weh-Bea, uh it's just wuh- uh as I say uh I-
            sometimes feel I'm too critical of these people,
            an' I have to restrain myself, an' I-cause I
            think "How do I know. I-I dunno what their
            mind works like,"
    A: Mn hm,
  → B: Uh y'know? -how it is,
    A: Yeah.

When no overt disagreement is made, the self-deprecating party tends to treat the self-deprecation as implicitly confirmed by the recipient. The prior self-deprecatory assertion(s) may be referred to by the self-deprecating party as already established and accepted between the parties in productions of admissions, justifications, explanations, laughter, and the like.

(80) (SBL:2.2.3.-7)

    B: I like 'er very much.
    B: But she still has that silly chatter about 'er.
    A: Mm hm,
    B: That is like a
          (1.0)
(SD) B: Oh, I'm not much of a teaser
(gap)   (1.0)
  → B: Well now this is my fault. I don't like teasing.
    A: Mm hm,
    B: And I know people love it.

   (79) (SBL:2.2.3.-27)

 (SD) B: ... I wasn't understanding anybody today.
(Ackn) A: Uh huh,
   → B: Course I was bidding poorly.
   → B: And uhm I couldn't remember, and I know
            it's just because I've had so much on my
            mind.
      A: Yeah,
   → B: And uh I have fer the last two 'r three months,
            you know, if I c'n get things settled Claire,
            then I c'n start think–w(hh)at I(h)'m do(hh)ing.

   (81) (SBL:2.2.3.-13)

 (SD) B: ... course I shouldn' be s'damn nosey either.
(Ackn) A: Mm,
   → B: Heh heh heh ⌈heh heh heh ˙hh
      A: ⌊Well I know she musta thought ...

When conversants agree with prior self-deprecations, the turns and sequences are shaped the same as when agreements are preferred and conversants disagree. For example, one turn/sequence shape associated with each of these actions in their respective environments is no immediate forthcoming talk by a recipient of the prior assessment. When an initial assessment invites agreement and the recipient is silent, the silence is a way of performing (and is interpretable as such) an unstated, or as-yet-unstated disagreement. When a recipient of a self-deprecation is silent, that silence is a way of performing (and is interpretable as such) an unstated, or as-yet-unstated agreement/coparticipant criticism. A question arises as to what the actions have in common if a silence is interpretable as an instance of disagreement in the one environment and of agreement/coparticipant criticism in the other.

An answer to this question may be found in the preference/dispreference statuses of these actions. In the first environment, the relevant alternative actions for recipients are agreement/disagreement; in the second, disagreements and agreements take the form of coparticipant praise/coparticipant criticism.

1
    A: Initial assessment that invites agreement
→ B: Agreement/Disagreement

2
    A: Self-deprecation
→ B: Coparticipant praise/Coparticipant criticism

Within each set of alternatives, one of the actions is normatively oriented to as offensive, compromising, wrong, or for some other reason uncomfortable to perform. As dispreferred actions in their respective environments, both disagreeing and criticizing one's coparticipants may be delayed, downplayed, or withheld. If a participant produces something that is not an *overt* instance of either of the two alternatives, such as a silence, it is interpretable as the dispreferred alternative: disagreement over agreement, criticism over praise.

The actions of praising a coparticipant subsequent to a self-deprecation and agreeing with a prior initial assessment that invites agreement also exhibit similarities. Both actions in their respective environments constitute ways of supporting and ratifying the interactants and interaction. Both actions in their respective environments are routinely performed as stated instances of the actions, have priority positioning, that is, are first actions performed by recipients, and occupy the entire turn unit with no contrastive prefaces.

The above discussion suggests that at least some features of turn/sequence organization operate with respect to the preference/dispreference status of actions – that diverse actions, by being preferred or dispreferred, may be performed in turn/sequence shapes specific to that status.[17]

Notes

1. This utterance contains B's report to A of Allen's declination. Whatever Allen may have said to B is inaudible on the tape recording of the telephone conversation between A and B, and is treated by B as inaudible to A. In B's report to A, B incorporates a disclaimer of Allen's knowledge ("doesn't know anything new") as a warrant for not proffering the requested assessment.
2. A speaker may claim insufficient knowledge to assess on his or her own behalf, and follow with a report of someone else's assessment, A_r, of the referent in question:

(JS:II:61)

```
no access  →  E:   No I haven't seen it
      A_r  →        Mae sed it 'n she said she
                    f- depressed her terribly
```

(SBL:2.2.-1)

```
qualified     A:   How is Aunt Kallie
access     →  B:   Well, I (suspect) she's better
              A:   Oh that's good.
      A_r  →  B:   Las' time we talked tuh mother
                   she was uh better
```

In reporting third-person assessments, speakers may affiliate with or dis-affiliate from the reported assessments. See Sacks's transcribed lectures and Pomerantz (forthcoming).

3. By proffering an assessment of the referent assessed by a prior speaker, a second speaker claims independent access to that referent. Subsequent to an initial assessment, a recipient may respond to the prior without claiming independent access to the referent assessed in the prior.

He or she may acknowledge a prior assessment:

(JS:II:61)

```
    E:   Oh I I:loved [it.
→   L:              [Yeah.
    L:   Ih w'z- en' we have never seen it.
```

(SBL:2.1.7.-1)

```
    B:   Well her niece is [here, and she's a lovely=
    A:                     [Yeah
    B:   =person.
→   A:   Uh huh
```

He or she may produce an assessment as a recipient of news just delivered:

(JG:R:1)

```
    F:   'hh how iz our fri::end
    N:   Oh: he'z much better I'm 'fraid --
         [hh h h h
→   F:   [Well uh that's marvelous
```

(Coliseum call 71)

```
    S:   Is there something going on down north there (   )
    D:   Yeah the Coliseum blew up.
    S:   It did?
    D:   Yeah, it's killed a bunch of people and I don't
         know how many's injured.  It's a hell of a mess.
→   S:   Oh, that's too bad.
```

(SBL:I:11.-2)

```
    B:   Say didju see anything in the paper last night
         or hear anything on the local radio, hh Ruth
```

```
              Henderson and I drove down, to, Ventura
              yesterday.
      A:      Mm hm,
      B:      And on the way home we saw the -- most gosh awful
              wreck.
                 .
                 .
                 .
                 .
      B:      Boy, it was a bad one, though.
  → A:        Well that's too ba:d.
```

He or she may proffer a qualified assessment of the referent assessed in the
prior, marking the assessment as based on other than direct access:

```
  (NB:PT:3:r:ca)

      L:      Jeeziz Chris'shu sh'd see that house E(h)mma
              yih av no idea h⌈hhmhh
  → E:                        ⌊I bet it's a drea:m ....
```

```
  (JG:II.1.-4)

      D:      ... oh I gotta n- I don'know th' las' time I
              talked t'yuh=I'm out here et Taft High School
              now, -- In the uh West Valley not too far frm
              home=I'm the boys' Dean out there, so I gotta
              new jo:b 'n=
      C:      =Yeah?
      D:      So it's a pretty good setup yihknow,
  → C:        W'l my God it sounds marvelous Don,
```

For a fuller discussion, see Pomerantz (1975), chap. 2.
4. How second assessments are coordinated with initial assessments are intri-
   cately bound up with how initials are coordinated with anticipatable nexts.
   In this chapter, however, features of initial assessments remain, by and
   large, unexplicated. References to some aspects of initial assessments are
   included only insofar as the analysis to date requires.
5. Whereas it is being argued that the initial complaint assessment invites
   agreement or a subsequent complaint assessment, it also should be mentioned that negative assessments, as a class, often are converted by one
   party or the other in a subsequent turn to positive assessments.
6. The sequential work that "though" does, that is, accompanying disagreements containing parameter shifts, may be seen in the following assessment
   series as well:

```
  (F.N.)

  A₁    A:      Good shot
  A₂¹   B:      Not very solid though
        A:      You get any more solid you'll be terrific
```

A's initial assessment is a praise assessment, incorporating the positive
descriptor "good." The second assessment is proffered as a *qualification* of
the prior: With the "though," B claims to accept the prior while proffering a
critical assessment ("not very solid"). The second may be formed as a quali-

fication of the initial assessment inasmuch as there is a shift in the parameter being assessed: The second specifies the solidness (or lack of which) as a feature of the shot to assess, moreover, to assess critically, that is, in contrast with the prior assessment.

In the assessment pair

(NB: IV: 11.–1)

A_1 A: <u>God</u> izn it <u>dreary</u>.

.

.

A_2 P: 'hh- it's <u>warm</u> though

P's assessment is proffered as a qualification in that it contrastively assesses a shifted parameter; A critically assesses the weather appearance, B non-critically assesses the weather temperature.

7. The prevalence of agreements that are organized as *preferred* actions is, clearly, not confined to assessment sequences. Research documenting that preference includes: Sacks (1973c) and Davidson (Chapter 5 herein).

8. The upgraded-agreement type being described is an upgraded assessment with no referent shift relative to the prior. In the corpus, one apparent exception is a second assessment that contains an upgraded evaluation and a rather subtle referent shift:

    (JS: II: 137)

A_1 A: They look nice to<u>g</u>ether.
A_2^1 B: Yes they're lovely.

In the second assessment, the evaluation term "lovely" is upgraded relative to the prior term "nice." The referent however is slightly altered relative to the prior. In A_1, "how they look together" is assessed. In A_2, the objects ("they") are assessed with an appearance assessment.

The modification in referent in A_2 relative to the prior can be seen to anticipate that speaker's partial disagreement with the prior speaker's assessment:

(JS: II: 137)

A: They look nice to<u>g</u>ether.
B: Yes they're lovely. But I particularly like
      the blue en gray, ⌜en white,
A: ⌞Yeah
B: What's so nice about this is you get <u>two</u>
      nice pieces.

A's initial assessment is of the objects "together" – B's subsequent assessment separates them, formulating them as "*two* nice pieces."

9. See note 8.

10. Same-evaluation second assessments may be strengthened or upgraded with intensifiers:

    (KC: 4: 35)

    K: 'n that nice
→   R: Yah. It really is

(SBL:1.1.10.-5)

```
  B:    Isn't that sad.
→ A:    Mm it really is,
```

Asserted agreements with intensifiers exhibit sequential features that are similar to those displayed by upgraded agreements – they do not normatively co-occur with disagreements.

11. Turn-taking apparatus is described in Sacks, Schegloff, & Jefferson (1974).
12. Some illustrations of turns containing pre-disagreement prefaces are provided:

(MC:1.-30)

```
  L:    Maybe it's just ez well you don't know.
        (2.0)
→ W:    Well, uh-I say it's suspicious it could be
        something good ┌too
  L:                    └Mmhm mmhm
        (1.0)
→ L:    Well-- I can't think it would be too good, ...
```

(SBL:1.1.10.-4)

```
  B:    Oh, how sad.
  B:    And that went wrong.
        (1.0)
→ A:    Well, uh --
  B:    That surgery, I mean.
  A:    I don't-
```

(MC:1.-27)

```
  L:    Maybe, en maybe by instinct, she took over
        from there, not really realizing, the extent
        of it?
→ W:    Uh:: hh
  L:    You think that's possible with her?
        (1.5)
→ W:    Uh well/ I'll tell you,
```

(SBL:2.1.7.-14)

```
  A:    ... cause those things take working at,
        (2.0)
→ B:    (hhhhh) well, they do, but-
```

13. A pattern that is observable in a large number of disagreement sequences is a movement from disagreement to agreement. Within those sequences, turns that occur subsequent to stated disagreements are modifications of prior assertions that partially concede to the coparticipants' discrepant positions.

(JG:II:2:33)

```
  D:    If y'go tuh Switzerlnd yer  payin about
        fifty percent a' yer money in ta:xes.
```

```
     C:   Not in Swi:tzerl'nd.
     D:   (No) I think it i:s.
     C:   'hhhh ((fri)) No̅:::,
          (0.7)
  → D:   Well you pay awful high ta(h)axes over
          there,
```

In D's modified assertion, the assessment "awful high ta(h)xes" replaces the prior estimate "about *fifty* percent." The replacement is a partial concession to the disagreement inasmuch as the assessment admits not only the original estimate but lower ones as well.

```
     (TG:1)
     B:   ... Yih sound HA:PPY, hh
     A:   I sound ha:p py?
     B:                 Ye:uh.
          (0.3)
     A:   No:,
     B:   N:o:?
     A:   No.
          (0.7)
  → B:   'hh You sound sorta cheerful?
```

Subsequent to B's disconfirmation, A modifies her initial assessment ("Yih sound HA:PPY"), restating it in a weaker form ("You sound sorta cheerful?"). The modified assessment is weakened via the inclusion of the qualifying descriptor "sorta" as well as having a question format.

14. Reversals and backdowns are rather special objects. They should not be accounted for as post-completion objects per se. Post-completers include "repeats" that are regularly *slightly* altered, and often upgraded, relative to the repeated prior:

```
     [MC:x]
     A:   How wz the trip?
     B:   O:h it was nice.
          (0.5)
  → B:   U:::h  It was very nice indee:d.
```

```
     (MC:1.-10)
     L:   ... they're robbing themselves blind.
          (1.0)
  → L:   Jus' robbing themselves blind ...
```

```
     (MC:1.-42)
     W:   ... somebody came along  and ju:st, didn't,
          like me,
          (1.0)
  → W:   They j(h)u(hh)st didn't.
```

15. There are sequential differences between performing an action with a "withhold" like a silence and with a stated component. When a withholdable is not withheld, such as a party stating a criticism, that talk may initiate a sequence in which subsequent withholdables may likewise be stated. Crit-

icizing a coparticipant may engender a return criticism. This sort of exchange is alluded to by F as an account for "not making any comments":

(NB:ITB:14) (T has just told F a 'fat joke' – purportedly said to him on an earlier occasion – that he jumped into the ocean and caused huge waves over the pier.)

```
F:    I: won't say anything.   I may come do:w:n.
      ┌eh-ha-ha:ha:-ha┐=
T:    └Oh(h)okhha(h)ay┘
T:    =hih hu:h hu┌h,
F:                └·huhhhhhh┌hhh
T:                          └Bring yer sui:t,=
→ F:  =Ah-ee-Well that's why I said I'm not g'nnuh
      say anything I'm not making any comments
      about anybu:ddy.
```

16. For a discussion of forms and functions of some repeat types, see Jefferson (1972).
17. The range of actions that are oriented to as preferred and dispreferred and how these actions are performed and recognized in turns and sequences constitute a promising research area. For example, refusing an invitation may risk offending the inviting party. A dispreferred-action turn shape, prefacing, may be used when speakers refuse invitations. Refusals are often prefaced with appreciative person assessments:

(SBL:1.1.10.–14)

```
B:    Uh if you'd care to come over and visit a
      little while this morning,  I'll give you a
      cup of coffee.
→ A:  hehh! Well that's awfully sweet of you.  I don't
      think I can make it this morning uh, I'm running
      an ad in the paper and-and uh I have to stay
      near the phone.
```

(NB:2.–14)

```
B:    Wanna come down 'n have a bite a' lunch with me?
      I got some beer en stuff.
→ A:  Wul yer real sweet hon, uhm, let-=
B:      ┌[D'you have sumpn else?
A:      └[I have-
A:    No, I have to uh call Bill's mother ...
```

5. Subsequent versions of invitations, offers, requests, and proposals dealing with potential or actual rejection

JUDY DAVIDSON
University of California, Irvine

1. Introduction

The doing of an object such as an invitation, offer, request, or proposal sets up a sequentially possible next object as either an acceptance or a rejection.[1] Furthermore, there is some evidence that producers of invitations, offers, requests, or proposals see this import of their actions not merely as a possibility but as an actuality, and therefore they may examine whatever follows the invitation, offer, request, or proposal for how that object is displaying or implicating either acceptance or rejection.

Consider the following instance:

(1) [Bike Ride]

```
1 A:   What time you wanna lea:ve.
2      (0.3)
3 B:   ((smack)) Uh:: sick clo:ck?
4      (0.5)
5 A:   Six (uh) clo:ck? hh=
6 B:   =Is that good.
```

In line 3, speaker B makes a proposal. This is followed in line 5 by speaker A's saying "Six o'clock?" Now whatever A was doing with this utterance in line 5, whether it was an understanding check or a challenge or whatever, B in line 6 displays that he is taking it as some sort of questioning or doubting of the acceptability of the proposal, such that its acceptability needs to be checked out.

Consider another instance:

This is a revised version of a paper read at the SSRC/BSA International Conference on Practical Reasoning and Discourse Processes, St. Hugh's College, Oxford, 1979.

(2)   [SBL:Tape 2: Side 2: Conv.3, p.43]

```
1 A:    'hh Yihknow id be kinda ni::ce, (.) to:o,='hh
2       uh(m): (0.4) 'hh I was thinking about goin- when
3       we go over tuh church w::why wouldn't it be nice
4       tuh play ↑pa:rt↓ners.
5       (0.3)
6 A:    Or wouldja li:ke that.
```

In lines 1–4, speaker A makes a proposal, which is met with a silence in line 5. A subsequently displays that she is taking this silence not as lack of understanding, difficulty in hearing, puzzlement, or whatever, but instead specifically as some sort of doubt about the acceptability of the proposal. In these two instances, two different sorts of post-proposal objects were taken by the proposer as having to do with issues of the acceptability of the proposal, and more specifically, as displaying the possible unacceptability of the proposal.

This chapter examines a variety of objects occurring after an invitation, offer, request, or proposal that can be taken as displaying either potential or actual rejection.[2] Given either the potentiality or actuality of rejection, the producer of an invitation or offer may then issue some subsequent version of his or her invitation or offer to attempt to deal with this potential or actual rejection.

2. Silence as potential rejection

Silences occurring immediately after an invitation, offer, request, or proposal may be taken as displaying that it is possibly going to be rejected. Consider the following instances:

(3)   [NB:31, pp.19–20]

```
1 A:    Well?=I'll tell yuh.= Call information.
→ 2        (1.4)
```

(4)   [NB:38, p.92]

```
1 A:    C'mon down he:re,=it's oka:y,
→ 2        (0.2)
```

(5)   [NB:43, p.150]

```
1 C:    Well yih c'n both sta:y.
→ 2        (0.4)
```

```
    (6)   [NB:40, p.116 ]

  1 A:   We:ll dih you wan(na) me tuh (me) tuh jus' pick
  2       you ken you:- get intuh Robinson's suh yih could
  3       buy a li'l pair a slippers?
→ 4      (0.2)
```

Pomerantz (1978c:4)* examines sequences in which an object such as an assertion is followed by a silence:

> What was taken for granted as adequate for its purposes at time of delivery can be called up for review by virtue of what it engenders. Gaps, faltering starts, hedges, etc. may accountably occasion a review of the prior assertion motivated to find a way of altering it to now-clear-and-understandable.

Although Pomerantz was talking about such objects as assertions, her findings can be generalized to the instances under consideration here: given a silence following an invitation or offer, then the inviter or offerer may take this silence as a display of some sort of trouble or problem that the recipient is having with the invitation or offer. Pomerantz further states: "One domain that may be critically reviewed is the initial assertion's formulation with respect to referential adequacy." Again generalizing her findings to the sequences under consideration here, an inviter or offerer, on hearing a silence after an invitation or offer, may then examine the invitation or offer for what was possibly inadequate, troublesome, or problematic about it.

Now in contrast to the sorts of sequences Pomerantz examined, in which the initial formulation was examined for its clarity or understandability, in the sequences in instances (3)–(6), by virtue of the fact that the relevance is acceptance/rejection, an inviter or offerer when faced with a silence may examine the initial formulation for any inadequacies of that initial formulation that may be adversely affecting its acceptability. Given such an analysis on the part of an inviter or offerer, he or she may then subsequently display an attempt to deal with the inadequacies of the initial formulation of the invitation or offer and thereby to deal with the possibility of rejection. In instances (3)–(6), the inviter or offer, following a silence, produces what I shall call a "subsequent version" of that invitation or offer:

```
    (3)   [NB:31, pp.19-20 ]

  1 A:   Well?=I'll tell yuh.=Call information.
  2       (1.4)
→ 3 A:   We c'n call information 'n find out.
```

*A revised version of this essay is included as Chapter 7 of this book [Eds.].

(4)   [NB:38, p.92]

```
1 A:   C'mon down he:re,=it's oka:y,
2      (0.2)
→ 3 A:   I got lotta stuff,=I got be:er en stuff 'n
```

(5)   [NB:43, p.150]

```
1 C:   Well yih c'n both sta:y.
2      (0.4)
→ 3 C:   ⌈Got plenty a' roo:m,
4 B:   ⌊Oh I-
```

(6)   [NB:40, p.116]

```
1 A:   We:ll dih you wan(na) me tuh (me) tuh jus' pick
2      you ken you:- get intuh Robinson's suh yih could
3      buy a li'l pair a slippers?
4      (0.2)
→ 5 A:   I mean or ken I getchu something?=Er: somp'n?=Er
6      somp'n? hh!'
```

The arrowed utterances are displays[3] of the inviter's or offerer's attempts to deal with some inadequacy, trouble, or problem with the initial formulation, where such an inadequacy, trouble, or problem may be adversely affecting the acceptability of the invitation or offer. The subsequent version, in dealing with this inadequacy, trouble, or problem, thereby displays that the inviter or offerer is attempting to make it now possible, desirable, or necessary for the recipient to accept. And this in turn displays that as far as the inviter or offerer is concerned, the preferred outcome is acceptance.[4]

Another feature of these subsequent versions of invitations and offers is that they provide a next place for recipient to do a response,[5] presumably an acceptance, which is the preference displayed, but also of course, possibly other responses, such as rejections or rejection-implicative objects. That is, not having obtained a response after the initial formulation,

Initial Formulation

Possible response point   →   (Silence)

then the doing of a subsequent version provides a next place for a response:

Initial Formulation
(Silence)
Subsequent Version

Possible response point   →   ─────────────

In instances (3)–(5), a response occurs after the subsequent version:

(3)   [NB:31, pp.19–20]

```
1 A:    Well?=I'll tell yuh.= Call information.
2       (1.4)
3 A:    We c'n call information 'n find out.
4       (2.6)
→ 5 B:  'h We:ll let's see,=(Iw) I w'z- I'm jus' startin'
6       t' look in the book,
```

(4)   [NB:38, p.92]

```
1 A:    C'mon down he:re,=it's oka:y,
2       (0.2)
3 A:    I got lotta stuff, I got be:er en stuff 'n,
→ 4 B:  Mm hheh heh heh "beer 'n stuff" huh
                                [
```

(5)   [NB:43, p.150]

```
1 C:    Well yih c'n both sta:y.
2       (0.4)
3 C:    ┌Got plenty a' roo:m,
4 B:    └Oh I-
5       (.)
→ 6 B:  Oh(h)o(h)o please don't tempt me,
```

A subsequent version may itself be met with silence, and the inviter or offerer may then produce yet another version (in instance [6], the silence in line 7 is "filled" with an inbreath):

(6)   [NB:40, p.116]

```
1 A:    We:ll dih you wan(na) me tuh (me) tuh jus' pick
2       you ken you:- get intuh Robinson's suh yih could
3       buy a li'l pair a slippers?
4       (0.2)
5 A:    I mean or ken I getchu something?=Er: somp'n?=Er
6       somp'n? hh!'=
7(A):   ='hhhhh=
8 A:    =Mean yuh don't haftuh walk around cuz all I'm gonna
9       do is just I'm just gonna go up their patio dresses.
10      =I'm not gonna put a lot of money in (yihknow) intuh
11      clo:thes. 'hh A:nd,=I thought I'd probly go over
12      around thre:e:,=I think the traffic might be (.) less
13      in the middle a the afternoo┌n.
14 B:                                └Mm hm.
```

The subsequent version in lines 5–6 is followed by the "filled" silence in line 7, and thereafter the inviter produces yet another subsequent version, which eventually gets a response in line 14.

It should be parenthetically noted that what I am terming "subsequent version" may come from different classes of objects. There are several ways of doing subsequent versions, such as adding more components, providing inducements, or giving reasons for acceptance, but these different sorts of objects nonetheless can be grouped together because they have in common the following features: (1) they display that the inviter or offerer is attempting to deal with some trouble with or inadequacy of the initial version, where this trouble or inadequacy may be adversely affecting the acceptability of the invitation or offer, and (2) they provide a next place for a response, such as – but not necessarily – acceptance or rejection.

3. Subsequent versions after actual rejection

Just as a silence after an invitation or offer may be taken by the inviter or offerer as a display of some trouble with or inadequacy of the invitation or offer, so an actual rejection may similarly be taken as a display of some trouble with or inadequacy of the invitation or offer. And given a rejection, an inviter or offerer may then display that he is attempting to deal with whatever inadequacy in the initial version led to the rejection, where this attempt is displayed through inviters' or offerers' doing a subsequent version.[6] In the instances below, an initial version of an invitation or offer is rejected, and thereafter, the inviter or offerer produces a subsequent version:

```
     (7)  [NB:52, p.248]

   1 P:    Wul lissid-  (.) uh:: d'you wah me uh come down'n
   2       getche t' ┌ morrow er anythi┐ng?
   3 A:              └ N o: d e : a r .┘
   4       (.)
   5 A:    No:, ┌I'm  fi:ne. ┐
→  6 P:         └To the store┘ er any┌thing,
                                      └

     (8)  [NB:52, p.266]

   1 P:    Don'tchu want me tuh come down'n getchu t'morrow
   2       en take yih down: duh the beauty parlor,
   3       (0.3)
   4 A:    What↓ for.=I jus' did my hair it looks like pruh
   5       uh pruhfessional.
   6       (0.4)
→  7 P:    Oh I mean uh: you wanna go t'the store er anything
→  8       over et the Market ┌Basket er anything?
                              └
```

(9)   [TV – II]

```
1 A:    °Gee I feel like a real nerd° you c'n ahl come up
2       here,
3       (0.3)
4 B:    Nah that's alright wil stay down he re,
→ 5 A:                                      ⌊We've gotta
→ 6     color T.V:,
```

(10)   [Computer]

```
1 A:    Oh I was gonna sa:y if you wannid to:,='hh you
2       could meet me at U.C.Be: an⌐ I could show yih some
3       a' the other things on the compu:ter, (.) maybe
4       even teach yuh how tuh program Ba:sic er something.
5       'hhh
6       (0.6)
7 B:    Wul I don' know if I'd wanna get all that
8       invo:lved, hh' hhh!  ⌐('hh)
→ 9 A:                       ⌊It's rilly intresti:ng:.
```

Just as in the instances where an initial version was followed by a silence, so in these instances, after an actual rejection, the doing of some
subsequent version provides a place for another response, presumably
an acceptance, but of course possibly a rejection or rejection-implicative
object. That is, not having obtained acceptance after an initial version,

Initial Version
→ Rejection

then the doing of a subsequent version provides a next place for a
response:

Initial Version
Rejection
Subsequent Version

Possible response point →   _____

In instances (7)–(10), the subsequent version gets another rejection:

(7)   [NB:52, p.248]

```
6 P:    To the store er any ⌐thing,
→ 7 A:                      ⌊'hh I've got evrything bought
8       dear,
```

(8)   [NB:52, p.266][7]

```
7 P:    Oh I mean uh: you wanna go t'the store er
```

```
   8        anything over et the Market ⌈Basket er anything?⌉
   9 A:                                 ⌊˙hhhhhhhhhhhhhhhhhhh⌋
→ 10        h=Well ho⌈ney I–
                     ⌊
```

    (9)   [TV – II]

```
   6 A:    We've gotta color T.V:,
→  7 B:    ˙tch ˙hh I know but u– we're watchin:g the Ascent
→  8       'v Ma:n, ˙hh en then the phhreview: so: y'know wil
→  9       miss something if we come over.
```

In instance (10), the subsequent version gets a silence in line 9, and thereafter offerer produces yet another version (lines 10–12), which leads to acceptance:

    (10)   [Computer]

```
   9 A:    It's rilly intresti:ng:.
  10       (0.2)
  11 A:    I showed Tom how tuh pro– (.) how doo uh program a:
  12       ˙hhh the computer doo: make a ra:ndom number cha:rt,
  13       eh heh! ˙hh An' that rilly turned 'im o:n,
  14       (.)
→ 15 B:    Hih! heh! huh! huh! huh! (.) ˙hhhh ((sniff))
→ 16       We:ll,=how 'bout if I do meet you in the computer
→ 17       center tomorrow then.
```

In this section, subsequent versions after an actual rejection have been examined. Now it sometimes happens that an inviter or offerer, in hearing just the start of what apparently was going to be a rejecting utterance, may produce a subsequent version. In particular certain kinds of sentence prefaces or beginnings may be taken by inviters and offerers as being the starts of what might turn out to be rejection. In the instances that follow two such sentence prefaces, "well" and "uh:" are displayed:

    (11)   [SBL, Tape 2, Conv. 6, p.4]

```
   1 B:    Do you want any pots for coffee or a⌈ny(thing).
   2 A:                                        ⌊We:ll I have:
```

    (12)   [SBL, Tape 2, Conv. 5, p.10]

```
   1 A:    You should uh<listen that could be a job for
   2       Sa:mmy:*.=
   3 A:    =˙hhhh ⌈h
→  4 B:          ⌊Uh:, we:⌈ll, (he        )
                          ⌊
```

(13)   [Moving Day]⁸

```
 1 A:    I was gonna call Sue tomo:rrow an'- 'hh ask if
 2       I could uh::
 3       (0.9)
 4 B:    (Drop ⌈in.)
 5 A:         ⌊Bring over lu:nch.
 6       (0.2)
 7 B:    ⌈(    )⌉
 8 A:    ⌊On:::⌋ Saturday.
 9       (0.9)
→10 B:   ↑Oh↓:.=Uh:⌈:
                    ⌊
```

(14)   [NB:52, p.266]

```
 1 P:    Oh I mean uh: you wanna go t'the store er
 2       anything over et the Market ⌈Basket er anything?⌉
 3 A:                                 ⌊'hhhhhhhhhhhhhhhhhh⌋
→ 4      h=Well ho⌈ney I-
                 ⌊
```

As Pomerantz (1975:66) points out, "well" is often used as a preface to disagreements, where the response relevance is agreement/ disagreement. In the case of such objects as invitations and offers, where the response relevance is acceptance/rejection, then "well" may be both used and taken as the preface to a rejection. "Uh:," on the other hand, is an object that, according to Jefferson (1974:194), may be used in error-avoidance formats, occurring immediately before a problematic element and displaying "I am thinking about how to put it." The use of "uh:" to preface an utterance that will be some sort of response to an invitation or offer may therefore already display some sort of problem or trouble, and this in turn may be taken by the inviter or offerer as being trouble with the acceptability of the invitation or offer. In the instances below, "well" and "uh:" as sentence prefaces apparently are taken by the inviter or offerer as being the start of what could possibly turn out to be a rejection, and the inviter or offerer then produces a subsequent version to attempt to deal with this possible rejection. Note that in instances (12)–(14), the subsequent version is produced in overlap with the apparent beginning of a rejection; that is, in just hearing "well" or "uh," an inviter or offerer may already be able to take what's upcoming as possibly going to be a rejection:

(11)   [SBL, Tape 2, Conv. 6, p.4]

```
 1 B:    Do you want any pots for coffee or a⌈ny(thing).
 2 A:                                        ⌊We:ll I have:
```

```
  3          (.)
→ 4 B:      You know, I have that great big glass coffee m-
→ 5        'hhh maker< it makes ni:ne cu:ps.
```

(12)   [SBL, Tape 2, Conv. 5, p.10]

```
  1 A:      You should uh< listen that could be a job for
  2         Sa:mmy:*:.=
  3 A:      ='hhhh ⌈h
  4 B:             ⌊Uh:, we:⌈ll, (he
→ 5 A:                      ⌊And his station wag⌋on.
```

(13)   [Moving Day]

```
  1 A:      I was gonna call Sue tomo:rrow an'- 'hh ask if
  2         I could uh::
  3         (0.9)
  4 B:      (Drop ⌈in).
  5 A:            ⌊Bring over lu:nch.
  6         (0.2)
  7 B:      ⌈(    )⌉
  8 A:      ⌊On:::⌋ Saturday.
  9         (0.9)
 10 B:      ↑Oh↓:.=Uh:⌈:
→11                   ⌊Since you're going to be moving en'
→12         you won't wanna fool with uh:: (0.3) I'm sure
→13         she won't wanna fool with cooking an' (all that
→14         ja:zz)
```

(14)   [NB:52, p.266]

```
  1 P:      Oh I mean uh: you wanna go t'the store er anything
  2         over et the Market ⌈Basket er anything?⌉
  3 A:                         ⌊'hhhhhhhhhhhhhhhhhh⌋ h=Well
  4         ho⌈ney I-⌉
→ 5 P:        ⌊Or  Ri⌋chard's?
```

Again, the doing of a subsequent version provides a next place for some sort of response, presumably an acceptance, but possibly a rejection or rejection-implicative object. In instances (11) and (13), the subsequent version gets acceptance, while in (12) and (14), the subsequent version gets rejection:

(11)   [SBL, Tape 2, Conv. 6, p.4]

```
  4 B:      You know, I have that great big glass coffee m-
  5        'hhh maker< it makes ni:ne cu:ps.=
→ 6 A:      =Well say now that's an idea, Ye:s.=I would like
→ 7         to use ⌈(tha:t)
                  ⌊
```

    (12) [SBL, Tape 2, Conv. 5, p.10]

  5 A: And his <u>s</u>tation wagon.=
→ 6 B: =Oh he <u>c</u>ouldn't get them i:n:.

    (13) [Moving Day]⁹

12 A: Since you're going to be <u>m</u>oving en' you won't wanna
13   fool with uh:: (0.3) I'm <u>s</u>ure she won't wanna fool
14   with <u>c</u>ooking an' (all ⌜that ja:zz).
15 B: ⌞<u>Oh</u>.=Uh:
16   (.)
17 B: <u>Hm</u>:.
18   (0.4)
→19 B: ee<u>Ye</u>:ah. hh˙ hih! ⌜hih!
20 A: ⌞hhhh!
→21 B: <u>Yeah</u> I'm sure she <u>w</u>ould (.) heh!

    (14) [NB:52, p.266]

  5 P: Or <u>R</u>ichard's?
  6   (0.2)
→ 7 A: I've <u>bou</u>:ght ev'rythai:ng,

4. Subsequent versions after weak agreements

Another kind of object occurring after an invitation or offer that may display
that the invitation or offer in its initial version is not adequate for acceptance is what Pomerantz (1975:82) calls "sequentially weak agreement
forms." These are objects such as "hm," "uh huh," and "yeah." She
states:

> While they occur in agreement sequences . . . they also occur in
> disagreement sequences, for example, as passes past possible dis-
> agreement points.
>
> Given the relevance of agreement/disagreement, the production
> of weak agreements may be disagreement implicative.

Pomerantz refers to sequences in which the response relevance is dis-
agreement/agreement, but her findings may be generalizable to the sequences under consideration here, in which the response relevance is
acceptance/rejection. Given that a recipient produces a weak agreement
after an invitation or offer, then the inviter or offerer may take this weak
agreement as being possibly rejection-implicative. The inviter may then
display, through the doing of a subsequent version, that he is taking this
possibility of rejection as coming from some inadequacy in the initial
version.

In the sequences below, an initial version gets in response to it a weak
agreement, and thereafter the inviter or offerer produces a subsequent
version:

(15) [NB:48, p.201]

```
  1 A:    ˙hhhhh Uh will you call 'im tuhnight for me,=
  2 B:    =eYea:h,
  3        (.)
→ 4 A:    Plea::se,
```

(16) [SBL, Tape 3, Conv. 4, p.3]

```
  1 B:    So I jus' wan' duh tell yih if you'd come we-
  2        we're inviting the kinnergarden teachers too becuz
  3        we think it's a good chance tuh get tuh know the
  4        mothers.
  5 A:    Uh huh.=
→ 6 B:    =˙hh So if yer free*, (.) It's et the youth ho**:use.
```

(17) [SBL, Tape 2, Conv. 7, p.20]

```
  1 A:    ... I- if you want to uh(b) (1.1) maybe get up a
  2        game some ↑morning↓ while˙yer out the:re,=why that's
  3        always fu:n,
  4 B:    Mm hm.
  5        (0.5̄)
→ 6 A:    So let me ↑kno:w.
```

(18) [Wednesday Night]

```
  1 A:    Uh: if I let To:m know ahead a' ti:me,=˙hh uh: I
  2        don't think we'll have school that week I'm almos'
  3        su:re,=
  4 B:    =⌈eeYeah,        ⌉
  5 A:  · ⌊(˙hhhh)⌋ =Before Chrismas, (.)an' so: maybe
  6        Wensdee ni:ght.=
  7 B:    =eYa:h
→ 8 A:    I could yih know if I c'n tell 'im not tuh: ˙hh
→ 9        book anythi⌈ng.
```

Again, the production of a subsequent version provides a next place for a response, presumably an acceptance that will in some way be more emphatic than the initial weak agreement:

(15) [NB:48, p.201]

```
  4 A:    Plea::se,
→ 5 B:    eYe:a⌈h
```

(16) [SBL, Tape 3, Conv. 4, p.3]

```
  6 B:    ˙hh So if yer free*:, It's et the youth ho**:use.
  7        (0.2)
→ 8 A:    We:ll? (.) ez far ez I kno:w, (0.8) I will be.
```

(17)   [SBL, Tape 2, Conv. 7, p.20]

```
  6 A:    So let me ↑kno:w.
  7        (.)
→ 8 B:    B:  Yah ↑will ↓do:.
```

In contrast, it is of course possible for the recipient to produce yet another weak-agreement form in response to a subsequent version, and this in turn can lead to the doing of yet another subsequent version. In the instance below, a first version of a proposal is met with a weak-agreement form (line 7). The subsequent version (lines 8–9) also gets a weak agreement, and thereafter, the proposer does yet another subsequent version (lines 11–12), which also gets a weak agreement at first and then a possible acceptance:

(18)   [Wednesday Night]

```
  6 A:    An' so: maybe Wensdee ni:ght,=
  7 B:    eYa:h.
  8 A:    I could yih know if I c'd tell 'im not tuh:
  9        ·hh book anythi ng.
 10 B:                  ⌊eeYa :h.
 11 A:                       ⌊·hhh Then maybe we could
 12        get tuhgether that night er some thing.  ⌉=
 13 B:                                  ⌊eeYah:.  ⌋
 14 A:    =hh hhhh·
 15 B:       ⌊That probly'll ⌈(work out ril well).
                             ⌊
```

Another instance will be quoted at length to display several occurrences of weak-agreement forms followed by inviter's doing subsequent versions, and these subsequent versions appear to be pursuing a definite acceptance or commitment from the recipient. The definite acceptance or commitment is never obtained, and instead the recipient "escapes" from the sequence by changing the topic (the weak agreement forms have arrows):

(19)   [Hospitality Night[10]]

```
  1 A:    You (oughta) bring 'em do:wn sometime.
  2        (0.6)
  3 A:    You en' ⌈Maggie (you know) ⌈have  ⌉a date.=
→ 4 B:            ⌊°eYah.°            ⌊°Yeh.°⌋
  5 B:    =[°Yeh.°]
  5 A:    ⌊ ·hhhh ⌋ =Uh:: week from Fri:day is the
  6        hospitality night.
  7        (.)
```

```
 8 B:    °A week from Fri day.°
10 A:                  (Yih know) when all the stores
11       are open in the evening.
→12 B:   °eeYea:h.°
13       (0.4)
14 B:    °Yeah well maybe we can do tha:t.°
15       (.)
16 A:    ˙hh (And someti-) they usually have: some a'
17       the high school ba:nds (        )
                                      [°Uh huh.°]=
→18 B:
19 B:    =˙hh (Wul)-
20 A:         If it's nice weather it's fun tuh (go.)
→21 B:                                      [eeY e a h. ]
22       (0.2)
23 B:    Yeah it is fun.=(˙h) We did it with you once
24       reme mber?
25 A:         eeYa:h.=Go tuh all the sho:ps,
26       (0.4)
27( ):   ˙hhh
28 B:    En' you won  some thing.
29 A:               [( )]
30       (1.0)
31 A:    Hm?
32 B:    En' you wo:n something.
33       (.)
34 A:    Yea:h ca:ndles
35       (0.2)
36( ):   ((falsetto)) Ye:ah.
37 A:    [(          )]
38 B:    [huh huh huh] huh huh.=
39 A:    =So: if yuh feel like (it) 'n if it's a real
40       pleasant evening you might come do:wn.
41       (.)
→42 B:   °eYeah.°<˙h Yih know what we got a Christmas
43       card tuhday,
44       (.)
45 A:    Oh no.=
46 B:    =An˙ we don't even know who it's fro:m.
```

5. Subsequent versions after absence of response at possible completion points

Jefferson (1973a) has shown that speakers have the technical capacity to start up immediately after a possible sentence completion point and in overlap with address terms occurring after this possible completion point. Analogously, recipients of invitations and offers can and sometimes do produce a response, such as an acceptance, immediately after a possible sentence completion point and in overlap with whatever might occur after this possible completion point:

```
(20)   [SBL, Tape 1, Conv. 5, p.2]

1 A:   We:ll, will you help me  ⌐ou:t.
2 B:                            ⌊I certainly wi:ll.
```

Furthermore, there is some evidence that when an acceptance is not done at this point, that is, immediately after a possible sentence completion point and in overlap with any components occurring after this point, that an inviter or offerer may take this absence of acceptance at this point as being possibly rejection-implicative:

```
(21) [Visit]

1 A:   Uh: would it be: alright if we came in a little
2      early or
3      (0.2)
4 A:   Would that upsetchu ⌐r
5 B:                       ⌊I: don't think so.
```

In this instance, a possible sentence completion point is after "early," and speaker A displays in line 4 that, having heard no response such as an acceptance at this point, he is taking this absence of response as being possibly rejection-implicative.

In each of the following instances, the offer or invitation has a possible sentence completion point that is not actual utterance completion, such that components occur after this possible completion point (these post-completion components are in capitals):

```
(22)   [NB:52, p.266]

P:    Oh I mean uh: you wanna go t'the store ER
      ANYTHING

(23)   [NB:38, p.85]

B:    Wanna come down'n have a bite a' lunch WITH ME:?

(24)   [SBL, Tape 2, Conv. 7, p.20]

A:    I- if you want to uh(b)(1.1) maybe get up a
      game SOME ↑MORNING ↓WHILE YER OUT THE:RE,

(25)   [Walk]

A:    ˙hh I was goin' tuh call you tuh see if you
      wannid tuh go fer a walk WITH ME.
```

Jefferson (1973a:73) comments about such "tag-positioned" components (i.e., those occurring after a possible sentence completion point):

> A question [You want sumpn to do Carol?] that invites its recipient
> to do a task may be "well-constructed" if it orients to such issues;
> if, for example, it designs its components to make it possible to
> scrutinize the elapsed time between question and answer for a
> recipient's willingness or reluctance, not merely to speak, but to
> take up the task.

Analogously, in the instances under consideration here, the components occurring after a possible completion point may be providing the
inviter or offerer with a *monitor space* in which he or she can examine
what happens or what does not happen there for its accep-
tance/rejection implicativeness. Given the absence of a response such as
acceptance immediately after the possible completion point and in overlap with the tag-positioned components in the monitor space, then an
inviter or offerer may take this absence as rejection-implicative, that is,
as a display that the recipient is having some trouble or problem with
the acceptability of the invitation or offer as it stands so far. And if the
inviter or offerer cares to display an attempt to deal with this possibility
of rejection, the inviter may then latch onto the components in the
monitor space some subsequent version of the invitation or offer:

```
(22)  [NB:52, p.266]

1 FIRST VERSION   P: Oh I mean uh: you wanna go
2                    t'the store
3 MONITOR SPACE      er anything
4 SUBS. VERSION      over et the Market  Basket er
5                    anything?          [
```

```
(23)  [NB:38, p.85]

1 FIRST VERSION   B: Wanna come down'n have a bite
2                    a' lunch
3 MONITOR SPACE      with me:?=
4 SUBS. VERSION      =I got some be:er en stuff,
```

```
(24)  [SBL, Tape 2, Conv. 7, p.20]

1 FIRST VERSION   A: I- if you want to uh (b) (1.1)
2                    maybe get up a game
3 MONITOR SPACE      some ↑morning ↓while yer out the:re,=
4 SUBS. VERSION      =why that's always fu:n,
```

```
(25)  [Walk]11

1 FIRST VERSION   A: 'hh I was goin' tuh call you tuh see
2                    if you wannid tuh go fer a walk
```

```
3 MONITOR SPACE      with me.='hh=
4 SUBS. VERSION      =I need ā walk.
```

Again, just as with subsequent versions produced after silences or rejections, in these instances the subsequent versions have the features of (1) displaying that inviter or offerer is attempting to make the invitation or offer now acceptable, and (2) providing a next point for response, the prior possible response point having been passed over:

(22)   [NB:52, p.266]

```
  5 P:    ... over et the Market  ⌈Basket er anything?⌉
→6 A:                             ⌊'hhhhhhhhhhhhhhhhhh⌋h=
→7        Well ho⌈ney I–
              ⌊
```

(23)   [NB:38, p.85]

```
  4 B:    I got some be:er en stuff,
  5       (0.4)
→6 A:     Wul yer real sweet hon;=u::hm: (.) le⌈t I
  7       (hev)--                              ⌊
```

(24)   [SBL, Tape 2, Conv. 7, p.20]

```
  4 A:    Why that's always fu:n,
→5 B:     Mm hm.
```

(25)   [Walk]¹²

```
  4 A:    I need ā walk.
  5       (0.7)
→ 6 B:    ⌈A (what)?
  7 A:    ⌊I need a lo:::ng walk.hh
  8       (0.4)
  9 B:    Bout how lo:ng.
```

Jefferson points out another feature of utterances designed with tag-positioned components (1973a:73):

> Tag-positioned address terms, however, can operate to add to the length of an ongoing utterance; they can be included among a series of utterables which provide that a speaker has not stopped talking although a possible complete utterance has been produced, where if he were to "have stopped," an informative pause might occur.

If these utterances were designed so that the tag-positioned components were excluded, there might very well have been silences. Designing invitations and offers to include tag-positioned components avoids a silence and at the same time provides a monitor space during which an inviter or offerer can monitor for acceptance and, in then not hearing acceptance, can immediately latch on a subsequent version. Since a silence following an invitation or offer may be explicitly rejection-implicative, then designing invitations and offers with tag-positioned components may be a technique for avoiding such an explicit rejection-implicative occurrence as a silence.

6. Subsequent versions after other monitor spaces

In instances (22)–(25), the monitor space consisted of components occurring after a possible sentence completion point. Another type of monitor space is suggested by Jefferson's (1973:78) finding that speakers have the capacity not only to scrutinize and act upon whole words, but also to do so merely upon parts of words, such as the initial sound or sounds. Given this technical capacity, then another type of monitor space may consist of a stretch on a possibly final component, as in the following instances (the stretched possibly final components are in capitals):

(26)   [SBL, Tape 3, Conv. 4, p.3]

B: ˙hh So we're inviting (.) the teachers bt I
       didn't send you an invitation cuz I was gonna
       tell YOU:.

(27)   [SBL, Tape 2, Conv. 6, p.6]

B: Dih yuh need any CA:RDS

(28)   [SBL, Tape 1, Side 1, Conv. 10, p.10]

B: I think I'll ca:ll her and ask her if she's
       (interested) because she's a goo:d NU:RSE,

(29)   [Cookout]

A: Why don't we get together Fri:dee NI:GHT,

In these instances, the monitor space consists of the stretch on a component that is a possible completion point. An inviter or offerer, on hearing no response such as acceptance in this space, may take this absence as possibly rejection-implicative. And if the inviter or offerer cares to display that he is attempting to make the invitation or offer more

acceptable to the recipient, then immediately after the stretched component, and latched onto it, the inviter may produce some subsequent
version of the invitation or offer. Again, the doing of this subsequent
version provides a next place for response, the first place (during the
stretched component) having been passed over by the recipient. As with
the sorts of subsequent versions previously mentioned, these subsequent
versions also have the feature of displaying that the preferred response is
acceptance, but, of course, other sorts of responses, such as rejections or
rejection-implicative objects like weak agreements, are also sequentially
possible. In each of the following instances, a response point and monitor
space, consisting of a stretched possibly final component, is passed over
by the recipient, and immediately thereafter the inviter or offerer produces a subsequent version that does get a response:

```
 (26)  [SBL, Tape 3, Conv. 4, p.3]

1 FIRST VERSION  B:  'hh So we're inviting (.) the
2                    teachers bt I didn't send you an
3                    invitation cuz I was gonna tell
4 MONITOR SPACE      you:.=
5 SUBS. VERSION      =En' Martha Maynard's gonna spea:k.
6                    (0.6)
7 RESPONSE      A:  Uh ho:┌h.
                         [

 (27)  [SBL, Tape 2, Conv. 6, p.6]

1 FIRST VERSION  B:  Dih yuh need any
2 MONITOR SPACE      ca:rds=
3 SUBS. VERSION      =I have (.) I have a couple decks
4                    thet'v never been ┌opened.┐
5 RESPONSE      A:                     [·hhhhhh]hh So have I:,

 (28)  [SBL, Tape 1, Side 1, Conv. 10, p.10][13]

1 FIRST VERSION  B:  I think I'll ca:ll her and ask her if
2                    she's (interested) because she's a
3                    goo:d
4 MONITOR SPACE      nu:rse,=
5 SUBS. VERSION      =An' I think they would like her
6                    don'tchu?
7                    (.)
8 RESPONSE      A:  ·hh Well I'll tell you I haven't seen
9                    Betty for ye:ars.=I should- as I
10                   remember,=Ye:s:.

 (29)  [Cookout][14]

1 FIRST VERSION  A:  Why don't we get together ↑Fri:dee
2 MONITOR SPACE      ni:ght,=
```

```
 3 SUBS. VERSION          =An' have a cookout er sumpin.
 4                         (.)
 5 RESPONSE           B:  F:riday ni:ght.┌hh
 6                    A:               └See see (watsh) up
 7                        on yer schedule
 8                        (0.5)
 9                    B:  Fri::day ni:┌ght.
10                    A:             └(Ya:h) we thought thad
11                        be °a good (night).°⌐(.) °(night tuh
12                        do tha:t).°
13                    B:  °Friday night.°
```

A stretched possibly final component may be followed by a micropause (that is, a pause of less than two-tenths of a second). In the instances below, the monitor space consists of the stretch on a possibly final component plus the micropause:

(30)   [SBL, Tape 3, Conv. 4, p.3]

```
                               *
B: ˙hh So if yer FREE:, (.)
```

(31)   [Computer]

```
1 A: ˙hh You could meet me at U.C.Be: an' I could
2    show yih some a' the other things on the
3    COMPU:TER, (.)
```

Again, an inviter or offerer, upon not hearing a response such as an acceptance in the monitor space, may take this absence as being possibly rejection-implicative, and he may thereafter produce a subsequent version as a display of attempting to deal with this possibility of rejection. This subsequent version provides a next place for a response:

(30)   [SBL, Tape 3, Conv. 4, p.3]

```
1 FIRST VERSION   B:   ˙hh So if yer
2 MONITOR SPACE        free:, (.)             **
                           *
3 SUBS. VERSION        It's et the youth ho:use.
4                      (0.2)
5 RESPONSE        A:   We:ll? (.) ez far es I kno:w,
6                      (0.8) I will be.
```

(31)   [Computer]

```
1 FIRST VERSION   A:   ˙hh You could meet me at U.C.Be:
2                      an' I could show yih some 'a the
3                      other things on the
4 MONITOR SPACE        compu:ter, (.)
5 SUBS. VERSION        maybe even teach yuh how tuh program
6                      Ba:sic er something. ˙hhh
```

```
7                            (0.6)
8 RESPONSE        B:   Wul I don' know if I'd wanna get
9                            all that invo:lved, hh· hhh!  [(·hh)
                                                          [
```

Another instance shows a succession of passed-over response points in the monitor spaces and subsequent versions after these passed-over response points:

```
(32)   [SBL, Tape 2, Side 2, Conv. 3, p.43]
 1 FIRST VERSION   A:   Well instead of doing that why don't
 2                       we p:lay: uh:::m (.) ·hh uh:: the
 3                       two rubbers:,=Uh:: an' then: uh cha:nge
 4 MONITOR SPACE         pa:rtners,=
 5 SUBS. VERSION         =That way: well we'll have two tables
 6                       en then we c'n dist- (0.3)
 7 MONITOR SPACE         cha::nge arou:nd, (.)
 8 SUBS. VERSION         An' dust play with the ones th't we
 9                       haven't played wi:[th
10 RESPONSE        B:                      [°Uh huh.°
11                 ( ):   ·hhhhhhhh
12                       (.)
13                 A:   Do[n'tchu th]ink that would better.
14                 B:     [e Y a h.]
15                       (.)
16                 B:   eYeaow.
```

The response point during the stretch in "partners" is passed over, and speaker A then produces a subsequent version (lines 5–7), in which a next possible response point is in the stretch in "change," and then in the monitor space consisting of the stretch in "around" plus the micro-pause (line 7). These next response points have been passed over, A then produces a next version (lines 8–9). This does get a response, but it is a weak agreement form, which was discussed earlier as being possibly rejection-implicative. Subsequent to this weak agreement form, A does a more overt solicit of acceptance.

Another sort of monitor space consists of a stretch on a possibly final component plus what might be called a "filled" pause, that is, either breathing or laughing or both:

```
(33)   [Computer]

1 A: It's rilly intresti:ng:. (0.2) I showed Tom
2    how tuh pro- (.) how doo uh: program a: ⁻hhh the
3    computer doo: make a ra:ndom number CHA:RT EH
4    HEH! ·HH!
```

(34)   [Walk]

```
1 B: I (wannid) tuh call t'ask if you'd come up (0.2)
2    en' have a piece of strawberry (stuffed) PI:E,=˙HH
```

(35)   [Rahman:II, p.20-21]

```
1  A: An' ih eh-ih ahs Paulo said, if evuh you wanted
2     tih cuu:m you £cuum£15 Minnie,
3  M: eOh:?hhh ┌heh heh┐ ˙*eh┌h: ˉh h h i : h┐=
4  A:         └Hon↑ˉes┘   'ly┘iˉt's mahv'lous,┘=
5  M: =hn┌˙hhh
6  A:     └It's only en hou:eh,
7     (.)
8  M: iYe┌::h,
9  A:    └from hahlf pahst eight to hahlf pahss ↓NI:NE.
10    ˙HH
```

(36)   [NB:40, p.116]

```
1 A: I mean or ken I getchu something?=Er: somp'n=Er
2    somp'n? hh!˙=
3(A):=˙hhhhh=
4 A: Mean yuh don't haftuh walk around cuz all I'm
5    gonna do is just I'm just gonna go up their
6    patio dresses.=I'm not gonna put a lot of money
7    in (yihknow) intuh CLO:THES. ˙HH
```

Again, the monitor space provides an opportunity for an inviter or offerer to examine whether or not a response such as an acceptance is being done at this point, and again, an inviter or offerer, in the absence of an acceptance at this point, may then produce a subsequent version, which provides a next place for a response:

(33)   [Computer]

```
1  FIRST VERSION   A:  I showed Tom how tuh pro- (.) how
2                      doo uh: program a: ˙hhh the
3                      computer doo: make a ra:ndom
4                      number
5  MONITOR SPACE        cha:rt eh heh! ˙hh!
6  SUBS. VERSION        An' that rilly turned 'im o:n
7  RESPONSE        B:  Hih! heh! huh! huh! huh! (.) ˙hhhh!
8                      ((sniff)) We:ll,=how 'bout if I do
9                      meet you in the computer center
10                     tomorrow then.
```

(34)   [Walk]

```
1  FIRST VERSION  B:  I (wannid) tuh call t'ask you if
2                     you'd come up (0.2) en' have a
```

```
3                         piece of strawberry (stuffed)
4 MONITOR SPACE          pi:e,=˙hh=
5 SUBS. VERSION          =An' A and W root beer,h=
6 RESPONSE        A:     =˙h Susan (kih-)=˙hh I was goin'
7                        tuh call you tuh see if you wannid
8                        tuh go fer a walk with me.
```

(35)   [Rahman:II, pp.20-21]

```
1 FIRST VERSION   A:    From hahlf pahst eight to hahlf pahss
2 MONITOR SPACE         ↓ni:ne. ˙hh
3 SUBS. VERSION         En we were bahck herre et twenty tuh
4                       te:n.
5 RESPONSE        M:    ˙hh (W'l) it mekshu feel bett'r if
6                       yih do a little exihcise b't really
7                       you w'd need t'do it ev'ry da:y don't
8                       you. This i⌐s (the thi:ng).
                                    [
```

(36)   [NB:40, p.116]

```
1 FIRST VERSION   A:    Mean yuh don't haftuh walk around
2                       cuz all I'm gonna do is just I'm
3                       gonna go up their patio dresses.=I'm
4                       not gonna put a lot of money in
5                       (yihknow) intuh
6 MONITOR SPACE         clo:thes. ˙hh=
7 SUBS. VERSION         =A:nd,=I thought I'd probly go over
8 MONITOR SPACE         around thre:e,=
9 SUBS. VERSION         =I think the traffic might be (.) less
10                      in the middle a' the afternoo⌐n.
11 RESPONSE       B:                              [Mm⌐hm
                                                      [
```

Instance (36) provides another case in which successive response points are passed over and in which the inviter produces successive subsequent versions. The possible response point in the monitor space "clothes. ·hh" (line 6) is passed over by the recipient, and the inviter produces a subsequent version (lines 7–8). This subsequent version itself has a monitor space consisting of a stretch on "three." This possible response point is also passed over, and inviter produces yet another subsequent version, which does get a response.

7. Concluding remarks

A variety of objects and occurrences may be taken by an inviter or offerer as constituting either potential or actual rejection. Following these sorts of objects or occurrences, an inviter or offerer may then display an attempt to deal with this possibility or potentiality through the doing of some subsequent version. The phenomena examined here are by no means unique to sequences containing invitations, offers, requests, and proposals in which what is being pursued is acceptance. As Jefferson, Sacks, and Schegloff (forthcoming) and Pomerantz (Chapter 7 herein) show, other sorts of responses such as displays of intimacy, agreements, and the like may also be pursued by using a variety of techniques other than those described here.

Notes

1. Transcript sources of instances are as follows: Gail Jefferson's transcripts, (9), (35), (iii); my parasitic retranscriptions of Jefferson's transcripts, (2)–(8), (11), (12), (14)–(17), (20), (22)–(24), (26)–(28), (30), (32), (36), (i), (ii), (iv); my transcriptions, (1), (10), (13), (18), (19), (21), (25), (29), (31), (33), (34), (v), (vi). All names of persons in all instances are fictitious.
2. Throughout this chapter, the term "invitations and offers" is used as a shorter version of "invitations, offers, requests, and proposals." These objects have been grouped together for consideration because of their sequential features. Of course, there may be other objects having the same sorts of sequential features that have not been considered here.
3. It should be emphasized that the doing of some subsequent version of an invitation or offer is a *display* that the producer is attempting to deal with some possibly unacceptable feature of the initial version. Such a display may sometimes be required by considerations of politeness or etiquette and may actually have very little to do with whether or not the inviter or offerer cares if the invitation or offer is accepted or rejected.

   I want to parenthetically note that, given a silence after an invitation or offer, an inviter or offerer may of course do nothing, as in the following instances:

   (i) [NB:47, p.193]

   ```
   1 P: I'll take yih up Wensdee.
   2    (0.5)
   3 A: Well I gotta- (0.6) Oh yeah bt will it thaw out
   4    by then.
   ```

   (ii) [NB:52, p.266]

   ```
   1 P: Don'tchu want me tuh come down'n getchu t'morrow
   2    en take yih down: duh the beauty parlor,
   3    (0.3)
   4 A: What ↓for.=I jus' did my hair it looks like
   5    pruh uh pruhfessional.
   ```

   (iii) [F:TC, Reel 1, Call 1, pp.15–16]

   ```
   1 A: So if you guys want a place tuh sta:y.
   2    (0.3)
   3 B: 't 'hhh Oh well thank you but you we ha-
   4    yihknow Thomas.
   ```

Whether or not an inviter or offerer, on hearing a silence, chooses to produce a subsequent version involves a variety of interactional considerations.
First of all, it may be one thing to be rejected after just an initial version
rather than after some subsequent version, where the doing of such a subsequent version may display that the inviter or offerer has a stake in getting
acceptance. Second, it may be one order of interactional event to get an
acceptance after having to do a subsequent version, where this subsequent
version, for example, provides inducements or enhancements, and quite
another sort of event to be able to get acceptance immediately after an initial
version without the "necessity" of having to provide inducements or
enhancements.

4. Objects occurring after a possible rejection-implicative silence may of course
display something other than that the preferred outcome is acceptance. In
the instance below, Agnes invites her widowed sister, who lives alone, for
Thanksgiving dinner:

    (iv) [NB:53]

    1 A: W'l Helen? ₍now I'd lo:ve ˙tuh have you join us?
    2 H: ⌊I-
    3   (0.3)
    4 A: If you: feel as though you'd like tuh come over,

Following the silence, Agnes deals with the possibility of rejection by changing the nature of what is being offered from an invitation to dinner in line 1
to something in line 4 that now sounds more like a favor that Agnes would
be doing for Helen were Helen to accept. In this way, Agnes may be displaying that she really does not have that much stake in getting acceptance.

Invitations of course may be designed to display that the preferred outcome is in fact not acceptance:

    (v) [BBQ Chicken]

    1 A: Do you wan' do that er do you wanna go dow:: (ow::)
    2   (.) have (a) ˙hhh we're: having: barbeque chicken but-
    3   or:: I mean uh rotisserie chicken ₍but-
    4 B: ⌊(˙hhhhhh)
    5   (.)
    6 A: I:t will be kinda la:te.

5. This point is based on two of Jefferson's papers. In the first (Jefferson
1978a:233-4) she talks about instances in which the recipient of a story,
rather than doing something such as an appreciation of the story, produces
tangential talk:

> Storytellers do not explicitly challenge or complain of tangential recip-
> ient talk (as they do not complain of recipient silence). Instead, they
> propose that the story was not yet completed by offering a next story
> component. Upon completion of that component, a next point occurs
> at which the story can be responded to, and thus, at least an oppor-
> tunity for, and perhaps an invitation to, a different order of response –
> in the case of tangential talk, a more fitted response – is provided by
> an added story component.

Second, in Jefferson et al. (forthcoming), several mentions of an impropriety
are described. The teller of the impropriety, in not getting affiliative re-

sponses in initial tellings, then does subsequent tellings in pursuit of such a response, where each subsequent telling provides a next place for the recipient to do the pursued response. I am taking these two phenomena as instances of perhaps a more general phenomenon: The producer of some kind of object, in not getting a desired response at an initial response point, may then do some sort of subsequent versions of or additions onto that object in pursuit of the desired response. See also Pomerantz (Chapter 7 herein) for a consideration of pursuit of responses in different sorts of sequences.

6. Just as an inviter or offerer, if faced with a silence after his invitation or offer, may choose *not* to do a subsequent version, so an inviter or offerer, if faced with actual rejection, may choose *not* to do a subsequent version, and may instead do something that conversely indicates going along with the rejection:

```
(vi)   [Trip]

1 A: You wan' me bring you anything?
2    (0.4)
3 B: No: no: nothing.
4 A: AW:kay.
```

"Okay" is an instance of a class of objects that display that the inviter or offerer is going along with the rejection and is not (for the time being) going to produce any subsequent versions. For a detailed consideration of these objects, which I term "rejection finalizers," see Davidson (forthcoming).

7. In line 10, A was apparently starting to do another rejection when she was cut off by P. For more instances of an inviter's doing a subsequent version after recipient's starting to do what could be a rejection, see instances (11)–(14) and the discussion of these instances.

8. This may be an instance in which the silence in line 6 is taken as puzzlement or lack of clarity about exactly what's being offered. "On Saturday" in line 8 may be providing such clarification and may be the result of offerer's analysis of the initial version as being confusing with respect to which day the offer is for.

9. Lines 15–17 provide another instance in which the recipient displays through "uh:" and "hm" something like "thinking about how to put it" and thereby some possible trouble. This is followed in line 18 by a (0.4) silence, which, as earlier proposed, could be taken by the offerer as prerejection, but note that here, in the face of these rejection-implicative objects, the offerer does *not* produce a subsequent version. That she does not may have to do with the fact that she has already done one subsequent version (lines 12–14); how many subsequent versions are done may have to do with how strongly the offerer wants to display something such as "urging" to accept or "eagerness" to get acceptance.

10. Line 8 is an instance of another sort of object that displays something like "thinking about it" or "pondering," and may thereby be taken as rejection-implicative. For another instance of this, see (29), also discussed in note 14, lines 5, 9, and 13.

11. Strictly speaking, the monitor space in instance (25) consists of the tag-positioned component "with me" plus the inbreath. See instances (33)–(36) for more instances in which at least part of the monitor space consists of either an inbreath or outbreath.

12. This may be an instance in which the (0.7) silence may be a display of not hearing or not understanding, as B in line 6 may be producing a repair request. Although this may be an instance in which the silence may not necessarily be rejection-implicative, the inviter nonetheless apparently takes it as such and points up the need for a walk in line 7.
13. Lines 1–2 may be an instance of the provision of successive response points and monitor spaces. A first possible response point that is passed over by the recipient is after "call her," a second response point also passed over is after "if she's interested," and the next is after "nurse."
14. "Friday night," as it displays something such as "thinking about it" or pondering, may be an instance of another sort of object that an inviter may take as rejection-implicative. In this instance, what the inviter does in lines 6–7 seems to be acknowledging that a rejection is a possibility.
15. The pound sign indicates suppressed laughter.

6. Speakers' reportings in invitation sequences

PAUL DREW

University of York

1. Introduction

Instead of saying that they did not or are not going to do something, speakers commonly assert an inability to do it.

(1) (Her:01:6:2)

```
G: Okay I cahn't get through t'ni:ght e-an: d I'm-
J:                                        No:
   fair enough=
G: =going tih chuhr:ch later o:n t'say muh prayers?
   hhhhh
```

In "Okay I *cah*n't get through t'ni:ght" G formulates a failure to contact someone as an inability to do so, rather than an unwillingness or decision not to. The failure is thereby portrayed as being the result of some circumstances that prevented her contacting the person in question, for example, there was no answer/they were not there, though some attempts were made. Those circumstances, however, are not reported. An account for G's failure to speak to someone is implied, but it is not explicitly provided. So "not getting through" is portrayed as being the consequence or upshot of some circumstances, though those are not reported.

Subsequently in (1) G does the reverse, by reporting something without providing the upshot or import. In the context of G's initially stating that she can't get through, G's subsequent report "e-an:d I'm going tih

I am grateful to Gail Jefferson for providing the majority of the data used in this paper, and for her detailed comments on an earlier version. She is, of course, not responsible for what I have made of those comments, or for my retranscriptions, particularly of examples (3), (6), and (13). I am also grateful to Anita Pomerantz for her suggestions, at an earlier stage, on some of the issues discussed here. I have also benefited from talking about these issues with Emanuel Schegloff, Charles and Marjorie Goodwin, and Richard Holmes.

chu*h*::ch l*a*ter o:n t'say muh pra*y*ers?" can be heard to imply that she will
not (cannot) now make any further attempt that evening to "get
through." By reporting an activity for later on that evening, G is not just
reporting some ingenuous or inconsequential news about how she will be
spending the evening. What is reported can be seen to have a consequence for the project or activity in question (calling someone), but she
does not state what that consequence is. By only reporting/detailing
some activity for the evening, G leaves it to the recipient (J) to see what the
upshot is (i.e., that she will not be trying again later).

   Two similar instances of this occur in the following example; C is
calling about a trip which C and I arranged to make together.

(2) (Trip to Syracuse:2)

```
 1   C: So tha: ⌐:t
 2   I:       ⌊k–khhh
 3→  C: Yihknow I really don't have a place tuh sta:y.
 4   I: ‾hhOh::::: .hh
 5      (0.2)
 6→  I: ·hhh So yih not g'nna go up this weeken?
 7      (0.2)
 8   C: Nu::h I don't think so.
 9   I: How about the following weekend.
10      (0.8)
11→  C: ·hh Dat's the vacation isn't it?
12→  I: ·hhhhh Oh:. ·hh ALright so:- no ha:ssle, (.)
13       s⌐o
14   C:   ⌊Ye:h,
15   I: Yihkno:w::
16( ): ·hhh
17   I: So we'll make it fer another ti:me then.
```

First, in reporting "I *r*eally don't have a place tuh *sta*:y" (line 3) C only
reports some circumstance, without saying what a consequence of that
might be for their arranged trip. The upshot of that reported circumstance is subsequently proposed by I, for C to confirm, as "So yih not
g'nna go up this weeken'?" Second, when in line 9 I makes an alternative proposal to go instead the following weekend, C just reports/ details some circumstances – "*D*at's the va*c*ation isn'it?" – but again without explicitly stating what the upshot of that is for the proposal. I is left
to find what the consequence is; I does so in an acknowledgment that
treats the proposal as having been rejected – "*Oh*:. ·hh ALright so:- *no*
ha:ssle" – and in then making another proposal, in line 17, to go "another time." All C has done in (2), at least officially, is to report some
circumstances, leaving it to the recipient to judge and address the im-

plications of the reportings for the originally planned arrangement, and for I's subsequent proposal. Whatever position C is taking on going/not going on the trip is conveyed unofficially, by his not explicitly stating the upshot of the reported circumstance for the plan/ proposal.

In (1) the speaker at first explicitly formulated an upshot of some circumstances, which was that she could not get through, though the details of how that upshot came about are not revealed. A contrasting option is exemplified in the second instance in (1), and in both cases in (2); speakers just report or detail some circumstances and activities without stating their upshot. This chapter examines the option in which the recipient is left to determine the consequences of a report for some proposed or projected arrangement. The chapter starts with a consideration of how, through reporting, speakers can avoid taking an official position with respect to some prior or anticipated proposal, and considers some of the properties of reportings that enable speakers to elicit or prompt, or otherwise *initiate* arrangements' proposals in quite unofficial ways. That is, by just reporting some activities/circumstances, speakers can get recipients to make proposals for arrangements arising from what is reported, hence avoiding making a proposal themselves.

2. Solicited reportings, and availability

Where, as in such instances as (1) and (2), speakers' reportings seem to be designed to have implications for a plan or proposal, those implications specifically concern their ability or availability to do something. From the reportings, recipients can detect whether the circumstances that are detailed will permit or prevent the speakers to phone later, go on the trip, and so on. For example, when in line 11 of (2) C reports that the following weekend is the vacation, that is treated by I as preventing him from going then – even though precisely how it being the vacation has that consequence is left unelaborated. Not only does the recipient treat it as having that upshot, but from its sequential position as a response to I's proposal it can be seen to have been designed to convey that he would not be able to go then.

Elsewhere, however, the consequentiality of a report as regards the speaker's availability is officially the product of the *recipient's* work, for example, in cases where initial inquiries solicit reportings.

(3) (NB:II:2:14)

```
1    E: w*Whadiyih doin.
2       (0.9)
```

```
 3   N: What am I d oin?
 4   E:            ⌐(Cleanin')
                   (Mmhm)        ?
 5   N: 'h I'm i:rening, wouldju believe that (h).=
 6   E: =Oh: bless it s heart.
 7   N:             ⌐In fact I: ir- I start'd ir'ning en
 8      I'd.I. Somehow er another ahrning dis kind uv
 9      lea:ves me: co:l d
10   E:               ⌐Yea:h
11      (.)
12   N:  °(Y'know)°
13   E: ⌐Wanna cum down'n av a bighta lu:nch with me:?=
```

This sequence begins with E making an inquiry, "w*Whadiyuh *doin.*," which solicits from N a report of her current activities; after N's report, E invites her for lunch. That invitation *arises from* N's report, by being made at just the point where E can detect the likelihood that N might be free to come over. In response to E's inquiry, N first of all reports (line 5) "I'm *i:*rening," which portrays what she's doing as a continuous present activity, as something she is currently doing. But then, in the course of E's sympathetic appreciation of that report (line 6), N continues in ways that qualify her original report. Some doubt as to whether ironing is indeed her current activity is introduced by the elaboration "I start'd ir'ning" in line 7. In now selecting the "starting" and not the "doing" as reportable, N may be contrasting the starting with continuing that activity; or the starting may be contrasted with its current non-progress. What follows in line 8 – "*Somehow er another ahrning dis kind uv lea:ves me: co:*ld" – portrays why ironing might not be, or would preferably not be, her current activity. And at this point, instead of doing an appreciation as she did in line 6, E minimally acknowledges the elaborated/qualified report, and then invites N over for lunch.

Although E's initial inquiry in line 1 can now be seen to have been made with an invitation in mind, to check N's freedom to come over, it does not do that at an *official* level. Officially, all that the inquiry "w*Whadiyuh doin." asks about is the recipient's latest news, how she's spent the morning, finding out how she is filling her day; it is a version of "catching up with the latest." Whether or not N anticipated that E had some other reason to ask, she replies just in terms of the inquiry's official business, in reporting the news of her current activities. The subsequent invitation is thereby managed (again, officially), as occasioned by N's report, as an upshot of finding in that report that N may be ambivalent about continuing with her ironing, or may have already given up on it. Thus the original inquiry's "innocence" is maintained by having the invitation interactionally generated in this conversation, as locally occasioned by N's report.[1] Happening to find that N has nothing better to do and might welcome a break from a tedious and possibly intermittent chore, an invitation is here-and-now being thought of and made.

The way in which an invitation/proposal is managed as an upshot of a prior reporting is nicely illustrated in the following extract.

(4) (JGII(b):8:14aff)

```
    J: So who'r the boyfriends for the week.
       (0.2)
    M: 'k'hhhhh- Oh: go::d e-yih this one'n that one yihknow,
       I jist, yihknow keep busy en go out when I wanna go
       out John it's nothing 'hhh I don'have anybody
       serious on the string,
    J: So in other words you'd go out if I:: askedche out
       one a' these times.
    M: Yeah! Why not.
```

In his subsequent invitation/proposal, J treats M's report – given in reply to his inquiry "So *who'r* the *boy*friends for the week" – as amounting to that she would be free to go out with him. By forming his invitation as a paraphrase of what her report amounts to – "So in other words you'd go *out*" – it is claimed as an upshot implicated in M's detailing her activities.

In such cases as (3) and (4) an invitation has been occasioned by the immediately prior reporting of the other's activities, albeit a reporting that was solicited (and possibly just for the purpose of making an invitation). The subsequent invitations treat the prior speakers' reports as implicating their availability/freedom, the reported activities not seeming to otherwise commit them. Whereas the coparticipant treats that implication (availability) as an upshot of the reporting, it is not stated as such in the reporting itself. In reporting/detailing, a speaker takes the prior inquiry to be just a request for news: it is left to the speaker who solicited the reporting/news to find the implication concerning the other's availability.

3. Reportings relevantly get upshots

In cases like (4) it is possible that recipients of such inquiries (i.e., those that solicit reportings) may anticipate that the inquiries are preliminary to asking or proposing something else. However, in responding to inquiries by just reporting some activities, speakers avoid taking a position

regarding the anticipated actions, at least at an official level.[2] This avoidance is perhaps more clearly so in instances like (2), in which a reporting
follows a proposal. It will be recalled that after I's proposal to go instead
on the following weekend, C reports some circumstance, without explicitly saying what its upshot is for I's proposal.

(from 2)

```
 9  I: How about the following weekend.
10     (0.8)
11→ C: ˙hh Dat's the vacation isn't it?
12  I: ˙hhhhh Oh:.   ˙hh ALright so:- no ha:ssle, ....
```

C thereby avoids officially taking a position about I's proposal, in the
sense that he does not explicitly reject it. What he does in reporting is to
provide her the materials from which she can see for herself that it will
not be possible to go then. It is left to I to find and address that upshot
from the materials provided in the reporting, as she does in line 12.
   A similar case is the following, in which J and L are trying to arrange a
family gathering on a suitable day around Christmas; it begins with L
proposing that they have it on "the *twunny thi*:rd."

(5) (TC1(b):16:18)

```
 1  L: W'l I w'z gunnuh say maybe th'day before that.
 2     (.)
 3  L: Yihknow the:: (0.2) the twunny, thi:rd.
 4     (0.4)
 5  J: hhh heh-huh-hn-hn ˙nh ˙hhhhh Ye::us? hhh
 6      ⌈h u h - h n
 7  L: ⌊Why what's tha:t.=
 8  J: =˙uh ¯hhh˙hhh ⌈hhhhhhhhhhhhhhhhhh
 9  L:              ⌊( ) you work that ni:ght,
10     (.)
11  J: Ah:: no:, the Twunny Thirdy Club is g- ther
12     gitting s'm boats tihgether tih go on the para:de,

    .
    .  ((further detailing by J of the parade, continues
    .     for 16 lines))
    .
    .

28→ L: We:ll what about the day before tha:t.
```

L's proposal is met first with a short silence (line 4), and then other signs
of hesitation on J's part, including her doubtful-sounding "Ye::us?" (line
5). L treats these as signs of J's difficulty in agreeing to the proposal, by
asking "Why *what's* tha:t . . . ( ) you work that ni:ght," (lines 7 and 9).

Although J disconfirms that she'll be working (line 11), she then reports at some length a parade in which members of her family might be interested/involved (lines 11 and 12, and in the omitted lines). As was the case with C's reporting "Dat's the vacation isn't it?" J just details the circumstances of the parade, and leaves it to L to find the consequence for the suggestion for the "twenty third." L does so by making an alternative proposal for the day before, in line 28. So again, the recipient of a report formulates its upshot, in an action (i.e., an alternative proposal), in both (2) and (5); the upshot displays what the report is taken to implicate (i.e., in each case, a rejection of the first proposal).

In other words, following such a reporting a recipient may relevantly formulate what the upshot/implication of the report is taken to be: in (2) and (5) recipients do not, for instance, continue talk about what is reported (e.g., inquire further about preparations for the parade, what is going on in it, etc.). What is reported is not then appreciated by recipients for its news value; instead it is treated for its consequences for the prior proposals.

This sequence can be contrasted with what happens after E's lunch invitation to N in (3).

(6) (NB:II:2:14)

```
 1   E: Wanna cum down'n  ┌av a bighta l:unch with me:?=
 2   N:                   └°(              )°
 3   E: =I got s'm bee:r en stu:ff,
 4       (0.2)
 5   N: Wul yer ril sweet hon:, uh::m
 6       (.)
 7   N: ┌l e t- I: ha(v)┐
 8   E: └or d'yuh'av sum┘ p'n el┌se (t')
 9   N:                         └N o :, I haf ta uh call
10      Rol's mother. ˙h I told'er I:'d ca:ll 'er this
11      morning=I g┌otta
12   E:            └°(Ahh.)°
13   N: letter from 'er en (.) ˙hhhhh A:n'dum
14      (1.0)
15   N: p.So sh- in the letter she sed if you can why
16      (.) yih know call me Sa:turdih mor:ning en I
17      jist haven't hh˙
18→  E: Mm┌hm
19   N:   └˙hh T's like takin' a beating. (.) mhh
20      heh˙┌heh heh ┌hh˙
21→  E:      └Mm::    └('N th' hav'n) heard a word huh.
```

```
((N then reports, and talk continues on, her
ex-husband's failure to get in touch with any
of the family))
```

When N responds to her invitation with some hesitancy,[3] E – anticipating that N may be going to decline – inquires into a possible reason for her difficulty in accepting, by asking "or d'yuh'av sump'n *else* (t')" (line 8).[4] Just as happened after a similar inquiry in the preceding example, the recipient reports/details some planned activity. Here N reports something planned for that morning; the report is formulated as a commitment ("I haf to uh call Rol's *mother*," in lines 9–10), and portrayed as such through detailing the history of how the plan/commitment came about (lines 10–17). As in (5), a declining of the invitation or any other upshot is not explicitly stated in the reporting; it is left to E to determine what it implicates for getting together at lunch.

It will be recalled that subsequent to the reporting in (5), L treated the consequence as being that J could not make the first suggested date by making an alternative proposal (line 28). After N's report in (6) about having to call her mother-in-law, however, E does *not* formulate, or otherwise attend to, the implication of N's report. Instead, where she might relevantly have done so in line 21, she encourages further talk about N's relations with her ex-husband,[5] as a continuation of the topic of her mother-in-law (i.e., "Rol's *mother*" referred to in line 10). E thereby avoids explicitly recognizing and treating what N's reported commitment might implicate for her invitation.

Whereas recipients of a reporting may subsequently formulate the consequence of that report, as in (2) and (5), they are not constrained to do so. Because a reporting, officially, only gives some news (activities, circumstances, etc.) a recipient has the option of initiating further talk about the report, as E does in (6). Hence a reporting may make the formulation of an upshot relevant, but not obligatory. Insofar as a recipient may relevantly address the reporting's implications, however, *not* to do so – to opt instead to inquire/talk more about the report – is a withholding of sorts. So that in (6), E can be seen to withhold proposing a consequence of N's reported commitment, and thereby to resist what the reporting could be taken to imply (i.e., that N might not be able to come for lunch). Hence a decision concerning E's invitation is left unresolved, not because one is not stated explicitly by N herself, but as a result of E's withholding proposing an upshot. Leaving the outcome unresolved in this way provides E the opportunity to reinvoke the invitation, in a manner to be discussed below.

4. Some properties of reportings

Some properties of reportings can now be reviewed. The instances discussed above show the following properties:

(1) Reportings recurrently involve a speaker detailing some activities or circumstances without explicitly stating the implications of the reporting, an upshot or consequence. By just detailing some activities or planned activities (or other circumstances), speakers withhold officially taking positions about the possible implications of their reportings.

(2) It is left to recipient to discover the upshot of a reporting. What is reported/detailed provides the materials from which the recipient can see for him/herself the consequence regarding the speaker's (non-)availability. Apart from thereby avoiding directly or explicitly rejecting a proposal or invitation a speaker manages, through reporting some circumstances, to have the recipient collaborate in determining those circumstances' upshot. Thus instead of a proposal's rejection being a matter of the speaker's decision (or congruously, the speaker's choice), it is managed as a "seen-by-anyone" consequence of objective circumstances.

(3) In their turns subsequent to reportings, recipients may relevantly address what their upshot is taken to be. In such cases as (2), (4), and (5) they do so by subsequently performing an action that relies on a particular version or understanding of what the report amounted to regarding the speaker's availability (i.e., by inviting M in [4], and making alternative proposals in [2] and [5]). However, because in reporting a speaker is only officially telling some news about current or future activities or circumstances the recipient has an option to attend to, appreciate, or further discuss that news for its sake, that is, to attend to what is newsworthy, rather than to what the reporting might implicate. Reportings provide for the relevance of recipients' finding and addressing their upshot, without constraining them to do so. But where a recipient does not so respond, the absence of action can be recognizable as a withholding,[6] as not going to make an upshot official, or as resisting a possible upshot.

(4) In just detailing some activities/circumstances, the speaker is officially responsible only for the reporting, and not for what is made from (detected in) that. Determining what a reporting amounts to (e.g., for a proposal) is managed as a recipient's work/responsibility. It is a matter for recipients to see that the activities/circumstances that are reported account for the speaker being unable to accept (agree to a proposal); and because treating what is reported as accounting for a declining is properly done by the recipient, it is the recipient's responsibility, not the speaker's. A speaker may not be committed to a position initially attributed to them by the recipient. A speaker may wait to see what the recipient will make from a reporting, what consequence the recipient will treat it as having, and subsequently revise (correct) that attributed position by further reporting.

This happens in the following example; earlier in this telephone call E has announced to N (who is the caller) that she has recently had an operation to remove an infected toenail, and she asks N over to visit her. N responds that she had called to ask E along on a shopping trip with her, which she portrays as something of a commitment ("*I've* got *to* uh ·hhh I have *go*:t ·hh to: get.h ·hhh a couple of things to wear Emma=I (.) *just* don't have enough clothes to: to go to work in"). To N's proposal/ invitation E replies with "Oh:::: darling I don't kno:wº uh it's bleeding a little." She then gives an elaborately detailed report of the trouble she's had with the toe, the operation, who else she knows had that infection, and so on. During all of that reporting, which continues for 130 lines (not reproduced here), E does not explicitly state any upshot for N's proposal to go shopping (i.e., whether she can or cannot go shopping with N). After that reporting (the last couple of lines of which are shown), the following occurs.

(7) (NB:II:4:1)

```
    E:  ... and I had to have my foot up on a pillow
        for two days, youknow ┌and- ˙hhhmhh
    N:                         └Yah?
    E:  But honey it's gonna be alright I'm sure,
    N:  Oh I'm sure it's gonna be alri:ght,
    E:  Yeuh,
 →  N:  Oh:: do:ggone.  I ┌thought maybe we could┐
 →  E:                    └I'd  l i k e  to  get ┘some
        little slippers but uh,
```

After E's detailing of the trouble with her toe, N expresses disappointment ("*Oh*:: do:ggone. I thought maybe we could"), which treats the upshot of E's report to be that E will not be coming along on the shopping trip. She does so *without* proposing the alternative, that she would visit E instead. Thus it is available to E that her report concerning her toenail operation has failed to persuade N to visit her, and that N still intends to go shopping instead, moreover without her. At which point E sets about repairing the position N attributed to her, revising the apparent consequence of her first report, by then reporting "I'd *like* to get some little slippers but uh." From this N can detect a different implication, that E might wish to come on the shopping trip. E's subsequent report of something she would like to buy accordingly has N offer "We:ll, do you want me to just pick you–" (not shown in [7]).

What is therefore illustrated in (7) is that by not being responsible for formulating an upshot, and thus not being committed to a position, speakers can subsequently revise a position attributed to them by further reporting. Should the consequence/position attributed to a report by the recipient be unwanted, the speaker can have that upshot revised and a new one substituted through adding to/subsequently continuing the reporting. Not having taken a position explicitly, the speaker can change or concede a position, make an accommodation to the recipient, and so on (as E does to N in [7], having seen that N will not put off her shopping trip in order to visit her), without any of these actions being a speaker's official business.

(5) Finally, since the actions that reportings achieve (e.g., a rejection, in [2]) are managed through *recipients'* determinations, what is reported is not, officially at least, dependent upon the speaker's explicit purposes (e.g., to receive an invitation or to reject one). What a speaker reports is independent of an action/purpose achieved through that reporting, which is thereby cleansed of being an interested, motivated production. Whatever is detailed is not, officially, being reported to pursue or support a stated purpose or action; the activities, commitments, or circumstances that are reported are to be treated as, and can be locally portrayed as, objective, as independent of, and not being manufactured for, any local sequential concerns.

5. Speakers' reportings can prompt self-invitations by recipients

The properties of reportings discussed above coalesce in showing how speakers can prompt self-invitations or proposals from recipients in such a way that speakers thereby avoid officially or directly making an invitation/proposal themselves.

We have seen that the work accountably done in reporting[7] can be to implicate a consequence (for a plan, proposal, etc.), in and through telling some news.[8] That work of reporting is evidenced in cases where speakers make invitations, having first reported some (forthcoming) event or activity or circumstances, in more or less elaborate ways.

(8) (Kamunsky:3:3)

```
    A: Uh nex'Saturday night's a s'prize party here
       fer p-Kevin.
       (0.2)
 →  A: 'p! Egnd if you c'n make it.
    M: OH RILLY::::=
```

(9) (NB:I:1:2)

```
    G: 'hhhhhh Hey uh, hh My son'n law's down, 'nd uh,
       thought w'might play a little golf either this
```

```
  →      afternoon er tomorrow, Wouldju like tuh
         (0.9)
  → G:   hh get out? hh
    E:   Well, this afternoon'd be alright, but I don't
         think I'd better tomorrow,
```

(10) (F:TC:1:1:15)

```
 1   S:  't'hhh Okay lemme tellyuh something. Uhm 'hh my
 2       second cousin: (.) probably will be in town aroun'
 3       then. 'hhh She has a house in San Francisco.=
 4   G:  =[ U-huh,
 5   S:   [ 'hhhh
 6       (.)
 7   S:  with her two ki:ds end her husband who will also be
 8       here with her. 'hhhhhh Mike en I er thinking about
 9       going.
10       (0.3)
11   S:  and if we do:, (.) we're g'nna stay et her hou:se.=
12   G:  =M-[hm,
13   S:     ['hhhh So: it's a four bedroom house.
14       (0.2)
15   G:  M-[hm,
16 → S:    ['hhh So if you guys want a place to sta:y.
```

In fragments (8)–(10) events are reported (the surprise party next Saturday in [8], that G's son-in-law is staying and they are going to play golf
in [9]) as a prelude to inviting recipients to coparticipate in those events.
In this way the invitations are managed as arising from the events/ circumstances that have been detailed. They are proposals that are portrayed, through the reporting, as being upshots of something already
planned to take place (notice in [10] that S's invitation to G to stay with
her is constructed as an upshot through the initial "So"). Detailing the
story behind an invitation can allay or mitigate its possible intrusiveness
in the recipient's (unknown) plans, by forming an event as a sociability
already planned independently of the recipient. Hence the speaker is
not being presumptuous in expecting or depending upon the other's
availability; though he may emphasize his desire for the recipient to
attend, and both may express disappointment if the recipient is unable
to, the reporting displays that a declination will not jeopardize the
event.

   An important feature of these instances is that there is evidence that,
even before the invitation is explicitly made, recipients already attend to
the reportings not simply as telling some news but as having some
further import (which they might perhaps easily guess is going to be an
invitation).[9] That attention can be exhibited in their withholding any

assessment or acknowledgment of the news immediately after the reportings, as in example (8).

(from 8)

    A: Uh nex'Saturday night's a s'prize party here fer
       p–Kevin
 →   (0.2)
    A: ˙p! Egnd if you can make it.

The short pause after the telling about the party was an opportunity for M to have receipted the news in some way, had she taken "news telling" to be the reporting's work. And in (10) S reports several things that the recipient might have treated as news; but throughout G holds off from anything more than minimal continuers ("U-huh" and "M-hm" in lines 4, 12, and 15) and passes over three other opportunities to acknowledge the news (i.e., in the pauses in lines 6, 10, and 14). Such withholdings of any appreciations/receipts of news display the recipients' treatment of the reportings as preludes to something arising from them.

But of course in their withholdings in (8)–(10), the recipients are simultaneously not stepping in to address what they might anticipate the speakers are leading up to. This is emphasized in (9), where E does not respond to the invitation in progress until finally, after a pause, G completes it.

(from 9)

    G: ... Would'ja like tuh
       (0.9)
    G: hh get out? hh
    E: Well, ...

In (8)–(10) this waiting, before responding, until the invitations have been fully and officially made, can be a cautious or even modest position for the recipients to take. Should they foresee that they are going to be asked (to the party, to play golf, to stay), they nevertheless hold off until an invitation has unequivocally been made.

The following instance offers a marked contrast.

(11) (MDE:MTRAC:60–1:3)

    M: Ye:h I I wa:s, (.) en n:ow I'm take- I have
       taken a leave en I'm:uh (0.2) ˙t I'm doing drug

```
        counseling down in Venice:.
        (0.2)
    M:  which I really (0.6) 'm crazy abou:t end as a matter
        fact (0.3) we hev written a pla:y, en we er putting
        that on un the tenth'v December.
  → R:  Ken I go see it?
    M:  Love tuh s:- Oh: thet'd be great.
```

Here M reports that "as a matter of fact (0.3) we hev written a pla:y, en
we er putting that on un the tenth'v December." This not only reports
news concerning her current activities (writing a play), but also portrays
those activities as a social occasion, by detailing that the play is to be
performed, and the date of the performance. This report closely resembles G's report in (9) that "My son'n law's down, 'nd uh, thought
w'might play a little golf either this afternoon or tomorrow," by formulating what is reported as a social occasion. In response to M's report
in (11), R straightaway asks to attend the play's performance. A similar
case is the following.

(12) (Rahman:B:1:1:12:1)

```
    I:  Ye:h 'h uh:m (0.2) ah'v jis ruung tih teh- eh
        tell you (0.3) uh the things ev arrived from
        Bahrkerr'n Stone'ou ⌐:se
    J:                        └Oh:::::.
        (.)
  → J:  O⌐h c'n ah c'm rou:nd,h ⌐h
    I:   └An'                    └Ye⌐s please ⌐that's w't=
    J:                             └h a h a  └'a : h
    I:  =I wantche tih come rou:nd.
```

Again initial speaker (I) reports an event (".the things ev arrived from
Bahrekerr'n Stone'ou:se,"), to which recipient (J) responds by asking
"c'n ah c'm rou:nd." Thus in both (11) and (12) the upshot or consequence of a reporting is a proposal to get together, to go to M's play, and
to come round to see I's furniture.

As before, the reportings in (11) and (12) ostensibly only detail some
news, without overtly suggesting how recipients (R and J respectively)
might be co-implicated in the reported events. However, conventionally
and contextually those events can have a special reference for a sociability involving the recipients,[10] by announcing the play's performance to a potential audience (especially as eighteen lines before example [11] M has described R's identity as "The writing for television
Rob . . . Ro::b: Rob writing for t(h)elev(h)isio(h)n"; and by announcing

the arrival of the furniture, to a friend who has plainly shared the anticipation of its arrival (through the announcement's initial position in, and reason for, the call; and J's needing no explanation about what "the *things*" refers to). The reports of these events leave it to the recipients to determine and address their coparticipation in the events. In other words the recipients' proper task is to inspect these reports/ announcements for their upshot in regard to their coparticipation. Were recipients to treat the reportings as no more than news announcements, for example, with expressions of pleasure on behalf of the prior speakers, or of congratulations, wanting to know more, and so on, they might be recognizably disattending or declining to attend the formulation of the events as something like special or social "occasions," occasions that might involve them (recipients) in some sociability.[11] But since the initial reportings only provide the opportunity for the recipients to address their possible involvement/participation, without constraining them to do so, any such withholding (i.e., just treating the reportings as news) would be as unofficial as the sociability/invitational relevance of the reportings themselves.[12] And because any proposal that a recipient makes is left as an option for them to do, they – and not the prior speakers – are responsible for the proposals (i.e., the self-invitations).

The official character of reportings, as just telling recipient about some occasion, is oriented to and sustained by the way in which recipients, as in (11) and (12) straightaway invite themselves, without first waiting to see whether an invitation would be forthcoming, as recipients conspicuously did in (8)–(10). In neither awaiting nor attempting to engineer an invitation, recipients in (11) and (12) treat their presence/participation as something that prior speaker would desire (e.g., to have a friend come and admire her new furniture). So that in inviting themselves – and in seeming assured of their probable success, through the directness and position of their requests to go to the play/come round – the recipients are requesting/offering to do things that they can tell from the prior reportings would be welcomed by prior speakers. Hence, the reportings in (11) and (12) can be cautious ways of finding out whether recipients are available and would like to come to the play or come round. Not knowing the chances of whether the recipients are free/willing to come, speakers can use reportings of a forthcoming or present occasion as a means of providing an opportunity for a sociability involving the recipients' coparticipation, yet leaving that coparticipation (as an option) for them to determine. This use would contrast with, for instance, a speaker being pretty sure that the recipient might be free/willing to do something (e.g., having heard, as in [4], that recipient is not otherwise involved), and displaying that certainty by just asking them.[13]

6. Reintroducing an invitation after its initial nonacceptance

After having discussed reportings being managed as cautious and unofficial ways of finding out whether the recipients are free and would like to do something, and prompting them to propose a sociability, we can now look at how E manages to reintroduce her invitation (see example [6]) to N to come over for lunch. It will be recalled that in response to E's invitation, N reported a commitment to call her mother-in-law. That response possibly implied (though it did not state) a difficulty with accepting. E subsequently encouraged N to tell more about her mother-in-law, and thereby avoided treating N's report as a declination. Thus N has not accepted the invitation, but neither has the upshot been explicitly treated as a declination; which leaves the matter unresolved.

However, it is returned to approximately three minutes later, in the following extract, in which E can be seen to attempt to reintroduce her original invitation. But she does so quite unofficially, through reportings that in the context can hint at N's coming over for lunch, without directly referring to or suggesting that action. At first these promptings are unsuccessful in getting N to reconsider whether she will come, and in the end are only partially successful.

```
(13) (NB:II:2)

 1   E: AW:::righ ty I don'know what ti:me izit, I- I=
                 [
 2   N:          °(allri-)°
 3   E: =woke up et s::six this mo:rnin g=
                                        [
 4   N:                                  Oh: my G*od
                                             [
 5   E:                                       =God w't izit.
 6      Quarter after 'leven?
 7   N: Yea(n)h
 8      (1.0)
 9   N: Yea (h°yeh ave got°)
            [                 ]
10   E:      T h e    S U : N  S comin ou(pt)
11   N: I know it.
12   E: Bee::utiful=
13   N: =(Jus')  beautiful.
14       (It's)
15      (0.2)
16   N: So: anyway, let me uh hhh' call Rol's mother,
17      (.) and uh,
18      (0.5)
19   N: (Don't)
         [
20   E:  Well give me a bu:zz if you- (.) u*g'mon down if
21      you- I'd like tih have yih come down fer ....
```

E's first attempt to return to her invitation seems to be her asking (line 1) and then reporting (line 6) the time, as a matter of surprise ("God w't izit. Quarter after 'leven?''). The time is depicted as remarkable, and hence reportable, because of her having lost track of the time and her surprise at its discovered lateness. "Lateness" is relative to something, and reporting the time can be designed to recall the invitation by implicitly invoking the closeness to lunchtime. Also E initiates her drawing attention to the time in line 1 in a way that is hearable as beginning to close the call ("AW:::righty"), and thereby occasion the relevance of arrangements talk.[14] But of course E makes no direct reference back to her earlier invitation; she leaves it to N to attend to the possible relevance of the time report in initiating a closing.

However, in response N just confirms the time (line 7, "Yea(n)h"). Thus she disattends any further implication of that being the time, for example, that she should get on and call her mother-in-law if she's going to manage to make lunch with E. Nor does she suggest or otherwise attend to the possible import of the "time/lateness" report, in the pause that follows her confirmation (line 8). After (and perhaps where she recognizes from line 8 that N is not about to mention "coming over for lunch") E does a further reporting in line 10 ("The SU:NS comin ou(pt)"). In the context of the prior report, alluding to the morning slipping away seems to pursue the implicit effort to encourage N to (re)consider the lunch invitation. Once again N disattends any consequentiality of that report by another confirmation of sorts (line 11). E's third discernible attempt is in line 12, where she makes an assessment ("*Bee*::utiful"), which continues her prior report. As in her two previous responses, N attends to just the report's/assessment's official character, in repeating it in line 13/14. We can notice that up to this point E has remarked on or reported things that contextually can have to do with getting together for lunch, and that thereby could prompt N to reconsider her invitation. And when N passes over those opportunities, E does not develop the talk in other directions. Nor does she allow N to do so: For example, at a point when, in line 9, it appears that N might have been going on to further detail her morning's/day's activities (that is, further declination-relevant reporting), E cuts in with something else relevant to having lunch together, which is that "The SU:NS comin ou(p)t" (line 10).

After a slight pause following her repeat of E's assessment of the weather, N says "*So*: anyway, let *me* uh hhh˙ call *Rol's mother*, (.) and uh," (lines 16–17), in which she seems to return to the invitation. But she does so quite implicitly, by not directly referring to lunch at E's, but reinvoking what she earlier reported she was going/had to do (i.e., at that time E made the invitation; see fragment [6], lines 9–11). By reinvoking and thus holding firm to the commitment to call her mother-in-law, N leaves it equivocal whether she will come after the call; or is making a lunchtime visit conditional on how long the call lasts, and thus does she defer a decision. Again it is left to the recipient to detect what the upshot is; E renews her invitation (lines 20–21), though in a particularly conditional form which is responsive to N's equivocality (i.e., treating N as not accepting, but being sufficiently encouraging to try again). In the end E's successive reportings, which avoid direct mention of a lunchtime visit, are at least partially successful in unofficially and implicitly prompting N to initiate reconsideration of E's earlier invitation.

7. Conclusion

If a recipient wishes to decline an invitation or reject a proposal of some sort, one option is simply to decline or reject it. But another (generally used) option, which has been discussed here, is to report some circumstances or activities, without concluding what the report's upshot is for the invitation/proposal. From what is reported the inviters/proposers are enabled to see for themselves that their invitation is being declined. Thus through just reporting, recipients not only manage to avoid outrightly or directly doing a rejection; particularly, they also have speakers (coparticipants) collaborate in seeing that, objectively or reasonably, an acceptance is not possible. In providing for the circumstances that prevent recipients from accepting, reportings go toward absolving their consequences from being the outcomes of personal preference, choice, unwillingness, and the like. Though certainly another's (un)willingness, (dis)preference, or (dis)inclination may be detected from the reporting, what gets treated officially is the recipient's (lack of) freedom/availability to do something.

If a speaker wishes to invite a recipient to come over or do something together, again there are options available: to go ahead and explicitly invite them, or to hint at an opportunity for some sociability, and leave it to the recipient to propose an arrangement explicitly. That hinting at, or putting the recipient in mind of a sociability, is achieved through the speaker reporting but withholding saying anything about what that reporting might implicate (for a getting together).

It may be worth mentioning two practical interactional concerns that may be associated with speakers using reportings that leave it to the recipients to see what the reportings could implicate, thereby withholding the actions that the reportings in effect achieve or generate (i.e., rejections, (self-)invitations, or proposals). First, in negotiations participants can be interested in discovering what the other will do or concede were a particular position to be taken, but without revealing their hand. Reportings can enable speakers to test recipients' likely reactions, by finding what they do in response to a position implied through the reporting. But because they thereby avoid taking an official position, speakers leave themselves the option of subsequently revising their position in the light of the other's initial reaction, though any such revision may itself be done implicitly through further reporting (see the discussion of [7]). Thus participants may negotiate positions, make concessions, stand firm or hold out on some matter, but without any of these activities having been done officially. A turn's official business is reporting; what the reporting may accomplish is done implicitly, at least as regards the speaker's involvement in the action that a reporting can be seen to have eventually managed, through something like its upshot. This approach has implications for the work that reportings may achieve in negotiations more generally, beyond the environment of invitations.

A second kind of consideration involved in reporting, rather than outrightly making an invitation, has to do with avoiding intruding on another's plans, commitments, or routines. Speakers who initiate an arrangement through either soliciting a reporting or themselves just reporting orient to the difficulty that their proposal may have by conflicting with or intruding upon the other's commitments (which of course may be unknown to the speakers in advance). Solutions to this difficulty are to check out the recipients' plans through an inquiry, or to provide materials for the recipients to make a proposal, to volunteer a proposal or self-invitation. Hence reportings are cautious ways of proceeding. We have seen how in fragment (13) E uses reportings of certain circumstances to try to bring N back to reconsidering the invitation to come over for lunch, after she has already had some indication that N may have something else to do, and hence is aware that the intrusiveness of the invitation is at least a possibility.

The use of reporting to have recipient attend to and determine coparticipation in, for example, some reported events, relates back to avoiding having "rejecting" as some talk's official business. If what is proposed turns out to intrude upon the other's (unknown) commitments for the time, it stands to be rejected. An orientation to this possible consequence is seen in the speakers initiating a proposal for an arrangement indirectly, by reporting. Although the opportunity or occasion for a sociability may be discovered by the recipient in the report, it is not announced as such by the speaker. The recipient is thus in a position to deal with that opportunity in the light of his or her own commitments, by proposing a sociability or withholding such a proposal – in the latter case without officially having rejected a proposal, as one was not officially made.

Notes

1. In his lectures Sacks has compared invitations that are interactionally generated in the course of a conversation, with invitations that generate the conversation (for example, inviting the recipient as the reason for a call being made). He discusses the differences in the placement of the two kinds of invitation, and in their possible treatments by recipients. See especially lecture 6, spring 1972, pp. 8–10.
2. They avoid doing so in at least two respects. If they should recognize or suspect what the prior inquiries are leading to, they do not acknowledge or attend to that matter explicitly; thus they take no position on whether they recognize an invitation being made. If they do recognize the speaker's purpose in soliciting a report, they do not take a position on whether or not they would accept an invitation if it is made.
3. For a more detailed consideration of how inviters treat recipients who do not take up early opportunities to accept, and hence are seen to have "trouble with" the invitation, see Davidson (Chapter 5 herein).
4. Pomerantz (1978c) concludes: "If a recipient of a solicitation withholds a reaction, hesitates responding, or hedges on answering, the solicitor accountably observes, infers, or queries what may account for the reaction. In the next turn, the solicitor may try a solution to the inferred difficulty, the difficulty that was not directly or overtly expressed. The combination of the recipient expressing himself or herself implicitly and the solicitor reading the implicit expression, that is, observing, inferring, or identifying what the recipient is doing/thinking, provides for the absence of an on-the-record, overtly stated formulation of an action that is nonetheless implicative and interactionally consequential. The absence of the on-the-record formulation provides for the doing of the reaction as voluntarily initiated and performed." (A revised version of the quoted paper is Chapter 7 herein [Eds.]).
5. It is noticeable that E somewhat delays a response to N's reporting, passing over a first opportunity to address its upshot in her first "Mmhm" (line 18). To that extent she has already encouraged further reporting, which N does in "T's like takin' a *beating*"; that reporting perhaps provides E the resources for the encouragement being pointed to here, that is, the inquiry about whether N has heard from her ex-husband.
6. On a recipient's option to address what is only implicitly done in a turn, but the recognizable (yet still unofficial) sense of withholding when recipient does not exercise that option, in another organization, see Pomerantz (1980a), especially p. 196.
7. "Accountably" is used here in the sense that the recipient of such a reporting as, for example, "Dat's the va*ca*tion isn't it?" might be likely to formulate that report (e.g., in describing it to some third party) as a rejection of the proposal. Thus the further action "rejecting" can be attributed to the "reporting."
8. We have analytically and empirically the puzzle (which will not be pursued here) of how reportings come to be treated as just telling some news. And of course on occasions it can be a matter of practical conjecture whether, in reporting something, a speaker means no more than to report/inform, or

intends the recipient to act on something being sought/done through the vehicle of reporting.

9. One of the bases recipients may have for doing so, at least in (10), is the preliminary announcement "Okay lemme tellyuh something." Another example is (8); just before the fragment reproduced here, A has said "Okay Well the reason I'm calling." In both these instances recipients are warned of something coming by the preliminary announcements, though these do not give any particular clue about what is being led up to. The preliminary announcements displace the actions (invitations) they lead to. For an extended treatment of what can be involved in speakers prefacing an action with closely related preparatory moves (e.g., "I wanna ask you something,") which are preliminaries to certain questions, see Schegloff (1980); see also Terasaki (1976).

10. By "conventionally," I mean that the way in which an event is portrayed in a reporting establishes the relevance of a particular kind of involvement/ coparticipation by the recipient through some conventional tying between the kind of occasion/activity and a relevant action by the recipient. Cases that in some essential respects are similar to those being considered here are reportings that prompt, or at least get, offers from recipients; for example:

    (NB: IV: 1)

    ```
    E: Wul 'anyway tha's: the deal. so I dunno what to do
       about Sandra (.) ˙hhh
       (.)
    E: Cuz yuh see she's depending on: him takin'er in tuh
       the el a: deepl s- depot Sundih s┌o ('e     )
    L:                                    └I:ll take er in
       Sund┌h
    E:       └˙hhOh:: no: Lottie
       Oh ┌my ga:d no Lottie
    L:     └Yea::(n)h
    E: No that's a he:ll uv a long trip.
    ```

    (but E comes back to the offer a little later, in proposing ".hhh I tell yuh what we could take 'er to thuh .hh *Grey*hound bus over here on the coa:st *high*way . . ."").

    In this instance E reports something that elicits an offer from L. Of course what E reports is portrayed as something markedly different from the events in (11) and (12), that is, as a problem, instead of a social or special occasion. Whereas for a social or special occasion another's involvement may be as coparticipant in a sociability (to be part of an audience, to come round), the telling of a problem sets up the relevance of helping – and it is help that L offers here. Part of seeing how one might be implicated by a reporting as a coparticipant *for the kind of recipient one is* is through such a conventional association (e.g., telling of a problem with helping).

    The conventionality of engineering offers by hinting through reports of troubles is recorded by Flora Thompson (1973:108) in her description of rural life in Oxfordshire around the turn of the century. She mentions that friends and neighbors "seldom asked directly for a loan, but would say, 'My poor old tea-caddy's empty,' or 'I ain't got a mossel o'bread till the baker comes.' They spoke of this kind of approach as 'a nint' and said that if anybody liked to take it they could; if not, no harm was done, for they hadn't demeaned themselves by asking."

11. In (11) R does no receipt of M's news, but straightaway asks, "Ken I go *see* it?": whereas in (12) J first of all does a news receipt of sorts, in her prolonged "Oh:::::." But even this action may not be just a news receipt, since it already seems, in the way it is delivered, to carry a sense of J recognizing how she is implicated in what I announces. Though no detailed case can be made for this here, elsewhere what might otherwise be characterized as news receipts do not just receipt the other's news, but instead (implicitly) treat the news as having some implications for a "getting together," as was discussed in the case of N's "Oh:: do:ggone" in (7), or for its meaning for themselves (i.e., for the recipients' plans). For instance, in the following case P's disappointed 'Oh:::::. Oh,' in receipt of E's announced/reported activities may treat E's report as posing some difficulty for what she has in mind (whether that would be just talking now, or as it turns out a plan to do something with E now) but without revealing what consequence the report happens to have.

    (NB:IV:9)

    ```
    E: Oh: I'm jis sittin here with Phil'n Martha'n
       haa:'eh fixin'm a drink they're goin out tih
       dinner:.
       (.)
    E: H e's-
    P:  Oh::::.  Oh.
    E: Why: whiddiyih waant.
       (1.0)
    P: hhuhh Well,h I wunnid um come down en I wannidju
       tuh call some numbers back to me b't it's not
       import'n
    ```

12. Again, on an organization that can provide for implicit, unofficial withholdings, see Pomerantz (1980a:196). A case of a recognizable but quite unofficial withholding occurs in the following extract. It comes toward the end of E's detailing the trouble she has had with her infected toenail and the operation to have it removed, and immediately precedes (7). At this point E seems to move from reporting the trouble, to reporting one of its consequences, that people have been nice to her and "come up and see how I am"; this report seems to more closely prefigure what she would like N to do (from her earlier invitation), that is, come and see her. However, N seems to resist the concession to her (E's) invitation that E can be angling for, and withholds treating the reports that "everybody's been nice" and "they all come up and see how I am" as anything more than news.

    (NB:II:4:6)

    ```
    E: So everybody's been nice in the apartment just
       like with my le:g ihh  hh heh heh huh?
    N:                         Yee:::a:::uh::,
    N: Well you- people should be nice to you Emma,
       you'r a, thoroughly nice person to be nice to.
    E: Oh::: well it was-
    E: They all come up and see how  I am and I have=
    N:                                Well su:re.
    E: to have my foot up on a pillow for two days,
       youknow  and- 'hhhmhhh
    N:          Yah?
    ```

13. Note, however, the conditionality of even relatively direct invitations, such as those in (4), and (8)–(10); for example, in "Egnd if you c'n *make* it" as a way of inviting M to the party.
14. On the relevance of arrangements for next meetings in initiating closings of conversations, see Schegloff and Sacks (1973, especially pp. 317–18).

7. Pursuing a response

ANITA POMERANTZ
University of Oxford

1. Introduction

If a speaker performs an action that solicits a response, it may or may not succeed. Recipients may not hear the talk or understand it. They may ignore it and continue to be involved elsewhere or even initiate other actions. They may hear and understand the talk but withhold their responses. If a recipient does not give a coherent response, the speaker routinely sees the recipient's behavior as manifesting some problem and deals with it. He or she may abandon the attempt to get a response, may infer the recipient's response but let it remain unarticulated, or may pursue an articulated response.

This chapter examines some procedures through which speakers pursue responses to their assertions. If a speaker makes an assertion to a recipient who is knowledgeable on the matter, he or she may expect the recipient to confirm (or disconfirm) the assertion. The recipient may directly address the prior talk, for example, confirm, elaborate on, challenge, query, or disconfirm the assertion. On the other hand, he or she may look blank or questioning, or may make hesitating noises such as Uhs, Ums, and Wells. The data for the study consist of fragments of talk in which a speaker fails to get a coherent confirmation or disconfirmation from the recipient and pursues the matter further. If a recipient fails to give a coherent response, his or her behavior is accountable: The speaker makes sense of it in terms of the recipient having some problem in responding. Different types of problems have different solutions appropriate to them. Three types of problems plus solutions are described in this chapter.

1. A recipient may not understand because a reference is unclear or a term unknown. To solve a problem of this order, a speaker may review his or her assertion, scanning for any troublesome word selections, for

I wish to thank John Heritage for his helpful comments on an earlier draft.

example, unclear pronouns or unknown vocabulary. If one is found, the speaker would offer a more understandable reference to replace the troublesome one.

2. A recipient may be confused because a speaker, in referring to a matter, presumes that the recipient knows about it when he or she does not. This type of reference problem results from a wrong assumption of some particular shared knowledge. To solve a problem of this order, a speaker would go over with the recipient the facts and information upon which he or she based the assertion.

3. A recipient may be hesitant to respond coherently because he or she does not support, or agree with, the speaker's assertion. To solve a problem of this order, a speaker may review his or her assertion, evaluating whether it is inaccurate, overstated, or in some other way wrong. If evaluated as wrong, the speaker would appropriately modify what he or she had asserted.

Clarifying, reviewing the assumed common knowledge, and modifying one's position are ways that speakers pursue responses. The success of these pursuits lies in whether the recipients subsequently voice their agreements and disagreements to the speakers' assertions. The remainder of this chapter discusses these three types of pursuits.

2. Dealing with no response by clarifying an understanding problem

The following datum is taken from a telephone call between two nurses, A and B. A is trying to persuade B to be a home nurse for a patient who has suffered a ruptured aneurism. When A identifies the nonlocal hospital and surgeon (lines 5–6), B recognizes (line 7) that she has already heard about it from another source.

```
1.    (SBL:1:1:10)

1    A:   It's uh it is really important.
2    B:   Yes. Well is it Dr. L.?
3    A:   No,
4    B:   Mm ⌈hm
5    A:      ⌊No, uh the uh surgery was done down at UCLA,
6         Dr. D.
7    B:   Oh, is this Mrs. T.?
8    A:   Yes,
9    A:   Have you been out there?
10   B:   No, I haven't I (met      ) who lives in
11        Little Rock
12   A:   Oh, Uh huh,
13   B:   And, uh she- And I heard about it at the time.
```

```
14     A:   Yes.
15     B:   And uh isn't she quite a young woman? Only in her
16          fifties?
17     A:   Yes, uh huh
18     B:   Oh, how sad.
19     B:   And that went wrong.
20          (1.0)
21     A:   Well, uh --
22  →  B:   That surgery, I mean.
```

After telling how she came to hear about the case (lines 10–11, 13), B takes the lead in discussing it. She begins by talking about the patient's age.

1.   (SBL:1:1:10)

```
15     B:   And uh isn't she quite a young woman? Only in her
16          fifties?
17     A:   Yes, uh huh
18     B:   Oh, how sad.
```

In this small exchange over the patient's age (as in the rest of their conversation), A's and B's respective aims bear on their descriptions of the case. In trying to convince B to work on the case, A portrays it in favorable and appealing terms. B, who does not want to take the job, gives it an unappealing and depressing cast.

Along with the chronological age ("in her fifties"), B gives a sense of that age relative to the age of the illness's typical victims. In relational terms, B proposes that it is a young age for a victim of that disorder ("quite a young woman" and "only in her fifties"). In characterizing the patient's age as "quite young" B portrays the event as more unfortunate or tragic than it would have been had the victim been old and soon to die anyway. In response, A confirms that B's information is correct but does not comment on it. B ends the topic of the patient's age with the assessment "Oh how sad," thus offering a reaction that is appropriate to the fact that the victim is "quite young." In this sequence, B portrays the case as sad both by reference to the "quite young" victim and with her subsequent assessment. A offers no evaluative response to this portrayal.

B then moves on to discuss what happened in the case (line 19).

1.   (SBL:1:1:10)

```
19     B:   And that went wrong.
20          (1.0)
```

21   A: Well, uh --
22   B: That surgery, I mean.

The way that B raises the topic suggests that it is somewhat delicate. First, delicate topics sometimes are talked about with terms and glosses that refer to the topic without naming or identifying it. In the above instance, what went wrong is not identified as such but is referred to with the proterm "that." Second, making a judgment or assessment of the outcome of an event, for example, that it went wrong, is a way of initiating a topic. It invites a discussion of the event: what happened, how it happened, and so on. The type of event that B refers to is an unhappy event, an event having gone wrong. When such events happen, attributing responsibility is an issue: who, if anyone, is to blame (Pomerantz 1978b). In B's topic opener, no subjects are identified as actors who are responsible for the unhappy outcome. Blame attribution is there only by implication.

In saying "And that went wrong," B would expect A who also knows the details of the case, to talk about the event that went wrong. Rather than speaking on this matter, A hesitates one second and then responds in a hesitating manner ("Well, uh –"). A has failed to join in the discussion and instead has displayed some difficulty in responding.

If a recipient manifests behaviors that indicate that he or she is having difficulty or is hesitant to respond, the speaker is in the position of guessing or inferring or determining what the trouble is. One possibility is that the recipient may not know what (or who) the speaker is talking about because an identification is not clear. Or perhaps a word is used that the recipient does not know. Or the word ordering is confusing to follow. In short, a recipient may have difficulty in understanding because of the poor construction of the assertion.

Although B may have made no further notice of her own assertion had it been successful, its lack of success engenders her reviewing it. The review seeks to locate what may have caused the trouble.

In reviewing the assertion, B locates a proterm reference that may have been unclear: the "that" referencing the surgery. The previous reference to the surgery (A's identifying the nonlocal hospital and surgeon in lines 5–6), is not just prior to "And that went wrong" but several segments back.

Clarifying a proterm reference is a solution to a recipient's problem in understanding. It therefore casts a provisional definition on what the recipient's hesitancy may have been about. It would become the ratified definition if the clarification proved to be a success, the confusion were eliminated, and the recipient responded to the assertion.

A speaker's making an unclear reference is normatively a minor problem with a quick and easy solution. A speaker's making an offensive, insulting, silly, or wrong assertion may be more troublesome and more complicated to repair. In other words, a recipient's hesitancy may reflect different types of problems that are more or less serious to the interactants and their relationship.

Clarifying a term is a simple solution in several ways. First, the search for the problem seems to involve the relatively quick and easy operation of reviewing or replaying the words themselves for any that are unclear or inappropriate. Second, solving the problem is quick and easy in sequential terms. The speaker offers the clarification, for example identifying the unclear referent, and if the recipient responds to the assertion, the clarification is successful with no more made of the confusion. Third and relatedly, clarifying a reference usually is socially and interactionally uncomplicated. A speaker's making an unclear reference and/or a recipient's not locating the proper referent typically are not taken to be reflections of character or relationship deficiencies.

Datum 1 may exemplify a speaker's method of determining what the recipient's problem is. If there is some question as to why the recipient has not responded, a speaker may *try an easy solution first*. He or she may attempt to determine what is wrong by seeing whether the easy solution works. It may be not unlike what mechanics, doctors, and others who routinely diagnose problems do on occasion: try the least complicated and costly remedy first. Poor referencing seems to be a matter that speakers rapidly monitor for, easily remedy, and treat as minor.

3. Dealing with no response by checking presumed common knowledge

B's clarification in the preceding section did not succeed in having A join in a discussion of how the surgery went wrong. Rather, she responds to the clarification with further hesitation: a negation that she cuts off (line 23).

2.   (SBL:1:1:10)

19   B: And that went wrong.
20   (1.0)
21   A: Well, uh --
22   B: That surgery, I mean.

```
23    A:   I don't-
24    B:   Isn't she the one who- I think I heard about it-
25         the daughter in law told me- Wasn't she playing
26         golf ⌜at the Valley Club?
27    A:        ⌞Yes, that's the-  That's the one
28    B:   -and had an aneurism.
29    A:   Yes
30    B:   -suddenly.
31    A:   Mm hm
32    B:   They thought at first she was hit with a golf (1.0)
33         ball or bat or something, but it wasn't that.
34    A:     ⌜⌜Uh huh
35    B:   ⌞⌞It was a-a ruptured aneurism, and uh-th-they
36         didn't want Dr. L. at M.  They took her down to UCLA.
37    A:   Yes.  Uh huh.
38  → B:   And it- and it left her quite permanently
39  →      damaged I suppose.
40    A:   Apparently.  Uh he is still hopeful.
```

In saying "I don't-," A shows that she still is having trouble responding to B's assertion. As clarifying the referent apparently has failed, B tries a different tack next. A may be offering no response because she does not know that the surgery went wrong or has a different version of what happened.

B may determine if A knows what B had presumed she knows and if they have the same version of events by checking each of her facts with A. In her responses, A indicates what she knows and does not know, what she confirms and what she disputes. B engages in laying out, bit by bit, a description of the event that, in the end "went wrong." With each description, she leaves room for A's response. By allowing for successive confirmations, B is providing for the end-product to be a mutually endorsed version of what happened.

After a brief identification of the case ("wasn't she playing golf at the Valley Club," "and had an aneurism," "suddenly"), B describes two events that support her assertion that something went wrong. The first is that the initial diagnosis was wrong: "They thought at first that she was hit with a golf (1.0) ball or bat or something, but it wasn't that" (lines 32–33). The second and more consequential event is that apparently after the proper diagnosis was made "they" (inferrably the family members) decided against a local surgeon in favor of one quite a distance away. The trip would have meant several hours' delay before the surgery was started.

With "they didn't want Dr. L. at M. They took her down to UCLA," B describes "just the facts."[1] B is most cautious about indicating her view of the family members' decision to take the patient to UCLA for the surgery. Though she implicates her disapproval of their handling of the case, she does not state it explicitly. She gives as the explanation of their taking the patient to UCLA "they didn't want Dr. L. at M." By saying "they didn't *want*," she portrays it as their decision, a matter of choice or judgment rather than, for example, necessity.

In describing the action, "They took her down to UCLA," B does not give any account of how this action affected the outcome of the case – it going wrong. The issue of how long it took to get there and hence the delaying of the surgery is not referred to.[2]

In reporting just the facts, speakers rely on the recipients' seeing the import of the facts for the issues at hand. If she were receptive to B's line that the surgery went wrong, A might have commented on how taking the patient to UCLA bore on the outcome of the case, that is, the poor condition of the patient. Rather than commenting on or giving the import of the decision to have the surgery done at UCLA, A merely confirms (line 37), thereby acknowledging that this is her version, as well, of what happened.

As A has not commented on the event, B offers her comment. Her comment consists of giving a *consequence* of the event, "And it – and it *left her* quite permanently damaged I suppose" (emphasis added). Although B does not name the delay in surgery, as such, as responsible for the permanent damage ("*it* left her . . . ," emphasis added), the delayed surgery is a reasonable inference, given her description. Her sense, then, of the event is that it is unfortunate that the family members made the decision to have the surgery done nonlocally because the delay caused permanent damage. B has portrayed an event in which the family members (not so named) are responsible for delaying (not so formulated) the surgery, which in turn led to the condition, "quite permanently damaged."

The condition of the patient matters with respect to what sort of job it is for a home nurse. In general, the more damage suffered, the harder and perhaps the more unpleasant and depressing the work is. Likewise, the damage being permanent projects a job with no natural end other than the patient's eventual death.

When B gives the prognosis, "and it left her quite permanently damaged I suppose," A is notably resistant. She confirms it but with the weak term "Apparently." She then adds a contrary prognosis "still hopeful." In reporting the contrary prognosis, she does not report it as an objective fact, for example, "No there *is* hope of recovery," or as an authoritative source's opinion, for example, "Dr. L is hopeful." Rather, she gives the husband's opinion ("he is still hopeful"), which is rather weak and unconvincing. With her interest in convincing B to take on the case, she gives what seems to be her best argument against the case being hopeless and depressing.

To summarize, in the face of A's not coherently responding to B's assertion that the surgery went wrong, B checks whether A does in fact know about the surgery. B tells A her own version of the events leading up to the surgery. If A acknowledges B's information as correct, then B has succeeded in having A support the version that the family members are at least partially responsible for the present condition of the patient, which is that she is quite permanently damaged.

A speaker may check the presumed common knowledge if a recipient does not coherently respond and the source of the trouble is unclear. By going over the facts as he or she knows them, the speaker can see what, if anything, is not established and accepted as fact. These matters, then, may or may not be subsequently resolved.

In their conversation, the two nurses have opposing aims. The descriptions that each of them offers foster their respective aims. In resisting A's appeal to be the home nurse, B reports a depressing and unfavorable prognosis. In persuading B to take the case, A offers a more optimistic prognosis. Although their aims bear on which descriptions they ratify or challenge, the official terms of reference are whether the descriptions properly and validly represent the facts of the case. Giving the facts or one's basis for an assertion often is done when persons have different versions of events and/or different interests, as in both informal arguments and formal judicial disputes (Pomerantz forthcoming a).

4. Dealing with no response by changing one's position

As discussed earlier, if a recipient is hesitant or displays a difficulty in responding to an assertion, a speaker reviews his or her assertion to find the source of the trouble. In the first illustration, the speaker finds a proterm reference that may have been unclear, and she clarifies it by identifying the referent. In the following illustration, the speaker locates the source of the trouble not in the construction of her assertion but in what she asserted. She solves the problem by asserting a different position.

In the datum below, C and M are members of a club. They are engaged in selling fruitcakes as a club fund-raising activity. C tells M of a practice that she has adopted, that is, selling halves of fruitcakes. Her account is somewhat defensive: she presents it as what she is having to do and specifies that she does it only with people that she knows (lines

1–2). M reacts to C's information with surprise (line 4). C explains or justifies her selling halves by showing how badly the customers react to the price of a whole fruitcake (lines 6–8). M responds by complaining about the unreasonableness of the customers (lines 9–11).

3.   (SBL:3:1)

```
 1    C:   Anyway I'm ha- ah what I'm having to do to people
 2          I know is cut them up and sell them ˙hhhh uh a
 3          pound and a half for a dollar sixty five.
 4    M:   Oh you're doing that,
 5    C:   ˙hhhhhh Well I'm doing it to the few people I
 6          know because ever'time I say three twenny five
 7          they look at me like ˙hh (.) you must be nuts
 8          woman, (.) You┌know,
 9    M:              └Well I don't know what's the
10          matter with them because fruitcake is not cheap
11          and that's not an awful lot of fruitcake.
12          (1.0)
13  → M:   Course it is a little piece goes a long way.
14          (.)
15    C:   Well that's right
16          (0.7)
17    M:   Cause we don't eat an awful lot and I'm we Mark
18          and I are the only ones who eat on this one
```

Complaints and counter-complaints frequently are made with relational terms. M is countering what she takes to be the customers' complaints: that a whole fruitcake is too expensive, and that it is too large an amount. With relative measures, for example, "too expensive" and "too much," speakers propose that the amount is more than (or less than) what is the right amount. A relative measure may be used to justify a course of action, namely, one that leads to having the right amount.

In saying, "fruitcake is not cheap" (line 10), M suggests that the customers are unjustified in complaining about its price. It is not priced too high because fruitcakes generically are "not cheap." In subsequently describing the amount of fruitcake as "not an awful lot" (line 11), M suggests that the customers also are unjustified in complaining about the amount of a whole fruitcake. If a whole fruitcake were "an awful lot," that would justify the customers buying the right amount, for example, half. B denies the legitimacy of the complaint by simply asserting its negation: "that's not an awful lot of fruitcake."

In countering what might have been the customers' arguments for buying only halves, M is soliciting C's concurrence and support. C's immediate response is silence (line 12). C's delay in responding may be seen by M as being hesitant or having difficulty responding. The delay gives M both a chance and a motive to reflect on what she has just said. M reviews her assertions to find the source of the problem and perhaps repair it.

During the one-second silence, M comes to reconsider what she said and to reverse her position. It may be that this kind of rapid and complete reversal of position has to do with a speaker's seeing an implication or consequence that he or she had not considered when saying it. (This may be different from modifying one's position in the course of an argument as a way of making concessions.)

Recall that C was telling M in a somewhat defensive manner about selling halves of fruitcake. M does not directly comment on C's practice either positively with a show of support or appreciation, or negatively with a reprimand or warning. Rather, she treats the practice as customer-instigated and complains about the unjustified demands and complaints that customers make. However, if C sees herself implicated and responsible for the practice, she would hear it as a criticism of herself.

It may be that during the one-second silence M realizes that her criticism of the customers' buying halves implicates C as well. Moreover, she may realize that she has just devalued the fruitcake by shrinking its size, so to speak. After the silence, M reverses her position and defends the legitimacy of the customers' buying halves. Perhaps realizing in the silence that her assertion is either undiplomatic or offensive, M rapidly reverses her position. It would not be enough to assert simply a negation of the previous position; she would need to show that it is a credible position and that she believes it. She supports the newly affirmed position with a consumer's aphorism ("a little piece goes a long way") that expands the amount in a fruitcake. She further supports the new position by describing her own circumstances in a way that would justify her buying a half.

5. Concluding remarks

If a speaker expects a recipient's support or agreement and instead the recipient displays difficulty in responding, the speaker would be motivated to figure out what went wrong and to remedy it. In this chapter, three types of remedies have been discussed.

One type of remedy-pursuit is a clarification. Clarifying apparently is directed toward a recipient's being confused or not following what was said because of an unknown term or unclear reference. The remedy is to clarify the confusion by supplying a different reference term to replace the prior one.

Seeing a recipient as not understanding what was said is a different order of social event than seeing a recipient as disagreeing. Disagreeing typically is a more emotionally ladened action than not following some talk. In not following, the recipient may be cast as inattentive or not too competent; in disagreeing, he may be seen as critical.[3] Speakers may search for understanding problems as an initial means of resolving difficulties not only because such pursuits are generally unproblematic in interpersonal terms but also because such features as unclear references seem to be simple to scan for and repair.

Another type of remedy-pursuit is to check out the facts. This remedy apparently is directed toward a problem caused by a speaker referencing, as events known in common, events that are either not known or not accepted as such by the recipient. To find out where the breakdown occurs, a speaker can present to the recipient each relevant fact upon which he or she based the assertion. They may find that they have different versions of events. On the other hand, a recipient may be unable to deny convincingly or disclaim knowledge of the facts as presented. By laying out the grounds or the basis of an assertion to a recipient, a speaker may determine whether the recipient's difficulty in responding is based on rational grounds, for example, having different information, or is based on other grounds such as conflicting interests or some emotional commitment.

A third type of remedy-pursuit is for the conversant to take a different position from the one he or she had just asserted. This remedy apparently is directed toward a problem caused by the speaker having said something that was wrong. If a speaker suddenly reverses his or her position, he or she may have just seen an implication that had not been considered before. For example, it may be that, though the intended object of a criticism is not the recipient, the criticism may apply to the recipient as well. If a speaker suddenly realizes that what he or she had asserted is insulting or offensive to the recipient, he or she might modify the assertion in the direction of being less insulting or offensive. Part of the job would be to be convincing, to present the different position as a credible one.

Regarding remedy-pursuits, the remedy offered should not be taken necessarily to reflect the conversant's analysis of the problem. Clarifying may be done as a first thing to try even when something is only remotely unclear. Checking the facts may be done when a recipient is hostile, or has different interests from a speaker. Changing one's mind may be done when a speaker says or does something, for example, offends or insults a recipient, that was not intended.

Notes

1. Speakers describe "just the facts" in a variety of situations. One situation is if a speaker is concerned with being held accountable, for example, for criticizing a friend or making a libelous statement. A speaker may suggest a state of affairs by giving evidence for it without explicitly advocating the position. In this datum (illustration [2]) what B does not explicitly state is who or what is responsible for the surgery having gone wrong.
2. One may contrast presenting just the facts, as is done in "They took her down to UCLA" with presenting the facts plus the speaker's position, as was done in (1). Recall B identifies the patient's age with factual information ("in her fifties") and gives a sense or interpretation of the age ("quite a young woman"). By giving the sense of the age with a relational term, B portrayed it as more of a tragedy than if it occurred to, say, an old person. Also, giving a sense of the facts provides for an appropriately matched assessment or reaction to be given, for example, "Oh how sad." In this segment, including an analogous sense of the fact might have been something like, "They took her down to UCLA. It took them quite a long time to get there."
3. This observation would be supported by circumstances in which errors one way or the other are made. Persons complain that they are not being given enough credit when they really disagree but are thought to have not understood. Conversely persons defend themselves by saying that they are not being critical; they really do not understand.

PART III
Topic organization

Although the domain of topic organization might appear to be an obvious target of early investigations using conversation analytic techniques, research in this area has in fact proceeded slowly and cautiously. The obstacles here are formidable. Not only is topical maintenance and shift an extremely complex and subtle matter, but also, as Jefferson's discussion of "stepwise transition" illustrates, there are no simple or straightforward routes to the examination of topical flow. Thus "topic" may well prove to be among the most complex conversational phenomena to be investigated and, correspondingly, the most recalcitrant to systematic analysis.

Both contributions to the present part on topic organization focus on the phenomenon of topic transition and begin from Sacks's distinction between *stepwise* topical movement in which one topic flows into another and *boundaried* topical movement in which the closure of one topic is followed by the initiation of another.

Button and Casey's chapter focuses exclusively on the boundaried form of topic transition. Here they identify a particular type of topic-initiating utterance, prototypical instances of which include "What's new" and "Anything else to report" that invite coparticipants to furnish new topical materials. These topic-initiating utterances, which the authors term "topic initial elicitors," usually initiate a three-turn sequence in which a newsworthy event is offered as a possible topic and subsequently "topicalized" by the initiator of the sequence. Button and Casey show the detailed ways in which both speakers engage in intimate and structured collaboration so as to generate new topics through these sequences. Thus the recipients of topic initial elicitors routinely design their initial reports of newsworthy events so as to display them as "candidate" topics in response to prior inquiry, whereas the producers of the topic initial elicitors display a preference for topicalization. Finally the authors argue that the use of this method of generating topics is fitted

165

for, and sensitive to, specific structural locations in conversation – openings, closings, and following topical boundaries – where stepwise topical development is not being operated. Here it may be added that Button and Casey (forthcoming) have isolated two additional procedures for topic initiation – news announcements and itemized news inquiries – which are also fitted to these environments. Examining the use of all three procedures, they have suggested that a speaker's choice among them may be influenced by both the local availability of knowledge about potential topics and the relative power of the various devices to generate newsworthy materials.

Jefferson's chapter also begins with a consideration of boundaried topic shifts but with a focus on a specific, and problematic, context of their occurrence – immediately after a "troubles-telling" (cf. Jefferson 1980a, Jefferson and Lee 1981). She begins by noting that participants routinely treat prior troubles-tellings as constraining upon the subsequent introduction of other matters by engaging in activities, ranging from closings initiations to conversation restarts, which are both topically disjunctive and systematically other-attentive and hence interactionally cohesive. Other-attentive topical disjuncts, she argues, specifically orient "to the problematic character of a troubles-telling for the introduction of new topics."

Jefferson then proceeds to contrast these disjunctive topic shifts with an alternative process of stepwise disengagement from troubles-talk. The latter, she demonstrates, is accomplished through a systematic sequence of moves through which speakers (usually the erstwhile recipient of the prior troubles-telling) construct links between ancillary aspects of the trouble and what is, prima facie, an unrelated matter. A number of points may be made about her treatment of these complex extended sequences. First, the participants' management of topic flow is accomplished through an immense range of procedures whose implementation may be variously cooperated with or resisted. Some of the elements involved, however, apparently turn up in both disjunctive and stepwise topic shifts. Of particular interest in this connection is Jefferson's suggestion that "a display of interactional cohesiveness is a general technique for the management of topical rupture" (cf. Jefferson 1981b). Finally, Jefferson's study shows the value of examining a single sequence in detail. Many of the phenomena that she identifies in relation to datum (15) have now been systematically described in relation to topic shift (Jefferson 1981b) and are providing valuable points of entry into the difficult problems of analyzing topic flow.

8. Generating topic: the use of topic initial elicitors

GRAHAM BUTTON   NEIL CASEY
Plymouth Polytechnic   *Plymouth Polytechnic*

1. Introduction

Routinely, topics in conversation flow from one to another (one way in which this is organized, for example, is through stepwise progression [Sacks lecture, February 19, 1971]). It can be observed, however, that a limited number of sequence types may be used in "sensitive" sequential environments to produce a topic that is *segmented* from other topics. This chapter reports on one of these sequence types. It examines the use of topic initial elicitors and the sequence of talk they initiate. This sequence is designed to generate topic interactionally and mutually. It is comprised of three, speaker and turn-alternating parts. The first part consists of a topic initial elicitor that is packaged as an inquiry concerning the possibility of presenting a report of a newsworthy event. The second part is a positive response to the first part and produces a newsworthy-event-report that has the status of a possible topic initial. The third part is a topicalizer; that is, it topicalizes the prior possible topic initial and provides for talk on the reported event. The following three extracts are offered as a preview and illustration of the sequence operating to generate interactionally and mutually on-topic talk.

```
[NB:II:3:1]

A:  ...llo ::,
B:  G'morning Olivia,
A:  Howuh you::,
B:  Fine.
B:  How'r ┌you
A:        └That's good ehheh
→ A:  Whaddiyuh kno:w.
```

This chapter elaborates upon a conversational phenomenon that was reported on by G. Button in "No Close Closings" presented at the International Conference on Practical Reasoning and Discourse Processes, St. Hugh's College, Oxford. We have benefited from analytic sessions with Gail Jefferson in which issues in this chapter were discussed.

167

→ B: ˙hh Jis' got down last night.
→ A: Oh you di:d,?

((continues on topic))

[HG:II:15-16]

N: Anywa::y,=
H: =˙pk! A:nywa⌐:y,
N: ⌊So::: ,
   (.)
H: ˙p=
N: =You'll come abou:t (.) eight. Right?=
H: =Yea::h,=
N: =Okay
   (0.2)
→ N: Anything else to report,
   (0.3)
H: Uh::::::: m:::,
   (0.4)
→ H: Getting my hair cut tihmorrow,=
→ N: =Oh rilly?

((continues on topic))

[F:TC:I:1:12-13]

S: Y'know I teh-anyway it's a hunk a'shit goes on
   I don' haftih tell you.
   (0.7)
S: ˙hmhhhh ˙t˙ hhhhhh BU::::T? hhh SO HOW'R YOU:?
G: ˙t˙ hhh I'm oka:::y?
→ S: What's new,
→ G: We::ll? ˙t °lemme see° las'ni:ght, I had the
     girls ove⌐r?
→ S: ⌊Yea:h?=

((continues on topic))

Providing a newsworthy-event-report that has the status of a topic
initial, however, is only one of two options next speaker has. The other
is to respond negatively by making no-news reports.

[HG:II:1]

N: What's doin,
   (.)
→ H: aAh:, noth⌐i:n:,
         ⌊

[Frankel:TC:2:1:10]

```
  M: =What else,
→ K: Noth:in',
```

[JG:I(S):X15:3]

```
  M: How are things goin?
→ P: Oh-h-h-h nothin' doin.
```

Whereas a positive response that produces a newsworthy event report has features that require a topicalizing response from the next speaker in order to complete the process of topic generation, as will be developed later, a negative response that produces a no-news report has differing sequential implications for the next turn. The three-part sequence that is used to generate topic and that is initiated by a topic initial elicitor is, then, only one line of sequential development that may accrue from a topic initial elicitor. Topic initial elicitors can, accordingly, initiate a domain of talk that although relevant for, and related to, topic generation, permits specifiable varieties of sequential development. Nevertheless, within this domain the three-part sequence of topic generation introduced above is a sequence development organizationally "preferred"[1] by a topic initial elicitor. Topic initial elicitors then, produce a constraint system, with two options, for the next turn, and within which the production of one option over the other is preferred. Further, the production of either of the options can itself have related sequential consequences for the shape of the following turn.

Examining each of the turns within the various specifiable lines of development initiated by a topic initial elicitor reveals the organizational grounds for a preferred sequential development. Lastly some of the sequential environments in which topic initial elicitors are used will be reexamined in order to disclose and illuminate topic initial elicitors as a technique for generating topic that is sensitive to the production of topic in these environments.

2. Topic initial elicitors

Topic initial elicitors possess a number of features that are relevant for their operation as oriented to establishing a topic for conversation. Some of these features, together with a consideration of the sequential positioning of topic initial elicitors account for their design as preferring possible topic initial production in the next turn. By way of a summary these features are: (1) topic initial elicitors segment talk, (2) though making news inquiries they do not, themselves, present a newsworthy event, (3) they provide an open, though bounded, domain from which events may be selected and offered as possible topic initials. Each of these features can be elaborated upon.

First, topic initial elicitors segment talk. The particular ways in which they segment talk are sensitive to the sequential environment in which they occur. This characteristic can be displayed by observing the way in which they segment talk in three sequential environments. They are regularly found to occur: following closing components, following opening components, and following topic-bounding turns.

Utterances that operate as topic initial elicitors following closing components include components that mark out prior topic(s) and display that anything that is introduced in response to their news inquiry will be "further" for a conversation that is approaching termination.[2] "Else" is a component that is commonly used in topic initial elicitor turns to mark an orientation to a contrast between prior and further talk.

[JG:III:15:2-3]

```
     M: ... I'll ring you back.  Okay?
     N: H'ri ((brusque))
     M: Okay?
     N: Bye  ((brusquely))
  →  M: Okay.  Iz there anything else yo:u-happen
        today of any interest?
```

[Frankel:TC:2:1:10]

```
     K: =S- Ma so we'll see lat:uh,=
     M: =or maybe we'll go in the morn:ing.
        (1.4)
     K: ⌈⌈Uhrigh:
     M: ⌊⌊(We'll see)
     K: We'll s⌈ee
     M:        ⌊When you and Vicki comes home. when
        Mark comes ho:me.
        (1.0)
     K: Uhright.
        (0.2)
     M: Uhri:ght?
     K: Yeah.
     M: pt. Oka:y.=
     K: Uhri:ght.=
  →  M: =What else,
```

[HG:II:15]

```
  N: =You'll come abou:t (.) eight. Right?=
  H: =Yea::h,=
  N: =Okay.
     (0.2)
→ N: Anything else to report,
```

[Trio:2:6]

```
  P: Well you jis tell'er I think ih wz stoo:pid.=
  M: =eh heh heh he ┌h eh┐ eh  eh ┌uh ┌uh,
  P:               └ehhh┘ hhehheh┘   └Fa:1se ala:::rm┐
  M:                                               hhhh
  M: =O::ka ┌y,
  P:        └Okay hon=
→ M: Nothing else happen.=
```

[Krakowski:D+R:11-12][3]

```
  D: Ye:ah W'l okay, okay (.) w'l so: I-I don't (.)
     ˙hhhhhhhhhhh hh Okhhay.  hhhhhhhhhhhhhh
     (1.5)
  R: °Right,°
  D: Okay.
     (0.6)
  R: Awright.
     (1.5)
  R: Aw:::
     (0.4)
→ R: I don' know w't else t'say t'you David °(I really-)°
```

Thus, the use of "else" in topic initial elicitor turns that follow closing components makes a contrast between prior talk and talk that may proceed from their news inquiry. That is, they operate to segment talk. In so doing they display that further talk proceeds, not from out of any prior talk, but from out of their inquiry. The operation that these utterances perform in closings to segment talk is relevant to their orientation to topic generation and to their preference for the next turn to be occupied with newsworthy-event-reports over no-news reports.

Entry into and development of closings offer the relevancy of a sequential movement to conversation termination. The production of topic initial elicitors in a closing section occupies a turn that could be occupied with a closing component. In this respect they display an availability by the speaker for further or more conversation. In other words, topic initial elicitors move out of closings but without actually introducing new topical material, and provide an opportunity for the next speaker to

introduce topicalizable items. The very inquiry into a further newsworthy event report, and its display of continued availability for further
conversation, operates, within closings, to provide for the production of
new items for talk. In this respect topic initial elicitors in a conversation's
closing section are oriented to topic generation. And that they make a
display of availability for further talk but without, themselves, introducing topical material provides the opportunity for, as a preferred next
activity, a newsworthy event report in a next turn.

Topic initial elicitors are also to be found following opening components. As in closings they operate to segment talk, and again, as in
closings, their design is sensitive to their position following an opening
component. This sensitivity is displayed by components that mark an
inquiry into *immediately current* events as first newsworthy items, as
opposed to *further* newsworthy events that follow closing components.
Typically these components are oriented to what the coparticipant is
"doing."[4]

[HG:II:1]

```
N: H'llo:?
   (.)
H: Hi:,
   (.)
N: ↑HI::.
   (.)
H: Hwaryuhh=
N: =Fi:ne how'r you,
   (.)
H: Oka:⌐y,
N:      ⌊↓Goo:d,
   (0.4)
H: 'mkhhh ⌐hhh
→ N:        ⌊What's doin,
```

[Rahman:A:1:MJ(5):1]

```
J: Hello  Redcuh five o'six one?
M: Mum?
   (0.2)
J: Ye:s?
M: Me Mahthew,
→ J: Oh hello thehr whatche ↑doing.
```

[NB:II:3:1]

```
A: ... llo::,
B: G'morning Olivia,
```

```
   A: Howuh you::,
   B: Fine.
   B: How'r  you.
   A:          [That's good ehheh
→  A: Whaddiyuh kno:w.
```

To appreciate the particular way in which topic initial elicitors operate to segment talk when used following opening components it is necessary to observe that turns occupied with opening components – such as initial and returned greetings, inquiries and returned inquiries into personal states – can be used to move into reason-for-call and/or first topic (Sacks lectures, spring 1972). In the three examples above turns prior to topic initial elicitors are occupied with components making up a conversation's opening, and have not been used to begin a movement into reason-for-call and/or first topic. Topic initial elicitors that make an inquiry into newsworthy events operate to segment prior talk from talk that may develop from them, in terms of them being a first move into first topic. That is, they segment prior talk from following talk inasmuch as they display that the prior talk has not been topical, nor is it being topicalized, and that they are providing for further talk to produce the newsworthy and topicalizable material.

For the three examples above it is the called person who produces the topic initial elicitor. The caller not having previously introduced the reason-for-call and/or first topic, the called can then use a topic initial elicitor in order to move into the first topic. The called person does so in such a way that the opportunity to initiate the first topic is given to the caller who may have the reason-for-call.

Although in the three examples it is the called person who produces a topic initial elicitor, the caller can also utilize them. When used by the caller they can operate to delay the reason-for-call presentation by generating a first topic that is not a reason-for-call. In the following example it emerges that Dave – the caller – has a reason-for-call. But it is Dave who used a topic initial elicitor in the fourth utterance of the conversation. Dave may, then, attempt to elicit a possible first topic from Pete and thereby delay the reason-for-call presentation.[5]

```
   [Northridge 2:1]

   P: Hullo,
   D: Hello Pe↑te
   P: Yeah.
→  D: ˙(h)ts goin o::n.
      (0.8)
   P: Oh nothin to it Dave what's happen'n
```

```
   D: A(h) w::(h) you've go:t it
      (0.7)
   D: .hhh
   P: Shit you've go:t it kid
   D: Whatiya doin it home?
      (1.9)
   P: Sittin down watchin de too:: ⌈b
   D:                               ⌊hhhnn. huh huh
      watchin=*hccn-y-=*hncnn (*    ) (.) watchin day
      time stories, unh?
   P: No: I wuz jus' watchin dis u::hm
      (1.3)
   P: 'hh yih know one 'aum ga:meshows,
   D: U:nh
      (1.3)
   P: Watchih up to: fellah?
→  D: Tch We:ll, what I wanda caw-w'talk t'yah about
→     =wha'iyah doin next week.

      ((Dave goes on to invite Pete on a fishing
      trip - reason-for-call))
```

It was observed that in closings the segmenting operation of topic initial elicitors was related to their orientation to topic generation, and to the preference constraint placed upon the next turn to make a newsworthy-event-report. This relevancy also exists in openings. Following opening components, topic initial elicitors segment the prior talk from possible further talk, by displaying prior talk as not having generated the first topic. Topic initial elicitors, then, provide for further talk as being topicalizable, and inasmuch as they do not introduce topical material, they also provide for next turns to produce possible topic initials as a preferred activity in order to generate further talk for the conversation.

A last position in which topic initial elicitors are used to segment talk that will be considered here is following prior topic-bounding turns. Again, as for closings and openings, the design of the utterance is sensitive to the position in which they are used. In closings their design marks prior topics, and provides for any newsworthy-event-report to be "further" for the conversation. In openings their design marks "immediately current" events as first reportable items. Following prior topic-bounding turns their design is aimed at newsworthy events but without marking them as further for the conversation, and without marking them as immediately current. Here, the topic initial elicitors regularly take the form of inquiries into "what is new." In so doing, they provide for new topicalizable material as dislocated from prior topical talk, though they do not mark an orientation to the event that may be reported as a first for the conversation, as is done in openings.[6]

[NB:II:1:4]

```
  A: (Ih) was too depre ssing
  B:                    Oh::::: it' is 'te::rruhble-=
→ B: =What's new.
```

[NB:IV:13:2]

```
  A: 'hh oh the kids cried, they wan' duh stay on she
     did have liddle stuff pa:cked. But, uh, 'hhh I: s:uh
     uh we got up at five thirdy en left her et six
     yesterday so uh Guy had tuh
  P:                      Yuh
  A: work, I guess I told juh that.
  P: Yea:uh
  P: Uh huh,
→ A:    What's new with you.
```

[W:PC:I:MJ:(1):5–6]

```
  J: Huhr doctuh never ca:lled again yeh
     (know?)
  M:  No:: ahn't thih funneh.h'h hh
  J:                             Ye:s=
  J: ( )'
  M: It's ridiculous reahl l y yih know,
  J:               Ah mean it's no t good e nough.=
  M:                                     'hh
  J: ( )-
  M: ih tisn't.
  M: Ih tisn't
  J: Neo::.
→ M: 'hhhh En what'v you been doing this lahst week
```

Following topic-bounding turns topic initial elicitors can operate to segment talk by distancing from the prior topic any new topic that is generated from their inquiry. That is, the possible initiation of a new topic can be located in their inquiry and not in the prior topic. Following topic-bounding turns a possible new topic is produced as dislocated and distanced from the prior topic by the topic initial elicitor.

The segmentation of talk in relationship to the prior topic and new topic is relevant, as is segmentation in closings and openings, for the orientation of topic initial elicitors to topic generation, and for their preference for newsworthy-event-reports to be produced in the next turn. It has been observed (Schegloff and Sacks 1973) that topic bounding produces a sequential environment which closings can be moved toward. Topic initial elicitors which follow topic-bounding turns occupy a turn that could be occupied by components that offer the relevancy of closing initiation. Occupying these turn positions with utterances that make inquiries into newsworthy events and that operate to segment talk marks an orientation by the speaker to new topic talk over closing initiation, and over the retopicalization of prior material. Inasmuch as they provide for new event-reports they are oriented to topic generation, and inasmuch as they occupy a turn that could be used to initiate closing but instead orient to topic generation, they prefer newsworthy-event-reports in the next turn.

The first feature observed in relationship to topic initial elicitors, that is, that they segment talk in the turn positions following closing and opening components and following topic-bounding turns, is relevant for their production as oriented to the generation of topic and for their preference for the next turn to be occupied with a newsworthy-event-report. It is with respect to this preference that they operate as *elicitors*, and it is in respect to their orientation to topic generation but without actually providing a topic initial that they operate as *topic initial* elicitors.

The fact that they do not provide, themselves, a topic initial is the second feature that was originally observed. Though topic initial elicitors make inquiries as to newsworthy events they do not, themselves, provide such newsworthy-event-reports and so do not initiate a topic for talk. However, in providing for the next turns to make a newsworthy-event-report an availability for talk on topic is displayed. This feature is relevant for turns that follow the second turn, whether the second turn has produced a newsworthy-event-report or a no-news report. This relevancy will be developed in Section 4.

The third feature was that they provide an open, though bounded domain from which events may be selected and offered as possible topic initials. This domain of relevancies may vary depending upon the design of the topic initial elicitor. Thus its design in openings is aimed at immediately current events; and its design in closings is aimed at further events that may be reported; and its design following topic-bounding turns is aimed at reporting events that are dislocated from the prior topic and are new for the conversation. This domain of relevancies may be further constrained by the inclusion of components that mark out particular time periods in which a newsworthy event may have occurred.

[JG: III: 15: 3]

M: Okay.   Iz there anything else you-- happen today
   of any interest?

[W:PC:1:MJ(1):6]

M: ·hhhh En what'v you been doing this lahst week.

Although topic initial elicitors may provide a domain of relevancies for newsworthy events, they do not designate the particular event to be reported. Consequently the next speaker has the task of selecting an event for reporting, from out of that domain. This feature of topic initial elicitors provides for the fact that although speakers have displayed availability for topical talk they have not displayed a commitment to talk on the particular event that may be reported as a result of their news inquiry. This has a consequence for the sequential status of the next turn as a *possible* topic initial. This status will be examined in the following section.

3. The next turn

In making inquiries into newsworthy events, topic initial elicitors produce a constraint system for the next turn. Although within that constraint system newsworthy-event-reports may be preferred by the topic initial elicitor, nevertheless an option for the next speaker is to produce a no-news report. The next turns can respond to a topic initial elicitor's news inquiry either positively, by making a newsworthy-event-report, or negatively, by making a no-news report. The two options within this constraint system for the next turns can be examined.

(1) Positive responses. Positive responses that provide newsworthy-event-reports display two features that position them with relationship to topic initial elicitors. First, in their production, components are used that mark the newsworthy-event-report as the result of a prior turn. Second, positive responses have the status of possible topic initials. Both of these features can be examined in turn.

One or other of two techniques can be used in the course of a positive response that display that the utterance was produced as the result of the prior turn's inquiry into newsworthy events. Both of these techniques involve prefacing a newsworthy-event-report with components that mark the upcoming report as the result of the prior turn.

A first technique is to preface the event-report with components that mark the event as "searched for," and thereby produce the reported event as a looked for or searched for item.

[F:TC:I:1:13]

```
   S: What's new,
 → G: We::ll?  't °lemme see° las' ni:ght, I had the
      girls ove r?
              [
```

[HG:II:15-16]

```
N: Anything else to report,
   (0.3)
→ H: Uh::::::m::: ,
   (0.4)
H: Getting my hair cut tihmorrow,=
```

Using components in a prefacing position that mark a reported event as searched for operates to display that the event reported was not immediately available for reporting. In this respect, displaying a search for an event to report is sensitive to the prior turn that is oriented to topic generation because it displays that even in the absence of an immediately available topic that could be introduced, the coparticipant is still prepared to search for one.

A second technique is to preface the reported event with components such as "oh." These mark an orientation to a shift in talk and a new line of talk which was initiated in the prior turn.[7]

[NB:II:5:2]

```
P: What's new wih you.
→ A: Oh I wen tuh the dentist 'nd
```

[Rahman:A:1:MJ(5)1]

```
J: Oh hello thehr whatche ↑doing
→ M: Ohn jis ringin tih say ah'm still ali''ve en
   ah'm still 'eah
```

By using components that can operate to mark an orientation to a shift of talk and a new line of talk, the current speaker displays the utterance as the result of a prior turn having shifted talk and begun a new line of talk.

The fact that newsworthy-event-reports are produced in such a way as to display that they result from the prior turn is consequential for the status of the reported event as newsworthy. Using components that mark the reported event as the result of the prior turn can display that the event would not have otherwise been reported *here*. This observation should be readily understood for components that mark an event as searched for but it is also applicable for components that mark an orientation to a shift in talk and a new line of talk. By marking a reported event in this way, the event reported can be displayed as one that was not available for reporting in terms of the line of talk that was current prior to the topic initial elicitor. For both cases of prefacing a newsworthy-event-report, the reported event is produced as one that has been *elicited* by the prior turn, and is sensitive to the eliciting properties of the prior turn.

Producing newsworthy-event-reports as elicited reports operates upon the status of the reported event as newsworthy. Inasmuch as they are produced as the result of the prior turn, components that mark them as elicited and not immediately available for reporting downgrade their newsworthiness. The produced status of positive responses as downgraded newsworthy events operates within the preference constraint for next turns to produce newsworthy-event-reports over no-news reports. The next speakers positively respond even though, in the course of that response, they display that they are not in a position to report unequivocally newsworthy events.[8]

The second feature of positive responses, that they have the status of possible topic initials, derives from previously observed features pertaining to topic initial elicitors. Insofar as topic initial elicitors are oriented to the generation of topic and display an availability for talk on topic but without nominating or initiating topic, the next turn that provides a newsworthy-event-report presents that event as available to be talked to. Because they are presented as available for talking to, the status of newsworthy-event-reports is that of a topic initial, but a further feature of topic initial elicitors provides for the newsworthy-event-report as a *possible* topic initial.

Topic initial elicitors provide an open, though bounded domain from which events may be selected and offered by the next speaker. Although the current speaker provides a domain of relevancy he/she does not specify a particular event to be reported from within that domain. Accordingly the actual relevancy and topicality of any subsequently offered event will not have been attested to by the first speaker. He/she has the option of either going or not going with the subsequently reported event. Thus, the interactional and sequential status of a next turn that responds to a topic initial elicitor with the production of a topic initial is that of a *possible* topic initial.

This status has a consequence for the next turn as the recipient is now placed in a position in which he/she can topicalize the possible topic initial. The operation of turns that follow positive responses in the second turn will be examined in the next section. For the moment the second opportunity for the next turns produced by topic initial elicitors within the constraint system is considered.

(2) Negative responses. Negative responses to topic initial elicitors may take the form of no-news reports.

[JG:1(S):X15:3]

M: How are things goin?
→ P: Oh–h–h–h nothin' doin.

[Frankel:TC:2:1:10]

M: =What else,
→ K: Noth:in',

[Trio:2:II:6]

M: =Nothing else happen.=
→ P: =n:Nothin.

[HG:II:1]

N: What's doin,
   (.)
→ H: aAh:, noth⌈i:n:,
                └

Exercising this option has sequential implications for the next turn different from those that accrue from a positive response. This matter too
will be examined in the next section. At this juncture, though, it can be
noted that the production of negative responses can also display a sensitivity to the operation of a preference produced by topic initial elicitors
within the constraint system.

   Although negative responses are an option that can be exercised for
the next turn, following the exercise of this option, and within this turn,
newsworthy-event-reports can be made.

[Campbell:2]

A: Ooo my gawd. =Well whaddiyou been doing.
   ((smile voice))
→ M: Oh:: (n) not- I (ain') been doin much? (awll
                      (aven'
→   dah) I been (g) yih know (d) git (tin) a few
     things,
     (0.3)
→ M: I ed a 'ai:rcut

[NB:11:1:4–5]

E: ... What's ne:w.
→ L: Gee nothing Emma, oh ::uh:: gee w–uh:: Bud

goes out, oh let's see hoooez playing go:lf tih
day.   huh?=

  E: =Yah.

  (0.2)

→ L: Gee we wen' out–uh:: (.) Ja:ck Patterson en Faye:

→   eh w–en they–uh:: (0.2) have this li'l Boston

→   whaler'n we gotta slod `hh we wen' out the: (.)

→   mouth a th' jetty Tuesday en Jesus did we ketch (.)

→   ba:ss 'nd halib't=

Making newsworthy-event-reports within turns begun on negative responses is another way in which next turns can display an orientation to a preference operating within the constraint system for next turns, and a way of preserving that preference. This way can claim that, although nothing of newsworthy status has occurred, nevertheless, some event is produced as a response to the prior turn. In at least one way the shape of these turns resembles the shape of positive response turns; that is, prefacing components followed by a reported event. The newsworthiness of events that do become reported in turns begun as negative responses is again downgraded. Thus the next turn begun as a negative response can preserve the shape of a positive response. In this respect, turns that exercise the option to produce negative responses can display an orientation to a preference for newsworthy-event-reports in the next turn, even though a no-news report is initially provided.

4. Turns following positive and negative responses

Sequential consequences for the following turn are different depending upon whether a positive or negative response is produced in the second turn. Turns that follow a report on an event are produced as a third part of a sequence oriented to establishing a topic for the talk. Turns that follow a no-news report may be used either to attempt to again generate a topic for talk, or to abandon the generation of a topic.

(1) Following newsworthy-event-reports. In the preceding section it was seen that second turns that positively responded and produced a report on an event have the particular status of possible topic initials and down-graded newsworthy events. In both respects the next turn that follows a reported event, if it is to display an orientation to the topical nature of the event, has the task of attesting to its topical status. That is, for that event to become an established topic the next speaker has the task of displaying that he or she is orienting to the downgraded newsworthy item carried in the *possible* topic initial *as* a topic for conversation.

Next turns to newsworthy-event-reports can, accordingly, be used to
topicalize the reported event.

Topicalizers both upgrade the newsworthiness of the previously
downgraded reported event, and operate to transform a possible topic
initial into an item for talking to. They perform both tasks by providing
for continued conversation on that item without themselves developing
on that item. In providing for further conversation on the reported event
they upgrade its newsworthiness, and by marking it as a newsworthy
event they show that it is available for further talk. In so doing the
reported event is transformed from a possible topic initial to an event
that is talked to.

    [HG:II:15-16]

    N: Anything else to report,
       (0.3)
    H: Uh::::::m:::,
       (0.4)
    H: Getting my hair cut tihmorrow,=
 → N: =Oh rilly?

    ((continues on topic))

    [NB:II:5:2]

    P: What's new wih you.
    A: Oh I wen tuh the dentist 'nd
 → P: [Yea:h

    ((continues on topic))

    [F:TC:I:1:13]

    S: What's new,
    G: We::ll? ·t °lemme see° las' ni:ght, I had the
       girls ove r?
 → S: [Yea:h?=

    ((continues on topic))

    [NB:11:1:4]

    E: ... What's ne:w.
    L: Gee nothing Emma, oh:: uh:: gee wuh:: Bud goes
       out, Oh let's see hooeez playing go:lf tihday.
       huh?
    E: Yah.
       (0.2)

```
    L: Gee we wen' ou:t uh:: (.) Ja:ck Patterson en Faye:
       en w-en t hey-uh:: (0.2) have this li'l Boston
       whaler n' we gotta sled 'hh we wen't out the: (.)
       mouth a' th' jetty Tuesdee en Jesus did we ketch
       (.) ba:ss 'nd halib't=
  → E: °Didju really°,
```

```
       ((continues on topic))
```

It can be recurrently observed that a reported topicalized event is talked to by both participants as a topic for conversation. A speaker who has now topicalized the prior possible topic initial displays an orientation to talk on the reported event by providing for further talk on that item and the prior speaker has, as was noted previously, displayed that he or she is available for talk on that item should the next speaker display such an orientation. With the production of a topicalizer, then, a place is reached where both participants have displayed that they are available for talk on the event reported, and have provided for talk on that event.

However, turns that follow the possible topic initial may not topicalize in the manner so far described. In the following example Mathew responds to a prior topic initial elicitor with a reported reason-for-call. Jenny responds by repeating the reason-for-call but does not provide for Mathew to continue on topic by topicalizing Mathew's response. Rather, Jenny provides for Mathew to respond to her inquiry concerning tea.[9]

```
    [Rahman:A:1:MJ(5):1]

    J: Oh hello thehr watche↑doing.
    M: Ohn jis ringin tih say ah'm still ali:ve en ah'm
       still 'eah.
    J: Yih still ali:ve'n yih still theah.  Well thaht's very
  →    nice, en yih don' want any tea.
```

Although possible topic initials would seem to permit the next turn to be either occupied with topicalizers or, as in the above example, material that does not take up the possible topic initial, it is observed that routinely possible topic initials are topicalized.

This routine use of topicalizers in the next turn is a systematic feature of the operation of the prior two turns. The production of a topic initial elicitor establishes a constraint system for next turns that can respond in terms of one of two options. Within that constraint system a preference operates for the production of a newsworthy-event-report having the status of a possible topic initial. In terms of this preference between options, the speaker who produces a topic initial elicitor has displayed an orientation, and sequential commitment, to the generation of a topic for talk. The next speaker can reciprocate a displayed orientation and sequential commitment by producing the looked-for, possible topic initial. Thus, in two turns at talk both speakers can display a mutual orientation and sequential commitment to the generation of a topic. Though the design of the possible topic initial may sequentially allow non-uptake the previously displayed mutual commitments to the production of a topic provide for topicalization as a preferred response. The first speaker has, after all, received the object of a topic initial elicitors' preference constraint, a possible topic initial.

In the course of three turns at talk speakers interactionally and mutually generate a topic for talk.

(2) *Following no-news reports.* The exercise of the option in the second turn to report no-news, and in so doing not to present a possible topic initial, provides sequential opportunities for the next turn different from those provided by a positive response that produces a possible topic initial. Having not received a possible topic initial, the first speaker may use this turn again to attempt topic generation, by using a number of techniques. Two to be considered here are (1) recycling no-news reports, (2) topic nominations.

The following is an example of the recycling of a no-news report.

[JG: I(S):X15:3] [10]

```
  M: How are things goin?
  P: Oh-h-h-h nothin' doin.
→ M: Nothin' doin' huh?
```

Recycling is oriented to topic generation in two ways. First, it presents prior speakers with their own no-news report to speak to in the next turn. Current speakers do not introduce topical material but in providing for prior speakers to speak to their own no-news report, a recycle can actually operate to topicalize the no-news report. Recycling can operate in a similar manner to topicalizers by providing an opportunity for next speakers to continue to talk on the prior no-news report.

Second, recycling provides an opportunity for the next speaker to reassess a no-news report and present a newsworthy-event-report in the next turn. A turn following the no-news report may, then, be used by the first speaker to attempt topic generation again.

The continuation of the example above uses another technique that can be involved with topic generation. Following Marvin's recycling of the no-news report, Pete reiterates his no-news report and then *returns* a topic initial elicitor.

[JG:I(S):X15:3]

```
M: How are things goin?
P: Oh-h-h-h nothin' doin.
M: Nothin' doin' huh?
→ P: No-o-o, how's it with you?
```

In so doing, Pete declines to introduce material that could have the status of a possible topic initial, but provides an opportunity for Marvin to make a newsworthy-event-report having the status of a possible topic initial. In this respect Pete displays an orientation to topic generation, but in returning a topic initial elicitor places the onus upon Marvin to introduce material that could possibly be topical for the conversation. Marvin follows with a report of his "good time" from out of which Pete moves to his inferred bad time which turns out to result from his being unemployed.

[JG:I:(S):X15:3]

```
P: No-o-o, how's it with you?
M: (              ) everythin's great=
P:     =[Is it?
M:      [havin' a good time and-an just wonnerful.
P: Yeah well that's good.  I'm glad somebody's
   enjoyin' it.
```

A second technique that is oriented to topic generation used in the next turn to a no-news report is to make a topic nomination.[11] Briefly, in contrast to topic initial elicitation, topic nomination may *present* a possible topic initial to be talked to. The current speaker does not talk to that topic in the turns but provides for the next speaker to develop the topic. Routinely the nominated topic belongs to the coparticipant, as in the following example.

[F:TC:I:1:22-23]

```
S: 'hhhhhh ⌜Good w'l have coffee.
G:         ⌞°°(          )°°
   (0.3)
G: °Oka:y°
S: Alright?
```

```
G: Mm-h ⌈m:?
S:      ⌊D'yih talk tih Dāyna this week?
G: ˙hhh Yeh I talk 'tih Dāna uh::m (0.4) ˙tch
   ˙k˙hh (0.4) ⁰uh::m⁰ (0.5) Monday night I
   gue⌈:ss.
       ⌊
```

A topic nomination may be used in a next turn when a topic initial elicitor receives a no-news response. In the following example, Hyla does not, from the onset of her turn, unequivocally, produce material that could be found as having possible topic initial status. Nancy intercepts this turn with a topic nomination done on behalf of Hyla and thereby provides for Hyla to talk to that topic. In so doing she can also attempt to produce a similar activity to that of topicalizing by marking the absence of a report on meeting Grahame as newsworthy. Hyla responds and talk continues on topic.

```
[HG:II:1]

N: What's doin,
   (.)
H: aAh:, noth ⌈i:n:,              ⌉
→ N:           ⌊Y'didn't g⌋o meet Grahame?=
H: ˙pt˙ hhhhhahh Well I got ho::me,=

((continues on topic))
```

The turn following a no-news report may, thus, be used to make further attempts to generate topic. Two techniques are to recycle the no-news report and to produce a topic nomination.

No-news reports, however, do not constrain next turns to be used in this way, but the *sequential environment* in which the original topic initial elicitor was used may carry over to this turn and be consequential for turns following a no-news report. Where a topic initial elicitor has been used following opening components then an attempt to elicit a possible topic initial that is followed by a no-news report provides the technical possibility for conversation termination. First speakers in producing a topic initial display, as was previously noted, that they are not, in that turn position, introducing topical or topicalizable material. If they are followed by a no-news report and the absence of a possible topic initial, then no first topic for conversation has been developed. Both speakers have also previously passed over opening turns in which topic may possibly be initiated. Where both speakers have displayed that they are not introducing a possible first topic the systematic possibility exists that the conversation can move to closings. Thus, where a no-news report follows a topic initial elicitor used next to an opening component, the next turn may be occupied with other techniques for generating topic in order to avoid using that turn for initiating closings for a conversation that has not produced a first topic.

In contrast, in closings, the next turn to a no-news report may be used to reinitiate closings. Because both speakers have displayed that they are not introducing possible topic initial material, the next turn to the no-news report is ripe for reentering closings. In the extract that follows, M reinitiates closings following K's no-news report and the absence of a possible topic initial.

[Frankel:TC:2:1:10]

```
M: pt.  Oka:y.=
K: =Uhri:ght.=
M: =What else,
K: Noth:in',
→ M: Ok:ay.=
```

5. Generating a topic using topic initial elicitors

Three sequential environments in which topic initial elicitors are regularly used have been noted: following opening components, following closing components, and following topic-bounding turns. In these environments the routine flow of topic using techniques such as stepwise progression is not produced. For each of the environments there is a sequential basis for this fact.

Although components that are regularly used in openings such as the greeting exchange and an exchange of inquiries into personal states, and the turn positions they occupy, can be used to move into reason-for-call and/or first topic, topic initial elicitors may be used where those opening components and their turn positions have not generated a first topic. They may be used in order to move to reason-for-call or to delay reason-for-call presentation. Turns in which topic initial elicitors are used following opening components, and their turn positions, that have not been used to move to topical material may not be available for the use of techniques that produce a flow of topics, simply, because there has not been a prior topic form out of which a new topic can emerge. Topic initial elicitors may be used to generate topic in the positions where a flow of topic is not being produced and its design marks the basis of its nonproduction, that is, the absence of a prior topic.

Turns that are occupied by topic initial elicitors following closing components are also turns in which flow is not operating because the prior closing turn is occupied by a closing component that is bereft of topical features. Thus the next turn cannot be occupied with techniques – such as stepwise progression – that organize a flow of topic because these techniques need to reference the topical feature of a prior turn. Again, topic initial elicitors may be used to generate topic in a position where the routine flow of topic does not operate, and its design following a closing component can mark the basis of this nonoperation as further talk for a conversation near termination.

Topic-bounding turns are oriented to the closure of a topic that has been in progress, and mark its sequential completion. For next turns to a topic-bounding turn to be used to continue a flow of topic it would be necessary to retopicalize the prior topic. Using topic initial elicitors in these turn positions may then be a way of generating topic without having to retopicalize the prior topic. Again, the design of topic initial elicitors following topic-bounding turns marks the basis of the absence of flow, in that they provide for a new topic to be dislocated from the prior topic.

The use of a technique for generating topic that involves the interactional and mutual generation of topic is particularly apt for the three positions in which they have been seen to operate because openings, closings, and topic-bounding turns function as sensitive sequential environments for the overall structure of conversation. Openings are sensitive in this respect because they can be used to organize a movement into a first topic. This movement is necessary if the conversation is to proceed. However, if opening components and the turn positions they occupy are not used to move a first topic, then both participants have passed up opportunities for movement to a first topic. Topic initial elicitors may then be apt for topic generation following opening components inasmuch as both participants, having passed up opportunities to move to a first topic, can now interactionally and mutually generate and determine a first topic.

Closings are sensitive environments for the overall structure of conversation because they may be used to move to conversation termination. It has been observed (Schegloff and Sacks 1973) that closings are not appropriate places for new material. Hence the use of topic initial elicitors as a way of generating topic in closings is then apt for closings as speakers can interactionally negotiate for topic generation in an environment in which the introduction of new material may well be interactionally problematic.

Topic-bounding turns are sensitive areas for the overall structure of conversation because, as was previously noted, the next turn may be used to initiate closings. Using topic initial elicitors in this turn position is also, again, apt, for both speakers can interactionally negotiate with one another for the generation of a topic that will continue the conversation in an environment that is sequentially appropriate for initiating closings. They can mutually suspend this appropriateness through the generation of topic. Thus topic initial elicitors are a way in which conversationalists can mutually generate a topic in particular sequential environments. These environments are sensitive with regard to the overall structural organization of conversation and the *generation* of topic is, in its turn, sensitive to the concern for conversational continuation and closure that such environments manifest.

Notes

1. For a consideration of "preference" see Schegloff, Jefferson, and Sacks (1977), and Pomerantz (1975), and the contributions to Part II of this book.
2. The use of topic initial elicitors in closings has been briefly examined elsewhere (Button forthcoming a). That work also analyzes them as moving out of closings, and therefore will not be elaborated upon again. Schegloff and Sacks (1973) deal with a conversation's closing section.
3. This example takes a form different from the others. Here the first speaker orients to the initiation of a topic as one for their own development. The operation of topic initial elicitors in all other examples provides for the second speaker to be the one who develops the topic.
4. Sacks's frequent discussions of opening sections and their components (for example, lectures 1–5, spring 1972) display that such inquiries are related to what the coparticipant is doing at the moment of the call.
5. Interestingly enough Pete also uses a topic initial elicitor to get to Dave's reason-for-call, and this use may be related to the previous unsuccessful attempts to generate a first topic.
6. Schegloff and Sacks (1973) introduce the idea of topic-bounding turns. For the first and third example topic has been bounded by drawing the moral or the lesson of the topic. For the second, topic is bounded by the proposal that what is being introduced is already known, and by the agreement to that. The third example takes a "what is doing" form, but the immediacy of this form is offset by the components: "this lahst week." Two of the examples were taken from material being used in an SSRC-funded project on "Talking about Troubles" (Jefferson and Lee). Jefferson has observed that, following the bounding of troubles talk, "buffer topics" are used before moving to another topic. She has suggested that the utterances being considered here as topic initial elicitors are one way in which a buffer topic is produced.
7. These components are considered by Heritage (Chapter 13 herein) as "change-of-state" tokens.
8. There is a systematic basis for the routine downgrading of the newsworthiness of elicited reports. To produce them as downgraded in newsworthiness is also to account for their nonpresentation elsewhere and to avoid the possibility that a report of the event can be found by the recipient to have been withheld.

9. The fact that Mathew may have produced what might qualitatively appear as an impoverished possible topic initial does not account for the fact that Jenny does not topicalize it, for it is not bereft of topicalizable features. That is, although it might seem, as a qualitative matter, insubstantial, it is, nevertheless, topicalizable.

10. This extract is briefly introduced elsewhere (Button forthcoming a) though the points made here move beyond Button's observations.

11. This is not the place to provide an extended elaboration on topic nominations. It can be noted, however, that they can take the form of sequence initials that are oriented to the generation of topic. Their decisive feature seems to be whether or not the sequence initial utterance can provide for extended talk over a number of turns, or just provide for the immediate next turn. Thus in the example that follows in the text, the next speaker could respond in one of two forms. She could respond minimally with a positive or negative item or she could respond elaboratively. In the latter case she could display an orientation to a prior turn as a topic-nominating turn. A minimal answer, however, could curtail the topic potentiality of the prior turn. Topic nomination is given more comprehensive coverage elsewhere – Button and Casey (forthcoming). See also Casey (1981).

9. On stepwise transition from talk about a trouble to inappropriately next-positioned matters

GAIL JEFFERSON
University of Manchester

1. Introduction: disjunctive movement from a troubles-telling

In one of his unpublished lectures (April 9, 1976, p. 9) Harvey Sacks proposes that some topics (he mentions "embarrassing" and "controversial" topics) pose a particular sort of problem for conversation. To get *off* them and to go anywhere else from them, one has specifically to *do* "getting off of them."

In the course of an SSRC-funded project focusing on conversations in which various troubles are talked about, it became clear that talk about a trouble poses the sort of problem for conversation considered by Sacks. Indeed, it appears that a primary orientation to a troubles-telling is that from it, there is nowhere else to go; that getting off a troubles-telling is tantamount to getting out of the conversation itself.

That is, a massively recurrent device for moving out of a troubles-telling is *entry into closings*. Following are two prototypical instances, in which the entry into closings is offered with a reinvocation of prior arrangments. (See Schegloff and Sacks, 1973:317; and for a consideration of a phenomenon similar to that of fragment (2) lines 2–3, see p. 313; and G. Button, forthcoming a; forthcoming b.)

```
(1)   [JG:I(S):X15:6]

1   P:    'hhh But I think it'll iron itself out,
2   M:    I sure hope ⌈so.
3   P: →            ⌊I'll see you Tuesday.

(2)   [Rahman:B:1:(11):5]

1   A:    Never mind it'll all come right in the end,
2   J: →  Yeh. Okay you go and get your clean trou⌈sers on=
3   A:                                            ⌊Yes.
4   J: →  =ehh hhahh(h)I'll see ⌈you in a few⌉ minutes
5   A:                          ⌊See you then⌋
```

As it happens, these two conversations, and many others, do rapidly
.erminate. However, as Graham Button's work on close-sequences
shows (forthcoming a, b), entry into closings does not automatically
provide for termination, and further (and substantial) conversation can
emerge. What is being noticed here is the *orientation* to a troubles-telling
as constraining subsequent introduction of other matters, that orientation exhibited by the recurrent phenomenon of post–troubles-telling
entry into closings.

Another troubles-telling exit device may be seen as a close associate of
entry into closings. It involves *reference to getting together*, a matter that
can entrain the making of arrangements. The making of arrangements is
an activity recurrently associated with, and strongly implicative of, conversation closure.

(3) [Frankel:HB:LL:12]

```
1   J:   So: m—everything'll be good and—=
2   P:   =That's goo d.
3   J:  →              M:aybe·t'hh maybe next weekend if you
4        and Freddy want to come up,
```

(4) [W:PC:III:1:3]

```
1   S:   Oh: God we had the (.) police round all (0.2)
2        ni:ght, hh it was hectic. ·hhhh So  I hardly got
3                                            ((beep beep   =
4   S:  =  any wo:rk done.
5         beep beep beep 13 X))
6   S:   So: consequently I didn't get any wo:k done hardly.
7        (0.6)
8   S:   Anyway.
9        (2.0)
10  D:  → So you think— Can you come out for a drink tonight.
```

The matters in fragments (3) and (4) that are introduced following a
troubles-telling may be characterized as *initial* references to matters
which in fragments (1) and (2) are being *reinvoked* to provide for entry
into closings.

Whereas the recurrent device for moving out of talk about a trouble,
that is, entry into closings, and its related activity, reference to getting
together, exhibits an orientation to such talk as drastically constraining
the introduction of other matters, there is a device that stands in strong
contrast. This device, in effect, provides carte blanche for subsequent
talk. Nevertheless, it may be seen to exhibit an orientation to the prob-

lem posed by a troubles-telling for movement to other matters. This device is the *conversation restart*.

In his discussion of problematic topics cited earlier, Sacks proposes that a prototypical way to *do* getting off a problematic prior topic is to produce something that specifically marks that a new topic is going to be done; something that proposes "let's start a new topic"; for example, "So what have you been doing?"

Just such a device is recurrently used as a way to move out of talk about a trouble. Such a device may be characterized as not merely proposing to start a new topic, but as proposing to start the conversation afresh; thus the name "conversation restart." Following are two instances.

(5) [JG:II:(a):3–4]

```
1    M:    But anyway I figure that maybe he can, hh give me
2          something to: uh (.) you know bring this do:wn.
3          Cause God I can't afford to you know. (0.2) get
4          like tha:t?
5          (0.3)
6    S:    °Ye:ah°
7          (0.6)
8    M:  → 'hhh'tch How are you,
```

(6) [W:PC:1:(1):3]

```
1    J:    I mean it's not good e[nough. [(      )-
2    M:                          ['hh    [It isn't. It isn't.
3    J:    No::.
4    M:  → 'hhhh And what've you been doing this last week
```

In effect, a new conversation is begun with a "How are you"–type utterance; an utterance that massively occurs, and may be said to have its home just after the greetings that start off a conversation. Thus, other matters will not occur as a next topic to a troubles-telling, but as a first topic in a distinctive, freshly started conversation.

A close associate of the conversation restart is the *introduction of pending biographicals*, which may be characterized as a specific version of the restart's "How are you"–type inquiries.

(7) [NB:IV:14:7]

```
1    E:    'hhhhhhhhh But hell if it costs five hundred bucks
2          I'm gonna get- we:ll,
```

```
3    L:    Well don't you have insur┌ance on that? ┌Huh?┐
4    E:                             └Yeah.         └Yeah┘::.=
5          =Yeah.
6    L:    On:.
7          (0.3)
8    L: →  So you're coming down in Ma:rch hu:h?
```

(8)   [W:PC:1:(1):35:S]

```
1    M:    ˙hh Well you never kno:w do you someti:mes you
2          feel as if you don't want to stay in the sa:me
3          pla:ce, ˙hh that where you've been with your
4          pa:ren┌ts: ˙hh
5                └Ye:s.
6          (.)
7    M:    Mm┌:. ˙hh
8    J:      └But uh:: anyway,
9          (0.3)
10   J:    ˙mptlk ┌(              )
11   M: →         └By the way Janet did you get my annive:rsary
           car:d
```

A weak and general characterization of the range of troubles-telling exit devices displayed in the foregoing array is that they are *topically disjunctive*. Whatever happens after a troubles-telling does not emerge from it, is not topically coherent with it, but constitutes a break from it.

Another feature that can be observed across the array may be characterized as *interactional cohesiveness*. Specifically, the one who proposes to depart from talk about a trouble does so with talk that is other-attentive. Whether blandly conventional – "I'll see you Tuesday" and "How are you" – or designed for this particular recipient – "Okay you go and get your clean trousers on . . ." and "Janet *d*id you get my annive:rsary car:d" – the talk that breaks from a troubles-telling exhibits attention to the coparticipant.

This recurrent other-attentiveness may constitute a special warrant for the activities that follow a troubles-telling. In effect, a breaking away from talk about a trouble exhibits deference to it by preserving the interactional reciprocity that is a feature of such talk.

In the current corpus of troubles-tellings there are only two cases of talk that break away from a troubles-telling but are not other-attentive; that is, self-attentive disjuncts.

(9)   [Frankel:TC:I:1:17–18]

```
1    G:    I mean there wasn't nuh– anything that didn't
2          happen. that could've happened.
3    S:    Right
```

```
4    G:    'hhh
5          (0.2)
6    G:    So,
7    S: →  I'm not surprized. 'hhh Listen, u-something very
8          very: cute happened last night at the Wherehouse.
```

(10) [NB:II:4:10:r]

```
1    E:    Ah::, (0.2) it's not worth it to be on my feet.=
2          =you ⌜know
3    N:        ⌊Ye:ah. Ri:ght.
4          (.)
5    N:    Ah hah?
6          (0.2)
7    N: →  'hhhh Oh I was just ou:t wa:shing window:ss: e-a:nd
8          ah (.) my mother ca:lled so I came in I thought well
9          while I'm in here and I looked at the clo:ck and
10         it's eleven thirty and I thought well: (.) they're
11         'hhhhh they're un- surely they're U:P. you know I
12         knew it w⌜as kind of a:: ⌜sleep in da:y=
13   E:          ⌊Yeh          ⌊(      )
14   N:    =but uh I didn't get home til 'hhhh two last night
15      →  I met a very,h very, n:ni:ce gu:y.
```

First, each of these instances may be seen to be exhibiting a version of
a special warrant for the introduction of other matters after a troubles-
telling. It happens that each of the only two self-attentive disjuncts in
the current corpus are introduced with superlative assessments; something being characterized as "very very X." In fragment (9), "something
very very: *cute* happened last night," and in fragment (10) "I met a
very,h *very*, n:ni:ce gu:y."

Second, in fragment (10), in the lead-up to the self-attentive new
topic, are features that may be seen to orient to the appropriate post–
troubles-telling procedures. There is a version of a restart (in this case,
not the "How are you"–type utterance, but another object that recurs,
and may have its home, at conversation openings, a report of "how I
came to call you"),[1] and an exhibit of other-attentiveness in the making
of the call (where the reported encounter may be a crucial item on the
agenda of this call).

Thus, all of the disjunctive exits from a troubles-telling in the current
corpus may be seen to be orienting in one way or another to the problematic character of a troubles-telling for the introduction of new topics.

A question raised by the foregoing array and its characterization is,
what sort of talk would be specifically inappropriate after a troubles-
telling? The following two fragments are offered as instances of such
talk. In these cases a matter is introduced following talk that has not

been produced as a troubles-telling. The new matter is disjunctive and
self-attentive, and is in no way processed to exhibit any particular warrant for its occurrence here and now.

(11) [Rahman:B:2:(14):8]

```
1   G:    I was gonna take it in for you and get the
2         ticket.=
3   L:    =Oh no- it doesn't matter Gwe-ah actually I think
4         it's one on Vera's ticket anyra┌te I think it's┐=
5   G:                                    └Oh : : : .┘
6   L:    =in the name of Manners=
7   G:    =[┌Oh ye- hhhh┐  ┌heh heh ˙eh:-:
8   L:     [└but I'm not┘su└re, but one of them are:=
9   G:    =[┌˙hhhhhhhh┐This i┌s th-
10  L:     [└you know,┘      └So- I'll take them all in,
11        ┌an:d uh:m ⎕
12  G:    └Ye:s::.  ⎕Mm,
13        (0.3)
14  L:    ┌┌check them
15  G: →  └└I'm gonna do some spaghetti an:d ( . ) n-eh::m
16        meatballs for tea for this lot now,
17  L:    Oh lovely.
18  G:    Cause they didn't have u they only had fish
19        fingers and chips for dinner,
```

(12)   [TCI(b):16:59-66]

```
1   J:    I went with uh::m ( . ) Fay one day, ahhndh iht was
2         really wierd. ˙hh I went in there because she
3         wanted to get some clothes for her little (.)
4         girl.=
5   L:    =Ye┌ah,
6   J:       └for her doll for Christmas. ˙hhhhh And so we
7         go i::n and she starts looking through them and I
8         start looking through them

      .   ((ca. 65 lines omitted re finding all sorts of
      .   nice gifts for her own children))

74  J:    Oh I came outta there and here I was only going in
75        with her and I came out with almost nine dollars hh=
76  L:    =┌┌Yhhhh-hhhh┐          ┌↑˙h u :h┐˙h u┐˙ehh┐
77  J:     └└worth of s┘t(h)u(h)u(h)u└↑huh-huh┘-huh┘˙hhh┘Just
78        those thi(h)i(h)ngs. ┌huh┌    ˙he:hhh┌hh.
79  L:                         └˙hh└ °n°     └O h┌ :::::.┐
80                                              └A::ow┘::
81        bo::y, ˙h┌hnhh and I┐ charged it=
82  L:             └M m : : :.┘
83  J:    =and if Jack °ever finds out I'm gonna be
```

```
84           murdered.° hh-h ┌hhhh                  ┌ˈhu:hˈhuh=
85    L:                     └hheh-hheh-hhe└h
86    J:      =ˈhhhh ┌hh    ┌Right on the spo:t. uh-huh heh huh=
87    J:           └ˈhhh └hh
88    L:      =knhhhh-hhhh-hhh-hh

        .    ((ca. 20 lines omitted re  managing it so that
        .    Jack won't find out, by being first to pick up
        .    the mail))
        .
        .

111   J:     But I thought well I'll go ahea:d, and, ˈhh and pay
112          for it when it comes and °he'll never kno:w,°=
113   L:     =°Ye:h,°=
114   J:     =°(we, ┌got anything)° ┌heh-heh-huh=
115   L:          └hheh huh ehhuh┘
116   L:     =[┌°ˈuhhhh ˈuhhhhhhh ┌hh ┌hhh°
117   J:      └└huh e-huh huh huh┘ └ˈhhehh
118   J;     Ex ┌cept when Christmas co ┌:mes a-a-┐ and ˈhhhh=
119   L:      └°°Oh°°               └Y e a h h┘
120   J:     =he says where'd you get all thahheh heh ┌hn huh┐=
121   L:                                            └mehheh┘
122   J:     =huh hu ┌h huh°huh° °hn°
123   L:            └ˈh h h h h┘Santa Claus.hhheh-h ┌eh
124   J:                                          └ˈhh↑Santa
125          Clause brou:ght it. (in his sle::d).=
126   J:     =hn ┌hih   ┌hn-hn- ┌hen huh=
127   L:        └Y e : └a h.  └ˈhh
128   L:     =Uh:: ┌:m,
129   J:           └ˈhhhhehhhhh°(        ┌      ).°
130   L: →                               └I found a recipe: that I'm
131          gonna try:,
132   L:     (0.5)
133   L:     O think,
134          (.)
135   J      ┌┌°Uh huhm °┐
136   L:     └└It's  u h ┘, for popcorn balls that you make it
137          with ˈhh-ˈhh you melt butter: an:::d miniature
138          marshmallows.=
139   J:     =↑Oh:: ┌::.        ┌°Gee:.°┐
140   L:           └And then you└a d d┘just one package of
141          raspberry flavor Jello.
142          (.)
143   J:     °ˈhhhh° ┌↑Oh: ┐ ┌:: ┌::::::::
                    └D└ry┘-ˈ└You just┘sprinkle that in there.

        . ((ca. 30 lines omitted re the recipe))
        .
        .

175   L:     So I thought oh that'd be fun I think I might, let
176          LeAnne do it. You know . . . and help her.
```

The utterances that are located as disjunctive and self-attentive introductions of new topics with no particular warrant for their introduction here and now are, in fragment (11): "I'm gonna *do* some spaghetti an:d (.) n-eh::m *m*eatballs for tea" (lines 15–16) and in fragment (12): "*I* found a *r*ecipe: that I'm gonna try:" (lines 130–131).

The bland introduction of such matters may exhibit/propose the topical non-problematicness of the prior talk, that is, may exhibit/propose that *any* next topic is appropriate here and now.

It is just this sort of blandly self-attentive topical disjunct that in the current corpus is absent from, and may be generally constrained from, the next position to a troubles-telling.

2. Stepwise transition from a troubles-telling

Whereas exit from a troubles-telling is for the most part done by means of other-attentive topical disjuncts, there is an alternative troubles-exit device; one that is not disjunctive and thus does not abruptly boundary off the talk about a trouble, but that *gradually disengages* from it over a span of talk. This device operates in what Harvey Sacks talks of as a stepwise fashion. He proposes:

> A general feature for topical organization in conversation is movement from topic to topic, not by a topic-close followed by a topic beginning, but by a stepwise move, which involves linking up whatever is being introduced to what has just been talked about, such that, as far as anybody knows, a new topic has not been started, though we're far from wherever we began. (lecture 5, spring 1972, pp. 15–16)

Several instances of stepwise transition out of troubles-tellings are evident in the current corpus. Of those, three have been selected that have in common a particular sort of work this device can accomplish.

In one of his discussions of stepwise movement, Sacks notes that it can be exploited to introduce otherwise "unconnected" matters: "If you have some topic which you can see is not connected to what is now being talked about, then you can find something which is connected to both, and use that first" (lecture, February 19, 1971, pp. 15–16).

Just such a procedure may be used in the two following fragments to arrive at matters that may not merely have no particular topical connection, but that may be inappropriate next topics to a troubles-telling.

(13)   [NB:IV:10:18-21]

```
1   E:1→ If  I'd just gone down there and spent my
2        Thanksgiving like, Tillie wanted me to, why
```

```
 3           I would of had no problems, and hell with the
 4           Thanksgiving dinner. I'm through. I'm not gonna
 5           do anything anymore.
 6           (0.6)
 7    L:     ⌜Yeah.
 8    E:   [[I'm n- ... I'm not gonna plan things anymore. I
 9         mean this is ridiculous, course I know Mister
10   2→   Cole's sick, let's God let's hope he gets well, but
11          'hhhhh I know the problem hhh you know, hh
12   L:3→ What does he ha:ve.
13    E:    'hh Oh he's got this gallbladder, and uh, they-
14          he's vomiting and everything they took him to the
15          hospital and I don't know how long he's gonna be
16          in or what the t- well he's gonna be eighty four:r,
17          (1.0)
18    L:    Yea:h. ⌜Well-
19    E:          ⌊And he's quite a playboy, you know,
20   L:4→ Yeah, you just got to be caref-well see, 'hh Dwight
21          only has- one gall bladder?
22          (1.0)
23    E:    Mm hm,
24    L:    He had- and then he has to be careful what he eats,
25          he can't eat anything greasy or anything you know,
26    E:    Mm hm,
27    L:    Go:d what a ma:n. He was out there this morning and
28          he- they have these great big olive trees all over
29          you know,
30    E:    Mm hm,
31    L:    And the wind was so bad that the-the-th- the
32          branches were hitting the house, and God, (0.3) uh,
33          I got up about well, it was about eight o'clock,
34    E:    Mm ⌜hm,
35    L:       ⌊ and here he's up there sawing those off, you
36          know,
37    E:    Mm::: ⌜wonderful.
38    L:          ⌊M a n   he's ⌜(   )-
39    E:                        ⌊God  he's about sixty seven or
40          eight.
41    L:    Yeah. Sixty seven.
42    E:    God love him.
43    L:    But man, I mean they really, They've really got ul-
44          oh: God what a house. You have no idea.
        .
        .   ((ca. 11 lines omitted re the house))
        .
56    E:    'hhhh eh: Is the swimming pool enclosed with the
57          gla:ss bit?=
58    L:    =No::, it's uh: ou:ts- (.) eh no outside the big
59          (.)
60    E:      ⌜°Mmhm,°            ⌝
61    L:    [[uh:::::: ⌋ gla:ss doo⌜rs.
62    E:                           ⌊°Ah: hah,°
```

```
63  L:    u-I got that wro:ng,
64  E:    Oh that's, that's ⌈okay,  ⌉ ·hhhhhhhh⌉
65  L:                     ⌊mBut ⌋ the water⌋is, eighty
66        ⌈fi:::ve.⌉
67  E:    ⌊Oh I kno⌋w  it. Isn't it gorgeous,=
68  L:    =But you know when you get out it's kind of co:ld.=
69  E:    =⌈⌈(Oh: oh) ya :h⌉
70  L:5→   ⌊⌊Well it was,⌋ ⌋two o'clock in the morning and
71        ⌈then⌉last ⌈°night°⌉
72  E:    ⌊°huh⌋haw h⌊awh  ha⌋:w.°
73  E:    ⌈⌈Oo I(h)  bet⌈that was (fu:n.) ⌉
74  L:    ⌊⌊n h h h h h ⌊hn-hn-hn with no:⌋c-
75  L:    ·hh⌈hh
76  E:       ⌊·hhh⌈·hh
77  L:          ⌊clothes⌈on God it's good.⌈hu-uh huh⌈huhh⌉=
78  E:                 ⌊↑aaaaaaa::::::::::⌋I s n 't ⌊that⌋=
79  L:    ⌈·hh
80  E:    =⌊exci:ting,
81  L:    Uh: ⌈:?
82  E:       ⌊Oh: that's wonderf⌈ul,
83  L:                          ⌊Oh:: God we had. we, I never
84        had so much fun in my li:fe.
```

(14) [NB:IV:14:12-14]

```
1   L: 1→ But eh-it's-it's terrible to keep people ali:ve and
2          ⌈you know and just let them suffer⌈day in and day=
3   E:    ⌊Right.                            ⌊r:Right.
4   L:    =out,⌈it's-
5   E:         ⌊They don't do that with an animal.((sniff))
6         (0.5)
7   E:    (You kno⌈:w,)
8   L:            ⌊Yeah.
9   E:    Oh well⌈bless his heart Well, we don't know what=
10  L:           ⌊((sniff))
11  E:    =it's all about I g-I-((sniff)) Don't get yourself=
12  L:    =⌈⌈O h  I'm  n o t . I  j u s t- you know I wish⌉=
13  E:     ⌊⌊Honey you've got to get aho:ld of your- I know⌋
14  L: 2→ =I'd- I'd kind of liked to gone out there but I was
15        afraid of the fog I was gonna drive him in::- l-'hh
16        last⌈ni:ght. but,
17  E: 3→     ⌊·hh Oh it was terrible coming down ev⌈en this=
18  L:                                              ⌊But-
19  E:    =morning.((sniff))
20  L:    But San Diego? I c- I couldn't believe it last
21        night. We left there about,·hh eleven thirty (.)
22        and it w- (.) it⌈was clear all the way up until we=
23                        ⌊((sniff))
24  L:    =hit, (1.0) u-uh:: the, the uh Fashion Square here
25        in Balboa.⌈I couldn't believe it⌈and we went into,=
26                  ⌊((sniff))             ⌊( )
```

```
27 L:     =you couldn't even see:.
28 E: 4→  Oh God it's terrible. ((sniff)) That's why well we
29        didn't get home til two o'clo:ck. Got it's-
30        (0.2)
31 E:     [ [beautiful- ]
32 L:     [ [It was ter]rible in to:wn?
33 E:     ·hhh [hh
34 L:          [((snort))
35 E:     ·h Oh we just got into bed at two:.I wasn't gonna
36        (.) go down, wait let me turn this fa- uh:
37        (0.5)
38 E: 5→  You know we w-this par:ty and then we went to
39        another little party a:fterwards and oh I met so
40        many f:fa::bulous pees- (.) people and danced with
41        my poor old toes with no t(h)oenails and I was
42        [in- ·hhhh hh(h)igh (h)h(h)eels and ·hahhh and oh:=
43 L:     [hmh hmh
44 E:     =we (.) just had a (.) beautiful time.
```

Most roughly, although each fragment starts up in the course of a troubles-telling, at its end a coparticipant is reporting a very good time. In fragment (13), starting with a troubles-teller's "*I'm* through. *I'm* not gonna do anything anymore," the talk somehow arrives at a point where the coparticipant is reporting "*I never had so much fun in my li:fe.*" In fragment (14), starting with a troubles-teller's "But eh-it's- it's terrible to keep people ali:ve and, you know, and just let them suffer day in and day out," the talk somehow arrives at a point where the coparticipant is reporting "*Oh:* we (.) just had a (.) *beautiful time.*"

Whereas in fragments (9) and (10) a shift from a troubles-teller's "I mean there wasn't nuh- *any*thing that didn't *hap*pen. that could've happened" and "*Ah*::, (0.2) it's not *worth* it to be on my fee:t" to a coparticipant's "something *very* very: *cute* happened" and "I met a very,h *very*, n:ni:ce gu:y" occurs disjunctively, as the introduction of a new topic, in fragments (13) and (14) the report of a good time is worked in such that, as Sacks has it, "a new topic has not been started, though we're far from wherever we began" (lecture, April 9, 1971, p. 9).

The latter pair of fragments exhibit features in common; features by which the "somehow" arrival at a report of a good time may be seen to be systematically achieved.

Following is a rough sketch of a series of moves that can be located in each fragment. Across the series, a troubles-telling may be seen to be itself moving away from the trouble per se, and the movement provides a resource that is taken up by the coparticipant and turned to the introduction of otherwise inappropriate materials.

(1→) The fragments start up in the course of a troubles-telling at a point that might be characterized as *summing up the heart of the trouble:* In fragment (13) lines 1–9, "If I'd just gone down there and spent my Thanksgiving like, Tillie wanted me to, why I would of had no problems . . . I'm not gonna plan things anymore. I mean this is ridiculous," in fragment (14) lines 1–13, troubles-teller's "But eh-it's-it's terrible to keep people ali:ve . . . etc." through troubles-recipient's "Honey you've got to get aho:ld of your (I know)."

(2→) *The troubles-teller turns to matters that,* although on-topic with and part of the trouble, are not at the heart of the matter, but *are ancillary:* In fragment (13) lines 9–11, "course I know Mister Cole's sick . . ." (In this case, Mister Cole's illness stands as a possible obstacle to the problematic Thanksgiving dinner that is being produced, in part, to reconcile a rift between the troubles-teller and her husband.) In fragment (14) lines 14–15, "I'd kind of liked to gone out there but I was afraid of the fog I was gonna drive him in . . ." (In this case, the troubles-teller's husband's mother is dying and he has flown out to be with her; troubles-teller is accounting for not having driven him to the airport.)

It is possible that the combination of (1) summing up the heart of the trouble and (2) turning to ancillary matters constitutes a recognizable movement by the troubles-teller toward closure of the troubles-telling. If that is so, then the recurrent and perhaps most appropriate sequel to troubles closure is projected; that is, termination of the conversation itself. Although there are other options, that is, the troubles-recipient can find some other-attentive pending biographical with which to sustain the conversation, or might hope that the troubles-teller will produce an other-attentive restart, such as inquiring into the troubles-recipient's circumstances, a most local and elegant resource is taken up.

(3→) Perhaps specifically at a point where the talk is recognizably moving toward closure of a troubles-telling, the *troubles-recipient* produces talk that *topically stabilizes the ancillary matters:* In Fragment (13) line 12, by reference to Mister Cole's illness, the question "What does he ha:ve"; in fragment (14) lines 17–19, by reference to the fog constraining the troubles-teller from driving her husband to the airport, "Oh it was terrible coming down even this *morning."*

Whereas each of these utterances can be seen to be working on behalf of a telling in progress and its teller, fragment (13)'s "What does he ha:ve" soliciting further talk, and fragment (14)'s "Oh it was terrible . . . etc." warranting the troubles-teller's disinclination to drive in the fog, each of them *potentiates further talk by the troubles-recipient.*

The ancillary stabilizer of fragment (13) is a question. In various lectures Harvey Sacks proposes that it is not merely that a question sequentially implicates an answer, but that following the answer, the questioner has the right/obligation to talk again (to comment, to ask another question, etc.).[2] That is, a question projects not only a next slot occupied by talk of the answerer, but a post-answer slot in which the questioner will talk.

The ancillary stabilizer of fragment (14) "Oh it was terrible coming down even this *morning*" invokes the relevance of the troubles-recipient's own experiences, via which she was enabled to make such an observation.

So far, then, it can be observed that a troubles-recipient may be taking up an opportunity to topically stabilize a troubles-telling at a point where it has moved away from the heart of the trouble but has not yet arrived at closure of the telling (such closure being potentially problematic for further conversation or for the introduction of other materials), that is, to sustain conversation at some distance from the trouble per se, and, further, to potentiate talk by the troubles-recipient.

(4→) *The troubles-recipient produces a pivotal utterance;* one that, though recognizably on topic, has independent topical potential: In fragment (13) lines 20–21, by reference to the troubles-teller's report of Mr. Cole's gallbaldder condition, "Well see, ˙hh *Dwight* only has- one gall bladder" (Dwight being a member of the couple with whom the troubles-recipient has just spent a vacation);[3] in fragment (14) lines 28–29, by reference to the troubles-teller's report of last night's unbelievable fog, "That's why well *we* didn't get home till two o'clo:ck."

In each case the pivotal utterance constitutes the talk potentiated by the ancillary stabilizer. In fragment (13) it occupies the post-answer slot projected by the prior question, and in fragment (14) the troubles-recipient's own experience, invoked by her warranting of the troubles-teller's fears, now begins to emerge.

Thus, move (3), the ancillary stabilizer, may be seen as a possible move toward some other matters, and move (4), the pivot, as a possible emergence of those matters. In move (3) each fragment is strongly other-attentive. The inquiry of fragment (13) constitutes a display of special interest; the warranting of the troubles-teller's fears in fragment (14) constitutes an affiliation with her.

What may be an initial move from a troubles-telling toward other matters, then, is produced with the interactional cohesiveness of the transparently disjunctive shifts considered earlier. In like manner, the strong other-attentiveness observable in this pair of fragments may constitute an orientation to the problematicness of the shift now under way.

(5→) Thereafter, matters that may specifically constitute the *target* of a series of moves are arrived at. In fragment (13), someone with a similar condition having been mentioned, he is focused upon, "Go:d what a ma:n" (line 27); his activities vis-à-vis the house are mentioned (lines 27–36); the house itself is focused upon, "God *what* a house" (lines 44), with its various facilities, including the swimming pool (lines 56–68), and mention of the swimming pool leads to mention of nude swimming (lines 70–77) about which the assessment is produced, "Oh:: God we had. we, *I* never had so much fun in my li:fe" (lines 83–84).

In fragment (14) the arrival at the target matter is achieved rapidly once the fact that "*we* didn't get home til two o'clo:ck" is introduced, with the report of the event that accounts for that late arrival (lines 38–42), about which the assessment is produced, "we (.) *just* had a (.) beautiful time" (line 44).

In these two fragments, as Sacks proposes, the coparticipants are "far from where they began," but there has been no point at which someone has started a new topic. Rather, there has been a "linking up" of two unconnected topics via materials related to both.

3. An exploration of a single problematic instance

A third instance of stepwise transition from a troubles-telling will be elaborately considered. Its features are remarkably similar to those of fragments (13) and (14) but at a point they part company. Specifically, the sort of material that, in fragments (13) and (14), have been identified as the possible target of some prior stepwise movement; that is, the report of a very good time, is produced, not by the troubles-recipient who has done moves (3) and (4), but by the troubles-teller.

The troubles-recipient has been working toward another sort of talk that may be constrained from occurrence in the next position to a troubles-telling, the blandly self-attentive type of material instanced in fragments (11) and (12). In various ways, however, the environment is so nicely ripe for the introduction of otherwise inappropriate materials that such talk is produced by the troubles-teller, preempting and delaying the introduction of the matter toward which the troubles-recipient has been moving.

(15)   [Rahman: I: 4–6]

```
1  G:    And [Danny] didn't get in so I didn't go: typing
2        last ni:ght,=
```

```
 3  L:      =Didn't y┌ou::
 4  G: 1→             [↑No: I┌ca- I thought well I c┌an't leave=
 5  L:                     [Oh : : : : : ]
 6  G:      =him for┌two hours if I'm if he's crying when I've=
 7  L:              [n:No.
 8  G:      =left him for one.
 9          (.)
10  L:      Oh: dear me.
11  G:      So: I euh you know as I say I didn't get
12          t┌o  t y p i n g.┐
13  L:       [Oh:::::: you're┘well tie:d dow:n aren't┌you.
14  G:                                               [Well I am
15          rea: ┌lly:┌°Yah,°
16  L:            [°Ye:[h,°
17  G:      Ye:s you know┌cause he do┐esn't he ↑hates being in=
18  L:                   [°Y e a : h°]
19  G:      =on his ow:n for┌some pec┐uliar reason and I mean=
20  L:                      [Y e : h?]
21  G:      =he always kno(h)ws: where I'm going a┌nd┐ ┌okh!'hh
22  L:                                            [y:]:[Ye:s.
23  L:      ┌┌Yes:.
24  G:      [[↑you know approximately what time┌I'll be,┐
25  L:                                         [°Y e s°]Ye:s.
26  G; 2→  Cause Norman said in the morning would I take him
27          to Saltbern and I said well uh'hih hI don't kno:w
28          the roads are so ba-ad I(h) mi(h)ght not (.) make
29          ↑i:t.=
30  L: 3→  =No:? No- Were they very ba:d, Gwenn┌ie, ( )
31  G:                                         [Ehm,- no it
32          wasn't it's just that you can't go: so fas:t=
33  G:      =you kno┌w-you-You kn┐ow you┐just have to: be that=
34  L:              [N o : : : :,]  N o .]
35  G:      =little bit more ca:┌reful.
36  L: 4→                      [I ↑think it's that little bit
37          wa:rmer toni:ght┌i:sn't it ┐
38  G:                      [Oh it is i]t's not so┌bad it's::┐]=
39  L:                                            [It's  not ]
40  G:      =[┌really┐n o t┐
41  L:       [[qui:te]as se]vere┌toni:ght, n┐o┌:.
42  G:                          [M m  :  .  ]└[No, but it's
43          it's eh (.) melted, but I th- if it freezes tonight
44          it'll be wo:rse tomor┌ro┌w↓mor:ning┐I think,┐
45  L:                           ['h[tomorrow, ] that's ]the
46          only thing, y┌e:s,
47  G:                   [Ye:h,
48  L:      Well┌I think I┐'ll stay in bed in the mor:┌ning
49  G:          [Y e : h ]                           [hHAH!=
50  G:      =I do┌n't bla:me ┐you?┐
51  L:           [nhh hnh hnh]heh [heh he┌h 'hk,
52 G:(5)→                             [·h h [H e y]listen 'hhh
53          You should have come on Tue:sda:y,
```

```
54 L:    Was it goo :d,
                    ⌐
55 G:               ⌊·hh Oh ↓it was ↑mar:velous=
56 L:    =⌈⌈Oh  w a s   i t .⌉
57 G:    ⌊⌊ I ↑thoroughly en⌋jo:yed it.
```
```
.     ((ca. 12 lines omitted re the movie))
.
```
```
70 G:    I jumped (.) e shot about three feet in the air I=
                      ⌐
71 L:                 ⌊°O h : : : : : : : :°⌋
72 G:    =think ↑he h heh⌉
                  ⌐
73 L:             ⌊Y e s⌋:.
74 L: 5→  ·hh Eh::m, we didn't go to have our hair done by
75        the wa:y,=
76 G:    =·h No well I gathered not
```

The series of moves similar to those of fragments (13) and (14) can be
briefly sketched out.

(1→) A summing up of the heart of the trouble, lines 4–15, the troubles-teller's "I ca- I thought well I can't leave *him* for two hours *if* I'm if
he's crying when I've left him for one," through the recipient's "Oh::::::
you're *well* tie:d dow:n *aren't* you" and teller's "*Well* I *am* rea::lly:
°Yah, °."

(2→) A turning by the troubles-teller to ancillary matters, lines 26–29,
"Cause *Norman* said in the *morning* would I take him to Saltbern and I
said well uh˙hih hI don't kno:w the roads *are* so ba-ad I(h) mi(h)ght not
(.) *make* ↑ i:t."

(3→) A topical stabilizing of the ancillary matters by the troubles-
recipient that potentiates further talk on her part; in this case a question
that reserves a post-answer slot, line 30: "Were they very ba:d, Gwennie" (cf. fragment 13 "What does he ha:ve").

(4→) A pivotal utterance by the troubles-recipient, by reference to the
answer to her prior question, "Ehm- no *it wasn't* . . . you *just* have to:
be that little bit ca:reful"; lines 36–37: "I ↑ think it's that little bit
wa:rmer toni:ght."[4] Once again the pivotal utterance occupies the slot
reserved by the prior ancillary stabilizer.

The troubles-recipient of fragment (15) can thus be characterized as
doing similar work to the troubles-recipients of fragments (13) and (14).
In this case, however, the troubles-recipient does not go on to introduce
a report of a very good time she had. Instead, with rather eerie symme-
try, the prior troubles-teller introduces a report of a very good time the
prior troubles-recipient *could* have had, lines 52ff., "*Hey* listen hhh You
should have come *on* Tue:sda:y."

The prior troubles-teller's introduction of such a matter differs from
the procedures used by the troubles-recipients in fragments (13) and (14)

and is similar to the technique considered earlier; that is, to the other-attentive disjunct that topically breaks away from, and/but preserves the interactional cohesiveness achieved in a prior troubles-telling.

The prior troubles-teller, unlike the introducers of reports of good times in fragments (13) and (14) who have worked to disengage from the relevance of a troubles-telling, may be orienting to the prior talk as still troubles-relevant. Consequently an orientation to its topical problemat-icness is appropriate, where, however, somehow the context has be-come ripe for just such a report. And the "somehow" can be understood by reference to the work done to that point by her coparticipant.

Then, what is the work done by the coparticipant in aid of? It may be a matter of terminating a troubles-telling yet sustaining a state of conver-sation; that is, the troubles-recipient finds that she has nothing in partic-ular to say, but wishes to remain in conversation, and thus works to avoid closure of the troubles-telling and its recurrent entailment, closure of the conversation, by producing a series of moves that will gradually disengage from the troubles-telling and provide at least a context in which other matters might simply emerge.

However, various features of the data suggest that something rather more pointed is being done. Specifically, it is possible that from an identifiable place in the course of the troubles-telling, the troubles-recip-ient is working toward the introduction of a particular item; an item that has been brought to mind, *occasioned* by something said in the course of the troubles-telling, but that is inappropriately introduced then and there, or even upon conclusion of the troubles-telling, that is, the blandly self-attentive item that is eventually produced, "We *didn't* go to have our *hair* done" (line 74). The argument that will be developed is that this item is occasioned by the report within the troubles-telling, "I didn't go; *typ*ing last ni:ght" (lines 1–2, reiterated at lines 11–12).

To start off with, the phenomenon proposed to be occurring in frag-ment (15) is not uncommon, and can have its consequences manifested then and there. For example, in the following fragment, the utterance in which the occasioning item has occurred is intersected by that which it has occasioned.

(16) [GTS: II: 2: 64]⁵

```
1   R:     The cops don't do that, don't gimme that shit I
2          live in the Valley.
3          (0.5)
4   K: →   The cops, over the hill. There's a place up in
5          Mulholland where they've- where they're building
```

```
6              those hous┌ing projects?
7    R: →               └Oh have you ever taken them Mulholland
8              time trials?─ ˙hh You go up there with a girl . . .
```

In the following two fragments the occasioned item appears in close
proximity to the utterance in which the occasioning item has occurred.
In the following fragment, one participant has momentarily gone "off
line" to talk to her child.

(17)   [TCI(b):16:41-42]

```
1    L: → Honey you have to put a shirt on with that.
2         (.)
3    L:   Not ┌just ┌tha┌:t.
4    J: →     └°n˙ └˙hh└Oh:. Shirt. ˙t˙hhh I have a red
5         shi:rt,
6         (0.2)
7    L:   Uh hu┌:h?
8    J:        └Si::::ze,hh (0.3) fou:r?
```

(18)   [SBL:2:1:5:12]

```
1    T:   But uh then when I found out the water was off, and
          I saw everything just (drooping) its head, even
3         the dahlias,
4    B:   Uh huh,
5    T:   I thought well good lord, I can't let the yard do
6         ┌that, so-
7    B: → └Saying-
8    B: → Saying dahlias, I just cut some fresh dahlias at my
9         nighbor's this evening, and had fresh flowers m-
10        all fixed up for you.
```

The relationship between the occasioning item and that which it occasions can be rather less concrete as, for example, in the following fragment.

(19)   [BH:IA:17:ST]

```
1    B:   Don't they have those new snaggies, or, you know,
2         non-snaggies?
3    S:   Mesh?
4    K:   I'm gonna get me (        )
5    S: → If you, uh, if you, uh put them, they run up, they
6         don't run down.
7    B:   Oh boy!
8    S: → But if you, you know rip it here it runs up -- and
9         then it doesn't run down.
```

```
10 B:  → Oh say! I've got something I want you to do,
11        running, up, running down, that reminds me
```

Recurrently, the fact of occasioning is not announced; the occasioned materials are simply presented as an appropriately introduced next matter.

(20) [SBL:2:1:8-9]

```
1  B:  → I still haven't my dishes done, I'm right in the
2         middle of doing them, but I stopped₁to call you.
3  J:  →                                     ⌐Well I worked
4         on my- medicine cabinet again, I'm so mad at that
5         painter,
```

(21) [Rahman:C:1:(16):8]

```
1  J:  → I've been cleaning ↓be:drooms and things₁so:
2  I:                                             ⌐Yes I've
3         done the bedrooms and the living roo:m,
```

(22) [Frankel:TC:I:1:26]   ((re their respective boyfriends))

```
1  G:  → He'll be down here₁for Christ₁m a s .₁
2  S:                       └·hh       └Good. m┘aybe we can
3         get together for dinner.
4  G:    Mm-↑hm?
5         (.)
6  G:    ₁₁Su:re.
7  S:    ||└(    ) ·hhh You know Michael's in the midst of
8      →  moving this weekend.
```

(23) [MC:II:36-37]

```
1  W:  → You know very often Lila I-I come across uh, a
2         library in a- at an estate sale, ·hh where I get uh
3         oh a whole pile of-of Masons uh books from Masons
4         you know₁and,
5  L:            └Really,
6  W:    Oh yeh OH I've got the most GORgeous things. ·hh I
7         have Masonic poems that are just out of this
8         worl₁d.
9  L:        └Really?
10 W:    Books of poetry I mean you never never see them in-
11        in library shelves any₁where.
12 L:                           └We::ll.
13 W:    Just- just absolutely beautiful. I'll show you one
```

```
14          or two┌(
15 L:   →        └Well- ·hh incidentally I picked up a signed
16          edition of an old man that only had a limited
17          edition printed . . .
```

(24)   [W:PC:1:(1):21-22]

```
 1  J:  → Lore:tta came,ṳ oh: they all came┌over all of┐them=
 2  M:                                      └for Easter ┘
 3  J:  =o:n┌uh (        )
 4  M:      └Did the::y, oh: goo:d.┌·hh
 5  J:                             └Eh (.) just (0.2) came
 6          here for a cup of tea in┌the after┌noon
 7                                  └i        └Ye:s.
 8  M:     Did they li:ke it?
 9  J:     Oh ye┌::s.
10           └Ye::s I'm ↓su┌:re they  d i d.┐
11  J:                     └Well they've bee┘:n befo:::re,
12        (0.2)
13  M:    When i┌t was:
14  J:          └Not uh:
15        (0.3)
16  J:    You kno┌w not when it was all the ca┌rpets there┐=
17  M:           └                            └ ca:rpeted ┘
18  M:    =No::,┌No::,
19  J:          └No:.
20  M:  → Oh lovely, ·hh h By: the way=
21  J:                 (        )
22  M:  → =I: got a nice surpri:ze last wee:k,┌·hhh
23  J:                                        └Ye:s
24  M:    On the Tue:sday night. [[An old girlfriend from
          London was in the area briefly and invited her
          out for dinner]]
```

Across the array, materials that are introduced immediately or at a bit of a distance, announced as occasioned or simply presented as an appropriate next matter, can be seen to have been occasioned by some prior talk. That relationship was proposed between "I didn't go: *typing* last ni:ght" and the far-distanced "We *did*n't go to have our *hair* done."

Features of the intervening talk tend to support the possibility. Specifically, it appears that the troubles-recipient, who can have just had something brought to mind, is through and through attempting to provide for its introduceability.

For one, upon initial mention of "I didn't go: *typing*," the recipient moves to stabilize it topically, first with a news receipt, "*Did*n't you::" and, upon the confirmation, with an emphatic and prolonged "*Oh*:::::" which may specifically be competing with troubles-teller's return to talk about the trouble (see lines 1–5). If the matter of the missed typing class can become stabilized as a topic in its own right, then perhaps the matter of the missed hair appointment can be introduced then and there (cf., e.g., fragments [20] and [21]), or when the topic has run its course as in fragments [22], [23], and [24].

The troubles-teller, however, pursues the troubles-telling, and the coparticipant aligns as a proper troubles-recipient with an expression of sympathy, "*Oh: dear me.*" (lines 4–10). With such an alignment of the coparticipant, the troubles-teller again offers the report, perhaps specifically not to be treated as news and as a possible topic in its own right, but for its relationship to and conveyance of the trouble. Indeed, the coparticipant, now aligned as a troubles-recipient, can be seen to be producing just the sort of response the report was, from the first, pursuing, "Oh::::: you're *well* tie:d dow:n *a*ren't you" (line 13).

However, summary assessments appear to be implicative of closure for a topic, and are recurrently deployed prior to various forms of topic shift. So, for example, the following fragment, taken from an institutional setting, a suicide prevention center, instances a dramatic use of the close-implicature of the summary assessment. In this case it is used prefatory to interruption of the conversation.

```
(25)  [SPC:10:3:9]  ((re M's possibly suicidal child))

1    M:   Cause this little guy will stand in the railroad
2         tre-uh track and holler (.) where's the trai:n
3         where is the trai:n.
4         (0.3)
5    K:   Ah-ha⌐h,
6    M:       ⌊And that's what he's done before is stand
7         there (he's) standing at the last minute and
8         jumps awa:y.
9         (0.7)
10   K: → Oh:. Well that that that's serious kind of uh
11        behvior and it could be extremely dangerous. ˙hh
12        ˙hhh Do you want to hold on half a minute? o⌐r-˙hh⌐
13   M:                                              ⌊Mm hm⌋
14   K:   I have a: booklet here and I think I could get you
15        the extension number to the Children's Clinic,
```

In the following fragment, a recipient who eventually declares herself as having had something she wanted to tell a current speaker can be seen to be using a range of devices to bring some current talk to a close, including a flurry of acknowledgment tokens ("Right," lines 6, 7, 11, and 12), a summary assessment "So he's doing alright" preceding a momentary interruption of the conversation to give some information to someone else (lines 16–18), coming back on line with a more elaborate

summary assessment, "Well I'm glad to hear he's doing reasonably
well," which is followed by the announcement of something to say (line
23).

(26) [Frankel:TC:I:1:24-25]

```
 1  G:    Bu:t, he does feel tha:t (1.0) you know, (.) he's
 2         proud of the fact that he got into the finals.·hhh
 3         and he doesn't ca:re if he doesn't make the finals
 4         and go o:n ·hh      t o - Berkeley or wherever,=
                         Ri  :ght.
 5  S:  →              Ri  :ght.
 6  G:    =·h h and then-
 7  S:  →     Ri:ght.
 8         (.)
 9  G:    become a Harvard attorney I mean he doesn't care
10         about ↓that. at all.↓
11  S:  →                 Right.
12  S:  → Ri ght.
13  G:      So.
14  S:    ·hh So he's doing alright.
15  G:    Ye:ah
16  S:  → Two twenty Joey,
17         (0.4)
18  S:    ·hhhh Twenty after two.
19         (.)
20  S:  → ·hh Well I'm glad to hear he's doing reasonably
21         well.
22  G:    Ye:ah,
23  S:  → ·hh Uh:m what was I gonna tell you.
```

In the following fragment a flurry of assessments is followed by an
enormously elaborate summary assessment (lines 12–21), itself followed
by a return to a matter talked of much earlier in the conversation (line
24).

(27) [NB:IV:10:46-47]

```
 1  L:    And then coming home I bought, they had tangerines
 2         ten pounds for a dollar, so I got  ten pounds and=
 3  E:                                        Mm::::.
 4  L:    =I got some casaba and then I bought uh::, uh Edna
 5         back a box of dates  cause          you know.
 6  E:  →                       Oh that's ni ce.
 7  L:         She-
 8  E:  →  [[That's  nice Lottie,
 9  L:               She fed the ca:t, and
10  E:  →                              That's beautiful
11         (0.4)
```

```
12   E:  →  'tch'hhhh  Well₁you had a beautiful-
13   L:                 [I-
14   E:  →  Now you feel like a new gal.·hhh
15   L:        ₁Mh-
16   E:     [[Your ne:rves've
17          (0.4)
18   E:  →  You know there's so many other wonderful people
19          around you, 'hhhh uh- it's good to get away from,
20          your family sometimes zhi-n-can be yourself. you
21          ₁know what I mea:n?
22   L:     [Yea:uh
23   L:     Yeah.
24   E:  →  'hhh Uh getting back to this Viafor::- foam,
25          Lottie . . .
```

The use of summary assessments can be far more discrete and in aid of rather smaller topical shifts, as in the following fragment. An item (line 6) is followed by acknowledgment tokens (lines 11 and 12) and a shift from the speaker's activities and rationales to a request for information the recipient is interested in (line 14).

(28)   [Heritage:I:11:3]

```
1    I:   Uh::m: d-Bessy was mated um (0.3) oh about three
2         weeks ago:.
3    N:   hhOh:. ₁(   )
4    I:          [A n d (.) Mitzi was mated about two weeks
5         ago₁:.
6    N:  →     [Oh my goodness you do a₁sk for i₁t,((suppressed
7    I:                             [eh-h e h̄]
8         laughter))
9    I:   'h he-Well 'h I a-always feel it's best to get it
10        all over at ₁the same ↑ti:me y₁ou know,
11   N:  →           [Well  y e :̲ : s .]
12   N:  → Ye:s.=
13   I:   =₁₁It's  u h :₁
14   N:  → [[And-and who]did you go: to.
```

Earlier it was noted that the ancillary stabilizer utterances in fragments (13) and (14) (and fragment [15] can be included as well), which may constitute initial moves toward a topical shift, are produced with the interactional cohesiveness of the transparently disjunctive shifts. The summary assessments, which are recurrently used as pretopical-shift devices, are strongly other-attentive. It is beginning to appear that display of interactional cohesiveness is a general technique for the management of topical rupture.

In fragment (15), then, upon the reintroduction of the proposed occasioning item (indeed, intersecting it in its course, see lines 11–13), the troubles-recipient produces an item that recurrently precedes a shift (and as may be the case in fragments [25]–[28], a shift that can have been pending across some greater or lesser portion of the coparticipant's talk).

Thereafter, as the troubles-teller continues on about the trouble, for a spell the troubles-recipient's talk consists, in toto, of a flurry of acknowledgment tokens (line 16, line 18, line 20, lines 22 and 23, and line 25). This flurry ceases as the troubles-teller moves into the ancillary topical talk, whereupon the next utterance by the troubles-recipient is the ancillary stabilizer question, "Were they very ba:d, Gwennie" (line 30).

From the point of the proposed occasioning item, the troubles-recipient's activities can be characterized as in various ways promoting an opportunity to produce the proposed occasioned item.

Further, features of the item's introduction (lines 70–76) tend to support the possibility that it was occasioned by and has been pending since that much earlier point in the course of the troubles-telling. These features become available *as* features by comparison with another fragment considered earlier, in which a blandly self-attentive report is introduced in virtually identical fashion, that report can be seen to have possibly a similar history to that of fragment (15); that is, can have been occasioned by prior talk and can have been delayed in its introduction.

The fragment in question is fragment (12). At one point in the talk, one of the participants is reporting some impulse-buying of Christmas gifts for her children (lines 1–78). Somewhat later, the coparticipant introduces a recipe she has found (lines 130–131). For one, it may specifically be a Christmas candy. The description of the recipe yields a red sphere analogous to a Christmas-tree ornament (see lines 136–144). Second, it is reported to have been seen at the time of discovery as a possible coproject with her own little girl (see lines 175–176).

There is, then, a discoverable relationship between the materials produced by one participant, the buying of Christmas gifts for her children, and those subsequently produced by the other, the finding of a Christmas project for one of her children. Were it not for the sizable delay between the two items, this fragment could stand as another instance of an occasioned item for which the fact of occasioning is not announced, the occasioned materials simply presented as an appropriately introduced next matter (see fragments [20]–[24]).

A comparison of details from fragment (12) and fragment (15) yields a series of identical components produced in an identical order by which the proposed occasioned-and-pending matters are introduced.

(12) [Detail]

```
J:     0→  ·hh ↑Santa Claus brou:ght it. (in his sle::d).
J:     1→  hn⌈hih⌉ ⌈hn-hn⌉=
L:     2→     ⌊Ȳ e⌋:⌊a h .⌋
J:     3→ =⌈⌈heh huh⌉ ⌈·hhehhh °(   ⌈     )°
L:     3→  ⌊⌊·hh    ⌋⌊Uh::⌋        ⌊I found a recipe:
```

(15) [Detail]

```
G:     0→  I jumped (.) e⌈shot about three feet in⌈ the air=
L:                     ·⌊°Oh : : : ⌉: : : : : °⌋
G:     1→ =I think ↑⌈he⌈h heh⌉
L:     2→           ⌊Y⌊e s⌋::.
L:     3→  ·hh Eh::m, we didn't go to have our hair done
```

(0→) A little joke is made.

(1→) The current speaker starts to laugh. The onset of laughter by a current speaker can initiate a "laughing-together," with the coparticipant joining in (see Jefferson 1979:80–3) and can lead to an expanded joke-laughter series via re-reference to the joke (see Jefferson, Sacks, and Schegloff forthcoming) as, for example, occurs at an earlier point in fragment (12).

(12) [Detail 2]

```
J:   → and if Jack°ever finds out I'm gonna be murdered.°=
     → hh-h⌈hhhh
L:         ⌊hheh-hheh-hhe⌈h              ⌈·hhh⌈hh
J:                       ⌊·hu:h·huh·hhhh⌊hh ⌊Right on
     → the spo:t. uh-huh heh huh□
L:                         knhhhh-hhh-hhh-hh
```

That is, at the current focal point in fragments (12) and (15), the current speaker has potentiated further activities by reference to the topic in progress.

(2→) Just after the onset of the current speaker's laughter, a point at which a coparticipant can join in a laughing-together, as in fragment (12) detail 2:

```
J:     hh-h⌈hhhh
L:         ⌊hheh-hheh-hheh
```

the coparticipant in each of the focal fragments produces an acknowledgment token:

```
J:      hn hih
L:        [Y e : a h .
```

and

```
G:      the h heh
L:        [Y e s :.
```

By starting to speak after the onset of laughter, a coparticipant can be recognizably (and consequentially) declining to join a laughing-together (Jefferson 1979:83–6), and thus, for example, declining to take up the topical expansion potentiated by the prior speaker.

Further, acknowledgment tokens, as has been seen, can be accomplice to topical shift. A recurrent phenomenon is the production of a token just prior to a shift, as in the details, for example, from fragment (2) and fragment (28):

(2) [Detail]

```
A:      Never mind it'll all come right in the end,
J: →    Yeh. Okay you go and get your clean trousers on
```

(28) [Detail]

```
I:      I a–always feel it's best to get it all over at
        [the same ↑ti:me y]ou know,
N:      [Well  y e : : s .]
N: →    Ye:s. And–and who did you go: to.
```

(3→) The acknowledgment token is, indeed, followed by a topical shift, but not immediately. It is immediately followed by a "floorholder" (in fragment [12] "Uh::" and in fragment [15] "Eh::m").

Floorholders can be used for a range of tasks, one of which may be systematically being produced in the materials under consideration. Most roughly, such an item as "uh" can be used to mark a "getting back to" some prior talk.[6] For example, it frequently appears among a set of devices used to get back to interrupted conversation. Following is a single, representative instance.

(29) [TCI(b):16:15–17](J is listing items purchasable via gift parties which turn out to be cheaper in the shops))

```
1  J: → That's al most two and a half mo :re.
2  P:         [YEGHHHAGHHHHH : : : : : : : :[: : : :]=
3  L: →                                    [O h ]
```

```
4  P        = [::::::::::
5  L:         [s:stop it.] Pammy

           . ((ca. 15 lines omitted, L and her children))
           .

21 L:    There. You can have that one.
22       (.)
23 L:    khh!
24 J:    hh hn-hn-h-hn-⌐hn
25 L: →                ⌊Uh:::⌐m
26 J:                       ⌊˙hhnhhh
27 L: → ˙t˙hh I didn't Oh: bo:y. That's really a  lot
28       cheaper.
```

A multistage process by which the interrupted talk is returned to
includes a return to interaction with a little laugh by reference to the
interruption (line 23), which is reciprocated by the coparticipant (line
24), followed by the floorholder *"Uh:::m,"* which precedes and may
specifically mark a "getting back to" the interrupted topic (lines 25 and
27–28).

Another sort of getting back to may be seen in the following two
fragments in which some new matter is explicitly announced as having
been pending. The latter fragment has already appeared as an instance
of the pretopical-shift work of the summary assessment.

(30) [HG:28]

```
1  H:   he:h huh,
2       (0.2)
3  N:   ˙hhh
4       (0.5)
5  N:   A::nywa::y,
6       (.)
7  H: → eh-eh ˙hhhhhhh Uh::m,
8       (.)
9  N:   (u-Wha:t.)=
10 H: → ˙k˙k There's something else I was gonna say,
```

(31) [Frankel:TC:I:1:25]

```
1  S:   ˙hh Well I'm glad to hear he's doing reasonably well.
2  G:   Ye:ah,
3  S: → ˙hh Uh:m what was I gonna tell you.
```

Some materials that are proposed as having been intended to be
placed somewhere and having found an appropriate place to occur here,
are prefaced with the floorholder. If this object works as these materials

suggest, that is, exhibits that the matters now being introduced have been pending, then in fragments (12) and (15) it may operate to introduce a new topic, not, as earlier proposed, as any next topic, but specifically as a topic that has been pending.

In these two instances, just how these particular topics came to be pending topics may be accounted for in terms of an earlier occasioning and a delay until an appropriate opportunity for introduction.

Thus, by reference to fragment (15), a detailed examination of the talk following a candidate occasioning item ("I didn't go: *typing*") and of the talk preceding the introduction of a candidate occasioned item ("We *didn't* go to have our *hair* done") tends to support their respective candidacies.

In contrast, then, to fragments (13) and (14), it appears that the troubles-recipient in fragment (15) is not in the first place working toward a report of a very good time. Rather, the target of the work in this case may be the arrival at an appropriate environment for introduction of the occasioned materials.

Such an environment might consist of the sort of light conversation that precedes the blandly self-attentive, occasioned-and-delayed "*I* found a *recipe*: that I'm gonna try" of fragment (12). And indeed, just such an environment may have been arrived at with the troubles-recipient's little joke in fragment (15), "Well I think I'll stay in bed in the mor:ning" (line 48), a joking solution to the projected hazards the morning might bring.

A story-recipient offers a similar device in fragment (12), in which a joking solution to the husband's discovery of the impulsive gift-buying and occasioned matters await introduction, that is, that the husband be informed that the gifts were brought by "Santa Claus.hhheh-heh" (fragment [12], line 123).

Whereas in fragment (12) the joking solution is expanded into a little joke-laugh series, the expansion at some point intersected by the story-recipient's introduction of her occasioned-and-pending topic, in fragment (15) a similar trajectory may be under way but it may be curtailed in a particularly interesting way.

Specifically, in fragment (15) the joking solution, with its reference to avoiding, missing out on the projected hazards of tomorrow morning, may itself occasion a matter for the troubles-teller, that is, bring to mind the recent occurrence of the troubles-recipient's having actually missed an event, the movie that turned out to be such fun.

In purposefully achieving an appropriate environment for the introduction of her own occasioned materials, the troubles-recipient has inci-

dentally (1) achieved an appropriate environment for a range of matters
inappropriately introduced directly adjacent to a troubles-telling, and (2)
occasioned a topic for her coparticipant, who, with an appropriate environment to work with, introduces it then and there, thus preempting
introduction of the prior-occasioned, worked-toward topic.

Again, details of the relevant segment of talk tend to support such a
view.

(15) [Detail]

```
L:    Well I think I'll stay in bed in the mor:ₙning,
G:                                            ⌐hHAH!=
G:    =I doₙn't bla:me ₙyou?ₙ
L:        ⌐nhh hnh⁻hnh ⌐heh ⌐ʰheh he ₙh ˙hk⌐
G:                         [˙h̅ h ⌐H e̅ y⌐listen ˙hhh You
      should have come on Tue:sda:y,
```

Following the joking solution, the joke-recipient overlaps the final
syllable of the joke with a single laugh particle. The laughter, the appreciation of the joke, is both early and brief, and is followed immediately
by talk. First, the talk moves to curtail the possibility of an expanded
joke-laughter series. Second, the talk constitutes a warranting of the
coparticipant's position, "I don't bla:me you?" In combination, the appreciation of the joke and warranting of the coparticipant's position can
be characterized as other-attentive/interactionally cohesive, and it may
be not incidental that such activities are occurring just prior to a topical
shift. The talk in toto produced by the joke-recipient may be analogous
to the summary assessments considered earlier, and may specifically be
being deployed as a topical pre-shifter.

Thus, as with the prior consideration of a candidate occasioning and
the introduction of an occasioned item, but here in a drastically more
condensed way, the talk following the candidate occasioning item and
preceding the candidate occasioned item tends to support their respective candidacies.

Finally, the joke-teller's activities by reference to the possible pretopical-shift activities of the coparticipant, when examined in detail,
yield features that tend to support the view being developed.

At some point she herself starts to laugh. That laughter is neither
immediately after her own joke (cf. the various details of fragments [12]
and [15] considered earlier), nor immediately after onset of the coparticipant's laughter (cf. fragment [12] detail 2); that is, it is neither proposing
a laughing-together nor joining in on one. Rather, it starts up immediately after onset of the coparticipant's talk.

(15) [Detail 2]

```
    G:    hHAH! I do n't bla:me  you?
    L:             [nhh hnh¯hnh [heh
```

At the point she starts to laugh, the joke-teller may not yet have access to just what the talk is, with only "I" and the first part of "don't" to work with. But the series of activities – the early, brief laugh followed by onset of speech – may be recognizably problematic for the trajectory she is operating, and its designed arrival at the introduction of her occasioned topic. By starting to laugh at this point, she may be countering a trajectory potentiated by that series; specifically, the closure of the expansion potential of the little joking solution, and a taking of the floor by the coparticipant.

Not merely does she start to laugh at such a point, but she continues to laugh across the coparticipant's utterance; and then continues to laugh beyond completion of that utterance.

(15) [Detail 3]

```
    G:    I do n't bla:me  you?   ˙h h
    L:          [nhh hnh¯hnh[heh ]heh heh
```

The laughter may be specifically being deployed to outlast the talk, and to be laughing upon utterance-completion, thus (re)inviting the coparticipant to join in a laughing-together, which can be intersected, as in fragment (12), by the joke-teller's introduction of her occasioned topic. As a further detail, the laughter is escalated just prior to completion of the coparticipant's utterance; it shifts from "nhh hnh hnh" to "*h*eh *h*eh heh," becoming louder and open-positioned. Such an activity can constitute an appreciation of the utterance overlapped by the closed-positioned laughter (see Jefferson, Sacks, and Schegloff forthcoming); a joke-laughter series is already in progress, the coparticipant now having produced a re-reference to the initial joke, that re-reference now constituting the source of a next round of laughter.

If this is the joke-teller's strategy, however, it is defeated, since the laughter that continues beyond completion of the talk is overlapped by the introduction of the coparticipant's occasioned topic.

(15) [Detail 4]

```
    L:    heh he h ˙hk
    G:    [˙h h [H e y]listen
```

Indeed, the laughter appears to be "caught by surprise" by the precipitous introduction. Note the little hiccuping inbreath " `hk`" that follows the onset of the *"Hey"* and is the terminal particle of the prolonged string.

Thus, detailed examination of this segment yields a competition for a slot that may constitute a first appropriate opportunity for the introduction of new topics after a troubles-telling.

Fragment (15), then, may be characterized as a manifestation of the consequence of a convergence of two distinct aspects of topical talk; that (1) some topic-types are open to immediate introduction of any next topic whereas others, such as a troubles-telling, are closed, that is, constrain what sort of talk properly comes next, and (2) topics may be occasioned in the course of ongoing talk. Whereas topics occasioned in the course of a closed topic-type are properly delayed until an open environment is achieved, topics occasioned in the course of an open topic-type can be introduced immediately.

A systematically based hazard, then, for matters occasioned during a closed topic is, as in fragment (15), that the deployment of an open topic to arrive at the introduction of the occasioned matter can incidentally provide an environment ripe for introduction of other matters aﬁd, as in this case, can itself occasion other matters. Inasmuch as those matters are properly introduceable immediately, there is the possibility (again manifested in fragment [15]), of a preemption and still further delay of the introduction of the matters occasioned during the course of the closed topic.

Notes

1. For a consideration of this fragment see the unpublished lecture of Harvey Sacks, SS 158X, February 19, 1971, pp. 17–18.
2. So, for example, in the unpublished lecture 2 (revised), spring 1966, p. 9, Sacks refers to the questioner's "reserved right to talk again, after the one to whom he has addressed the question speaks."
3. The proposal of Dwight's similar condition, that he only has one gallbladder, may be discarding facticity for local aptness; that is, if it is so that he "only has one," then what he problematically only has one of is probably a kidney.
4. Each of the pivotal utterances may be seen to be exhibiting a spurious fittedness to the talk from which it is departing. In fragment (13) there is the factually wrong but topically apt identification of a similar complaint, *"Dwight* only has-one gall bladder." In fragment (14) there is the utterance-initial proposal of a strong relationship to the prior talk, *"That's why . . . ,"* that the relationship obscured as the utterance develops into a report of this speaker's circumstances, "well *we* didn't get home til two o'clo:ck." And in fragment (15) the fragile topical relationship is augmented by a lexical echoing, that is, the prior utterance's "that little bit more ca:reful" echoed by "that little bit wa:rmer."

5. This fragment is taken from G. Jefferson (1978a:220). (Some consideration of the phenomenon can be found in this chapter.)
6. The oriented-to power of such an object as "Uh::m" and its capacity to mark such an activity as "getting back to" was initially noted by Graham Button in his consideration of bids to move out of a closing sequence back into a state of conversation (forthcoming a; forthcoming b).

PART IV
The integration of talk with nonvocal activities

Although most of the chapters in this book (and in the literature of conversation analysis more generally) report on studies of audiotape recordings of interaction, it does not follow that conversation analysts are therefore uninterested in or content to ignore the possible significance of nonvocal activities. Indeed, the widespread use that has been made of recorded telephone calls as a focus for analysis recognizes a major methodological advantage precisely in the fact that the interactants themselves cannot see each other. The analyst can thus proceed to the study of audio recordings without having to worry about how nonvocal activities may have been involved in any particular sequence. The same obviously cannot be said of interactions where the participants are copresent with one another and, for investigating these, videotapes and films can provide a much fuller record of what occurred. As the relevant technologies become more sophisticated and more readily available, then, research in conversation analysis is likely to pay more attention to issues that can be addressed with reference to an audiovisual data base, and the chapters in this part reflect some of the directions such work is taking.

The range of practical, ethical, and technical problems associated with the use of video recordings for analytic purposes cannot be discussed in detail here (but see, for example, C. Goodwin 1981a). One that becomes quickly apparent, however, from the chapters here is the difficulty of publishing visual records of the data in such a way as to permit readers easy access to the activities about which observations are being made. Anyone who has ever attempted to produce a detailed description of some sequence of bodily movements will know only too well how daunting a task it is. And anyone who has been present at oral presentations where video-recorded fragments were played and replayed will appreciate the sorts of losses that are inevitably involved in attempts to represent the data in other ways. The authors of this book are deeply aware of these problems, and have sought to resolve them for present purposes by using Jefferson's transcription conventions for representing the talk, and other symbols for marking where particular nonvocal activities occur in relation to what is being said. The readers do not, of course, have access to features of the settings other than those discussed in the reports, and it is not at all clear how this access could ever be facilitated, unless it eventually becomes possible to issue copies of the original videotapes (or discs) to accompany published research reports.

Although conversation analytic research has been influenced by and has a good deal in common with studies of nonvocal communication by social psychologists, it is less concerned with quantitative analyses of phenomena like gestures, gaze, and bodily movements. A distinctive feature of the approach is that greater emphasis tends to be given to the sequential positioning of nonvocal activities in relation to particular details in the production of an ongoing flow of talk. Just as utterances are not analyzed and treated by recipients as having occurred "out of the blue," so also is there growing evidence that movements of the head, eyes, hands, and bodies of coparticipants are also oriented to with reference to precisely *where* and *when* they occur in the unfolding context of an interactional sequence. The chapter by Goodwin, for example, shows how various nonvocal activities of both the teller of a story and her recipients are finely coordinated with particular stages in the course of the storytelling. Similarly, Heath reports on the way in which noticeable shifts in nonvocal activity can be effectively used as a method for displaying recipiency, and thereby eliciting talk from a previously silent cointeractant. The chapter by Schegloff explores some implications of an observably recurrent feature in the timing of gestures that depict, represent, or relate to something being said by the speaker who uses them.

Taken together, the studies in this section provide further evidence of how talk and nonvocal activities are closely coordinated and oriented to by interactants in the production and monitoring of each other's actions. If participants themselves are routinely sensitive to the ways in which vocal and nonvocal phenomena are integrated, the puzzle of how they work is unlikely to be resolved by studying one or the other independently of the overall context of the sequence of interaction. Great skepticism should be shown toward some of the claims that have been given wide currency in the popularized literature on body language, and particularly those that propose or presuppose that there is a simple, invariant, and "one-to-one" relationship between any particular nonvocal activity and its meaning.

10. Notes on story structure and the organization of participation

CHARLES GOODWIN
University of South Carolina,
Columbia

This chapter investigates the interactive organization invoked and sustained through the telling of a single story in natural conversation. Among the phenomena examined are (1) how the participants organize themselves in relation to each other through the telling, with particular attention to how telling-specific identities, such as teller, addressed recipient, nonaddressed recipient, and principal character, are made relevant, displayed, and differentiated from each other; (2) ways in which the distinguishable subcomponents of the story are analyzed; (3) how participants display with their bodies as well as with their talk orientation to the alternative possibilities for action that the different subcomponents provide, and (4) how participants, through attention to both the internal structure of the talk and their place within it, manage shifting but concurrent involvement in other activities also taking place within the setting.

The story to be examined occurred during a dinner at the home of John and Beth at which another couple, Ann and Don, were guests. The dinner was videotaped.[1] Analysis focuses upon both the vocal and nonvocal behavior of the participants.[2] The following provides a simplified transcript of the talk producing the story.[3]

[G:26:5:55] (Simplified Version)

```
1                (4.0)
2   Ann:    Well- ((throat clear)) (0.4) We coulda used a
3           liddle, marijuana. tih get through the weekend.
4   Beth:   What h⌈appened.
5   Ann:            ⌊Karen has this new hou:se. en it's got
```

Earlier versions of this chapter were presented at the 77th Annual Meeting of the American Anthropological Association (Los Angeles, 1978); Wolfson College, Oxford (1979); and the Fifth Annual Institute of Ethnomethodology and Conversation Analysis, Boston University (1979).

225

```
 6            all this like- (0.2) ssilvery:: g-go:ld
 7            wwa:llpaper, ·hh (h)en D(h)o(h)n sa(h)ys,
 8            y'know this's th'firs'time we've seen this
 9            house.=Fifty five thousn dollars in Cherry
10            Hill.=Right?
11                 (0.4)
12 Beth:     Uh hu:h?
13 Ann:      Do(h)n said. (0.3) dih-did they ma:ke you take
14           this ⌜wa(h)llpa(h)p(h)er? er(h)di ⌜dju pi(h)ck⌝=
15 Beth:          ⌞hh!                         ⌞Ahh huh huh⌟
16 Ann:      =⌜⌜i(h)t ou(h)t.
17 Beth:      ⌞⌞huh huh huh ⌜huh
18 Don:                     ⌞Uhh hih huh hu⌜h
19 Ann:                                     ⌞UHWOOghghHHH!=
20 Ann:      =Y'kno(h)w that wz ⌜like the firs' bad one.
21 Beth:                        ⌞Uh:oh wo::w hh
22                 (0.2)
23 Don:      But I said it so innocuously y'know.
24 Ann:      Yeh I'm sure they thought it wz- hnh hnh!
```

1. Some initial observations

The story that Ann produces here exhibits one of the characteristic shapes that stories take in conversation. A multi-utterance turn (lines 5–16), the body of the story, is preceded by specific moves by both the teller and the recipient: a preface offering to tell the story (lines 2–3) and a request to hear the offered story (line 4). At the conclusion of the story proper the participants engage in further talk relevant to it (lines 17–24). Sacks (1974) has analyzed how such a shape represents an adaptation to some of the basic features organizing turn-taking within conversation. For example, the preface and recipient answer to it provide one technique for negotiating the systematic occurrence of a subsequent turn consisting of multiple turn-constructional units.

The body of the story contains a number of distinct sections.[4] It begins with relevant background information, the fact that Karen has a new house and that it has a certain kind of wallpaper (lines 5–7) and then at the end of line 7, with "(h)en D(h)o(h)n sa(h)ys," moves to what will turn out to be the climax of the story. At this point, however, rather than producing what Don in fact said the speaker begins to provide further background information, the cost of the house and its location (lines 9–10). Only after the acknowledgment of this information by a recipient (line 12) does the speaker return to where she had left off, saying (line 13) "Do(h)n said" and then reporting what he said.

The story thus contains not only preface, background, and climax sections but also what may be called a parenthesis, a section of background information embedded (disjunctively) within the climax.

The differentiation of these subsections is not merely an analytic device for studying the story but poses a practical problem for the participants themselves. Alternative tasks are raised for them in different sections. For example, recipient action different from that called for during background sections becomes appropriate and relevant at the conclusion of the story, during (see line 15) or after the climax segment. (Other examples of alternative recipient action in different segments are examined later in the chapter.) The parenthesis poses the issue of differentiation with particular clarity. Syntactically the talk produced there could be the next component of the sentence begun with "Don says." Recipients fail, however, in their ongoing analysis of the story if they interpret "y'know this's th'firs'time we've seen this *house*" as something Don said over the weekend to Karen rather than as something the present speaker is now telling them about that event.[5]

The way in which the speaker articulates her talk is relevant to this issue in that it has the effect of heightening the contrast between adjacent segments of her story. For example laugh tokens, indicated in the transcript by "(h)"'s, occur extensively in talk constituting part of the climax, but only there. Presence of laugh tokens thus clearly differentiates " ˙hh (h)en D(h)o(h)n *sa*(h)ys," in line 7 from both the background segment that precedes it and the parenthesis segment that follows it. The parenthesis is in fact precisely bracketed by laugh tokens, as the speaker places another in the very first syllable of her return to the climax segment in line 13. Laugh tokens are not simply comments by the speaker on the talk being produced but rather, as has been noted by Jefferson (1974b and Jefferson, Sacks, and Schegloff forthcoming), may constitute invitations to laugh, moves making relevant particular types of subsequent actions by a recipient.[6] The distribution of laugh tokens thus both emphasizes the disjunctiveness of adjacently placed segments and provides a recipient with different guides for his action within alternative segments. Contrast between segments is also manifested in other ways, not to be dealt with here, such as changes in voice and intonation. The fact that the speaker's articulation of her story is highly textured and differentiated rather than homogeneous thus constitutes a resource for the accomplishment of some of the interactive and interpretative tasks facing the participants.[7]

Several additional features of the conversation may also be noted. First, the principal character in the story, Don, is present at its telling. He is in fact seated next to Ann. Second, the talk being investigated takes place in what may be called a multi-activity setting. In addition to conversation the participants are also engaged in a variety of other activities such as eating, distributing food, and child care. Among the phenomena to be examined in the present report are ways in which participants display different types of alignment to competing activities as well as the coordination of these multiple activities relative to each other.

2. Teller's body position

Through the way in which she handles her body during this sequence the speaker performs a number of actions relevant to the telling of her story. These include displays about the nature and extent of her orientation to the conversation itself as well as displays about the type of talk she is producing, and relevant differences within that talk.

For the telling a distinctive body posture is adopted. Ann clasps her hands together, places both elbows on the table, and leans forward while gazing toward her addressed recipient, Beth. With this posture the speaker displays full orientation toward her addressed recipient, complete engagement in the telling of her story, and lack of involvement in any activities other than conversation. The posture appears to mark the production of a focused, extended turn at talk, that is, to constitute a visual display that a telling is in progress.

Support for this possibility is provided by the sequential placement of the teller's position and by its contrast with the position of the speaker's body before and after this turn. The speaker's elbows reach the table over the word "new" in line 5 and leave the table over the word "out" in line 16, the very last word of the story. The boundaries of the position thus coincide almost precisely with the boundaries of the multi-unit turn containing the body of the story.[8]

Not all talk receives the exclusive involvement of the speaker that Ann gives hers here. For example, just after this turn Ann picks up a glass of water so that her talk in line 24 is done while displaying concurrent involvement in multiple activities, conversation and eating. By holding the glass just to the side of her face during this turn she displays that that strip of talk is being done in the shadow of another, interrupted activity which, though being held off during the talk, is nonetheless awaiting accomplishment when the talk comes to completion. The story proper stands under no such shadow but has the full and exclusive engagement of its speaker.

The speaker's actions at the beginning of the story provide further evidence that a display of full engagement in it by its speaker is in fact an oriented-to feature of its production. Just before the story begins Ann, and all of the other participants, are fully occupied with eating. Ann places food on her fork and starts to raise it to her mouth. She then hesitates, however, puts the loaded fork back on her plate, raises her head, and produces the story preface. The activity of eating is not simply interrupted (in which case Ann might have continued to hold the fork in readiness, as she later did the glass) but noticeably abandoned in midcourse in favor of the talk. Thus even before the talk has been produced the activities of the speaker's body provide a display about the status she is proposing for it, that is, that it is something she is putting aside other activities to engage in and thus not simply a comment or remark, but potentially something such as a telling.

As was noted earlier, the production of the story is not up to the speaker alone but rather something accomplished with the collaboration of a recipient, this collaboration being established through a preface/request sequence. During her preface Ann does not adopt the distinctive teller's position used in the body of the story but rather engages in a number of actions that seem to display preparation for some upcoming activity. Specifically she raises herself in her seat, adjusts her hair and glasses, and rearranges the space in front of her by moving a glass from one side of her plate to the other. With the way in which she handles her body Ann thus differentiates the preface from the body of her story and displays that she is treating them as quite different types of events.

Other units in the talk are also differentiated by the speaker's body. For example, though her elbows remain stable throughout the body of the story the speaker's hands are mobile, their movements being coordinated with subunits within the long, multi-utterance turn in lines 5–16. This coordination is perhaps most clearly seen over the parenthesis segment, where the hands are unclasped and rubbed back and forth. The movement of the hands stops precisely when the speaker closes the parenthesis and returns to the climax segment. Subsections within the parenthesis itself are also marked. For example, just after "Right?" which transfers the floor briefly to the recipient, the speaker's hand noticeably closes.

Ann's telling is thus made visible not only in her talk but also in the way in which she organizes her body and activities during the telling. With these resources she is able to provide relevant displays about both her alignment to the talk and its sequential organization.

3. Gaze between speaker and addressed recipient

One characteristic way that orientation toward the other is displayed within the turn at talk is through gaze. Other research (Goodwin 1979a, 1981a) has provided some demonstration that participants both orient to particular states of gaze within the turn and have systematic procedures for achieving these states. The gaze of the speaker and addressed recipient in the present data forces this analysis to be expanded to take into account the distinctive sequential organization for talk provided by a story. To establish necessary groundwork for examining this, some relevant features of the organization of gaze within the turn are briefly summarized.

One principal rule organizing the gaze of speaker and recipient within the turn can be stated as follows: When a speaker gazes at a recipient that recipient should be gazing at him. When speakers gaze at nongazing recipients, and thus locate violations of the rule, they frequently produce phrasal breaks, such as restarts and pauses, in their talk. These phrasal breaks both orient to the event as a violation by locating the talk in progress at that point as impaired in some fashion and provide a remedy by functioning as requests for the gaze of the hearer. Thus just after phrasal breaks nongazing recipients frequently begin to move their gaze to the speaker. The following provide examples of this process. The gaze of the speaker is marked above the utterance, that of the recipient below it. A line indicates that the party marked is gazing toward the other. The absence of a line indicates lack of gaze. Dots mark the transition movement from gaze to nongaze, commas indicate the dropping of gaze, and the point where gaze reaches the other is marked with an "X." If gaze arrives within a pause each tenth of a second within the pause is marked with a dash.

```
Beth:     . . . .X_____
          Terry- [Jerry's fa[scinated with elephants
Don:            . . . . .x_____

Joe:      . . . . . . .X_____
          My mother tol'[me th't We had a col[d wadder flat
Pat:                 . . . . . .[x_____
```

The rule organizing gaze also provides organization for the sequencing of the gaze of the parties at a turn beginning. If the speaker brings his or her gaze in first, as happens in the above examples, the speaker will find a nongazing recipient and thus violate the rule. Therefore if the rule is to be satisfied gaze should be sequenced in the order first recipient and only then speaker.

The present data show that the gaze of the speaker and addressed recipient during the preface satisfies the rule.[9]

```
Ann:                              . . .  ⌐X_____
           Well (--- ⌐-) We coulda used  ⌐a liddle, marijuana.=
Beth:            .  ⌊X_____
```

```
Ann:                                 .  ⌐X___
           =tih get through the wee ⌊kend.
Beth:      _____
```

However, during the first segment of the body of the story, the addressed recipient withdraws her gaze from the speaker:

```
Ann:       _____
           Karen has this new hou:se. en it's got all this
Beth:      _____      ,  ,  ,
```

When this happens a clear violation of the rule stated above occurs. The speaker is gazing at a nongazing recipient.

The participants do not, however, orient to this event as a violation. For example, the speaker does not immediately produce a restart to request the recipient's gaze but rather continues with the talk that she is producing and indeed advances the development of that talk further even after she has lost the gaze of her recipient.

Such behavior by the participants suggests that the looking away of the recipient at this point is permitted. This raises the possibility either that it is a lawful exception to the rule or that the rule has been relaxed.

To explore this possibility two phenomena are examined: first, the sequential position of the look-away, and second, the demands being made upon the participants by the multiple activities within which they are engaged.

The recipient's look-away occurs during a background segment within the body of a story. This position is a sequential one with somewhat special properties. First, by virtue of the sequence preceding it the party who is now looking away has already displayed orientation to the talk that the speaker is currently producing in several different ways: vocally, by explicitly requesting that the speaker tell her story and, nonvocally, with her gaze during the preface and at the beginning of the body. Because of its placement after these events the present look-away is quite different from lack of gaze at the beginning of an isolated turn at talk, for example, the beginning of a turn just after a lapse, where the orientation of recipient to speaker has not yet been established.

Second, this position is also special with respect to the contingencies for action operative at the termination of the unit. In general within conversation speaker transition is a relevant possibility at the end of each turn-constructional unit (Sacks, Schegloff, and Jefferson 1974:704). However here, through the preface sequence, speaker and recipient have specifically negotiated the production of a turn that is to consist of multiple turn-constructional units. The unit within which the recipient looks away is recognizably not the last unit in the turn but the first. As such it is a unit within which the tasks that will face the recipient at the climax of the story, and completion of the turn, are not then to be posed.

The sequential position of the look-away is thus consistent with the possibility that the recipient is orienting to the talk then occurring specifically as a multi-unit turn and using that feature of it, and in particular the embedded position of this unit, as one reference point for the organization of her activities.

It may also be observed from the videotape that the recipient does not simply turn her eyes away from the speaker but while she is looking away engages in another activity achieved in part through the use of her gaze: putting food on her fork. Eating makes use of some of the same body material, the mouth and gaze, for example, used to do conversation, and the demands made on this body material by these different activities are not always able to be satisfied simultaneously. Insofar as multiple activities are occurring the participants are faced with the on-going task of coordinating these separate activities with each other.

The present data suggest one possibility for accomplishing such coordination. In particular sequential positions the rule that a recipient should be gazing at a gazing speaker may be relaxed, permitting the recipient to look away and attend to competing activities. If the rule is only being relaxed, and not ignored, the participants may still provide some demonstration of their orientation to it even though it is not being strictly adhered to.

The data show that shortly after turning away the recipient does a nod:

```
Ann:
      Karen has this new hou:se. en it's got all this
Beth: _____  , , ,              ((Nod))
```

By producing the nod the recipient is able to display that even though she is not gazing at the speaker she is still orienting to her talk.

Further, the nod is done in a different sequential position, mid-turn-constructional unit,[10] from the nods performed while the speaker is being gazed at. These occur at the boundaries of turn-constructional units:

```
Ann:  _____
      Karen has this new hou:se. en it's got all this=
Beth: _____     , , ,            ((Nod))
```

```
Ann:  _____
      =like- (0.2) ssilvery::   g-go:ld wwa: ┌llpaper, `hh=
Beth:                      . . . . . . └X      ((Nod))
```

```
Ann:  _____
      =(h)en D(h)o(h)n sa(h)ys, y'know this's th'firs'=
Beth: _____
```

```
Ann:  _____
      =time we've seen this house.=Fifty five thousn dollars=
Beth: _____((Nod))_____ , , ,
```

```
Ann:  _____
      =in Cherry Hill.=Right?
           (0.4)
Beth: Uh hu:h?
```

The data are thus consistent with the argument that the recipient, by doing special work to display that she is still orienting to the talk of the speaker, is attending to the possibility that her look-away is a dispreferred activity.

The speaker also performs actions relevant to the dispreferred status of the recipient's lack of gaze. Shortly after the nod the speaker produces a phrasal break, an act that may function to request gaze but here has the effect of soliciting a second nod from the recipient:

```
Ann:  _____
      Karen has this new hou:se. en it's got all this=
Beth: _____     , , ,            ((Nod))
```

```
Ann:  _____
      =like- (0.2) ssilvery::
           ((Nod))
```

Both speaker and recipient thus perform specific actions relevant to the recipient's lack of gaze at this point. The data are therefore consistent with the argument that the rule about gazing at a gazing speaker has not been abandoned but relaxed. Further, even though relaxed, orientation to the rule has consequences in detail for the actions of the participants.

Some other phenomena relevant to these issues are more tenuous but nonetheless suggestive in the data. After the phrasal break solicits a nod but not the return of the recipient's gaze, the talk of the speaker becomes noticeably more textured with phenomena such as elongations of sounds and slight hesitations. One word after this texturing begins the recipient raises her eyes from her plate so that her head is directed to the speaker while she places her food in her mouth (this position is marked in the transcript with asterisks). Once this has been done Beth raises her head higher and moves into a position of full orientation toward the speaker:

```
Ann:      _____
          Karen has this new hou:se. en it's got all this=
Beth:     _____  , , ,              ((Nod))
```

```
Ann:      _____
          =like- (0.2) ssilvery:: g-go:ld wwa⌐llpaper.
Beth:          ((Nod))           ******* . .⌊X_____
```

The perturbations in the talk of the speaker and the two-stage return of the recipient raise the possibility that they are still negotiating the recipient's lack of gaze. The speaker provides further solicitations in her talk, and the recipient, with her first head movement, displays that even though she cannot yet return to full orientation she recognizes that this should be done and is in fact making a display of doing it as soon as possible.

The perturbations in the talk of the speaker also function to coordinate the production of her talk with the return move of the recipient. This function is most noticeable in the word "wwa:llpaper" where the sound stretch of the speaker positions the recipient's gaze arrival at a syllable boundary, but stretches in "g-go:ld" may also function to delay the beginning of "wwa:llpaper" until the first stage of the recipient's movement has been completed.[11]

Though gaze is returned by the end of the initial background segment it soon emerges again as an issue between the participants.

Just after the speaker enters the climax segment and, through the use of phenomena such as laugh tokens, differentiates it from the unit that preceded it, the addressed recipient leans toward the speaker (this movement starts in the midst of the word "D(h)o(h)n"). With this change in her position the recipient manages to show heightened orientation within the framework of full engagement that has been reestablished just before the beginning of this unit. It thus appears that the movement of the story from background to climax segments is achieved and ratified through the coordinated actions of both the speaker and the recipient. The recipient, with the return of her gaze at the end of the background segment (something that may be managed in part by adjustments in the speaker's talk), displays that she is prepared for the speaker to move to the climax. The speaker then does so, and then the recipient, by moving toward her, displays that she recognizes what has been done and is treating the current talk differently from the talk that preceded it.

However, after the recipient's display, instead of continuing with the climax, the speaker returns to background material by entering the parenthesis. The recipient holds her climax orientation and continues to gaze at the speaker throughout the first turn-constructional unit of this new, unprojected background segment. But shortly after the speaker enters a second turn-constructional unit in the parenthesis, thus displaying that the parenthesis will be extended, the recipient withdraws her gaze from the speaker:

```
Ann:   _____
       Karen has this new hou:se. en it's got all this=
Beth:  _____   , , ,            ((Nod))


Ann:   _____
       =like- (0.2) ssilvery:: g-go:ld wwa:┌llpaper, ˙hh=
Beth:       ((Nod))                . . . . . .└X____ ((Nod))


Ann:   _____
       =(h)en D(h)o(h)n sa(h)ys, y'know this's th'firs'=
Beth:  _____


Ann:   _____
       =time we've seen this house.=Fifty five thousn dollars=
Beth:  _____((Nod))_____  , , ,


Ann:   _____
       =in Cherry Hill.=Right?
               (0.4)
Beth:  Uh hu:h?
```

At the end of the turn-constructional unit in progress when the gaze withdrawal occurs the speaker appends an explicit request for a display of coparticipation, the tag question "Right?" The recipient does not provide an answer to this request for four-tenths of a second but the speaker waits for an explicit response before producing further talk. When the response from the recipient has been obtained the speaker returns immediately to the climax segment of her story.

Although the speaker is permitted to produce a parenthesis in her talk, to project the punchline and then insert further background information, the continued production of the parenthesis is contingent upon the cooperation of the recipient to the talk, the party who provided the speaker with the opportunity to produce a multi-unit turn in the first place. Thus (1) the recipient shows that she will not continue to display full orientation during an extended parenthesis; (2) the speaker then explicitly requests a display of her coparticipation; and (3) closes the parenthesis as soon as this display has been obtained.

After providing an answer to the speaker's "Right?" the addressed recipient does not return her gaze to the speaker. Rather, like her answer to the speaker's explicit request, her principal response to the story is displayed vocally, with laughter.

The recipient's withholding of her gaze during the final climax segment may be sensitive to the details of the particular interactive event being created through the telling of this story. For example, in that her gaze is not returned she is not put in the position of looking at the principal character in the story[12] while she is laughing at what he did.[13] Such issues will not, however, be investigated in the present chapter.

The telling is thus organized not only by actions of the speaker but also by actions of the addressed recipient. The actions of these two parties, however, are not performed mechanically with reference only to structures in the stream of speech but are also achieved and given shape through a continuous process of interaction with each other. Each takes into account both the demands being made upon her by the local contingencies of the talk and the actions of the other and, where appropriate, modifies her own actions in terms of what has been seen. Indeed, as such phenomena as the inclusion of the "Right?" in the parenthesis indicated, the talk itself may be changed.[14] This process of interaction is not however arbitrary and formless but rather quite precisely organized through the use of systematic procedures and displays that are not only relevant to the talk but in part constitutive of it.

4. Principal character

Don, the person whose actions are being reported by the speaker, has not only heard the story but lived through it.[15] Thus, unlike Beth, he does not need to listen to what is now being said to find out about the events being described. This does not, however, mean that he is freed from the task of attending in detail to the emerging structure of the story. Rather, the way in which his actions are presented makes it relevant for him to participate in the telling in specific ways at particular places within it.

Ann not only reports what Don said but also characterizes that action in a particular way. Through both the organization of the story itself and the details of its telling, such as the laugh tokens that punctuate the report of what was said, its principal character's actions are formulated as inappropriate, a social faux pas, an embarrassable, or, as the speaker herself says in line 20 "the firs' bad one." Given such a formulation, reaction from the party who produced the embarrassable is a potentially seeable event in its own right at a specific place in the telling: when what he said is revealed to the others present. The principal character may therefore be faced with the task of being available at a particular place in the story and of arranging his behavior there for the story-relevant scrutiny it will receive from others present.

These possibilities can be investigated by observing what Don does as the speaker reveals what he said to his hosts.

First, as the speaker produces the punchline of the story, Don's face is positioned so that it is pointed in the direction of the addressed recipient.

Second, Don uses his face to make displays relevant to the talk that the speaker is producing. These do not take the form of enactments of the events being reported but rather make visible an alignment to those events appropriate to the way in which they are now being formulated through the story. Thus as speaker's voice produces laugh tokens in the word "wa(h)llpa(h)p(h)er?" (line 14) his face begins to produce a smile. As both the speaker's and the addressed recipient's laughter is extended this smile is elaborated. Over the words "pi(h)ck i(h)t" the smile is noticeably escalated and renewed with a jerk of the head:

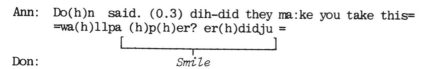

Ann: Do(h)n said. (0.3) dih–did they ma:ke you take this=
     =wa(h)llpa (h)p(h)er? er(h)didju =

Don: *Smile*

```
Ann:   = pi(h)ck i(h)t ou(h)t
         [_____]
              T
Don:      Escalation with
             Sharp
          Head Movement
```

The head movement that escalates the laughter is also used to begin a
shift in Don's gaze away from the nongazing addressed recipient and
toward the unaddressed recipient, John, who is found to be smiling
back at him. At this point the speaker also moves her eyes away from
the nongazing addressed recipient and to Don (the particular party
being gazed at by someone is indicated by placing that party's initial at
the beginning of the gaze line):

```
A:   B_____ ,·  · · · · · ·  ┌D
       wa(h)ll ┌pa(h)p(h)er? er(h)didju pi(h)ck i(h)t└ou┌(h)t.
D:       ·     └B_____  , , , , , , , , , , ,  · · ·└J____ , ,
J:                                                · · · · · ·└D____ , , ,
```

Thus just as the punchline of the story reaches its conclusion the principal character is the focus of the gaze of everyone who is gazing at
someone. While being gazed at he arranges his own behavior, and in
particular his face, for the observation it is receiving from others in terms
of the story.

The possibility will now be investigated that the displays made by the
principal character are a systematic part of the field of action created
through the story and that his orientation to the task of producing these
displays provides organization for his actions, not only when they are
being done, but before they are done.

Over "Do(h)n said." in line 13 Don, who has been gazing to his side at
something unrelated to the talk, moves his head back so that it is facing
the addressed recipient. He does not however display full engagement
in the conversation (for example, by openly gazing at the addressed
recipient) but rather keeps his eyes downcast, and at the point where his
face returns has his hand over his mouth and is rubbing his finger over
his upper lip:

```
Ann: Do(h)n said. (0.3) did–did they ma:ke you take this
          [_____]
                  T
Don: Face Returned but
     with Eyes Downcast
     and Mouth Covered
```

This position, somewhat like that of an actor who has moved to the wings but is not yet on stage, appears transitional. It places the party who adopts it in a position that is relevant to upcoming events in the sequence of talk (i.e., his face is available for story-relevant scrutiny by the others present) but the party adopting this position is not yet displaying full engagement with his coparticipants.

The data therefore suggest that this is a particular type of preparatory position that is tied to an event that has not yet occurred, but that can be legitimately anticipated from the materials provided by the sequential structure of the talk.

One way to investigate this possibility would be to see what would happen if such a position were adopted but the action it was supposed to be preparatory to was then withdrawn. Fortunately this story provides materials with which this possibility can be examined.

By the end of the initial background segment the principal character has moved into a position suitable for scrutiny for the first time:

```
Ann:   ssilvery:: g-go:ld wwa:llpaper, 'hh(h)en
                        ↑
Don:             Face toward
             Addressed Recipient
             with Hand over Mouth
```

However, after this has happened, instead of bringing the climax segment to completion, the speaker enters the parenthesis. The event that the principal character's body position is possibly preparatory to is no longer about to occur. If the body position is in fact tied to that event the removal of the event may have consequences for whether or not the body position can be maintained.

As soon as it can be recognized that a parenthesis has been entered the principal character moves his head to the side and shifts his gaze to a ladle of soup that is being passed there:

```
Ann:   'h (h)en D(h)o(h)n sa(h)ys, y'know =
       └─────────────────────────┘
                     |
Don:         Face toward Addressed
              Recipient with Hand
                  over Mouth

Ann:   =this's th'firs'time we've
                       ↑
Don:            Shifts gaze
            to Soup Ladle
```

Thus, when the parenthesis is entered the principal character abandons his scrutiny-relevant position and displays a shift in his involvement from the talk that the speaker is producing to other activities occurring within the setting. When the projected event is removed the body position preparing the principal character for participation in that event is dropped.

As soon as the parenthesis is closed, over "Do(h)n said." in line 13, Don returns his face to the focus of the conversation and again takes up his position next to the teller, even going so far as to rub his finger over his upper lip in the same way he had done before the parenthesis:

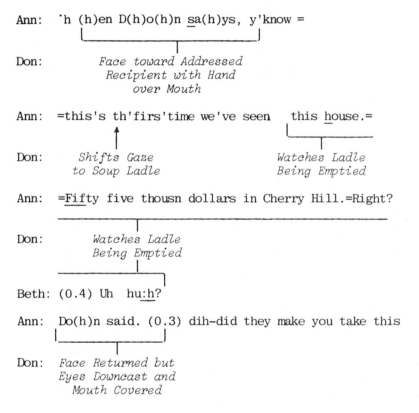

Thus, when the talk where scrutiny will be relevant is retrieved the body position appropriate to it is resumed. The way in which Don adopts this body position whenever scrutiny of him is visibly projected, but abandons it when that possibility recedes, is consistent with the argument that the this body position is in fact a preparatory position, not to be held in the absence of the event it is preparatory to.

Earlier in the telling the principal character engages in activities that systematically differentiate him from both the speaker and her addressed recipient. For example, rather than putting aside competing activities during the preface, as the speaker and addressed recipient do, he uses this time to take a drink. However, when the body of the story is begun he begins to perform preparatory activities similar to those performed by the speaker during the preface (and described on p. 229). After putting his glass down he moves an object on the table in front of him, puts his elbows on the table, looks toward the speaker, and then as the background segment is closed moves into his pre-position. Both the speaker and the principal character thus seem to perform similar activities just before they emerge as focal participants. However, because the structure of the telling places the emergence of each as focal at different points, over the same segments they are doing different things.

The actions of the principal character during the story, including his displays of disengagement from the talk of the speaker, are thus organized with reference to, and precisely synchronized with, the story that the speaker is producing. His adoption of a pre-position at a particular point in the talk, just before the focus of the participants shifts to him, is not accidental but rather something he works to achieve and is capable of renegotiating as contingencies within the interaction change.

His actions also provide some demonstration that participants are listening to the talk that is being produced not simply to comprehend the events being reported, but also in terms of the position of that talk in larger structures of talk, the possibilities for action provided for or constrained by that talk, the future talk or actions it projects, and the relevance of such material for the actions the participant doing the listening must perform.

5. Nonaddressed recipient

In a sense the position of John, the nonaddressed recipient, is complementary to that of the addressed recipient. Whereas conversation is the primary focus of the actions of the addressed recipient, and eating a subordinate activity, serving himself food is the primary activity that the nonaddressed recipient is performing and orientation to the conversation is subordinate to that. Indeed it initially appears that until John smiles at the punchline he has shown almost no attention to the speaker's story, though he does gaze at her briefly during the preface.

Closer examination reveals, however, that his serving activities are in fact being organized quite precisely with reference to the emerging structure of the story. As the speaker performs her background segments he is lifting a ladle full of soup from the soup pot. However he does not yet have the ladle to his plate when the background segment closes. He moves the ladle toward his bowl very slightly after the close of the background segment but when the speaker projects the arrival of the punchline with " hh (h)en D(h)o(h)n sa(h)ys," he stops this movement and holds the ladle in midair. The ladle is held in this position until it has become apparent that the parenthesis has been entered, over "this's," at which point John brings the ladle to his bowl.

The timing of this movement, and the hesitations within it, are consistent with the possibility that John, anticipating through the projection provided by the speaker that the punchline is about to be produced, delays his actions with the ladle so that he will not be involved with them when the task of appreciating the story is posed for him.

Further support for this possibility is provided by John's actions when the punchline is in fact produced. At this point John has returned to the pot for a second ladle of soup. He has a full ladle by the end of "wa(h)ll-pa(h)p(h)er?" the place where the job of doing appreciation arrives. Despite the fact that he has already filled the ladle he drops it back into the bowl again at this point as he looks toward the principal character in the story. He then takes another ladleful but holds it over the pot until "one" in line 20, the very end of the speaker's appreciation of her story. His activity of serving is thus done during background segments of the story but held in abeyance, by active work on his part, during focal segments. The alternative actions he performs during different types of segments are consistent with the possibility, first raised when considering the actions of the addressed recipient during the initial background segment, that participants might orient to background segments as places where competing activities can legitimately be done, thus differentiating parts within the body of a story in terms of the interactive possibilities they provide.

The recycling of the filling of the ladle provides an example in an activity other than conversation of a technique employed frequently in conversation to coordinate talk with the actions of a coparticipant: the addition of a new segment to that action so that synchronization with the actions of a coparticipant can be achieved.[16]

6. Conclusion

The actions of the participants during the telling of this story make visible some of the interactive tasks such an activity engenders, as well as the types of organization it makes relevant. For example, recipients to the story are faced with the job not simply of listening to the events being recounted but rather of distinguishing different subcomponents of the talk in terms of the alternative possibilities for action they invoke.[17] The actions of the addressed recipient, principal character, and nonaddressed recipient all demonstrate that the recognition of an event in talk such as a parenthesis poses not simply problems of comprehension but practical problems for the organization of action while it is being spoken. Further, such tasks involve not simply recognition of the type of story component then being produced but also an analysis of how the person doing the analysis fits into the activity in progress. Thus the speaker and principal character operating on the same subsection of talk, a background segment for example, find that it provides for the relevance of quite different actions for each of them. The participants are engaged in a local, situated analysis not only of the talk in progress but also of their participation in it and the multiple products of such analysis provide in part for the differentiated but coordinated actions that are constitutive of the story as a social activity.

The methods of analysis developed here are relevant to a range of issues that have emerged in other work on story organization. To note just one, contemporary work in the ethnography of speaking, and disciplines such as folklore that draw from it, lays great emphasis on obtaining the "participant's perspective" and on elucidating "emic" categories. In practice what is studied usually consists either of linguistic labels obtained from informants, or of data obtained in response to requests by the researcher for phenomena that the researcher has already decided are theoretically interesting. For example, what is studied as a story characteristically consists either of talk obtained when a researcher asks someone to "tell a story" or of talk that participants explicitly label a story. The ability of participants to deal in such a fashion with the category being studied is assumed to demonstrate its "emic" status. This assumption is not warranted. Pike (1966), in his seminal expansion of the etic/emic distinction beyond the scope of phonology, defined emic analysis in terms of how phenomena are utilized within specific systems of action, not with reference to labels recognized by informants.[18] In the present chapter, structures that participants attend to within a strip of talk (for example, "background" as opposed to "climax" segments of a story) have been specified, not by questioning the participants, but rather through study in detail of the actions they perform as the talk itself emerges. In addition to revealing some of the internal organization of multi-unit turns, such an approach embeds relevant structural units within the activity systems that give them meaning, and demonstrates how participants use this structure as a constitutive feature of the events they are engaged in.

Notes

1. I am indebted to George Kuetemeyer for providing me with this tape.
2. One strong limitation of a written format for the presentation of this analysis is the unavailability of the videotape to the reader. Attempts have been made to make relevant features of the visual material accessible through both transcription and description but these efforts have not provided a completely satisfactory solution to the problem.
3. I am indebted to Gail Jefferson for transcribing this material. What has been omitted from the version presented here is talk involving the children of the hosts who are also present at the dinner. The fact that their activity is not being examined in the present report should not be taken to imply that their actions are in no way relevant to the talk that is being examined.
4. The organization of story segments has been the subject of ongoing research by Gail Jefferson for a number of years. See, for example, Jefferson (1973b).
5. For more detailed consideration of the different entities who can talk through a speaker see Goffman (1974:496–559).
6. From this perspective it is interesting to observe that after the laugh token marking reentry into the climax segment, laugh tokens disappear from the final climax segment until the recipient produces an outbreath (line 15), a sound that may be interpreted as a preparatory laugh move. Thus, after raising the possibility of laughter, the speaker delays further production of it until a display of possible coparticipation has been received from recipient.
7. Within sociolinguistics the practice of style shifting has been treated as a phenomenon in need of some systematic explanation. However, when the task of marking distinctions between units in a strip of speech for a recipient is considered, stylistic homogeneity emerges as a far more problematic practice.
8. The elbows reach the table slightly after the beginning of the turn. However, not only is this movement fluid but other research now in progress indicates that a position such as this is not organized solely with reference to the structure of the stream of speech but rather with reference to relevant interaction between the speaker and hearer. Thus the position may be withheld if the recipient has not reached orientation toward the speaker by the beginning of the turn containing the body. In the present data it may be observed that the beginning of Ann's turn overlaps Beth's request for the story. Ann's elbows reach the table at just about the place where her talk emerges in the clear.
9. The movement of the speaker in the present data is consistent with the possibility that she is actively delaying bringing her gaze to her recipient. Thus her move into orientation is divided into several distinct stages. First, there is an initial movement from a posture of disengagement. This movement does not terminate with her gaze on one of her potential recipients but rather with Ann gazing directly in front of her. This position is held for a period of time during which the addressed recipient's gaze reaches the speaker. Only after this has happened does the speaker produce a second movement, bringing her own gaze to the addressed recipient:

```
Ann:    . . . . . . . . . . . .*************..
          Well- ((throat clear)) (-⌐--⌐-) We coulda=
Beth:                           . ⌐X_____
```

```
Ann:    . . .⌐X_____
          =used ⌐a liddle, marijuana.
Beth:         _____
```

The data also suggest that the recipient might utilize the expectability of a delay in the speaker's gaze to accomplish tasks of her own. Thus while the speaker is holding her pre-position the recipient wipes her lips with a napkin, finishing this job before the speaker's gaze reaches her.

10. Sacks, Schegloff, and Jefferson (1974:702) note that many different types of units, including sentences, phrases, clauses, and even single-word constructions can be used to construct a turn at talk but that any such unit allows in its course a projection of what will constitute an adequate completion of the unit. It is thus possible not only to locate stretches of talk containing multiple units (something that will be relevant to the analysis of the parenthesis in the present data) but also to locate systematically the middles of such units, places where they have recognizably not reached a point of possible completion.

11. The fact that these perturbations might be implicated in dealings relevant to the mutual orientation of the speaker and hearer does not of course mean that they are not also functioning in other ways, for example, providing displays about how the talk where they occur is to be heard and operated on.

12. Note that the fact that the climax would involve a laughable by Don was not available when the recipient returned her gaze to the speaker before the parenthesis but is available by the time of the parenthesis.

13. The actions of the principal character, to be examined in the next section of the chapter, indicate that receiving such looks from recipients is a possibility he anticipates and he orders his own behavior in terms of them.

14. For other analysis of how processes of interaction between the speaker and hearer might lead to changes in the emerging structure of the speaker's talk see C. Goodwin (1979a, 1981a) and M. H. Goodwin (1980).

15. The presence of someone who has already heard a story raises systematic issues for the conduct of a telling. For some consideration of these issues and the methods that participants have developed to deal with them see Sacks (October 17, 1971) and C. Goodwin (1981a, chap. 5).

16. For further analysis of this process see C. Goodwin (1981a, chap. 4).

17. The analysis that has been developed here, by showing how the story provides a field of action for a range of different types of participants, and how these participants analyze and make use of the emerging structure of the story, is thus relevant to some general questions about story organization that have been raised by workers in a number of different fields. For example, an attempt to uncover the natural units attended to by participants for the organization of speech events, such as stories, has become an important issue in both the ethnography of speaking and folklore (see, for example, Robinson's [1981] study of the "personal narrative" which deals explicitly with the place of listeners in such structures). I would, however, like to note that if analysis is restricted to "expressive" and "artistic" components of the storytelling process (see, for example, Bauman 1977:11–12) important fea-

tures of its organization may not be accessible to study. For example, the way in which the principal character during the parenthesis carefully displays *noninvolvement* in the field of action being sustained through the story is as appropriate, and interesting analytically, as his subsequent official participation during the climax. At this stage in our attempts to come to terms with such materials what is needed is less an analytic framework that specifies for us in advance the theoretically interesting phenomena in an event, than an awareness of our ignorance, and a willingness to be open to whatever phenomena the data reveal.

18. Indeed, as the study of phonemics proper amply demonstrates, the labels used by participants are not only irrelevant but frequently inaccurate. For example, the fact that three separate letters are used by speakers of English to describe the sounds in "the" in no way demonstrates the presence of three phonemes in the word. Similarly the absence of clear labels differentiating the voiced and voiceless versions of the sound spelled as "th" does not in any way mean that these variants are treated by speakers of English as phonemically equivalent. The analysis of emic structures deals with another order of phenomena entirely.

11. Talk and recipiency: sequential organization in speech and body movement

CHRISTIAN HEATH
University of Surrey

Social interaction requires participants to establish and sustain mutual involvement in the business or topic at hand and to coordinate systematically their actions and activities. Involvement in interaction however is rarely explicitly addressed; if it were it would shift the focus of attention from the topic at hand to the problems of being involved in it. Rather, participants sustain involvement through the ways in which they behave both as speakers and the recipients of the actions of others.

Within the course of interactional activity participants themselves orient to how their actions and activities are received and attended to by their fellow participants. As studies within conversation analysis have shown, an important focus for the demonstration of receipt and related interactional work is in "next turn," the utterance immediately following a prior. It is also found that a speaker actually within the course of an utterance may orient to the behavior of a coparticipant(s) in order to determine whether and how he or she is attending to what is being said. In this chapter I wish to explore the way in which a speaker may elicit a display of recipiency from a coparticipant and the way in which a display of recipiency is itself elicitive. By exploring the relationship between recipiency and speech I hope to cast a little light on the nature of sustaining involvement in social interaction.[1]

This chapter is drawn from a study concerned with nonvocal communication in social interactions. The study was funded by the (British) Social Science Research Council, HR/5148 and HR. I should like to express my gratitude to the late emeritus Professor P. S. Byrne and Professor D. H. H. Metcalfe for their support in the investigations and all those who cooperated in the research project.

I should like to express my thanks to Charles Goodwin, John Heritage, Gail Jefferson, Emanuel Schegloff, Anita Pomerantz, and Rod Watson for their extensive comments on earlier presentations, drafts, or sections of the materials examined in this study. Gail Jefferson should be especially mentioned for her detailed notes on a previous draft. I have not attempted to acknowledge their contributions in detail but they permeate the study. For the many problems that remain in the analysis, I alone am responsible. I should also like to thank Stephen Rigby of the University of Manchester for his invaluable technical assistance.

The examples in this chapter are drawn from videotape recordings of naturally occurring professional–client interactions in particular medical consultations. The data were gathered as part of a research project supported by the (British) Social Science Research Council concerned with the social organization of speech and body movement in face-to-face interaction in medical settings. The discussion is focused on a detailed examination of a number of brief transcribed segments drawn from this corpus of data.[2]

<u>Example 1. Transcript 1</u>

```
1        (door opening)
2        (0.5)
3    D: Hello
4        (2.3)
5    D: Mohammed Oola?
6    P: Yes
7    D: Yes could you sit down (.) please
8        (7.3)
9    D: What can I do for you?
10   P: °hhh (0.2) um:: (0.7) um: last week in
11       our::::fff holiday (0.7)
```

The patient enters, and a greeting is followed by a sequence in which the identity of the patient is confirmed. The doctor then asks the patient to sit. A (7.3)-second silence ensues followed by the doctor producing a turn at talk, an utterance that begins the consultation proper, the topic-initiating turn (line 9).[3] As the patient enters, he moves across the room and sits in a chair that is directly facing the doctor. Through these actions the patient establishes copresence with his coparticipant. Copresence is established approximately (5.0) seconds into the (7.3)-second silence (line 8). While the patient establishes copresence he only briefly glances at the doctor and the doctor reads the medical record cards. The particular area of interest is the latter half of the (7.3)-second silence and the topic-initiating turn (line 9).

A more detailed transcript will be helpful.

Example 1. Transcript 2

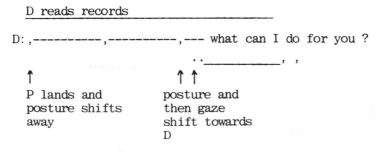

Approximately (2.3) seconds before the topic-initiating turn the patient lands in the chair and moves posturally backward away from the doctor. As he lands, the patient briefly glances at the doctor, who is reading the records, and turns away. The patient then moves posturally forward, not directly toward the doctor, but to one side. During this move forward the patient gazes away from the doctor. The patient then moves posturally backward; again he does not look at the doctor. The doctor continues to read. The patient then moves posturally forward, directly toward the doctor. As the patient moves forward he brings his gaze upon the doctor. Immediately following the patient's movement forward and his shift of gaze toward the doctor, the doctor produces the topic-initiating turn.[4] Copies of photographs of these movements and others referred to in this chapter are available on request.[5]

Throughout the (7.3)-second silence and the topic-initiating turn the doctor reads the records. The occurrence of the topic-initiating turn is not responsive to the completion of that activity. Moreover, by (5.0) seconds within the (7.3)-second silence the patient has established copresence with the doctor; he has completed the actions that enable him to display to his co-interactant availability or readiness to start the consultation proper. The doctor does not immediately respond to the patient's display of availability. The situation, at least toward the last (2.3) seconds of the (7.3)-silence, is one of free-floating opportunity, where the patient is available and the doctor could initiate talk on topic throughout a range of locations.

I wish to refer to a person's presentation of him/herself, through gaze and sometimes posture, directly toward a co-interactant as a display of recipiency. A display of recipiency can be contrasted with a display of availability where actors present themselves as available for interaction, but specifically do not point their gaze and perhaps posture directly at the coparticipant. In example (1) the actual production of the topic-initiating turn by the doctor, within an environment that until recently was one of free-floating opportunity, occurs immediately preceding the patient's gaze and postural shift directly toward the doctor. The patient's display of recipiency and the doctor's utterance are in immediate juxtaposition. The patient's display of recipiency appears to occasion the doctor's turn at talk.

Within our corpus of data, which includes hundreds of videotape recordings of professional–client interactions, there are few cases in which talk on topic does not occur following the completion of the activities of the participants establishing copresence. As in example (1) often a lengthy silence follows the preliminaries (such as greetings and identity checks, etc.), and the beginning of talk on topic. Either a display of availability or a display of recipiency can serve to mark the completion of establishing copresence and readiness for talk on topic. However, whereas a display of availability serves as a pre-initiating activity providing an environment for the occurrence of a range of actions, a display of recipiency specifically initiates a sequence. The former leaves the coparticipant open to decide when to begin, the latter declares an interest in starting at some specific point. The following data also contain a display of recipiency.

Example 2. Transcript 1

```
1    P: kn kn
2    D: Come:in::
3       (0.3)
4       (door opens)
5    P: (He⌐llo there)
6    D:    ⌊hello
7       (0.7)
8    D: Mississ Hodson
9       (.)
10   P  Yes::
11      (2.7)
12   D: Like to take a seat
13      (1.5)
14   D: Howav:: you bee:n:
```

The example is again drawn from an opening sequence of a doctor–patient consultation. The patient knocks on the door, enters, and then walks across the room and sits in a chair near the doctor. As the patient establishes copresence, she and the doctor exchange greetings, confirm her identity, and arrange to sit. The area of particular interest is the (1.5)-second silence (line 13) and the topic-initiating turn (line 14).

A transcript including nonvocal components is necessary.

Example 2. Transcript 2

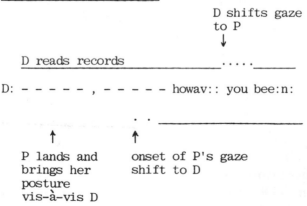

```
                                    D shifts gaze
                                    to P
                                    ↓
        D reads records                    . . . . ._____

D: - - - - - , - - - - - howav:: you bee:n:

                          . .
                                  _____

            ↑              ↑
        P lands and    onset of P's gaze
        brings her     shift to D
        posture
        vis-à-vis D
```

The patient lands in the chair approximately (.8) within the (1.5)-second silence. The doctor is reading the records. The doctor only brings her gaze from the records to the patient during her topic-initiating turn (line 14). As the patient lands, she moves posturally backward; she is looking down, away from the doctor. As she moves posturally backward, the patient's postural orientation is brought vis-à-vis the doctor. During this process, approximately (.3) seconds prior to the doctor's turn (line 14) the patient begins to bring her gaze upon the doctor. Immediately and sequentially following the arrival of the patient's posture and gaze toward the doctor, the doctor produces the utterance (line 14).

As in the previous example, an interactant, during a silence, presents herself, through posture and gaze vis-à-vis a co-interactant. Interactants display recipiency to their co-interactant and thereby elicit an action, a turn at talk. The display of recipiency is, in these cases, the first action in a two-action sequence, a sequence in which body movement elicits speech.

The following example is drawn from a discussion in a consultation concerning the troubles of the patient. We enter the data as the patient begins to mention the failure of the treatment she has received.

Example 3. Transcript 1

```
35   D: Ye::r:s::  [:
36   P:            [an I jus:t ca:n:t move:: atall now:
37      (0.2) an I: can't sleep at night: en he gave me
38      as:pirins te ta:ke a(t) night:
39      (.)
40   P: °°hhhh
41      (0.2)
42   P: En theyen: jus:t (.) pointless taking them doctor:
43      (1.0)
44   P: Tch
45      (0.5)
46   D: °hhhhhhh right(.)well theres quite alot in tha::t
47      (.) lets:: jus:t: (.) err:: (1.0) give me a moment
48      to recap because: I: haven't seen you before::
```

The doctor does not produce a response to the patient's utterance (lines 36–38), and she continues with the utterance (line 42). As the patient begins to produce the utterance (line 42) she is looking at the doctor, but as she continues she moves her head, a couple of times, away from the doctor. These movements occur with "jus:t" and "taking." Coupled with the intonation contour of the turn, they appear to indicate prospectively that the patient is drawing to the completion of what she wishes to say. The head movements do not seem unlike the movements chronicled by C. Goodwin (1980) that occur just prior to disengagement in

conversation. Following the turn-completing "doctor:" (line 42) a (1.0)-
second silence occurs and then the patient produces "tch," a sort of
clicking sound with the tongue, a vocal shrug. As the patient completes
the turn (line 42), she looks away from the doctor. The doctor is leaning
back in his chair and his face is out of camera at this point. During the
(1.0)-second silence preceding the "tch" the patient stares at the desk at
which she is sitting. She produces "tch" and continues to look away
from the doctor. The doctor produces no response, neither to the prior
turn nor to "tch."

Example 3. Transcript 2

   (D out of camera)

D: ‐ ‐ ‐ ‐ ‐ °hhhhhhh <u>right</u> (.) <u>well</u> theres quite alot

         . . . ._____

      ↑

      onset of gaze shift to D

Approximately (.2) within the (.5)-second silence following "tch," the
patient begins to bring her gaze toward the doctor. Her gaze arrives at
the doctor about (.4) seconds within the (.5)-second silence. Immediately following the arrival of the patient's gaze at the doctor, the doctor
begins an in-breath and produces the turn at talk.

   As in the previous examples, vocalization by an interactant that
breaks the silence systematically occurs immediately following the shift
of gaze and, on occasions, posture to the speaker by a fellow participant.
Moreover, in example (3) the actual vocalization that occurs immediately
following the display of recipiency is a lengthy in-breath " °hhhhhhh."
It is followed by "right(.)" and a turn that actually postpones the doctor
providing an immediate answer/solution to the patient's troubles. The
lengthy in-breath provides the doctor with the ability to demonstrate to
the patient that he is responding to the display of recipiency, while
concurrently allowing him to delay his actual talk. The in-breath demonstrates the import of what the patient has done in producing the display
of recipiency.

   In this example, as with the previous two, a body movement, a display of recipiency is employed by one actor to elicit action from another.
In the cases discussed above the display of recipiency occurs within an
environment of continuous opportunity to speak by either participant.
Within the silence the display of recipiency fixes a point, locates a mo-

ment, at which one actor attempts to elicit an action from a coparticipant. The display of recipiency is sequentially implicative for an action by a coparticipant; it breaks the environment of continuous opportunity, and declares an interest in having some particular action occur in immediate juxtaposition with the display.

In the examples examined above the display of recipiency is the first action in a two-action sequence, body movement eliciting speech. In those cases it provides a systematic technique for the introduction of talk in silence. However, the display of recipiency does not necessarily elicit speech in response; for example, declinations to a display of recipiency are often produced through nonvocal action.[6] Moreover, the display of recipiency can occur in sequential positions other than a first action to a second; body movement eliciting speech does not exhaust its interactional possibilities.

At the beginning of the essay it was suggested that an actor, during the course or following the production of a particular activity, has an interest in whether and how it is received by coparticipants. Receipt can be illustrated vocally or nonvocally as with a display of recipiency. Hence even within the production of an actual activity, for example, a turn at talk, an actor may search for an indication that the potential recipient is attending to what is being said.

As with some of the earlier examples, the following extract is from an opening sequence.

Example 4. Transcript 1

```
1   P: kn kn kn
2   D: Yes:: cum in:::::
3      (1.5)
4   D: Hello
5   P: Hello
6      (3.4
7   D: Err: : (.) howah things: Mister (0.6) Arma n?
8   P:                                        Erm:::
9      (0.5) all:right (.) I just err:: (1.0) cum to:
10     (0.7) have a look you know about err::: (0.7)
11     heerrr: (0.4) have you got any information from
12     hos:pital:
13  D: No::: (0.3) I don't think so (0.3) urm:::
```

As the patient enters the room the doctor is reading the medical record cards. The doctor glances briefly towards the patient at the start of the topic-initiating turn (line 7), but by the completion of the turn the doctor is back reading the records. The doctor continues to read the records until "have a look you know" (line 10) when he looks at the patient. By "err:::" (line 10), the doctor is again reading the records.

Following his demonstrable receipt of the doctor's topic-initiating turn with "erm:::" (line 8), the patient continues following a (.5)-second pause with "all:right (.) I just err::" (line 9). The continuation of the turn with "all:right . . ." occurs precisely at the point at which the patient lands in the chair. Turn continuation is engaged following the completion, by the patient, of the activity of establishing copresence, with his co-interactant;[7] "erm:::" (line 8) allows the patient to show receipt of the doctor's turn and delay in producing an immediate response. It allows the patient to hold the floor until he had completed the activity of establishing copresence.

As the patient continues with his reply, his turn at talk is fraught with perturbations. There are a number of lengthy pauses, for example, "(1.0)," "(.7)," and "(.7)," and word stretches "err::," "err:::," and "heerrr:." These perturbations are perhaps not unrelated to recipiency.

A transcript including nonvocal components is helpful.

Example 4. Transcript 2

```
                   sharp postural
                   shift away
                        ↓


       _____
_____,   ._____  , ,     _____
P: cum to: - - - - - - - - have a look you know about err::::

                 .  _____  , ,
                        ↑
                   onset of D's
                   gaze shift
                   towards P
```

Transcript (2) begins actually within the patient's reply, at "cum to:" (line 9). Even within the turn up to this point there are a number of perturbations, including the lengthy pause of (1.0) second prior to "cum to:." Throughout the turn until this point, the doctor, the recipient of the patient's speech, is reading the records. Following "cum to:" the patient pauses once more, the reply still incomplete. As we enter the pause, which lasts for (.7) seconds, the patient's recipient continues to read. During "cum to:" and the patient is gazing toward the doctor. Approximately (.1) into the (.7)-second pauses the patient turns away from the doctor. He returns his gaze to the doctor approximately (.3)

within the (.7)-second pause, and then (.2) later turns away from the
doctor once more.

As the patient turns away from his recipient for the first time within
the pause, he begins to cross his legs. As the patient begins to turn away
for the second time in the pause he produces a sharp, sudden posture
shift backward, away from the doctor.

Immediately following the start of the patient's posture shift backward, actually during the postural movement, the doctor turns from the
records to the patient. As the doctor turns his gaze toward the patient,
the patient begins to turn back toward the doctor. The doctor's gaze
arrives at the patient approximately (.6) seconds within the (.7) pause.
Immediately following the arrival of the doctor's gaze at the patient, the
patient begins to speak, continuing his turn.

The patient's turn continuation with "have a look you know about
err:::" appears to be sensitive to the speaker's[8] receipt of his recipient's
gaze. The doctor's gaze shift, from the records to the patient, displays
recipiency in a way not dissimilar to the displays of recipiency discussed
in the previous examples. The doctor's gaze shift, his display of recipiency, elicits speech from the patient, in this case, turn continuation.

Unlike the previous examples, however, the display of recipiency
does not intervene in an environment of the "floating opportunity," but
rather occurs immediately following a posture shift by the patient. The
juxtaposition of the two actions, coupled with the speaker's absence of a
recipient, suggests a systematic relationship between the two actions.
The display of recipiency is responsive to the posture shift, just as the
patient's continuing turn is coordinated with the display of recipiency. It
is as if the speaker elicits the display of recipiency so as to enable him to
continue talk.

A little further evidence for the significance of the display of recipiency to the patient's speech can be discerned from a slightly more detailed
examination of the patient's turn up and till the next pause.

Example 4. Transcript 3

    P gazes at D

     ↓
 · · _____

P: have a look you know about err::: (0.7) ...

    _____, , ,
                    ↑
                  D turns
                  back to the
                  records

The speaker's turn remains unperturbed until he loses the recipient's gaze. At the end of the word "about," the recipient, the doctor, turns away from the patient and reads the records. As the recipient begins to turn away the speaker produces "err:::" followed by a (.7)-second silence. The speaker's turn becomes perturbed immediately following the loss of the display of recipiency.

The (.7)-second pause is broken by the patient producing "heerrr:" (line 10). A transcript including nonvocal components will be helpful.

Example 4. Transcript 4

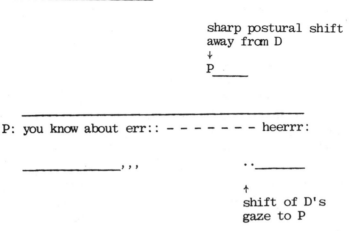

Immediately preceding the speaker uttering "heerrr:" the recipient shifts his gaze from the records to the patient. The patient's speech is responsive to the display of recipiency produced by the doctor. Interestingly the speech component produced by the patient is content free and appears to project that the speaker wishes to retain the floor and produce further talk, but is delaying the production of that talk; "heerrr:" delicately displays response to the elicit, produced through the display of recipiency by the doctor.

Like the previous instance, the display of recipiency does not occur anywhere within the pause, but rather immediately follows a nonvocal action produced by the patient. Approximately (.5) within the (.7)-second pause, the patient begins a sharp postural movement away from the doctor, a movement not unlike his previous postural shift. As the patient begins his movement, the doctor looks up, his gaze shift occurring within the postural movement. And, as has been suggested, on the arrival of the doctor's gaze at the patient, the patient utters "heerrr:."[9] The patient's postural shift elicits the display of recipiency from the doctor, just as the display of recipiency elicits talk.

Thus the second instance in transcript (4) is not unlike the first, in transcript (2). In both instances the speaker who does not have the gaze of his recipient pauses in the production of the turn, prior to turn completion. Within the pause the speaker produces a body movement that elicits the gaze, a display of recipiency, from the coparticipant. The display of recipiency consequently elicits further talk, turn continuation, from the speaker. Hence the actual construction of the turn at talk is sensitive to whether the speaker has the gaze of the recipient. Moreover, the speaker actually within the construction of the turn at talk has a systematic nonvocal technique to allow him to elicit the gaze of the recipient.

It can perhaps be suggested as it is elsewhere (Argyle and Cook 1976, C. Goodwin 1981a) that a significant aspect of gaze in social interaction is that the direction of an actor's gaze allows others to infer the focus of the actor's attention. So that a speaker, faced with a recipient who is looking at records, may infer that he or she is reading rather than listening to the talk of the speaker. This is not to suggest that speakers desire the gaze of their recipient throughout the talk they produce, but rather at certain junctures a recipient's gaze may be crucial to the construction of the talk; cf. C. Goodwin 1981a and Kendon 1977.

Unlike the previous examples, in example (4) the display of recipiency is a second action in a three-action sequence. The body movement elicits the display of recipiency and the display of recipiency elicits talk. Thus we find a systematic relationship not only between a nonvocal action (the display of recipiency) and a vocal action (turn continuation), but also between a nonvocal action such as body movement and a following nonvocal action, such as a display of recipiency.

A display of recipiency that occurs as a first action provides a relatively broad collection of opportunities to the respondent. It does not strictly delimit the action type appropriate in response. A display of recipiency that occurs in response to a preceding action that is sequentially implicative for a next action may delimit the appropriate response more strictly. In example (4) the display of recipiency elicits speech that can be heard as an appropriate continuation of the speaker's preceding talk. The display of recipiency is elicited so as to enable turn continuation by the speaker, not to provide the speaker with a broad range of optional action types.

If it is correct to suggest that body movement may be employed to elicit recipiency within a turn at talk, then it is only one among a number of strategies a speaker may use to achieve the gaze of his co-interactant. C. Goodwin (1981a) has investigated how a speaker may employ perturbations in the actual production of a turn at talk to summon the gaze of a hearer. In discussing perturbation Goodwin refers to, among other phenomena, pauses and word stretches. In example (4), the elicitation of recipiency through body movement occurs following previous attempts using vocal techniques. Both pauses and word stretches occur prior to the body movement–gaze elicitation. Moreover, the elicits through body movement not only occur following prior perturbations but also occur within actual perturbations, namely, pauses. In this example, therefore, gaze elicitations through body movement have an interesting relationship to other techniques in gaze elicitation. In this case body movement, is perhaps an escalated technique, a technique that proves successful where others have failed. Also, the body movement is separated from the talk; it fits snugly within the pauses.

One feature in the summons of gaze through perturbation is that the speaker is often gazing toward the recipient. In the elicitation of gaze through body movement this is not necessarily the case. In both instances in example (4), the speaker is looking away from the recipient in soliciting his gaze through body movement. The speaker only returns his gaze to the recipient, after the recipient's gaze begins to turn to the speaker. In the first instance in example (4) it intuitively feels that the actual gaze shift by the speaker away from his recipient, concurrent with the posture shift, works with that postural movement to elicit the display of recipiency from the doctor.

The elicitation of gaze, or a display of recipiency, through body movement, however, does not necessarily follow previous vocal attempts or occur only where the speaker's gaze is away from the recipient. Gaze elicitations through body movement occur in a range of interactional locations, for example, turn beginnings, in nonperturbed turns, and even outside talk.[10] They can also occur where the actor who is eliciting the gaze is or is not looking at his potential recipient.

Let us consider a rather different example.

Example 5. Transcript 1

```
1    S: and: I: w:ill
2       (0.3)
3    M: Um::
4    S: See him an tell him ⌈about this: interview: that=
5    M:                     ⌊(              )
6    S: =we've had
7    M: Yes
8    S: together::  °hhhhh I think he: will be able to:
9       prescri:be something ⌈°hhh
10   M:                       ⌊yes
```

11 S: <u>Which</u> <u>Elizabeth</u>: (0.6) Elizabeth: (0.3) youll have
12   to ta::ke °hh (0.3) regularly without let up

This example is drawn from a three-party conversation among a social
worker, a client, and the client's mother. The client is a teenage girl
whom the mother claims is depressed and being difficult at home. The
client, Elizabeth, has said little and spent much of the interview staring
at the floor. The bulk of the conversation has been between the social
worker and the mother, though the social worker has made a number of
attempts to stop the mother speaking and encourage Elizabeth to discuss her problem.

We enter the interview towards its end. The social worker is discussing what might be done to deal with Elizabeth's difficulties. As the social
worker begins to describe the treatment (line 8) that she is going to
recommend for Elizabeth, Elizabeth is still staring at the floor while the
social worker addresses her remarks to the client's mother. It is of course
Elizabeth for whom the treatment is recommended, and at "something"
(line 9) the social worker shifts her gaze from the mother to Elizabeth.

A more detailed transcript, including nonvocal components is necessary.

Example 5. Transcript 2

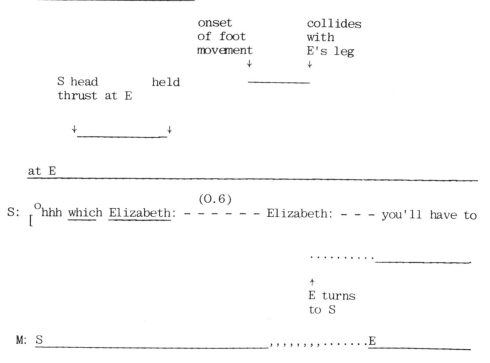

This extract begins immediately preceding the turn transition relevance point (cf. Sacks, Schegloff, and Jefferson 1974) at "something" line 9 (see transcript [1]). The social worker in-breaths " °hhh" to enable her to continue and the mother overlaps the in-breath with "yes" (line 10). With her gaze now directed to Elizabeth, who continues to stare at the floor, the social worker utters loudly *"which Elizabeth:"* (line 11). Coupled with *"which Elizabeth:"* the social worker produces a head thrust pointed at Elizabeth. The head thrust is organized to co-occur with the speech.

The speech *"which Elizabeth:"* coupled with the head thrust appears to be designed not only to mark, both to Elizabeth and the mother, that the proceeding turn is for Elizabeth, but also to elicit some response from Elizabeth. The social worker, in the way she produces these actions, appears to be eliciting a response from Elizabeth, a display of recipiency, prior to proceeding with the turn. Elizabeth continues to stare at the floor, and (.6) of a second later, following no response from Elizabeth, the social worker utters "Elizabeth:" (line 11). "Elizabeth:," like *"which Elizabeth:,"* is hearable as attempting to elicit a response from Elizabeth. (.3) of a second following the second attempt to solicit a response from Elizabeth, the social worker produces a turn specifically for Elizabeth, giving her instructions concerning the treatment.

The production of the utterance "you'll have to ta::ke . . ." (lines 11 and 12) occurs immediately following the arrival of Elizabeth's gaze at the social worker. Towards the end of the (.3)-second pause following "Elizabeth:," the client displays recipiency to the social worker, and the social worker in response, produces the utterance. As in the earlier examples, the immediate juxtaposition of a display of recipiency and speech, nonvocal and vocal action, occurs.

On first inspection of the data, the audiovisual record, one assumes that the display of recipiency by Elizabeth is produced with consideration to the second vocal elicit by the social worker, "Elizabeth:." However, the onset of the gaze movement by Elizabeth occurs rather late in the production of the second vocal elicit, at the "e" in "Elizabeth:." Moreover, the client has failed to respond to a previous vocal solicitation that was both louder and coupled with a head thrust. Closer examination of the data leads one to notice that the display of recipiency by Elizabeth may not be immediately responsive to the vocal elicits but rather a nonvocal action.

Toward the end of the (.6) pause, prior to "Elizabeth:" the social worker begins a leg movement. She moves her leg toward Elizabeth and thrusts her foot on Elizabeth's leg. The social worker kicks her client.

The social worker's foot lands on her client's leg at the "a" of "Elizabeth:." Immediately following the kick the client starts her gaze movement toward the social worker.

In this example, like the former, the speaker awaits the display of recipiency prior to producing further talk. Further talk is coordinated with, and produced in response to, a nonvocal action, the display of recipiency. Furthermore the speaker elicits the display of recipiency from the co-interactant through body movement. Speech relies upon the interactional coordination of nonvocal and vocal actions.

The body movement–gaze elicitation in example (5) is unlike the previous example inasmuch as it does not follow prior gaze elicitation through perturbations. There is, however, a prior failed attempt at eliciting recipiency from the co-interactant, but unlike in example (4) it is produced through an explicit naming of the candidate recipient.

In multiparty interaction, as in example (5), a speaker may have an interest not in gaining a display of recipiency from any of the co-interactants, but in achieving recipiency from a particular participant. The social worker, for instance, wishes to establish Elizabeth as the recipient of the instructions. Certainly a vocal naming, soliciting the recipiency of the co-interactant, is one technique of attempting to establish a particular recipient. Body movement is also recipient selective. The kick is unambiguously for Elizabeth. It selects her as the actor who should provide a display of recipiency. Through body movement the social worker establishes Elizabeth as recipient.

It was mentioned that a problem for the social worker during this interview was to encourage Elizabeth to participate and to reduce the amount the mother spoke. As the social worker goes to kick Elizabeth the mother turns from the social worker to her daughter. The vocal naming and the kick not only allow Elizabeth to see that the social worker is attempting to establish her as recipient, but also publicize this to the coparticipant, the mother. The social worker's actions achieve the cooperation of the mother who not only shifts her gaze to Elizabeth but allows her to speak on her own behalf. Recipient selection requires not only action from the candidate recipient, but also cooperation from the coparticipant(s).

The fact of a social worker kicking her client might seem a somewhat violent if not bizarre solution to the problem of establishing a particular recipient in interaction. Yet the kick successfully elicits a display of recipiency, when other movements might well have failed. Many movements by the speaker, such as the posture shifts in fragment (4) or the various gestures we find in other instances, would likely pass unnoticed by

Elizabeth. The kick is one of the few movements that would enter Elizabeth's field of vision and thereby be noticeable by the candidate recipient even prior to the pain it may have inflicted.[11] The speaker's movement unambiguously selects and establishes Elizabeth as the appropriate recipient to her utterance. The movement can be found to be carefully designed with respect to the circumstances faced by the speaker and the task of the action.

As a number of researchers have shown, for example, Condon and Ogston 1966, 1967; Birdwhistell 1971, and Kendon 1977, within social interaction there is a continual flow of body movement from eye and facial movements to major shifts in postural orientation. Within this flow and the process of nonvocal coordination relatively few movements attract gaze and posture shifts from coparticipants. The elicitation of a display of recipiency requires a particular movement on a particular occasion, a movement that stands out from the environment of goings on and draws the gaze of the coparticipant. Not unlike the way in which a movement can draw a taxi to the curb or attract an auctioneer's attention[12] so the speaker produces a nonvocal action which contrasts with the surrounding flow of movement. Frequently the movement that elicits a display of recipiency alters the spatial arrangements of the interactants and breaks the established rhythm of body movement coordination. In these and a variety of other ways the movement reflexively recasts the local scene, temporarily emerging into the foreground and rendering co-occurring movements into the background.

Given these considerations one might expect the most extraordinary movements to be used to elicit a display of recipiency, yet such actions are rarely used by speakers to attract the attention of the recipient. The movements used to attract a display of recipiency are designed to stand out from the environment of goings on, but not themselves to become the focus of attention. The speaker's nonvocal actions work on behalf of the course of actions with which they occur; they serve to establish a recipient for the speaker's utterance. In this fashion the speaker establishes a recipient who is then placed in a position of response to the utterance; the nonvocal actions of the speaker assist if not establish the sequential implications of the utterance with which they occur. The body movement generates an audience for the vocalization with which it occurs; it is the servant of the utterance with which it occurs. If the speaker were to use more exotic movements, the recipient's attention may well be shifted to the nonvocal action itself rather than the speaker and the utterance. Eliciting a display of recipiency through nonvocal action, without having the movement itself questioned or specifically attended to, allows the speaker to establish a state of mutual involvement if only temporarily without shifting the focus of attention from the topic or business at hand.

In examples (4) and (5) it is found that a speaker coordinates the articulation of an utterance with the nonvocal actions of the coparticipant(s). Either prior to the production of an utterance or actually within its course, the speaker withholds speech until there is evidence to suggest that the coparticipant is prepared to attend. In these and other instances (cf. Heath, forthcoming) the speaker uses a body movement to elicit a shift in orientation by the coparticipant, and as the recipient turns toward the speaker the utterance is begun or continued. Through a body movement, be it a postural shift, kick, gesture, or the like the speaker is able to establish a coparticipant as a recipient and thereby sustain involvement if only temporarily in the talk and topic at hand.

A display of recipiency itself does not leave the local environment untouched. A shift of gaze and, frequently, postural orientation toward another is itself elicitive and can be used to encourage speech. In the examples discussed at the beginning of the chapter we can notice the way in which a display of recipiency is used as a first move, a way of encouraging a co-interactant to begin to speak. In these instances the display of recipiency features in the process of reengaging talk following a lapse, in establishing a focus of mutual involvement. In later examples the display of recipiency is the pivotal action in a three-action sequence, responding to a prior action and eliciting a next.

Thus face-to-face interaction requires a delicate and precise coordination between speech and body movement. Of crucial significance in this process and the maintenance of involvement in interaction is the social organization that provides for sequential relationship between actions and activities be they vocal or nonvocal.

Notes

1. The first part of this chapter, especially the discussions concerning the display of recipiency, draws extensively from Heath (1982a). In investigating how gaze recipiency is solicited it was felt necessary to discuss some of that earlier material.
2. The data extracts employed in this study are taken from videotape recordings of naturally occurring, professional–client interactions. The transcripts employed for the spoken interaction were developed by Gail Jefferson. Details of the orthography may be found in Psathas (1979). The transcription system employed for gaze was developed by Charles Goodwin, and details may also be found in Goodwin (1977, 1981a) and Psathas (1979). Briefly, a

line above the talk refers to the speaker's gaze, a line below, the recipient's. A continuous line means that the speaker and/or the recipient are gazing at each other. A series of dots means that the speaker (and/or recipient) is bringing that gaze vis-à-vis the other party. A series of commas means that they are taking their gaze away. In more than two-party conversations the actual party to whom the gaze is directed is marked with a name. For the convenience of this chapter, I have tracked the gaze above the line during silences if that party is the next speaker, below if he is the next recipient. Silences are marked by the dashes, each dash equals (.1) of a second.

3. A discussion concerning the organization of talk in opening sequences in doctor–patient consultations may be found in Heath (1981). In that paper the discussion focuses upon the movement from opening talk, such as greetings and identity checks, to the start of talk on topic, namely, talk about the patient's trouble. Movement into topic in doctor–patient and other forms of professional–client interaction is typically achieved through the production of a topic-initiating turn spoken by the professional such as "what can I do for you" or "how are you." Such turns mark the movement from opening in to the business at hand. The record cards play a significant role in the organization of the topic-initiating turn and the opening sequence in general; see Heath (1981, 1982b).

4. Analytically it is perhaps interesting to inquire why the patient produces the posture and gaze shift toward the doctor at this particular point. In the data there does not appear to be any specific action by the doctor to which the patient's action is immediately responsive. There is however a slight head movement by the doctor immediately preceding the patient's posture and gaze shift. One wonders whether the patient may have treated this head movement as possibly projecting that the doctor was about to cease reading the records. However, recall that the doctor does actually continue to read.

5. On request the author will be pleased to send a collection of copies of photographs of some of the more significant parts of the data used in this paper. There are photographs for all the data extracts discussed in this chapter. Reading it with the copies of the photographs will greatly aid its comprehension. Please contact the author, at the Department of Sociology, University of Surrey, Guildford, Surrey, England, if copies of the photographs are desired.

6. Nonvocal responses also occur in an acceptance to a display of recipiency. In such cases the nonvocal response is often passing the floor back to the initial recipient to enable him to produce some next action, such as a turn at talk. Some displays of recipiency appear specifically designed to elicit the floor for the initial recipient. In fact, it might be suggested that the cases examined in examples (1) and (2) concern patients eliciting an invitation to report their troubles through a display of recipiency; cf. Heath (1982a).

7. In professional–client and perhaps other forms of social interaction, there is evidence to suggest that actors orient to establishing copresence prior to the beginning of talk on topic. Example (4) perhaps illustrates this orientation, rather clearly. As suggested, the patient receives the topic-initiating turn prior to the completion of the establishing of copresence. He demonstrates receipt of the turn with "erm:::" but only continues talk on topic following the completion of establishing copresence; "erm:::" not only projects further talk to the doctor, but in so doing, allows the patient to hold the floor, establish copresence, and then begin talk on topic. It should be added that example (4) is one of a very few instances, out of a collection of hundreds of hours of audiovisual recordings of various forms of interaction, in which talk

on topic is initiated prior to all parties having established copresence. These issues were discussed in more detail in the author's paper entitled: "Establishing co-presence and the display of the recipiency," which was presented at the German–English Colloquium on Ethnomethodology and Conversational Analysis at the University of Konstanz, 1980. Work is at present being conducted upon these issues.

8. I use the term "speaker" to refer to the patient throughout his production of this turn even when he is not actually speaking. In the pauses it remains the patient who has the floor and is in an incomplete turn and the doctor who is the (candidate) recipient.

9. The "heerrr:" as indicating response to the display does not seem unlike the long in-breath " °hhhhh" in example (3). For a further discussion see Heath (1982a) especially the examination of examples (4) and (5).

10. Examples are waving to a friend across the street, hailing a taxi, or catching the eye of a waitress.

11. In this interview there are a number of instances in which the social worker stretches forth and touches Elizabeth's knee. Some of them are instances of body movement–gaze elicitations. Others are instances of the social worker attempting not only to elicit recipiency from Elizabeth but also to establish her as next speaker. They are different from the cases being discussed in this chapter and they will be mentioned in more detail in Heath (forthcoming).

12. It should be mentioned that it is only a first bid among a possible series of bids by someone for a particular object that may be accomplished through a body movement–gaze elicitation. Subsequent bids may be made through some form of body movement, be it a wave, facial expression, or the notorious wink, but typically second, third, or nth bids for a particular object are actually produced in response to a specific elicitation by the auctioneer to the bidder. However, like other body movement–gaze elicits, the first bid may be designed to stand out in the environment among not only an audience of candidate bidders, but also others actually attempting to make a bid.

12. On some gestures' relation to talk

EMANUEL A. SCHEGLOFF
University of California,
Los Angeles

1

A common understanding of talking holds that at some point a conception or intent is formed in the mind of a speaker or potential speaker to say something or to use some word or construction, and that the talk that is eventually produced is an expression or realization of that intent, with something having occurred between conception and birth (I suppose we might call it "gestation") that converts the intent or conception into the form in which it emerges from the mouth.

This notion of talking has informed the professional literature as well. William James, for example, writes:

> And has the reader never asked himself what kind of a mental fact is his *intention of saying a thing* before he has said it? It is an entirely definite intention, distinct from all other intentions, an absolutely distinct state of consciousness, therefore; and yet how much of it consists of definite sensorial images, either of words or of things? Hardly anything! Linger, and the words and things come into the mind; the anticipatory intention, the divination is there no more. But as the words that replace it arrive, it welcomes them successively and calls them right if they agree with it, it rejects them and calls them wrong if they do not. It has therefore a nature of its own of the most positive sort, and yet what can we say about it without using words that belong to the later mental facts that replace it? The intention *to-say-so-and-so* is the only name it can

The chapter printed here is the same essay as was circulated in preparation for the Conference on Space, Time, and Deixis, organized by the Max Planck Institute in Nijmegen, The Netherlands in June 1978.

I want to thank Richard Fauman for research assistance and the Research Committee of the Academic Senate at UCLA for financial support. I have benefited from the extraordinarily careful reading and comments of Charles Goodwin.

266

receive. One may admit that a good third of our psychic life con- sists in these rapid premonitory perspective views of schemes of thought not yet articulate. (Vol. 1, 1950:253, emphasis in original) Or, later, Heinz Werner's "microgenesis of meaning," although some- what more concerned with reactive situations, speaks to a similar notion in referring to "inner experiences of the semantic sphere of the linguistic forms, that were apparently prior to any specific articulation of the words" (1956:348).

More recently, efforts at constructing "performance models" of speech production follow similar lines. For example, Fromkin (1971:49, 51) pro- poses a model of speech performance that would be consistent with her findings about "speech errors." The model begins with "Stage 1. A 'meaning' to be conveyed is generated," and ends with a stage "where automatic phonetic and phonological rules take over, converting the sequences of segments into actual neuro-motor commands to the muscles in the articulation of the utterance." In between, "generators" of syntac- tic structure, semantic features, intonation contours, the lexicon, and so on operate.

Although there are models available of the speech production pro- cess, empirical work in this area has proven more difficult than work on speech perception. In particular, attention to "naturalistic" materials as input to, or as constraints on, models of speech production has largely focused on speech error data (Fromkin, 1973, 1980), often with the errors detached from the surrounding talk of which they were a part.

In the sort of work I do (on the sequential organization of commonplace interaction and conversation), a topic of interest that has a bearing on these issues is what I will call "projection." That term collects a variety of interests in how and when earlier parts of turns, turn-constructional units like sentences, sequences, whole conversations, and the like adumbrate, foreshadow, or project aspects of possible later productions (sometimes with the consequent intervention of others to circumvent the projected possibility). For turn-constructional units in particular, the notion of a "projection space" is concerned with both the span in which some element of talk is "in play" before being produced, and with the evidence of that which a speaker's turn may make available to its recipient. For example, it appears central to the organization of tightly coordinated turn-transfer from one speaker to a next that aspects of some current turn are projected, and are available to analysis by a recipient/potential-next- speaker before their actual occurrence; for example, the type of turn (question, quotation, disagreement, etc.), and roughly where the turn might come to completion (Sacks, Schegloff, and Jefferson 1974). Another example is afforded by Jefferson's (1973a) discussion of "recognition points," that is, points in the production of a turn at which its recipient can recognize, and display recognition of, what is being done or said before it has actually been done/said, or before the doing/saying has been completed. A particular, and somewhat different, type of interest in projection has motivated the research direction reported here, and I shall try to give an abbreviated account of it.

In recent work on the organization of repair in conversation (cf. Schegloff, Jefferson, and Sacks, 1977; Schegloff 1979b), the initiation of a move to repair something in the preceding talk has been distinguished from other elements of the repair segment, and found subject to its own organization. This research has prompted efforts to specify the first signs in an ongoing flow of talk that repair is upcoming. The operationally critical items we have called "repair initiators." When the repair is initiated by the speaker of the talk being repaired, and in the same turn in which the talk being repaired (henceforth the "repairable" or "trouble-source") occurred, then the most common repair initiators are a "cutoff" (typically a "glottal stop" or "closure" indicated in the transcript by a hyphen) if the repair is initiated while a sound is in progress, or "uh" if not. In the vast majority of cases, the repair initiator is the first sign of the possible occurrence of repair, and is immediately followed by other parts of the repair segment, which are disjunctive with the talk otherwise projected.

However, there are sometimes indications of "trouble ahead" before the actual initiation of repair. Examination of our materials (audio- and videotapes, with detailed transcripts, of a range of mundane, everyday, in-real-life interactions) turned up cases in which a cutoff type of repair initiator is preceded by some "hitch" in the production of the talk. For example, a sound stretch – a prolongation of a sound (marked in the transcript by one or more colons following that sound) – in the talk immediately preceding seems to serve as a harbinger of trouble ahead, without yet displaying the start of a move to deal with that trouble. Such harbingers seem quite clear when they occur just before the initiation of the repair – in the word preceding the one in which the cutoff occurs, or within the two or three preceding words, as in the first two instances below. In (1), the repair initiation at "u-she's" is pre-indicated by the sound stretches on the immediately preceding words "the:re" and "fo:r." In (2), the word-search repair initiated at "uh" is pre-indicated at "na:med" (though this could be treated as itself the initiator of the repair) and further back at "wa:s."[1]

#1   (PB 3-4:6)

Robin: → She hadda wait up the:re fo:r u-she:s been there
             since eight uh'clock this morning'n at six thirty
             she called me.

#2   (Clacia: 17)

Clacia: B't, a-another one theh wentuh school with me
      → wa:s a girl na:med uh, (0.7) w't th' hell wz er
            name. Karen. Right. Karen.

In (3), the trouble which is involved at "theyd- they *do* b- . . ." and in
what follows is preceded by sound stretches at "i:n::" and yet further
back at "fie:ld."

#3   (TG:219-232, simplified)

Bee: Yihknow she really eh-so she said you know,
            theh-ih-she's had experience. 'hh with
            handicap' people she said but 'hh ih-yihknow
     → ih-theh- in the fie:ld.
            (0.2)
Ava: (Mm:.)
Bee: → -thet they're i:n::.yihknow theyd- they do b-
            (0.2) t!'hhhh they try even harduh then
            uhr-yihknow a regular instructor.
Ava: Right.
Bee: 'hhhh to uh instr- yihknow do the class'n
            evr//thing.
Ava: Uh huh.

However, as the last instance suggests, the further back before a cutoff
repair initiator a sound stretch occurs, the more problematic it becomes
whether or not it is a harbinger of the later occurring repair.

     There are specific sources of this "problematicalness." First, sound
stretches themselves are employed as repair initiators (Schegloff, Jefferson, and Sacks, 1977:367). Second, we know that sometimes repair is
initiated by a repair initiator and is then "canceled," that is, the repair
initiator occurs, but no other part of a repair segment follows; rather, the
turn at talk as projected before the repair initiator continues. We may
term these "nonethelesses," to catch the flavor of spotting trouble, stopping the turn-in-progress to address it, but then continuing the turn
"nonetheless." Thus:

#4   (MO: Chicken Dinner)

F: So the park is trucked at thee:: beginning 'a
              the pier, right?

The stretch of "the" could be the initiation of repair, especially in view of
the "error" just made ("park is trucked" instead of "truck is parked");
however, no further repair segment is forthcoming, and the turn's continuation is produced compatible with its projected shape. These two
points – that sound stretches can be repair initiators, and that sometimes
only the repair initiator occurs in a repair segment – make it unclear
whether a sound stretch that occurs well before a later initiated repair is a
pre-indication of that later repair, or whether it is an *independent instance of a
repair-related event*, initiated by a stretch and then canceled. (Of course,
not all sound stretches are repair-related, and this fact further complicates
making a judgment as to whether some particular sound stretch is a pre-
indication of a later repair.

The possibility that a sound stretch or other hitch well before a later
repair is a pre-indication of that later repair suggests a further possibility. As some item enters the "projection space," as it "comes into
play," as it first becomes a specifically planned-for item, if it is sensed or
recognized by speaker as a possible trouble-source (e.g., the exact word
is not available, a difficult sound pattern is involved, how to say it is
unclear, etc.), then a hitch appears in whatever is being produced –
whatever is in the process of being said – *at the moment*. (By momentarily
delaying the point at which the possible trouble-source is to be said, the
possibility is enhanced that the trouble will be solved before that point
arrives. Also, notice is given interactionally of possible trouble ahead.)
Then some hitches would mark the early ("left") boundary of the projection space, which would thereby become "visible." To establish, or
begin to work toward, such an investigation requires, however, some
anterior sense of which "early" hitches are candidates for "early repair
indication" status, and that sense requires some independent estimate
of how far back before the actual appearance of an element of the talk it
can be shown to have been "in play." That is, an independent estimate
of the size of projection space is needed in order to work toward establishing early repair harbingers as another type of evidence on this issue.
In the next section, I will try to show how one sort of independent
estimate can be derived from the organization of gesture.

The particular concerns described above do not exhaust the possible
interest of the projection space. It is, after all, one main arena in which
the machinery of speech production works. It is worth noting that two

different aspects of projection are potentially relevant: (1) when some later produced element of the talk comes into play, and (2) the evidences given and available to recipients, before their actual occurrence, of aspects of some elements of the talk. The two are linked here, by the use of the latter to gain leverage on the former.

2

In the remainder of the chapter I shall be drawing on aspects of the organization of gesture, and hand gestures in particular. It will be useful to mention some general points about hand gesturing as a point of departure.[2]

Hand gesturing is largely, if not entirely, a speaker's phenomenon. With few exceptions, which are themselves orderly and in keeping with this general proposition, hand movements by current nonspeakers are not, and are not seen to be, gestures. They may be/be-seen-to-be what ethologists call "self-grooms," self-manipulations, what Goffman calls "auto-involvements," fidgeting, and the like. I know of three main types of exception: (1) Current nonspeakers who initiate a hand gesture may show themselves thereby to be intending, and incipient, speakers, and the gestures may thus be used as a way of making a move for a turn at talk next (cf. also Duncan 1972), and "now"; this exception does not bear adversely on the larger claim. (2) Gestures may be used "in lieu of" talk, as when others are talking and a current nonspeaker tries to communicate without interrupting. In such cases it appears that the gesturing "nonspeaker" is a sort of covert speaker nonetheless; a simple case is the following, in which new guests are arriving to Pam's back yard while she is facing the opposite direction, and Carney calls attention to them by pointing:[3]

```
#5          (Pre–Auto: 2)

                          o.................a
Pam:        John'n Ca:rm'n A:bbey c'd all ge//t–
Carney:     ((points to direction behind Pam))
Pam:        ((looks over shoulder in direction of
            point))
```

(3) A third type of exception occurs when a current speaker is interrupted, and yields to the interrupter. Such at-that-moment nonspeakers may hold a gesture that was in progress at the point of interruption to show that they consider their turn still in progress and intend to resume after the interruption. In the following fragment, the guest is in the

midst of a hand gesture when she withdraws from an overlap with
"mother" at line 6:

```
#6              (MO: Chicken Dinner)  Gesture: guest has hands in
                front of her on table with palms facing each
                other but slightly facing up and "baton"ing
                together at the marked points of stress in the
                talk

Guest:          I've never thought about how it's done.=        1
                o.........................
                =I thought they just set the cameras=I          2
                                                                3
                ┌mean-┐
                [                                                
Father:            In    credible                               4
                (.)                                             5
                                                    h........
Guest:             I have néver (thou::ght)                     6
                [[
Mother:            (         ) all that- all   that cable       7
                ..1.....................................
                'n what if you got the wrong end when           8
                ........................
                you get where yer going.                        9
                h......................
Guest:          It never entered my mind.                       10
                (0.3)                                           11
                o...............
Guest:          'hhh I mean I never- when I watch (.)           12
                any kind of thing on television ...             13
```

```
1= Guest moves frozen gesture to slightly more "palms up"
   position, as if responding "I don't know" to prior
   talk unit by mother (ending with "all that cable"),
   and then holds that position until next marked onset.
```

The hand gesture the guest is in as she "drops out" of the overlap with
"mother" is frozen throughout the mother's talk, and through her response to the mother at line 10, and is remobilized only when the guest
resumes (line 12) the turn ("I mean I never") which was implicated in
the interruption. For much of this duration, she is not talking, but the
import of her holding the gesture is that she retains a claim to "speakership."
    None of these three classes of exception requires substantial revision

of the general rule that gesturing is a speaker's activity. Indeed, pictorial artists have long known that, in depicting a group of persons, they could indicate that, and which, one was talking by showing one person in mid-gesture. This close relationship between speakership and gesturing with the hands does not extend in quite the same way to other gesturing body parts, like the head.

The connection between speakership and hand gesture recommends the possibility that hand gestures are organized, at least in part, by reference to the talk in the course of which they are produced. Examination of video materials of everyday, naturally occurring interaction shows this organization to be the case. Various aspects of the talk appear to be "sources" for gestures affiliated to them. For example, hand gestures may be orderly and organized relative to the "stress" or "beat" organization of the talk, relative to lexical components of the talk, relative to the type of turn they occur in or some type of action done by the talk in a turn, relative to repair operations in the talk, and so on. Here, I will discuss only the first two aspects, with the focus on the second.

One class of gestures has as its primary organization the co-incidence of its "thrust" (its major energy pulse) or "acme" (its point of maximum extension) with a, or the, major stress or beat of the turn-constructional-unit (e.g., sentence) in which it occurs. The recurrence of this co-incidence is available to relatively casual inspection of video materials, and it has motivated the use of on-stress occurrence as a typological criterion in the professional literature (e.g., in Ekman and Friesen 1972). That this co-incidence is an organized achievement and not "mere coincidence," that it is a product of an organized effort and not a byproduct of some otherwise-focused organization, is most readily evident in two sorts of cases. One is when a series of stresses occur in close succession and have a series of gestures successively co-incident with them, as in fragments (7)–(10) (in which "´" marks the thrust of a gesture, and underlining marks stress in the talk):

#7   (Three Sisters)

S: I mean it's like <u>Ed</u>die says, (1.0) as t<u>í</u>me
           goes on it gets w<u>ó</u>rse 'n w<u>ó</u>rse 'n w<u>ó</u>rse 'n
           w<u>ó</u>rse

#8   (Salv. Army)

C: ... We had s<u>íx</u> f<u>óot</u> h<u>ígh</u>: s<u>nów</u>drifts.

```
#9              (MO:  Chicken Dinner)

F:              ... hhh an' they ca:rry o(h)ne b(h)oth

                ways.
```

```
#10             (MO:Chicken Dinner)

                            c............ ´
F:              ... What I'm saying is then the peacock

                feáthers chá:nge cólor because we put eh-

                different colors ...
```

The other occurs when the gesture is released from a held or prepared position. For example, the gesturing limb is moved to a "cocked" position (this movement not being seen as a gesture but as a preparation for one) and is held there; such a holding can be sustained or broken at various points. A release of the gesture from the cocked position so that its thrust or acme comes "on the beat" displays a designed and organized effort to achieve that co-incidence.

```
#11             (Auto Disc: 03:05)
                        o.........................
Mike:           ... settin there en 'e takes iz helmet

                c......t....
                off 'n clunk it goes on top a' the car ...
```

```
#12             (MO:Chicken Dinner)

                c...............................t
Guest:          Okay you have the male end for the trucks,
```

```
#13             (MO:  Chicken Dinner)

                            h.............t
Guest:          ... or:: (0.7) does he:: (0.8) particularly

                c.........t
                like the Washington tee shirt.
```

(Also, cf. [10].) This is especially striking when a momentary failure of coordination occurs and the co-incidence threatens to be missed. Then, an imminent gesture may be stopped and recoordinated with the talk so as to be delivered on the stress, as in the following fragment:

#14   (Auto Disc: 03:05) Gesture involves hand
               mimicking grasping substantial object, forearm
               raised in backswing prior to hitting down.

                                              o..
Mike: ... was up on the back of his pi̱ckup

              c   l   t........a
               truck with a,   (0.4) with a ja̱:ck

l = starts thrust, stops short and re-cocks.

"On-stress" organization can be the primary or sole organization for a
gesture which is thereby "affiliated" to the talk component on which the
stress fails. As we shall see, on-stress organization can also operate as a
secondary ordering principle for gestures otherwise organized in the
first place. On-stress organization aims at a version of simultaneity;
there are relevant temporal relationships, and relevant relationships between talk and gesture other than the temporal.

Another class of gestures I will term "iconic." These are gestures
whose shape links them to lexical components of the talk either seman-
tically (i.e., the shape that the gesture describes depicts a/the "meaning" or referent of a word)[4] or by word class (e.g., "locatives"). I will
work only with the most transparent iconic gestures, ones that, to my
eye and mind, require no text or explanation to link them to some
component of the talk.

Two occurrences are necessary for the composition of an iconic gesture: a bit of movement and a lexical component relative to which this
movement is depictive. Although iconic gestures are sometimes co-incident with their affiliated word(s) (as in fragment [9], which is iconic in
"both ways"),[5] for the most part the two occur in a regular order. The
gesture – both its onset and its acme or thrust – precedes the lexical
component it depicts, sometimes being released from a cocked or held
position to do so.

#15   (Staff Meeting) Gesture is circular motion of
               hand articulated around wrist; "hold" is
               midway between highest and lowest points of
               circle. Lexical Affiliate is "rotating."

                       o..................................
Brown: ... y'know we were rotating people in the

               ....h...
               office so th't it was o̱pen

#16   (Staff Meeting, directly following #15) Gesture
      is resumption (from #15) of circular motion
      until hand is at highest point of circle, where
      it is held with fingers pointing up. Lexical
      Affiliate is "up."

```
              .h..o.....h......r...
Brown:        `hhh b't nobody came u:p
```

#17   (MO: Chicken Dinner) Gesture is motion up and
      down of right hand with forefinger extended for
      two full cycles. Lexical Affiliate is
      "vertically."

```
                                o.....
F:            ... it u:setuh look like a sto:plight.

              ...................................
              B'cuz we usetuh use it vertically a lot.
```

#18   (Auto Disc: 13:30) Gesture is extension of
      forefinger. Lexical affiliate is "first."

```
                           o........a.....r.....hm
Gary:         ... he took t'the-(0.4) he gotta first down
              et uh ...
```

#19   (Salv. Army) Gesture involves right arm with
      hand open being extended straight up over
      head and held, then retracted by closing hand
      in "grasp" and lowering arm. Lexical affiliate
      is "reach" or "reach God."

```
W:            ... If I go tuh church mosta the ti:me, en

              `hh if I do all these goo:d things, (.)

              o......a....r........hm
              `hh maybe I'll rea:ch God,
```

The critical property of iconic gestures for the purposes of this chapter is
that they are pre-positioned relative to their lexical affiliates, achieving
their affiliation by means other than co-occurrence with them.

  The organizational design of this pre-positioning is further displayed
in another property of many iconic gestures. They are over before their
lexical affiliate is produced. In most cases, the gesture at least begins its
breakup or decay or retraction before production of the lexical affiliate,
as in the following (and cf. also fragments [16] and [19]):

#20   (MO: Chicken Dinner) Gesture is screwing
      motion; after end of that gesture, hands go

outward with thumbs pointing outward.
Lexical affiliate is "screw"; second gesture
may have "adapt" as lexical affiliate.

```
         o...............................
F:       =y'(h)kno(h)w th(h)et th(h)ey haveta

         o.......
         screw on, `HHH to adapt
```

Note that the iconic gesture here is a repeating screwing motion, one that could be ended earlier or extended further with no change in its "shape." It is stopped just before its lexical affiliate. (On its lexical affiliate, a further gesture is enacted that may well be designed to depict "adapt" in the electronic sense.) Similarly, in fragment [16], the gesture involves a held limb, a hold that could as well be broken earlier or later; it begins its decay before its lexical affiliate.

Furthermore, some iconic gestures not only begin their decay before their lexical components, they end before them. One way gestures can have their endings marked is by the return of the gesturing limb to the position from which it departed at the onset of the gesture – to "home position" (cf. Schegloff, Sacks, and Roberts 1975). A great many iconic gestures end with a return to home, some before production of their lexical affiliate, and in spite of immediate redeparture into another gesture, as in fragment (21).

```
#21          (Auto Disc: 03:15)  Gesture as follows: with
             right elbow planted on table and forearm
             extending upward, hand describes circular
             motion articulated at wrist as preparatory
             phase or "windup," and forceful downward thrust
             of hand as gesture.  Lexical affiliate is
             "down."  All markings refer to Mike.

Mike:        So they all // go dow//n
Gary:        A:ll
Gary:        All show
             (0.2)
             o.................
Carney:       Yeah, th//ey all,=
             ......t..
Mike:        They all-
             c.......
Gary:        =hn-//-hn:
             ....t      hm          o........
```

```
Mike:        They all go down th//ere,= No, some-
             somebody
```

The pre-positioned placement of iconic gestures may, thus, be found in
the pre-affiliate occurrence of the gesture's onset, thrust or acme, decay
onset, or termination at "home," although not all of these features are
present in every iconic gesture.

It is the property of pre-positioning that raises the possibility that
iconic gestures (and other pre-positioned gestures that are otherwise
linked to affiliates in the talk) might shed light on the extent of the
projection space. If the gesture is depictive of a particular element of the
talk, it is selected or constructed by reference to the particulars of that
element.[6] If it occurs before the element is said, then it can be proposed
that the element (e.g., lexical item) involved is "in play" – is in the
"projection space" – at least as early as the thrust/acme or perhaps even
the onset of the gesture selected or constructed by reference to it. Pre-
positioned gestures, therefore, potentially offer a minimum estimate of
the size of the projection space. The projection space extends back from
the production of the lexical affiliate "at least" to the acme, thrust, or
onset of its depicting gesture.

How far back, then, does the projection space extend? I would like to
begin to address that question on another body of materials. Before
turning to them, however, I want to note that the projection space may
not be "linear" with respect to the actually produced talk, and that for
that reason the appropriate way of talking about it may not be in measurement units that assume linearity, such as milliseconds. Rather, organizational units indigenous to the production of talk may be involved
– versions of what we have elsewhere termed "turn-constructional
units" (Sacks, Schegloff, and Jefferson 1974). Consider the following
fragment, in which the gesture involves both forefingers pointing to the
speaker's temples:

```
#22      (MO: Chicken Dinner)  Gesture has both
         forefingers pointing to speaker's temples.
         Lexical affiliate is "thinks."

                           o...........
F:       Jus' like a cl(h)a:ssic story,='HHH An'

         a..........................r
         now when I go out to a job, yihknow an'
```

```
                    o....a........
'HHH before we run the cable ev'rybody

.............................
thinks, 'hh "fuck the tru:ck."
```

The beginning of the gesture is around the boundary of a constructional unit; its shape – pointing both forefingers to the temples – to me clearly projects think(ing). But "thinks" does not arrive for quite a while, and between the onset of the gesture and the production of its affiliate, the gesture is dropped and then resumed. The dropping and resumption of the gesture occur around the boundaries of an insertion ("yihknow an" to "cable") into the initially projected shape of the turn unit/sentence; an insertion in which the "subject" of the talk gets shifted from "I" to "we" such that the final portion – "fuck the truck" – is attributed to "ev'rybody." Much is going on here, and the gesture is deployed, undeployed, and redeployed in a manner well fitted to the talk and the exigencies of its production. Units of talk construction of some sort, rather than physically standardized time units, would appear to be involved.

3

When references to space, place, or direction occur in conversation, they frequently are accompanied by gestures. Some of these gestures are depictive of the spatial element and are a type of iconic gesture (some were examined in the previous discussion). These are mostly direction terms such as "up," "down," "out," "in," "off," and the like. Others are not depictive in the same way, but are "points"[7] of varying degrees of clarity that occur in turns that contain place and space references of various sorts. Though the relationship is not iconic, these gestures seem affiliated to the place/space talk elements as the iconic gestures are affiliated to their lexical sources. Aspects of the construction of the gesture and its relationship to the talk element follow.

If the place referred to is visually accessible, then the point is in the direction of the referent, as in the following:

```
#23        (Auto Disc: 01:35) Gesture is a point by Gary,
           who is sitting in the yard, to the house.
           Lexical affiliate is "iz room."

Gary:      Whynche go put that up so thet it don't
```

```
                    g//et broke any worse,

                         .


                         .


Gary:               Go put it u//:p.
Curt:               Go on.
                         o...
Ryan:               Uh-WHE-E:RE?
                    .....a  .a  r.......hm
Gary:               Put-nah- In iz roo:m.


#24                 (MO: Chicken Dinner)  Gesture is point by F to
                    the end of the dining table.  Lexical
                    affiliate is "the end uh the table there."

                         o....a..r......hm
F:                  Why:nchu put that 't the end uh the
                    ta:ble there.
```

If the place referred to is not visually accessible, then it appears that the point is not necessarily in a direction selected to be the "actual direction" of the referent relative to the scene of the talk. For example, in segments that I will not display here, different "places" (which happen actually to be in different directions from the talk scene) are accompanied by points in the same direction, and two persons referring to the same place while talking together point in different directions. The behavior of recipients is compatible with this disengagement of gestures from "actual direction"; recipients of the talk rarely look in the direction to which the point is pointing in place-reference–related gestures.

Instead, sectors of local space relative to the speaker (or the gathering) may be identified with some place referred to.[8] Then:

(1) References to different places employ different local space sectors for their associated gestures, as in the following, in which "beginning" and "end" of a pier are marked:

```
#25                 (MO: Chicken Dinner)  Gesture marked at the
                    beginning of the excerpt is a point to the
                    right; the lexical affiliate is "the
                    beginning of the pier."  Gesture marked toward
                    the end of the excerpt is a point to the left;
                    the lexical affiliate is "end of the (pier)."
```

```
            o..c...........t...............
F:          So the park is trucked at thee::

            h...........r........
            beginning uh the pier, right? So

            they can't run the cable on top a'

            the pier, they haveta run the cable

            undernea:th  the pier. Right?
G:          Oh G(h)od
F:          So now yihknow they're (.) they're

            climbing on rafters and jumping

            from rafters, carrying this ca:ble

            that's about the size of a half dollar

            that stretches for maybe a thousand feet.

            `hhh An' they're running out an' running

                               p...........
            out, `hhh `course when they get tuh thee

            .................................
            end uh the (0.2) end uh the (0.2) instead of ...
```

(2) Subsequent references to a "same" place employ the same sector as previously used. (Fragment [26] immediately precedes [25].) Note that left points are used to refer to "on" or "end of" the "pier."[9]

```
#26         (MO:Chicken Dinner) Gesture has several parts:
            first right hand is cocked to the right, but is
            not released; then right hand moves to the left;
            then left hand points to the left. Lexical
            affiliate is "on the pier."

F:          He ran, they went down to the ocean,

            y'know P.O.P., the park,   t//o

                                      o..
            do a commercial, or do a scene.  So

            ....................r......c...............
            they had a video truck, `course parked

                r.......                 l......
            (0.3) ih can't park on the- on.the-

                          p....
            on the- on the pie:r
```

```
G:              Yeah
```

1 = right hand moves to left

(3) An apparent extension of this practice (on which I have only slight evidence) is the identification of a referred-to object or person with some referred-to place to which a point to some space sector is affiliated. Subsequent reference to that person or object is accompanied by a point to the same sector, even if no place reference is included in the subsequent mention; for example:

```
#27          (MO: Chicken Dinner)  Gesture is a point.
             Lexical affiliate is "the truck"

F:           You gotta have the female end for

             the cam'ra,

G:           Oh no::// :

                 o...t...h.....r...
F:           And the ma:le end for the truck
```

Here, "truck" is accompanied by a point to the space sector previously employed for "beginning of the pier" (cf. fragment [25]) with which the parking of the truck was associated.[10]

Place/space related gestures (henceforth "locationals"), therefore, are either iconic (as in the case of the "directionals") or they are shaped in other ways that display their organized affiliation to an element of the talk around them. Such connections allow independent exploration of the relative positioning of gesture and talk affiliate.

As in the case of iconic gestures, although they are sometimes co-incident with their talk affiliates, locationals are most commonly pre-positioned, and are methodically organized to be so.

(1) Some locational gestures are returned to home position before production of their affiliate, as in (24) above, or the following:

```
#28          (Auto Disc: 14:05)  Gesture is a point to the
             right with the left forefinger.  Lexical
             affiliate is "t' Florida."

Gary:        =of course he hast'take it down

             there (        //   )

Curt:        He can't sw//ap with someb'dy]
```

```
                       o........a r.......hm
Gary:              But eez takin it] t'Florida so, ...
```

(2) A great many more begin their decay or retraction before production of their affiliate.

```
#29        (Auto Disc: 06:35) Gesture is a point with
           whole of left forearm and hand to the left.
           Lexical affiliate is "over there."

                                    o....
Gary:      You always go o-over en ni-nice in

           ...................a.......r......
           the afternoon en (th'n) you go over

           ........hm
           there wi//th jus::t shirtsleeves on ...


#30        (MO: Chicken Dinner) Gesture is a point and
           touch to own forehead above hairline with
           right forefinger. Lexical affiliate is
           "on the front of your hair."

M:         (Ushh't) I got flou:r i(hh)n m(h)y nose.

           o..........a     a      r...
G:          W'll yih sure had it on the front of

           yer hai:r.
```

(3) Most commonly, even if the retraction or home position is not
before the lexical affiliate, the acme or thrust, and consequently the
onset of the gesture, precede the locational reference. They potentially
offer, therefore, the same resource offered by iconic gestures for estimating how early a component of talk may be said to be "in play" before its
actual production.

A consequence of this organization and a question it raises require
comment before proceeding. Because the acme or thrust constitutes the
core of the enactment of a gesture, and because the acme/thrust regularly occurs before its lexical affiliate, the possibility is afforded of a rupture
between the gesture and its affiliate, such that the gesture is produced
but its lexical affiliate is not. This possibility occurs when the speaker is
in overlap and drops out of the competition after the gesture has been
formed but before its lexical component has been produced, as in fragment (21) cited earlier, or the following:

#31   (Pre-Auto: 5) Gesture is point to left with
               left forefinger from extended arm.

Gary: Beer's in th'r'frig'rater,
Curt: hm-mghhm.
Mike: Yeah w'll leave it there.

Pam: Bring yer own co:ke.=

           =e┌n here we sto:cked up on┐
            └   ┘
            ┌ o.............a r.... ┐ hm
Gary: en└booze is settin on the ┘

           (0.3)

Pam: o:n coke for yeh,

   Or it may happen when the speaker cuts off the turn in progress in a
self-initiated repair, as in the following:

#32   (MO: Chicken Dinner) Gesture is repeated point
               at the table or something on it.

           o..a   a r...
G: Dih you: put- no you used a lot of

           flou:r
           (1.7)
G: Dih you pu:t- (0.2) 'n (1.0) spices?

In both cases, a full place reference seems to inform the turn, though
some or all of it is missing from the talk.
   Once these types of occurrences are noted, we can note that some talk
displays a gesture, apparently locational, with no lexical affiliate, but
seems to have been designed that way, and is not a conversational
casualty. For example:

#33   (Salv. Army) Gesture is a point with forefinger
               to each cheek -- first left cheek, then right
               cheek.

           o....a.......a....
L: En I'm getting a sun tan.

#34   (MO: Chicken Dinner) Gesture is a point to
             S's chair by G. All markings refer to "G".

G: <u>Don</u>' sit the:re.

S: Huh?

                            o.
G: Don' sit there.

             ....
F: C'mo:n

             a.......r.................ha
G: C'mo:n. Sit ⌐back up an' ta:lk to us
                          [
F: C'mon Stevie. Come sit down.

Here, I take it, "on my face" or "on my cheeks" and "here" or "there"
respectively clearly inform the talk, although they are missing from it.
Such occurrences, whose possibility is structurally provided for by the
organization of gesture in which these gestures are pre-positioned, un-
derscore again the importance of examining talk and body behavior
together as complementary aspects of talk in interaction.

There does not appear to be, nor should one expect, an invariant span
between the production of a bit of talk and the beginning of its projection space, invariant to the type of talk component, its placement in its
sentence or other turn-constructional unit, and the placement of that
unit relative to the turn it is in, in the sequence it is in. Nor should one
expect such a finding when looking at data that happen to afford a
resource for estimating a minimum value for that span. What can be
reported is a weak ordering principle for acme/thrust, a limit on empirically based theoretical possibility, and an application of the resources
that have been developed to a particular case.

(1) A general ordering principle for locational gestures has been noted:
before the lexical component to which the gesture is affiliated. There is
variation in *where* before its lexical affiliate a locational gesture is placed.
A weak auxiliary principle that orders a cluster of cases is: the acme or
thrust is positioned to be co-incident with a/the major stress most prox-
imately *preceding* the gesture's lexical affiliate, as in the already cited
fragments (21), (24), (27), (28), and the following:

#35   (Auto Disc: 02:55) Gesture is point out to
             right with right thumb. Lexical affiliate
             is "off."

Mike: 'n 'e <u>tr</u>ied it about four differn

```
                 times finally Keegan rapped im a good
                          o....c......l     a...
                 one in the a:ss'n then the-b- DeWald
                 r......hm.
                 wen o:ff.
```

l = starts thrust but cuts it off.

Note, furthermore, that in all these fragments the gesture's acme or thrust falls on a preceding stress even though the lexical affiliate of the gesture is itself stressed, and the gesture could have been placed there by reference to on-stress organization, further evidence that the pre-positioning of these gestures is organizationally designed.

(2) Although the acme or thrust is the core of a gesture, and is what we mainly refer to by "the gesture," it is not the earliest evidence of it, or productionally the first part of it. For estimating the earliest indication of the opening of the projection space for some component of the talk, the *onset* of a gesture is what is wanted, the first bit of movement that will become the gesture that is shaped by reference to that talk component. Here the question is, "How far back do such things go?" The answer will not hold for any case in particular, but can tell whether any entertained possibility in any particular case is within known-to-be-possible limits. In the materials I am dealing with, onsets of locational gestures can be found as far back as just before the beginning of the sentence or other turn-constructional unit in which the lexical affiliate occurs, even if the affiliate occurs at the end of that unit. Specifically:

(a) The gesture's onset may start at the end (in the last syllable or word) of the prior sentence or other turn unit in the same speaker's turn,[11] as in:

```
#36              (MO: Chicken Dinner)  Gesture is point with left
                 forefinger.  Lexical affiliate is "over here."


                 o....a.................:.....r.....
G:                 Wuh- (0.2) No:: sit over he:re and

                 ta:lk  //  to us.

F:               C'mon


#37              (MO: Chicken Dinner)  Gesture is point to S's
                 chair.  Lexical affiliate is "up there."

F:               Last time?
```

```
G:        Yea:h  'hhh This time he ate so fast.
F:        Mmhmm.
          (0.4)
                                    o......
G:        an' got down from the table so fast.=
          .......a  r......................hm
          Las' time he sat up there the whole ti:me.
```

```
#38       (Auto Disc: 09:55)  Gesture is sweep with right
          hand toward left and rear.  Lexical affiliate
          is "back."
```

```
Mike:     ... 'hh the guy come all the way with

          fifteen thous'n dollars, he had it right

          there in iz hhh(h)ha:nd man 'hh in iz

          trailer 'e sz I wantcher Cord, 'hh yer
                    o....t.............a
          not getting it. You might ez well turn
                hm
          around'n go back.
```

(b) The gesture's onset may start in the bit of time between the start of a turn's talk and the end of a prior turn by another speaker, as in fragment (30) above, or the following, in which the gesture has nearly returned to home position before the talk begins, though the place reference occurs at the end of the sentence there begun:

```
#39       (Auto Disc: 15:00)  Gesture is a point forward
          with left forefinger by Gary.  Lexical
          affiliate is "out there."

Curt:     ='n then he, uh:: seh-uh sent a couple of'm

          t'California.
                          o..a..r......hm
Gary:                    (-  -  -  -  -  -  -) Well he

          has a snowmobile out there'n, one guy ...
```

Note: each dash at the start of Gary's turn represents about one-tenth of a second of silence.

(c) The gesture's onset may start in the last word(s) of a prior turn by another speaker, as in the earlier cited segments (21), (23), and (34). This is not to say that the projection space of any component of a turn can be asserted to extend back to before the beginning of the turn unit in which it occurs. It does propose that if some occurrence is a candidate precursor of a later occurrence in a turn, then if it comes no earlier than just before the start of that turn unit, it is compatible with being within the projection space of the later occurrence.[12] A brief application of this logic to a segment follows.

4

I began by developing the question of the extensiveness of the projection space preceding the actual production of a component of speech with regard to the pre-indication of repair. I suggested that, in order to decide whether early possible pre-indications of repair were indeed that, we would need an independent estimate of the possible size of the projection space. I then proposed that such an independent estimate might be derived from iconic gestures, because an element of the talk depicted by a gesture could be said to be "in play" at least as early as the onset of the gesture depicting it. Locational gestures, which share the relevant properties of iconic gestures, can potentially serve the same ends. But does an indication of the beginning of the projection space derived from iconic or locational gesture have any bearing on the status of a sound stretch as a pre-indication of repair? Does the source of the solution I have proposed actually contribute to the problem that motivated it? I will finish with a treatment of a stretch of talk in which the two phenomena – pre-positioned gesture and early possible pre-indication of repair – both occur, so as to see how the solution resource fits to the problem.

```
#40          (Auto Disc: 13:30)   Gestures are all points by
             thumb or forefinger of right hand, either to
             the right or over his left shoulder.  All
             gestures are Gary's and are described by
             reference to his position.

Curt:        I  heard Little wz makin um, was makin frames'n
             sendin 'm t'California.

Gary :       (mn he might be, //          )

Curt:        (Is he:: w-)

Gary:        He's got iz one furse:ll. (1.0) en iz new
```

```
          o..(a:)..1    2     3      r.hm  o........4
    one:      (uh)’   he took t'the– (– – – –) he gotta

          r....hm                  o...5   r.....
    first down et uh,  ( – – – – – – – – – –) Bowling

    Green last week er, oh a couple weeks ago I guess
                  o.....
    ih was, inna car show,

              6....
Curt:     Hm.

          .r....
Gary:     Enna, place from Nashville Tennessee offered him
                                      o.....7....
    a hunner do:llars a, da:y, (– – – – – – – –) to

    ......r....hm
    bring it down tuh Nashville tuh show it.
```

1,2 = acmes of two points to the right by thumb.

3   = acme of point over left shoulder by thumb or
      forefinger.

4   = acme of point over left shoulder by forefinger.

5   = acme of point over left shoulder by forefinger.

6   = acme of point to the right by thumb.

7   = acme of vestigial point to the right by thumb.

Note first that when Gary comes to refer to "Bowling Green," he does so only after a bit of repair – a search initiated by "uh" and followed by a 1.0-second pause before he "finds" the name. Note second that there is a sound stretch well preceding this search, at "en iz *new* one: uh,." We have here, then, an instance of a repair preceded by a sound stretch that could be a pre-indication of that "trouble." But the sound stretch is so much earlier than the search; could "Bowling Green" have entered into play that much earlier? Could its projection space go back as far as that?

Note third that in the 1.0-second pause that is part of the search for "Bowling Green" Gary does a "point"; he does it in sequential environment at which a place reference is already projected as relevant, and he thus appears to be doing a pre-positioned locational gesture. (Indeed, such gestures are not unusual in the course of word search segments for place reference.) This point (identified in the transcript by the number "5") is "aimed" over his left shoulder.

Note further, that, during the production of the sound stretch, which we are treating as a candidate pre-indication of the later repair, Gary produces another gesture, indeed a series of gestures. These are points and are seeable as possible affiliates of an imminent locational reference. The third point in this set (the one identified by the "3" in the transcript) appears to be aimed over Gary's left shoulder – the same sector of local space to which he points when he "finds" the reference to "Bowling Green," and to which he points with the same finger at the position marked "4" in the transcript, which appears to be both an iconic gesture affiliated to "first," and a locational gesture affiliated to Bowling Green. The practice of pointing to a same sector of local space in connection with repeated reference to a same place has already been remarked on, and serves here to connect the repair preceding "Bowling Green" to the sound stretch well before it, at "new one."

Note finally that another set of gestures connects two parts of the talk substantially removed from one another, with repair of quite another sort being involved. Of the three points produced in the environment of "new one," only the third is a point over Gary's left shoulder. The first two (at the positions marked "1" and "2" in the transcript) are points to the right, and not with the forefinger but with the thumb. It is therefore notable that when Gary finishes the clause about "the first at Bowling Green," its very end is accompanied by the onset of a new gesture – a point apparently affiliated to the reference of a locational character to "place from Nashville Tennessee." This point, as well as the much reduced or vestigial point preceding the later reference to "Nashville" (at the number "7" in the transcript), are both to the right and both done by the thumb. We are thereby led to remark that these excerpts may be quite similar to (22) examined earlier, in which an iconic gesture was first deployed, then retracted, while a parenthetical remark was inserted before the gesture's lexical affiliate, reinitiated as the parenthetical remark was ended, and then redeployed in the usual manner – just before its lexical affiliate. Here, it appears that the utterance fragment beginning "en iz new one" is projected to incorporate a reference to Nashville, and a locational gesture – a thumb point to the right – was deployed in "anticipation" of it, marking its entry to the projection space. That utterance is then suspended for a bit in favor of a different one first, and with it, the locational gesture in progress is withdrawn, and another – fitted to the newly inserted talk – is deployed. As the inserted talk is brought to an end and the suspended talk is about to be resumed, the gesture that had been in progress before is resumed, now finding its proper place just before the locational reference to which it is affiliated.

In sum, this segment provides not only a specimen of the connection between repair and pre-indication of it being displayed by the deployment of related gestures in those two environments, but of a more general connectedness between two parts of discourse by the deployment of related gestures in them.[13]

5

A great deal of the talk in interaction arrives on a prepared scene. By the time any particular bit of it is produced, many of its aspects have been prefigured, sometimes in quite distinct ways (as with the "thinks" in fragment [22]), often in ways much harder to pin down. Posture, gesture, facial expression, preceding talk, voice quality, and the like all till the soil into which the words are dropped.

Iconic and locational gestures have, as one of their attractions, the property of being often connectable in reasonably clear ways to specific components of the talk. One of the findings proposed above about these classes of gestures holds for some other talk-accompanying behavior as well. This behavior is not distributed randomly or symmetrically around the talk that it accompanies. Rather, its distribution is skewed, and occurs before the talk it is built for, and up to co-incidence with that talk, and rather less after the bit of talk has been produced. This is even more the case if the onsets of these behaviors are considered.[14] Of course, a great many of these behaviors taken one by one are indefinite in their meaning and import, however pregnant with projected sense. Examining a gesture or a facial expression does not ordinarily allow any definite assertion about the character of the talk then in progress, and its interactional import. Isolated units of this sort are like so many chips. We regularly get their sense and contextual fit only when the bit of talk they were built to accompany arrives. These bits of behavior render the scene in which the talk arrives a prepared scene; the talk, in turn and in retrospect, renders the bits of behavior their coherence as preparation.

Appendix A. "This," "That," and the Placement of Deictic Gestures

The temporal relationship between a gesture and its affiliate has a direct bearing on aspects of deixis. I shall give only a brief illustration here, one concerning the choice between the indexicals "this" and "that" and the sensitivity of that choice to proximity/remoteness, not in space, but in time.

We are dealing here with indexical uses of "this" and "that." An object is referred to in the talk but not by a reference term or a descriptor, but rather by the insertion of a dummy item that is paired with a gesture of some sort that indicates the object the dummy "stands for." The gesture has its placement in the talk specified by the placement of the dummy – the indexical. It is crucial to note that it is the *gesture* that is thereby placed in the talk, not the object the gesture indicates. For what is brought into the talk by the dummy is not "the indicated object" but a "reading of" or an "analysis of" the gesture. The choice between "this" and "that" as alternative dummies can turn on the sort of analysis to be made of the gesture.

Consider the following three segments:

```
#41          (MO: Chicken Dinner)  Several gestures are
             involved.  F is holding a business card in his
             left hand and gesturing with right hand.  He
             first releases a prior gesture, then repositions
             the business card with his left hand.  He then
             points at (something on) the card and animates
             the point for a  few moments.  He then stops that
             gesture and points at a part of one of the
             listener's  garment at "this color."
                                    1.............2....
F:           ...y'know like three time lo:nger the bird. ˙HHH
             ......o.......3.....................4  o......
             an' then: u-thi:s stripe is in a li:ght (.) w'll
             5.................
             it's in this color.
```

```
1   =  release of prior gesture toward business card
2   =  repositioning of business card
3   =  point reaches its acme and moves back and forth over
       business card
4   =  stop back and forth motion
5   =  arrival at target of next point
```

In the cases of both "this"s here, the state of the gesture at the time the "dummy" is "due" is the "reading" of the gesture to be brought into the talk (I omit consideration of Wittgenstein's problem here). In the first case, methodical preparation brings the acme of the gesture to its initiation simultaneous with the indexical (and with its stress), and the gesture is sustained over the ensuing words. In the second case, the target seems to be arrived at in advance of the indexical, but is apparently in position as the indexical is said ("apparently" because the gesturing limb is hidden from view in the video picture).

A second case:

```
#42          (Auto Disc: 08:30)  Gesture involves both hands
             describing roughly the shape of a large bell,
             starting at the bottom and with hands just
             meeting at the top.

Curt:        Hey, Where c'n I get a::, uh 'member the old

                                    o..........c   t..
             twenny three model T spring, (0.5) backspring,
```

```
             ......................1
             't came up like that, (0.2)
```

```
1  =   gesture describing bell ends with hand at high point
       of gesture, hands are held there before being
       released to next gesture, which redescribes the
       figure but from the top down.
```

Note here that what is to be brought into the talk is a *shape* described *over the course of the gesture*, not a state displayed at its end point, or at the point at which the indexical is produced. The appropriate analysis of the gesture to be brought into the turn is, therefore, the course of a gesture largely already past, relatively remote, and the dummy that can indicate that is "that." Use of "that" may, thus, serve to display completion, and readiness for recipient's response. It is not that "this" could not be used; it seems likely, however, that were it used it might be accompanied by a repeated enactment of the shape, and, accordingly, extension of the turn. All of this depends in part on the speaker's judgment of the eyes of his recipients. Here, he sees them (or at least the one he is directly looking at) to be seeing the gesture on its first presentation. "That" is usable, and sensitive to its placement relative to the gesture and the analysis of it wanted for the turn, that is, "prior states of the gesture."

And a third case:

```
#43        (MO:Chicken Dinner)  Hands are held in front of
           body with palms facing each other about nine
           inches apart, and then are twice moved to be
           farther apart.  After final widening, hands are
           shaken up and down, animating the "measuring
           gesture."

                                 1     2
F:         ... an' the female to a ma:le,='HHH So these

           3 c    t................................r
           (0.3) ca:bles about th(hh)is l(h)o(heh heh)ng

           y'know ...
```

```
1  =   adopts first position of hands about nine inches apart.
2  =   increases distance between hands.
3  =   increases distance between hands again.
```

The "length of the cables" is to be brought into the talk. Elsewhere, just before the first data segment discussed in this section, the same speaker has described something as "incredibly long" with an accompanying gesture. There he chose a descriptor to do the work of "length," and perhaps here – in the (0.3)-second pause – a similar selection is at stake. Instead, a deictic function is employed. Whether or not such a selection in such terms is involved, note that a series of adjustments is made in the relative positioning of the hands which will be the analysis of "this long." Twice the hands are widened (the adjustments, quite apart from the finally achieved distance, helping to achieve a reading of "this long" as "very long") so that they are "current-state-of-the-gesture-readable" when the indexical that refers the recipient to them is produced. There is a trajectory to the gesture here as there was in the prior segment considered, but in that one the whole trajectory preceding the deictic was brought into the turn by "that," and here the earlier parts of the trajectory are replaced by the later, and the final, stage alone invoked by "this" (though the history of this final stage may have consequences, as previously noted).

Note in all three segments that (1) the onset of the gesture always precedes its deictic affiliates; (2) the acme, or beginning of acme, is on or before the affiliate; (3) therefore, the deictic is built not to point to something ahead, but to something just happening or already over.

Appendix B

Unless otherwise noted, transcript excerpts in which body behavior is included employ the following symbols marked above the line of talk in which they occur:

o	=	onset of movement that ends up as gesture
a	=	acme of gesture, or point of maximum extension
c	=	body part "cocked" or "poised" for release of gesture
h	=	previously noted occurrence held
t	=	thrust or peak of energy animating gesture
r	=	beginning or retraction of limb involved in gesture
hm	=	limb involved in gesture reaches "home position" or position from which it departed for gesture
p	=	point
. . . .	=	indicates extension in time of previously marked action
1, 2	=	numerals refer to legend describing special actions at end of data excerpt
(— —)	=	elapsed time of silence, each dash representing about one-tenth of a second; this representation of silence used only occasionally, to show placement of body behavior in it; otherwise silence is represented by numbers in parentheses, e.g., (0.2).

Notes

1. The word search that occurs in this utterance is analyzed in Goodwin and Goodwin (forthcoming). One finding of the analysis is that the gaze withdrawal and "thinking face" that accompany this word search begin at the word "wa:s," and make the "link between the stretch in 'wa:s' and the subsequent search . . . quite clear, and indeed literally visible to recipient." (Charles Goodwin, personal communication)
2. The chapter was prepared on the premise that a videotape of the relevant data would be available. The videotape was available at the conference but is not in this book. There is no satisfactory device for the presentation of the sort of material appropriate to the themes of this essay. Still pictures, tracings, stick figures, and the like all lose precisely what is at issue – the shape and pace of movement. Discursive description preempts the very analysis the material should bear on contingently; how to describe the body behavior is precisely the issue. Quasi-anatomical and topographical descriptions give a false sense of objectivity and precision, and are not the relevant terms of descriptions for the analysis; metaphorical and analogical descriptions "capture the flavor" but are not detailed accounts; in any case, the reader is

disallowed an independent judgment of the adequacy of the account to the materials. Every effort I have made to revise the essay has foundered on the issue of adequate representation of the data. Nor does coding the fragments and reporting statistically solve the problem; it merely hides it under a table. What is needed is a videodisc accompanying the text. For the present publication, I have fallen back on discursive description as an unavoidable expedient.

I most regret being unable to present in publication at this time a reworking of the essay to explicate the methodological import of some of the discussion now couched in substantive terms. Specifically, what is here, and elsewhere in the literature, treated as findings about the relationship of components of speech and their "affiliated" gestures, can be recast as a discussion of how we (analysts and coparticipants) come to see some bit of talk and some bit of body behavior as "affiliated." Rather than treating their affiliation as a given, and using it as a license to explore what is treated as "further findings" (such as their temporal relationship, their "semantic" relationship, etc.), the notion of "affiliated gesture" can itself be seen as problematic, and the "further findings" recast as those properties of talk-and-body-behavior by which they are constituted as an affiliated "package." When visual inspection of the behavior becomes possible, such a recasting of the discussion may be more feasible.

The conference version of the paper, substantially reproduced here, omitted adequate bibliographical references. Most glaring was omission of any reference to the growing literature on so-called nonverbal behavior, and on gesture, or as Kendon calls it "gesticulation," in particular. The most relevant references are to Efron (1941), Condon and Ogston (1966, 1967), Ekman and Friesen (1969, 1972), and Freedman (1972). Most directly pertinent is the work of Kendon, who as long ago as 1972 reported in passing a finding like those with which I am concerned. More recently, Kendon (1979b) takes up materials and findings just like those with which I am concerned. Our interpretation of these findings is different – Kendon finding in them grounds for a claim of some sort of priority, precedence, anteriority, or more fundamental status for body behavior as compared to speech. I treat the production of the talk as organizationally more fundamental, the body behavior being generally temporally and sequentially organized with respect to it, and not the other way around. Still, the convergence of findings is notable; the results were arrived at independently, and from different sets of (naturalistic) materials.

3. See Appendix B for explanation of symbols used in transcript.
4. The "meaning" depicted is not necessarily the one employed on that occasion of use; e.g., though "upness" is not involved in the "up" of "wake up," the gesture may depict "upness." Cf. (21).
5. The speaker's two hands move in parallel to the right, to the left, and to the right again.
6. Gestures may also be constructed as complements to the talk in describing something, and may then not be shaped by the particulars of talk elements; cf. examples (33) and (34) and related discussion.
7. As it happens, these are nongaze-directing points.
8. Richard Fauman first called my attention to some of these points.
9. Note in this fragment the similarity to fragment (22). In both, a gesture is under way, an insert is done in the talk that gets the gesture temporarily aborted, and when the originally projected talk resumes, the originally projected/enacted gesture is resumed.

10. These points are especially relevant to place/space references in stories told in conversation from which many of the fragments displayed are taken, but they seem to obtain outside storytellings as well. On the association of persons or objects with places as a mnemonic device with broad implications, cf. Frances Yates (1966).

11. Instances such as (37) and (38) are ones in which various aspects of the talk display that another sentence or other talk unit is to come. In other cases (e.g., [6]), incipient gestures, or as yet uncompleted ones, may serve to claim, or display an intention, to produce further talk. Charles Goodwin called my attention to the relevance of this point here (also cf. Goodwin 1981:29).

12. All the "harbingers of repair" cited at the beginning of this paper are compatible with this constraint.

13. My understanding of this segment was substantially enhanced by Charles Goodwin's detailed remarks on an earlier version of it.

14. Note that even gestures designed for co-incidence (e.g., with stress) will regularly need pre-positioned onset to achieve it, yielding access to their projection space as well.

PART V
Aspects of response

The chapters in this part examine some features in the operation of various commonly used nonlexical responses (the particle "oh," laughter, and applause) that recur across a range of interactional settings, but that have been relatively neglected as topics for detailed empirical research. That some conversation analysts have begun to study such phenomena is a result of the more general programmatic willingness to regard anything whatsoever that can be observed to occur or recur in the course of interaction as "anthropologically strange" (Garfinkel 1967), and hence also as sufficiently puzzling to be of potential analytic interest. Thus, insofar as these chapters show how such responses work in ways that are more subtle, systematic, and consequential than might initially seem on the basis of intuition, or in the light of existing research literatures, they provide further grounds for resisting attempts to impose a priori restrictions on what may or may not be subjected to detailed investigation.

Phenomena like the particle "oh," laughter, and applause tend to be commonly regarded, and to be referred to in dictionaries, as "expressive" responses through which emotions, amusement, approval, and the like are displayed. Also implied in this is the idea that there is something spontaneous or instinctive about the way such responses are produced. If, however, spontaneous actions are held to be ones that are done in a more or less unconstrained or disorganized fashion, the following studies provide little support for such a view. For they show that these responses are by no means random interjections or exclamations that can simply be inserted at any point in the course of any interactional sequence, but are deployed in a variety of quite systematic ways for the accomplishment of particular local practical purposes.

The particle "oh," laughter, and applause appear to have in common that they tend to occur in interactions where one or more participants are concerned to display, or elicit a display of, affiliation or alignment.

Heritage shows how "oh" can be used in a range of sequential environments to display to a prior speaker that something he has just said has brought about a change in the recipient's state of knowledge. Depending on what else is said in the turn within which "oh" occurs, it will be treated as having immediate and specific implications for the subsequent course of the interaction.

Jefferson's chapter explores a phenomenon that was noticeable, in the light of her earlier work on laughter (Jefferson 1979; forthcoming c; Jefferson, Sacks, and Schegloff forthcoming), as a deviant case. Whereas a focus in some of the previous studies had been on the ways in which the production of laughter and laugh particles in the course of a turn at talk can serve to elicit laughter from a recipient, the present chapter examines how laughter may be produced and treated quite differently in environments where talk about troubles or problems is being initiated.

Laughter is also found occurring in association with applause in the data from large-scale public gatherings, the focus of Atkinson's chapter on how politicians and others invite affiliative responses from their audiences. This study extends some of his earlier work on the organization of attentiveness in multiparty settings and suggests, among other things, that applause and laughter may be organized in quite similar ways across diverse settings.

One methodological *caveat* which should perhaps be noted in relation to the chapters in this part is that to focus on particular responses (whether lexical or nonlexical) that look alike or sound the same wherever they occur is not widely used or recommended by conversation analysts as a research procedure. For in so doing there is always a danger of presuming in advance that some particular word or nonlexical response will invariably have the same interactional implications wherever and whenever it occurs. As will be seen, however, none of the following chapters claim that "oh," laughter, and applause always operate in an identical fashion, or that the interactional work that they do cannot also be accomplished in other ways.

13. A change-of-state token and aspects of its sequential placement

JOHN HERITAGE
University of Warwick

1. Introduction

This chapter reports some preliminary findings on the work accomplished by the particle "oh" in natural conversation. Evidence from the placement of the particle in a range of conversational sequences shows that the particle is used to propose that its producer has undergone some kind of change in his or her locally current state of knowledge, information, orientation or awareness. Such a proposal is, in various sequence specific ways, informative for other participants and is implemented in, or accomplice to, the achievement of a variety of interactional tasks.[1]

A preliminary sense of the way "oh" can be used to propose some kind of change of state is readily available from such fragments as the following.

(1) [GJ:FN]

((three people are walking together: someone passes
them wearing a photograph teeshirt))
→ N: Oh that teeshirt reminded me [STORY]

(2) [Goodwin: G91:250]

A: Yeah I useta- This girlfr- er Jeff's: gi:rlfriend,
the one he's gettin' married to, (0.9) s brother.=
=he use'to uh,

Earlier versions of this chapter were presented at the Conference on the Possibilities and Limitations of Pragmatics, Urbino, Italy, July 1979, and at the British Sociological Association Sociology of Language Study Group Meetings, University of York, December 1980. I would like to thank the members of the Oxford–Warwick seminar in conversation analysis for their many informal observations and comments. Max Atkinson, Graham Button, Paul Drew, Bob Dunstan, and Tony Wootton have read earlier drafts and supplied valuable comments and examples. Finally, I am grateful to Gail Jefferson for her detailed comments and suggestions about data extracts and for her generous intellectual support over the past several years.

```
      ..... (( 13 lines of data omitted. During this
      ..... period the setting is disrupted by the
      ..... leaving of some of the participants))
  A:   What was I gonna say.=
→ A:   =Oh:: anyway.=She use'ta, (0.4) come over .......
```

In (1) a noticing is proposed with "oh." The noticing is subsequently described and used to furnish the basis for a storytelling.[2] In (2) a story-telling is temporarily abandoned in the face of the setting's disruption. The resumption of the story is achieved by a preliminary display that a search is being made for the next item of the narrative ("What was I gonna say.="). This is followed by "Oh:: anyway.=" and what is then subsequently recognizable as a resumption of the narrative thread. Here then the "oh::" displays a successful outcome of the search previously displayed as being in progress. The "oh's" produced in these fragments thus provide a fugitive commentary on the speaker's state of mind. Produced within ratified states of talk and as component elements of larger turns at talk, they are nonetheless fully fledged response cries: "signs meant to be taken to index directly the state of the transmitter" (Goffman 1981:116), through which evidence of an alignment taken to events is displayed, "the display taking the condensed, truncated form of a . . . non-lexicalised expression" (ibid:100).

In these cases, the speaker volunteers his production of "oh" and thereby injects an extraconversational contingency, adumbrated by the particle and subsequently elaborated upon, into the talk. However, the particle is also produced as a *response* to a variety of conversational actions, and it is these other occasions of its production that will be the central focus of this chapter.[3] The claim that "oh" makes a generic change-of-state proposal will be demonstrated by considering its place-ment in two major types of conversational environment – "informings" (Sections 2–4) and "repair" (Sections 5–7) – where the particle is regu-larly produced in response to prior turns at talk. In these sections, the sense of the particle's generic change-of-state proposal is particularized by reference to (1) the conversational sequences in which it occurs, (2) its precise placement within such sequences, and (3) the additional turn components that it commonly prefaces. In the final sections of the chap-ter a variety of aspects of the particle's sequential role are considered.

2. Informings

A major conversational environment in which "oh" regularly occurs is in response to informings. Thus in (3) I's report of the arrival of some furniture is, initially at least, responded to with "oh."[4]

(3) [Rah:B:1:1:12:1]

I: Ye:h. ˙h uh:m (0.2) I've jis' rung tih teh- eh tell
     you (0.3) uh the things 'av arrived from Barker'n
     Stone'ou⌐:se,
→ J: ⌊Oh::::::.
     (.)
J: Oh c'n I c'm rou:nd, hh

Similarly in (4) J's informing "I rang y'earlier b'tchu w'r ou:t" gets an
"oh" response as does I's subsequent accounting "I musta been at Dez's
mu:m's."

(4) [Rah:II:1]

J: =Hello there I rang y'earlier b'tchu w'r ou:t,
→ I: ↑Oh: I musta been at Dez's mu:m's=
→ J: =↓aOh::. h=

Moreover in (5) a more extended informing is similarly responded to
with "oh."

(5) [Trip to Syracuse:1]

E: Goo::⌐d
C: ⌊hhhen heh ˙hhh I was um: (0.3) I wen' u–
     (.) I spoke t' the gir- I spoke to Caryn. (0.2)
     ˙hh andum i' w'z really bad because she decided
     of all weekends for this one to go away
     (0.6)
E: Wha?
     (0.3)
C: She decided to go away this weekend.=
E: =Yeah
C: ˙hhh (.) So that (.) y'know I really don' have a
     place ti'stay
→ E: ˙hO:::h.
     (0.2)
E: ˙hh So you're not gonna go up this weekend?

In each of these three cases, we can minimally characterize the data by
suggesting that "oh" is used to mark the *receipt* of the informing delivered in the preceding turn or turns. Moreover we can additionally notice
that these "oh" receipts (1) occur in response to complete chunks of
information and (2) are produced at points at which the informings are
possibly complete. In this context, it is striking that, in (5), C's "She
decided to go away this weekend" is "continuation" receipted with
"yeah." This continuation also receipts a complete chunk of information

but, in eliciting further talk from C, it seems designed to propose that C's informing is not yet possibly complete. By contrast, E's subsequent "oh" receipt does not prompt further talk from C, who thereby treats it as proposing that his informing is now complete at this stage and, relatedly, that E has now grasped what he has left unstated.[5]

Free-standing "oh" receipts of prior informings, as illustrated in (3)–(5) above, are comparatively rare in the conversational data to hand. More commonly, the turn initiated with an "oh" receipt contains additional components that achieve other tasks made relevant by the sequence in progress. For example, it is common for recipients to attend to, and deal with, informings as tellings of good or bad news. Recipients do so by assessing the news delivered, and, in such contexts, "oh" receipts are commonly combined with assessment components to give an oh-plus-assessment turn structure. In such turns, the "oh" invariably occurs in the turn-initial position. Fragments (6) and (7) illustrate this format.

(6)   [TG:16]

A: ... Well <u>la</u>tely in the morning Rosemary's been
       picking me up. –Yihknow so I (haven' been) even
       takin' a <u>train</u> in [(the morning)
→ B: [hhO<u>h</u> that's grea:t.

(7)   [Rah:1:1]

J: I w'z <u>j</u>'st eh <u>ringing up t'say I'll be comin' down</u>
       inna m<u>o</u>ment,
       (.)
→ I: <u>Ohgh</u> goo:d,

And in fragment (8) the format is deployed twice in succession:

(8)   [JG:3C:5 simplified]

R: I fergot t'tell y'the two best things that
       happen'tuh me t'day.
       . . . .
R: I gotta B plus on my math test,
C: On yer final?
R: Un <u>huh</u>?
→ C: Oh <u>that's</u> wonderful
R: And I got <u>athl</u>etic award.
C: REALLY?
R: <u>Uh huh</u>.=From sports club.
→ C: Oh that's te<u>rri</u>fic Roger

Such assessments commonly occur at the end of an informing and are regularly terminal or topic-curtailing in character (Jefferson 1981b).

By contrast, where an informing is produced as a "hearably incomplete" news announcement, "oh" may co-occur with additional turn components that in various ways request or invite the informant to continue:[6]

> (9) [JG:3C:5]
>
> R: I fergot t'tell y'the two best things that
>   happen'tuh me t'day.
> → C: Oh super.=What were they

> (10) [Rah:B:1DJ(12):2]
>
> J: I ⌜saw Janie this morning=
> I: ⌊Yes
> J: =in in: uh Marks'n Sp⌜encers⌝
> → I: ⌊Oh you⌋ did didju yes,

> (11) [HG:II:2] ((re a visit to a dermatologist))
>
> N: My f:face hurts,=
> H: =°W't°
>   (.)
> → H: Oh what'd'e do tih you.

> (12) [Rah:I:8]
>
> V: Oh I met Jani:e, eh:::m yesterday an' she'd
>   had a fo:rm from the Age Concern about that
>   jo:b.h=
> → J: =Oh she has?

In each of these cases, a chunk of information is "oh"-receipted by the recipient who subsequently proceeds to promote further continuation of the informing by the production of a question as in (9) and (11), or a "newsmark" (cf. Jefferson 1981a and note 13 to this chapter) as in (10) and (12).

In order to develop an initial sense of the work accomplished with the production of "oh" in these sequences, it can be noted that conversationalists exhibit a pervasive orientation to the tellability of information. A major aspect of this orientation involves avoiding telling recipients what they already know. Thus in (13), A and D have "good news" to tell to B and C, which is announced by A with: "Hey we got good news."

When B then requests a telling of the news, C proposes (in overlap with
B's request) to know it already.

(13) [KC:4]

```
A: Hey we got good news.
B:  ┌What's the good ne┐ws,
C:  └I   k  n  o  :  w.┘
    (.)
A:  ┌Oh ya do::?
D:  └Ya heard it?
```

Rather than proceeding to tell the news, as requested by B, A and D
both address C's proposal that he knows it already.[7] Here then the
telling of the "good news" is deferred in the face of a claim by one of the
recipients to have prior access to it.

Although interactants may have a variety of resources with which
they can infer, a priori, whether a candidate recipient is informed or
uninformed about a potential "tellable," it is nonetheless the case that,
with respect to the specifics of an informing, the informed or uninformed status of recipients is commonly the object of active negotiation
and determination throughout the course of the informing itself. Negotiations over the informed/uninformed status of recipients have been
shown powerfully to structure the design of storytelling, joke telling,
and announcement sequences.[8] Through these negotiations, the parties
to the talk establish local identities of informed teller and uninformed
recipient with respect to the matter at hand, and these identities are
commonly sustained through to the termination of the informing sequence.

In this context, a particle that proposes that its producer has undergone a change of state may be nicely responsive to prior turns at talk that
are produced as informings. With the act of informing, tellers propose to
be knowledgeable about some matter concerning which, they also propose, recipients are ignorant. Correspondingly, in proposing a change
of state with the production of "oh," recipients can confirm that, although they were previously uninformed on the matter at hand, they
are now informed. With the use of "oh," recipients thus confirm the
presupposition, relevance, and upshot of the prior act of informing as an
action that has involved the transmission of information from an informed to an uninformed party.[9] "Oh" is thus a means by which recipients can align themselves to, and confirm, a prior turn's proposal to
have been informative. Furthermore, by the addition of specific types of

turn components, such as assessments or requests for further information, recipients can proceed to treat the local trajectory of the informing as complete (with assessments) or incomplete (with requests for further information).

Moreover, it can be further noted that "oh" is a *strong* indication that its producer has been informed as a result of a prior turn's talk. Specifically "oh" is scarcely ever (see note 9) associated with further turn components that assert prior knowledge of "oh"-receipted information. By contrast, receipt objects such as "yes" and "mm hm" avoid or defer treating prior talk as informative. Thus "yes" is regularly, and in contrast to "oh," associated with additional turn components that assert prior knowledge of just delivered information.

Thus in (14) and (15), "yes"-prefaced turns involve just such assertions.

(14) [PD:250]

```
H: Listen, Bud's alright.
→ J: Yeah, I know, I just talked to 'm.
```

(15) [Frankel:TC:1:1:19]

```
S: In any eve::nt? hhhhh That's not all that's ne:w.
G: W't e:lse.
S: ˙t˙hhhhh W'l Wanda'n I have been rilly having
   problems.
G: M-hm,
S: ¯hh An' yesterday I talk'tih her. ˙hhhh A:n'
   (0.3) apparently her mother is terminal.
→ G: ˙tch Yeh but we knew that befo:re.
```

In (16) prior knowledge of the high cost of a train journey is asserted at a slight distance from a "yeh" receipt of a turn that was intendedly informative.

(16) [WPC:1:MJ(1):18]

```
M: Well u- she's goin' by: trai:n.h All the wa:y.
   ˙hh An' it's seventy ni:ne pou:nds by trai:n.h
   ˙hh ˙hh=
→ J: =[Yeh
M.   [Isn't that aw:ful:. ˙h
→ J:                      [Well I know it is.=
```

```
    M:   =₋e-eYe:s
 →  J:   ⌊We inquir:ed abou:t ₋th'trai:-n,₋
    M:                        ⌊Y e : :s::.⌋
         (0.3)
    J:   Yihknow before we went by: coach.
```

Additionally receipt objects such as "yes" and "mm hm" are regularly used as continuers in extended tellings. In these tellings the production of "oh" or "oh"-prefaced turns is commonly reserved for significant story elements. Thus in (17) an initially bland description of a mother's state of health is continuation-receipted (arrow 1), whereas the subsequent detailing of the mother's progress gets a strong news receipt ("oh" + "newsmark") from M (arrow 2).

(17)   [WPC:1:MJ(1):2]

```
    M:   ˙hhhh (.) °Um::° 'Ow is yih mother by: th'wa:y.h
         (.)
    J:   We:ll she's a:, h bit better:,
1→  M:   Mm₋::,
    J:    ⌊eh- She came: do:wn on: Satidee:eveni₋ng
2⌐→ M:                                          ⌊↑Oh:
         did ₋s h e : : ,h₋
3→  J:       ⌊for the fir ⌋:s'ti:me.
4→  M:   Ye:s.
    J:   Ye₋s. (   )- I d₋on't know whether she came I: .....
5→  M:    ⌊O h ↑ : : . ⌋
```

This sequence is of additional interest is that M's " ↑ Oh: did she::,h" overlaps a further piece of information that J appends to her prior turn, namely, that Saturday was the first evening the mother had risen from her sickbed (arrow 3). This information, however, initially receives a simple "continuation" response from M (arrow 4). In this context, J begins her next turn with a resumptive "yes," and midway through its production, M, hearing the "yes" as a possible recompletion of the prior turn's talk as "the news," revises her receipt of the prior to a stretched and rise–fall intoned "Oh↑::." (arrow 5). Here then is delicate, but dramatic, evidence for the use of "oh" to respond to prior talk as significant and, by picking it out for such treatment, to mark it as information to be "foregrounded" from surrounding talk.

A return to (5) shows that E's continuation receipt to C's "She decided to go away this weekend" treats it as a "background" to an informing that is to come.

```
(5)  [Trip to Syracuse:1]

     C: She decided to go away this weekend.=
     E: =Yeah
     C: ˙hhh (.) So that (.) y'know I really don' have
        a place ti'stay
     E: ˙hO:::h.
1→      (0.2)
2→   E: ˙hh So you're not gonna go up this weekend?
```

Thus, E's later "oh" receipt to C's subsequent detailing "foregrounds" the latter as informative, and thereby treats it as the burden of his informing in a way that a further continuation receipt would not. Subsequent to such a receipt, which is strongly hearable as proposing a realization, C may thus wait (arrow 1) to see what E has made of his informing (arrow 2). Here the type of receipt object, its positioning in the sequence, and the way in which it is intoned all contribute toward this outcome.

In sum, it is proposed that "oh" specifically functions as an information receipt that is regularly used as a means of proposing that the talk to which it responds is, or has been, informative to the recipient. Such a proposal is not accomplished by objects such as "yes" or "mm hm," which avoid or defer treating prior talk as informative. Where tellings are chunked into segments, "oh" may co-occur with additional turn components, which in inviting or curtailing further talk to an informing exhibit the "oh"-producer's orientation to, and preparedness to collaborate in, the production of an informing as an event having recognizable stages of development. Finally, "oh" may be used by recipients to highlight or "foreground" particular elements of an informing.

3. Question-elicited informings

Just as "oh" receipts regularly occur in the environment of informings that are, in various ways, initiated by the informant, so they also regularly occur in response to informings that are elicited by questions. In each of the following cases, a simple sequence of (question) – (answer) – ("oh" receipt) (arrows [1]–[3]) is deployed.

```
(18)  [Rah:I:8]

     V: And she's got the application forms.=
1→   J: =Ooh:: so when is 'er interview d'd she sa⌈:y
2→   V:                                           ⌊She
```

```
         didn't u- Well u-she's gotta send their fo:rm ↓back
         ─̅S̅h̅┌e d'sn't know w┐hen=
3→ J:       [O h : : : .┘
    V: =the ┌interview i : s ┌yet.┐
    J:      [Oh it's just th'  [fo: ┘rm,=
```

(19)   [Campbell:4:1]

```
1 → A:          Well lis;ten, (.) tiz you tidju phone yer
                vicar ye:t,
                (0.3)
2 → B:      ___  No I ain't
    (A): (0.4) (·hhh)
3 → A:          Oh:.
```

(20)   [WPC:1:MJ(1):1]

```
1→ J: When d'z Sus'n g┌o back.=
    M:                  [·hhhh
    J:  =┌(            )
2→ M:    [u-She: goes back on Satida:y=
3→ J: =O┌h:.
    M:   [A:n:' Stev'n w'z here (.) all las'week ....
```

(21)   [Frankel:TC:1:1:13–14]

```
    S: ·hh When d'ju get out.=
1→
    S: =Christmas week or the week before Christmas
       (0.3)
2→ G: Uh::m two or three days before Ch┌ristmas,┐
3→ S:                                    [O h : ,┘·hh=
    S: =Tha┌t-
    G:     [See,
```

(22)   [Rah:A:1:IMJ(2):2]

```
1→ I: Ah thi- et-y-I: think there w'z only about three
      things ordered was it or four.
2→ J: eh-u-Four I think there w'z two: for Ken'n two
      for I:an.
3→ I: Oh:.
    J: B't I(c) I don't know what quite.
```

(23)   [Rah:B:2:JV(14):1]

```
1→ J: Oh:::. Have they'ave yih visitiz g┌one then,┐
2→ V:                                     [They've go┘:ne.
       Yes,
3→ J: Oh┌:ah
    V:   [A::n:' they've gone to ....
```

(24)   [Rah:C:1:JS(15):1]

1→ J: Whadiyih doing eating yer breakfast or
       someth┌ing
2→ S: └Yes,
3→ J: Ohgh(h)h hhuh huh huh ┌˙huh
   S: └˙hhh
   J: You're en↓joying life aren'tchu.

(25)   [Rah:B:1:1DJ(12):4]

1→ J: Okay then I w'z askin' and she says you're
       working tomorrow as well,
2→ I: Yes I'm s'pose to be tomorrow yes,
3→ J: O┌h:::,
   I: └Yeh,

Examining (18)–(25) shows that the production of an "oh" receipt is not
necessarily associated with the degree to which an answer is unexpected. The cases are arrayed in an order that roughly approximates the
degree to which the expectations of the questioner – exhibited in the
design of the question – are met. Thus in (18) the answer undercuts one
of the presuppositions of the question to which it responds (i.e., that an
application for a job that might lead to an interview has, in fact, been
lodged). This answer may be treated as "least expected" by the questioner who subsequently goes on to produce a display of understanding
(see Sections 6 and 7) that is hearably corrective of her prior misap-
prehension. In (19) and (20), open requests for information are responded to with the information requested, while in (21) and (22) information requests that propose alternative possibilities are responded to
with a selection of one of the alternatives. In (23) and (24), question-
formed likely inferences receive confirmation, while in (25) a source-
cited report receives confirmation.[10] In all cases, however, the responses
are "oh"-receipted by the questioner at, or near, the first point at which
the responses are possibly complete and the question is, at least in a
minimal sense, answered.

   In these simple (question) – (answer) – ("oh"-receipt) sequences,
which are massively recurrent in ordinary conversation, "oh" again
functions as an information receipt by proposing a change of state of
knowledge or information. Moreover, in proposing a change of state,
the "oh" receipt is once more nicely fitted to the Q–A sequence in which
it participates. For the producer of a question proposes, with the production of a question, to assume the status of presently uninformed
about its substance and thereby proposes as well that the respondent, in

answering the question, assume the status of informed with respect to the matter at hand. Given this organization, the questioner may be committed by the provision of an answer to have undergone a change in his or her state of information and may be required to propose just that.[11] Here then the production of "oh" confirms an answer as an action that has involved the transmission of information from an informed to an uninformed party.[12] Although it is but one of a variety of resources for such proposals,[13] the particle is an economical resource for their accomplishment. Moreover it is one that, as already noted in the context of simple informings, is readily combined with additional turn components – such as assessments or requests for further information – that accomplish associated sequential tasks.

These considerations further suggest that the production of an "oh" receipt (or some equivalent) may be avoided by questioners so as to propose that they have not been informed. Thus in (26) three Q–A – "oh" sequences (arrowed a, b, and c respectively) run to completion. Subsequently (arrowed d), a fourth such sequence, is apparently initiated with N's question-intoned utterance "Nice Jewish bo:y?."

```
        (26)   [HG:II:25]

       ┌→N: ='hhh Dz he 'av'iz own apa:rt ┌mint?┐
   a   ├→H:                                └'hhhh┘ Yea:h,=
       └→N: =Oh:,
            (1.0)
       ┌→N: How didju git 'iz number,
       │    (.)
   b   ├→H: I(h) (.) c(h)alled infermation'n San
       │    Fr'ncissc(h) ┌uh!
       └→N:              └Oh::::.
            (.)
        N: Very cleve:r, hh=
        H: =Thank you┌: I- 'hh-'hhhhhhhh hh=
       ┌→N:          └W'ts'iz last name,
   c   ├→H: =Uh:: Freedla:nd. ·hh┌hh
       └→N:                      └Oh┌:,
        H:                          └('r) Freedlind.=
       ┌→N: =Nice Jewish bo:y?
       │    (.)
   d   ├→H: O:f cou:rse,=
       └→N: ='v ┌cou:rse,┐
        H:      └hh-hh-hh┘ hnh'hhhhh=
        N: =Nice Jewish boy who doesn'like tih write letters?
```

This latter utterance appears little different from other likely inferences (e.g., [24]) whose confirmations are routinely "oh"-receipted. In this case, the respondent (H) confirms the inference with an utterance

"O:f cou:rse," which treats the inference as self-evident rather than merely likely. In turn, this confirmation is receipted by N with a repetition of the confirmation ("'v cou:rse"), which preserves this treatment and asserts it on her own behalf. In effect, the recipient withholds a change-of-state proposal and thus retrospectively proposes that her previous, question-intoned inference is to be heard as having been a comment on something self-evident rather than an inference concerning something still in doubt.

It was noted earlier in the context of informing sequences that the status of informed/uninformed may be the object of detailed negotiations over the course of a telling sequence. Similar issues can now be seen to arise in the context of questions and their answers where, for example, the avoidance of now-informed receipts can be used, as in (26), to implicate that an answer does not inform, or to confirm or revise the status of a prior question-formed utterance as one that did not request information.[14]

Finally, it may be noted that an "oh" receipt, in occurring at a point at which an answer is possibly complete, may be used to propose that its producer is prepared to treat the answer as, in fact, complete. In this context, it is relevant to observe that, whereas "oh" is routinely used to receipt information, its sequential role is essentially backward looking. Specifically, the particle does not invite or request further information. Since, in many Q–A sequences, questioners cite information gaps, which they request to be filled, an answerer/"oh" recipient may treat an "oh" receipt as proposing that the questioner's information gap has been made up and that the answer is, from the questioner's point of view, sufficient. Under these circumstances, the answerer may withhold the detailing of further tellable materials until invited to tell more, as in (26).

```
(26)  [HG:II:25  Detail]

N: ='hhh Dz he 'av 'iz own apa:rt ⌈mint?⌉
H:                                ⌊'hhhh⌋ Yea:h,=
N: =Oh:
→      (1.0)
N: How didju git 'iz number,
```

Alternatively where, as in (20) (see also [22] and [23]), the answerer does continue with further detailing after an "oh" receipt,

```
(20)  [WPC:1:MJ(1):1]

J: When d'z Sus'n g⌈o back.=
M:                ⌊'hhhh
```

```
   J:   =ₗ(                    )
   M:    ⌊u–She goes back on Satida:y=
   J:   =O⸢h:.
→  M:      ⌊A:n:' Stev'n w'z here (.) all las'week .....
```

this detailing is volunteered, that is, produced at the teller's initiative.
The issues raised by these observations will be considered in more detail
in sections 8–10.

In sum, "oh"-carried change-of-state proposals are commonly used to
receipt answers-to-questions as informative, while withholdings or sub-
stitutions of "oh" receipts may be used to imply either that an answer
was not, or not yet, informative or, alternatively, that a prior question-
formed utterance did not request information. Produced as a free-standing object, the placement of "oh" at, or near, a first point at which an
answer is possibly complete may be used to propose the "oh" producer's preparedness to treat the prior answer as complete for all practical purposes and may result in a curtailment in the production of
further tellables.

4. Counterinformings

Finally, in the context of informings, we briefly consider the placement
of "oh" in sequences where a first statement is met by a second "counterinforming" statement that is contrastive with the first. In this environment, the "oh" is regularly produced as part of the turn with
which one of the speakers revises a previous position. Once again, the
use of "oh" as a change-of-state proposal that is responsive to the informative character of a prior turn at talk is strongly implicated.

A simple case is shown below.

```
   (27)  [Goodwin: Family Dinner:13]

   B:  It looks like beef'n bean curd.
       (1.0)
   J:  Well I wan' lots of beef.
   D:  I think it's pork.
→  B:  Oh. Pork.
   D:  Mm hm
```

Here B identifies a package of Chinese food as "beef'n bean curd."
Subsequently another speaker (D) counteridentifies it as "pork." B subsequently accepts D's identification by repeating "pork," marking a
change of state of information with "oh." In this case, the production of
"oh" is closely associated with the acceptance of the counterinforming
as a correction.

In the following case, J's realization/recollection–intoned "oh" adumbrates a revision of her prior assertion, which is accomplished by an initial display of "thinking back" ("Well ¡ W'z it ↑la:s' night.") and a subsequent revision of her position.

(28) [Rah:I:1]

```
V: Where didje get to la:s' ni-ight,
      (1.0)
J: La:st- I dit (0.2) I di'n't go any↑where?
   (0.4)
V: W'l Andrew r:ang t'see if you were ↑there,
      (0.7)
→ J: ·hh °Ohh::.° hh Well ¡ W'z it ↑la:s' night.
   (.)
J: ↑Yes it w- Tha:t's right i' was la:s' nah-
   ·hh No I'd taken I:an: .......(continues)
```

A more elaborate case is (29). Here I's initial announcement is met, after a considerable gap, with a possible predisagreement object (see Pomerantz, Chapter 4 herein, and note 13 to this chapter) from J " ↑ *Janie* has." (line 4) and a subsequent counterassertion "*No* she has*n't*" (line 6).

(29) [Rah:B:1:1DJ(12):2]

```
 1 I: Ye- ·h Well she's gone to mm eh: eh: Chester:.
 2      (0.9)
 3 I: Ja┌nie:,
 4 J:    └↑Janie has.
 5 I: ↑Ey?
 6 J: No she hasn't
 7     (0.8)
 8 I: Yes. She's go::ne,
 9     (0.7)
10 I: She went just before dinner.
11     (0.2)
12→J: Oh↑:::. Oh ┌I (thought      ),┐
13            └She w'z in such a ┘rush,
```

After a further extended gap, I reasserts her own prior informing (line 8) and, after yet another gap, elaborates it with further detailing (line 10). It is only after this subsequent detailing that J announces the revision of her prior position with a stretched rise–fall intoned "oh" (line 12) and the beginning of a description of her prior misinformation which, in turn, is overlapped with further detailing from I (line 13).

The use of "oh" to project acceptance of another speaker's position in the above sequences can be highlighted by examining comparable sequences in which "oh" is absent. Thus, in (30), D's proposal that Rice is

in Louisiana is met with the intendedly corrective counterinforming
from M and F that it is in Texas. In her subsequent turn, D revises her
position by accepting that Rice is in Texas.

```
(30)  [Post Party:I:14]

    D: Rice? °is in Louisiana.°
    M: No :.
          [Tex as
    F:        [
    M:         [Texa s.
                   [
 →  D:              [Texas. Rice. °Yeh that's (right).°
    A: Heeyoosto:n
```

Here it is noticeable that D manages to revise her position while avoiding the production of an "oh"-carried change-of-state proposal. Instead,
by repeating "Texas. Rice.," she produces a display of consulting her
own knowledge of the location and only then produces a confirmation
(" °Yeh that's [right] °.") which accepts the position asserted by M and
F. In effect D manages to revise her prior assertion so as to show that,
although the revision is an interactional consequence of the interven-
tions from M and F, it rests not on a simple acceptance of their assertions
but, in part at least, on a consultation of her own independent knowledge of the location of Rice. Thus whereas in (27) B accepts a counterinforming as a correction with her "oh"-plus-repeat receipt, in (30) the
repeat-plus-acceptance is managed so as to avoid, with the withholding
of "oh," an acceptance that treats the counterinforming as an authoritative transmission of information (i.e., a correction) from M and F
to D.

Relatedly, in (31), C's "yes" receipt (line 8) to a hearably complete and
intendedly corrective counterinforming from the DJ (in lines 3–4 and 6–
7) is treated as insufficient to propose a revision of her prior position.

```
(31)  [JH:FN]

((From a radio phone-in competition titled "Beat
the Jock." Carla's question to "beat the jock"
was: "Name the second group to enter the British
'Top 20' at No.1"))

1  DJ: You'd better tell me then.
2   C: The Jam.  "Going Underground."  Nineteen eighty.
3  DJ: Uh no Carla.  That's why I asked you if you
4      thought Slade were the first.
5   C: Yes.
6  DJ: 'Cos the Beatles were first, Slade were second
7      and the Jam were third.
8 → C: Yes.
```

```
 9   DJ: No. The Jam were the third group to go straight
10        in at number one. Yeah?
11 → C:  Oh:.
12   DJ: See people forget that the Beatles were first .....
```

Here C's "yes" receipt to the DJ's itemized counterinforming is met (lines 9–10) with "no," a further assertion of the central component of the prior counterinforming (concerning "The Jam") and a tag-positioned request for acceptance/confirmation. Only after C's "oh" receipt of this turn does the DJ treat her position as having been adequately revised by observing that "people" (including C by implication) "forget that the Beatles were first."

In sum, in sequences in which contrastive proposals concerning a state of affairs are being made, an "oh"-carried change-of-state proposal may be used by one of the parties to propose a revision of his or her position that overtly responds to the other's talk as corrective. The data suggest that, while a free-standing "oh" may be sufficient to propose acceptance of a counterinforming (as in [31]), it is more normally accompanied by turn components (usually repetitions) that explicitly accept the counterinformation. Similarly, although it is possible to accomplish acceptance of a counterinforming without the production of "oh" (as in [30]), such cases are rare and instance the accomplishment of rather special interactional work. Finally, as (31) illustrates, "yes" is insufficient to propose a revision of position.[15]

Overall, in each of the informing sequence types considered so far, "oh" is used to propose a change of state of information. In each case, the sequential role of the particle is, *at the minimum*, one of accomplishing a retrospective reconfirmation of both the prior and the current knowledge states of the participants. The conclusions of sections 2–4 can be drawn together and summarized as follows: Through the use of the particle, informed, counterinformed, or questioning parties can assert that, whereas they were previously ignorant, misinformed or uninformed, they are now informed. Correspondingly, the informing, counterinforming, or answering party is reconfirmed as having been the informative, knowledgeable, or authoritative party in the exchange. By means of the particle, the alignment of the speakers in their sequence-specific roles is confirmed and validated.

5. Other-initiated repair

A second major sequential environment in which "oh" is regularly used as a receipt object is that of other-initiated repair.[16] In each of the following fragments, a second speaker initiates repair on a prior speaker's turn and, the repair having been performed by the first speaker, the second speaker receipts the repair with "oh."

(32)   [C & D:9]

```
       A: Well who'r you workin' for.
       B: ˙hhh Well I'm working through the Amfat
          Corporation.
1→     A: The who?
2→     B: Amfah Corpora⌐tion. T's a holding company.
3→     A:              ⌊Oh
       A: Yeah
```

(33)   [TG:3]

```
       B: Where didju play ba:sk⌐et baw.
       A:                       ⌊(The) gy:m
1→     B: In the gym? ⌐(hh)
2→     A:             ⌊Yea:h. Like grou(h)p therapy.
       Yuh know ⌐half the grou⌐p thet we had la:s' term...
3→     B:       ⌊O h ː ː ː  .⌋
```

(34)   [HG:II:4]

```
       N: But he goes, (.) he:- he goes yih 'av a rilly mild
          case he goes,
          (.)
1→     H: Of wha⌐:t.⌐
       N:       ⌊Yih⌋ sh-
          (.)
2→     N: A:cne-e,=
3→     H: =Ōh⌐:,  ⌐hhh⌐ (hhh)
       N:    ⌊seh⌋ ⌊you⌋ shouldn' even worry abou:t it.
```

In each of these cases, the producer of the repair initiation (arrow 1) proposes to have some difficulty with the prior turn's talk and specifically locates that difficulty through the repair initiation itself. In each case the producer of the prior turn remedies the difficulty (arrow 2) by repetition (32), elaboration (33), and specification (34) and in each case, the producer of the repair initiation receipts the repair with "oh," thereby proposing a change of state of information and, by implication, a resolution of the trouble previously indicated.

These cases contrast with the following in which the one (A) who initiates repair with "Who?" fails to respond to B's first repair attempt.

(35)   [NB:II:1:10]

```
       B: If Percy goes with- Nixon I'd sure like that.
```

```
    A: Who?
1→  B: Percy.
       (.)
2→  B: That young fella thet uh- his daughter was
       murdered,
       (1.0)
3→  B: =[(And)-
    A:  [OH YEA:::h.
    A: YEAH.
    B: They, said sump'n about his goin tuhgether uh-on
       th'ticket so,
```

Here it may be noticed that A's repair initiation (*"Who?"*), although locating a trouble source in a person reference, does not locate the trouble specifically (as between Percy and Nixon). Moreover the repair initiation does not discriminate the *type* of trouble being proposed as either a hearing problem or a recognition problem. In producing her repair, B first addresses the trouble as a hearing problem located to the person reference stressed in her prior turn by repeating "Percy" (arrow 1). Having got no immediate receipt, B then attempts to remedy a hypothesized recognition problem by elaborating additional particulars of the referenced person (arrow 2). A further period of one second elapses during which the initiator of the repair produces no receipt, after which B begins a third attempt at repair (arrow 3) which is overlapped by an "oh"-initiated receipt that proposes recognition of the referenced person ("Percy").

A similar case is the following. Here A proposes, with the use of a questioning repeat (*"Pixy dust?!"*) to be having difficulty in understanding R's prior turn (lines 1–2). In line 7, R proposes a remedy by elaborating an origin for the "pixy dust," namely, "the big boom."

```
    (36)  [GTS:2:2:19]

1   R: But the air's gotta come in dere an' the air is
2      sorta infiltrated with little uh pixy dust.
3      (1.0)
4   K: Doesn' bother me any.
5   A: Pi[xy dust?!
6   K:   [I ain't gonna live in it.
7   R: Y'know from the big boom?
8      (2.0)
9   D: Ra[dio-
10  A:   [Pixy dust,
11  K: heh hh
12  D: Radioactivity I think is what he means,
13 → A: (hh)OH. Okay.
```

The absence of any receipt for this repair attempt from A engenders a further repair attempt ("Radio-") from a further speaker (D) which is cut off as A initiates repair on the trouble source for a second time by re-repeating "*Pixy* dust." Finally D produces a remedy proposed as on behalf of the producer of the trouble source ("Radioactivity I *think* is what he means") which is "oh"-receipted by A.[17]

Once again, in proposing a change of state of knowledge or information, the "oh" receipt is well fitted to the sequence of repair initiation – repair – "oh" receipt in which it participates. For the initiator of a repair proposes, with the production of a repair initiation, to be undergoing some difficulty with the prior turn and thereby proposes that the respondent, in producing the repair, will resolve this difficulty. Given this organization, the initiator of a repair may be committed by the provision of a repair to have undergone a change in his or her state of information and may be required to propose just that. The particle "oh" is a major resource for the achievement of this proposal which, in turn, permits a mutually ratified exit from repair sequences. Although such exits may be achieved by other means,[18] "oh"-accomplished exits from repair sequences are a common form of exit in both simple repair sequences (32)–(34) and their extended counterparts (35)–(36).

6. Understanding checks

A closely related environment in which "oh" is used as a sequence exit device is instanced in (37).

```
(37)  [NB:III:1:2]

      ((Re an invitation for F's daughter to visit))

      F: When didju want'er tih come do::w n.
1→ S:                                      [ ˙hhh Oh any time
      between: now en nex' Saturday, hh
2→ F: A wee:k from:: (0.3) this coming Saturdee.
3→ S: Yeah.
      (.)
4→ F: ˙hhhh Oh:::.
```

In (37), F proposes a trouble (arrow 2) concerning S's prior time reference. Rather than initiating a repair with, for example, "Which Saturday," F proposes a remedy for the trouble by producing an understanding check which, in this case, takes the form of a best guess about the specific "Saturday" in question. This sequence involves a simple variation in the design of other-initiated repairs sketched above. Whereas the latter form of repair initiation proposes, and commonly locates, a trouble with a previous turn's talk for which a remedy is solicited, the understanding check identifies a trouble with a previous turn's talk by proposing a solution to that trouble. The understanding-check sequence, however, is not properly complete at this stage. For in proposing a *candidate* understanding of what an earlier speaker had intended, the producer of an understanding check thereby invites that speaker to confirm (or disconfirm) the adequacy of that proposal. The locus of the completed repair, therefore, is to be found in the responsive confirmation/disconfirmation of the understanding check (arrow 3). This responsive confirmation/disconfirmation is, once more, routinely receipted with an "oh" that reconfirms the previous understanding check as a candidate one.

Thus a basic format for other-initiated repair sequences is:

1. A: Repairable
2. B: Repair initiation
3. A: Repair
4. B: "Oh" receipt

Similarly, a basic format for repair sequences involving understanding checks is strikingly similar:

1. A: Repairable
2. B: Understanding check ((repair initiation))
3. A: Confirmation/disconfirmation ((repair))
4. B: "Oh" receipt

The format is clearly evidenced in (37) and in (38)–(40).

```
   (38)  [Rah:II:7]

1→ J: Derek's ho:me?
          (0.5)
2→ I: Yo:ur De rek.
3→ J:          [Ye:s m m
4→ I:                 [Oh:.
```

```
   (39)  [SF:2:5:simplified]

   B: So::: we thought thet yihknow=
1→    =if you wanna come on over early. C'mon over.
2→ M: 'hhhh- 'hhhh:::::: Ah::: hhh fer dinner
      yih mean? hh
3→ B: No not fer dinner. h=
4→ M: =Oh
```

(40)   [NB:II:2:17]

1→ N: I just uh, forward'iz mail, stick it in 'n
       envelope, (0.4) send it all on up to 'im en, ˙hhhh
2→ E: You know where 'e is then.
       (0.8)
3→ N: I have never had <u>any</u> of it <u>returned</u> Emma,
4→ E: Oh::.

It is noteworthy that this format is preserved throughout a wide variety
of cases, varying from those, e.g., (37) and (38), in which the understanding check is transparently clarificatory and is confirmed, through
(39) in which the understanding check is self-interested and discon-
firmed, to cases such as (40) in which the understanding check, in topicalizing a presupposition of the prior turn, can be heard to be investigative in character.

In both of the forms of other-initiated repair considered, "oh" is used
as a repair receipt. In each of them, as in the Q–A sequences treated in
Section 3, an information gap or difficulty is proposed and its subsequent remedy is receipted with an "oh"-accomplished change-of-state
proposal. Once again, the alignment of the speakers in their sequence-
specific roles is reconfirmed by this means. The work of such alignment,
moreover, is not always simply formal in character. For example, to
return to (40), E's investigative understanding check is deployed as a
means of inquiring into the present relationship between N and the
"he" of the fragment (N's ex-husband). N's reply, "I have never had *any*
of it re*turned* Emma," manages both to depict the absence of communication between them (and hence the state of the relationship) and to
implicate an unwillingness to develop the topic further. In this context,
E's "oh" receipt preserves the prototypical understanding-check sequence and hence avoids any overt or official treatment of N's unwillingness to elaborate. Through the understanding check an opportunity to develop the talk in a particular direction is offered (by E) and
declined (by N) without the offer or its declination ever reaching the
official surface of the talk.

7. Displays of understanding

In Section 6, it was suggested that the provision of a sequence-terminat-
ing "oh" by the producer of an understanding check confirms the latter
as a candidate display of understanding. That this is so is, we suggest, a
result of the production of the change-of-state proposal *after* a responsive confirmation/disconfirmation of the check. However, there are oc-

casions in talk where recipients may wish to show that prior talk has been adequately descriptive and/or that they have competently understood its import. Such recipients require resources with which they can display confidence or certainty in their displayed understandings of what another had intended.

One such resource simply involves the repositioning of "oh" from a fourth-turn receipt position to *preface* the turn within which the understanding is displayed. This use of "oh" is examined by reference to (41)–(45).

```
(41)  [Goodwin: G84:M:3]

G: He wz o:n the opposite side a'the driver ri:ght?
   (.)
G: °with iz::°
   (0.4)
M: No he w- (.) e-he wz on the sa-:me side ez the
   drive r
→ G:        [Oh on nuh ba:ck seat?=
   M: =Yeah i n d'ba:ck s eat
   G:         [Wu:1      [
   C:                    [hmm, hm-m-hm-m-hm
```

Example (41) is taken from an extended stretch of talk in which G is being told about an automobile escapade. It turns out that an understanding of the physical location of the major protagonist (the "he" of the fragment, who is not present in the conversation) within the automobile is critical for an appreciation of the story's details. G's first attempt to locate the protagonist's position within the car consists of an understanding check explicitly designed for confirmation: "He wz o:n the opposite side a'the driver ri:ght?." In disconfirming this attempt, M refers only to which *side* of the car the protagonist was located and does not explicitly state whether the latter was in the front or the back seat. He does, however, provide G with the resources with which to infer this last coordinate of the protagonist's position. G may thus, using the information provided, conclusively infer that "the back seat" is the location in question. G is enabled, in short, to work it out for himself. In this context, it can be seen that G prefaces his revised referencing of the location with "oh." Here he draws upon the "oh"-carried change-of-state proposal to assert that *then and there* is the point at which he has determined the location, a point which is *prior* to any possible confirmation. In proposing this as the point of realization, G thereby proposes its independence of subsequent confirmation and, hence, his confidence in his displayed grasp of the state of affairs.

Other materials provide support for the proposal that "oh"-carried recognition/realization claims in turn-initial position are associated with subsequent referencings that are, in various ways, confidently produced. Thus in (42) a firm assertion of recognition is "oh"-prefaced and followed by a word search that is finally successful.

> (42)   [S:1:1:12:23]
>
> A: Uh, she asked me to stop by, she brought a chest
>   of drawers from um
>   (4.0)
> A: What's that gal's name? Just went back to Michigan.
>   (1.0)
> A: Hilda, um
> 1→ B: Oh I know who you mean,
>   (1.0)
> 2→ B: Grady-Grady.
> A: Yeah. H̄ilda Grady.

In (43), the first speaker makes three attempts to secure evidence of the recipient's recognition of the location of "Pilgrim Lake." Following the third attempt, the recipient comes up with a firm re-referencing of the lake by reference to "Bakersfield" and thereby proposes independent recognition of the lake in question. Here again a turn-initial "oh" marks the initial realizing moment of the recognition that was solicited by the prior speaker.

> (43)   [Northridge 2:3]
>
> D: Like yih know wherah:: Pilgrim Lake is i(t)s-
>   that's on the other si:de u'th'Grapevine.=
>   =Yih know this side of the Grapevine.
> → P: Oh the's jus' up to Bakersfield.

A return to (41) further shows that M's confirmation of G's understanding check is not "oh"-receipted by G. A similar pattern can be observed in (44) and (45).

> (44)   [JH:FN]
>
> A: She's moving house soon.
> B: Where to.
> A: Just round the corner actually.
> B: From you?
> A: No.

1→ B: Oh (.) from where she lives now.
    A: Yeah.
2→ B: That won't be too difficult.
    A: No.

  (45) [DA:2:2]

  F: How long yih gunna be he:re,=
  B: ='hhhh Uh:t's (.) not too lo:ng. Uh:: justn'til:
     uh::uh think Monday.
     (1.0)
1→ F: Til, oh yih mean like a week tomorrow.
     (.)
  B: Yah.
2→   (0.3)
  B: Mm:hm,=
3→ F: Now you told me you ....

In (44), as in (41), disconfirmation of a first understanding check (B's "From you?") is followed by a second attempt that is "realizing" "oh"-prefaced as a confident inference. Confirmation of this second attempt is not subsequently "oh"-receipted (arrow 2). In (45), F revises a simple understanding check initiated with "Til" in favor of a "realizing" "oh"-prefaced display of confident inference. Once again, the subsequent confirmation is not "oh"-receipted by F (arrows 2 and 3).

Comparing (45) with the very similar instance in (37), we see a simple movement of the "oh"-carried change-of-state proposal from a fourth turn-receipt position (in [37]) to a turn-initial position to the understanding check (in [45]). This comparison yields the conclusion that the "oh" functions in (45) as a realization claim which, in occurring *prior* to the subsequent turn components conveying the substance of the understanding achieved, proposes confidence in the adequacy of the understanding subsequently displayed. Moreover, since a change of state is proposed to have occurred then and there, no further similar proposal subsequent to confirmation is required. By comparison, in (37) the producer of the understanding check that was not "oh"-prefaced thereby proposes the displayed understanding as a candidate understanding that requires subsequent confirmation before the process of realization is accountably complete. In this case the completion of the realization process is proposed with a fourth turn-receipting "oh." By means of these two alternative placements of "oh," therefore, a turn that proposes a confident display of understanding may be systematically discriminated from one embodying a less certain understanding check.

8. Aspects of the placement of "oh" in informing sequences

The aim of this chapter thus far has been to demonstrate that the production of "oh" generically proposes that its producer has undergone
some kind of change of state. In previous sections, it has been argued
that this generic proposal is particularized by reference to the sequence
types in which "oh" occurs and by the details of its placement in such
sequences. Finally, some attempt has been made to characterize the
formal or official sequence-specific tasks accomplished by the production of the particle. These tasks, however, are far from being the only
ones that the production of "oh" may be used to accomplish; indeed
they constitute the absolute minimum that may be claimed about the
uses of the particle and its placement. In the remainder of this chapter,
an attempt will be made to develop a broader appreciation of the particle
and its uses by considering its placement in the context of a wider set of
sequential relevancies than those treated so far.

We begin by reemphasizing that, while the particle may propose a
change of state that is appropriately responsive to a prior turn's informing or repair, its sequential role is essentially backward looking. Specifically, although the production of a free-standing "oh" is commonly
used to establish or confirm current speaker alignments, the particle
does not, of itself, request, invite, or promote any continuation of an
informing. Thus in (38), the "oh" receipt of the repair on an initial news
announcement ("*Derek*'s ho:me?"), which also receipts the announcement itself, is not treated by the announcer (J) as requesting further
elaboration.

```
   (38)   [Rah:II:7(extended)]

   J:  Derek's ho:me?
          (0.5)
   I:  Yo:ur De rek.
   J:            Ye:s m m
   I:                   Oh:.
1→     (.)
2→  I:  An'- is he a'ri:ght?=
3→  J:  =Oh he's fi:ne .....
```

Instead J withholds continuation or elaboration of the initial news announcement (arrow 1) until specifically invited to do so (arrow 2),
whereupon she responds promptly with a latched utterance (arrow 3).
Similarly, in (26), after N's "oh" receipt of N's affirmative answer to her
prior question "D'z *he* 'av 'iz own apa:rtmint?," a one-second pause

elapses before N initiates further on-topic talk with *"How didju git 'iz number."*

```
(26)  [HG:II:25 (detail)]

    N: ='hhh D'z he 'av 'iz own apa:rt ┌mint? ┐
    H:                                 └'hhhh┘ Yea:h,=
    N: =Oh:,
 →      (1.0)
    N: How didju git 'iz number,
```

In both cases, the informative party withholds further on-topic talk after an "oh" receipt until receiving a request to do so. While one factor contributing to these post-"oh" hitches may be the informative party's wish to avoid proceeding unilaterally with further talk, additional considerations are undoubtedly at work.

As noted in Section 2, free-standing "oh" receipts to informings are rare in the data to hand. Instead, the particle most regularly occurs in conjunction with additional turn components such as assessments or requests for further information. Moreover, in a range of instances (see, for example, [3], [18], [21], [24]), the production of "oh" is followed at a slight distance by further talk from the "oh" producer. Thus an informant/"oh" recipient may withhold further talk on the assumption that the "oh" already produced is prefatory to further turn components. And indeed such additional components are forthcoming, at a slight distance, in (38) and (26) above and (26 [detail]) below – (see also [5]):

```
(26)  [HG:II:25 (detail)]

    N: How didju git 'iz number,
       (.)
    H: I(h) (.) c(h)alled infermation'n San Fr'ncissc(h)
        ┌uh.
 →  N: └Oh:::::.
       (.)
 →  N· Very cleve:r, hh=
```

Here it is the "oh" producer who, as in the previous two examples, resumes the talk with an assessment – another turn component that commonly co-occurs with "oh." In this context, it may further be noted that, whereas "oh" may propose a change of state in response to an informing, it is entirely opaque as to the quality or character of the change of state proposedly undergone by its producer. Thus an informant/"oh" recipient may withhold from further talk with a view to permitting/inviting the "oh" producer to elaborate what lay behind the production of the particle.

An elaborate version of this post-"oh" withholding is the following:

```
(46)  [Rah:II:2]

         ((Re a previously announced change of
           arrangements for coffee))

      J: C's uh:  ┌there's no ba:dmint┌on,
      I:          └I : s   V e r a  s ┘
         (.)
      I: Pardon?
      J: There's no ba:dminton:, tomorrow so┌: wuh:r,┐
      I:                                     └ O h : .┘
  1→     (.)
  2→  J: Yeh.
  3→     (.)
  4→  J: S┌o I thought well┐  lah-
      I:  └e e  Y  e  h  . ┘
      J: It'll be an opportunity for me: to do it.
```

Here J abandons a projected extension to her repaired accounting ("There's no ba:dminton, tomorrow so: wuh:r,") in the face of I's disappointed-sounding "oh" receipt. Here it appears that J, hearing I's "oh" receipt, abandons her accounting so as to permit I to elaborate her "oh" with some comment or query (arrow 1). In the absence of any move by I, J recompletes her prior turn (arrow 2) and thus creates a further opportunity for I to produce some talk (arrow 3) before proceeding with a continuation of her account (arrow 4).

A final type of evidence that informants/"oh" recipients treat the production of "oh" as projecting further turn components arises from sequences such as (20) and (23).

```
(20)  [W:PC:1:(MJ)1:1]

      J: When d'z Sus'n g┌o back.=
      M:                 └ˑhhhh
      J: =┌(                    )
      M:  └u-She: goes back on Satida:y=
      J: =O┌h:.
   →  M:   └A:n:' Stev'n w'z here (.) all las'week .....
```

(23)   [Rah:B:2:JV(14):1]

```
J: Oh:::. Have they'av yih visitiz g┌one then, ┐
V:                                     └They've go┘:ne.
   Yes,
J: Oh ┌:ah.
→ V:   └A::n:' they've gone to .....
```

In each of these cases, the production of a receipting "oh" is intersected with a stretched version of "and" with which the prior speaker displays continued turn occupancy and a commitment to extend the prior question-initiated informing with further talk.[19] In these cases, the informant/"oh" recipient's production of overlapping talk appears designed to stifle, or otherwise sequentially delete, the production of additional turn components projected by the production of "oh."

In considering the tasks accomplished by this overlap competitive talk, it will be recalled that possible additional turn components projected by the production of "oh" include additional inquiries and assessments. Since either item may disrupt trajectory of talk intended by the informant – inquiries by redirecting the talk along a different track, assessments by being topic-curtailing – neither may be desired by an informant who wishes to elaborate on prior talk and to control its direction. Thus the "oh"-intersecting elaborations instanced in (20) and (23) appear designed to forestall the possible production of such additional turn components in the service of retaining control over the future development of topical talk.

With these considerations to hand, we can now proceed to consider recipient conduct in two systematically organized sequence types used to develop new topics in conversation. We will find that a free-standing "oh" is an unsatisfactory receipt item, though for different reasons, in both sequence types.

9. Recipient conduct in new topic beginnings

Button and Casey (forthcoming) have described two distinctively organized procedures – news announcements and itemized news inquiries – through which speakers can initiate talk that involves an abrupt shift from an immediately preceding topic to a new one.

In news announcements, intending informants initiate a new topic by partially describing, or headlining, events in which they, or known-to-recipient third parties have been involved.

(10)   [Rah:B:1DJ(12):2]

```
      I: Yes he's he re,
      J:          [mHm.
             (.)
  ┌→  J: I  saw Janie this morning=
 1│    I:    [Yes
  └→  J: =in in: uh Marks'n Sp encers
 2→   I:                      [Oh you] did di dju  y e s, =
      J:                                [Mm: :. [ 'hh ]=
 3→   J: =She w'z buyin' a whole load of stuff .....
```

(11)   [HG:II:2]

```
      H: 'hhhh I c'n live without 'er, °'hhhhhh (.) That's
         a'right,°
             (.)
      N: u-h Oh::,
             (.)
      H: = Bu:t
 1→   N:   [My f :face hurts,=
      H: =°W't-°
             (.)
 2→   H: Oh what'd'e do tih you.
             (.)
 3→   N: ↑GOD'e dis (.) prac'ly killed my dumb fa:ce,=
```

(12)   [Rah:I:8]

```
      J: ... 'cuz she said she wouldn' be going if Janie
         w'z going t'that keep fit thing.
  ┌→  V: uRight yeh 'hh Oh I met Jani:e, eh:::m yesterday
 1│     an' she'd had a fo:rm from the Age Concern about
  └→    that jo:b. h=
 2→   J: =Oh she has?
 3→   V:  So: eh she w'z sending the fo:rm back .....
```

In each of these cases the initial news announcement (arrow 1) is disjoined from previous talk and is hearably incomplete in intimating that
there is more to be told than has emerged thus far. Similarly, in each of
the cases, the recipient orients to this hearable incompleteness by creat-
ing a further opportunity for an elaboration of the news (arrow 2),
whereupon the news announcer engages in such elaboration (arrow 3).
The recipients of news announcements, in each case, progress the projected sequence with the use of a receipt of an "oh" plus inquiry (in [11])
or of "oh" plus newsmark (as in [10] or [12]). These receipts are well
fitted to the news announcements to which they respond. For a news
announcer unilaterally proposes a new topic of conversation and may

require a strong display of recipient commitment to the proposed topic before continuing.

By contrast, a simple "oh" receipt may be insufficient to promote such topical development, as in (38).

```
(38)   [Rah:II:7 (extended)]

    J: Oh (well) let's hope something comes o:f i :t
    I:                                          [Yes:.
    J: Mm:  ˙h
    I:      [Ye s
1→ J:          [Derek's ho:me?
       (0.5)
    I: Yo:ur De rek.
    J:          [Ye:s m m
2→ I:                   [Oh:,
3→     (.)
    I: An'- is he a' ri:ght?=
    J: =Oh he's fi:ne .....
```

Here, as we have already noted, I's "oh" receipt of J's (repaired) news announcement does not progress the topic. In this context, "oh" is systematically weaker than an "oh" plus inquiry or "oh" plus news-mark receipt in that (1) it fails to invite the informant/news announcer to tell more and (2) in projecting additional turn components, it may invite the announcer to await them by withholding from further talk. Given these features, in the environment of news announcements as unilateral new topic proposals, a mere "oh" receipt is systematically insufficient to promote further talk from the news announcer/"oh" recipient.

In the context of itemized news inquiries, by contrast, the reverse is the case. Here it is the intending recipient who nominates a possibly newsworthy event by inquiring into a coparticipant-related event as in (17) and (47).

```
(17)   [WPC:1:(MJ)1:2]

→ M: ˙hhhh (.) °Um::° 'Ow is yih mother by: th'wa:y.h
```

```
(47)   [Rah:II:5]

→ J: When are you gettin' yer: ↑dining room suite.
```

Such inquiries are regularly understood, not as requests for information to be answered in abbreviated form, but as news inquiries – requests to be brought up to date on current recipient circumstances or troubles to which the inquirer displays partial access (Button and Casey forthcoming). Recipients display this understanding by giving elaborated, but hearably incomplete, responses (arrow 2) and thus establish themselves as the intending tellers of further information topicalized by the prior inquiry (ibid.). In turn, inquirers regularly promote such further telling by means of the production of a continuation (arrow 3).

    (17) [WPC:1:(MJ)1:2]

```
1→ M: ˙hhhh (.) °Um::° 'Ow is yih mother by: th'wa:y.h
       (.)
2→ J: We:ll she's a:, bit better:,
3→ M: Mm┌::,
   J:    └eh- She came: do:wn on: Satidee:eveni┌ng.....
   M:                                          └↑Oh: did ...
```

    (47) [Rah:II:5]

```
1→ J: When are you gettin' yer: ↑dining room suite.
2→ I: Well not ye:t i- eh we ca:lled last wee:k.h
3→ J: eYe┌:s,
   I:    └°(But) Jilly:°........
```

In these cases, by contrast with the news-announcement sequences, the elaboration of the news is invited by the production of a more-or-less passive continuation object, most commonly, "yes" and "mm hm."[20] Again such continuation receipts are well fitted to the sequences in which they participate. For the would-be recipient of the informing has already displayed substantial commitment to the to-be-developed topic by the initial production of an itemized news inquiry. Moreover, since the projected informant has already begun a to-be-completed informing in response to the prior inquiry, the alignment of both speakers to a trajectory of topical development is largely accomplished and requires only that the inquirer/projected recipient *sustain* the role of recipient. The production of a continuation is the standard means to this end.

In this context, an "oh" receipt is doubly inappropriate. Firstly, since it regularly co-occurs with additional turn components, it may be heard to project early recipient intervention in the informing sequence. Thus in (48) an itemized news inquiry (arrow 1) gets an elaborated but hearably incomplete response (arrow 2). The subsequent ("oh"-plus-assessment) response (arrow 3) is overlapped by the projected informant with two stretched "uh::m"s, after which the informant proceeds in the clear with further detailing (arrow 4).

(48)   [Her:I:11:3]

```
1→ N: =˙h have Are: you ex:pecting ┌any (puppies)?┐
2→ I:                               │˙h Well I hope│so::=
3→ N:  =┌°Oh. How e┐xci┌ting.°┐
4→ I:   │ u h : : m┘   ┘U h ::│m: d-Tessa w'z mated .....
```

In this case of overlap competition, the intending informant (I) overtly contests both the "oh" receipt and the subsequent object it projects – an early and topic-curtailing assessment. Whereas N and I begin their overlapping turns simultaneously, I's first "uhm" is stretched across N's "oh" and the initiation of her assessment so as to claim continued turn occupancy, and this claim is reinforced by the initiation of a second stretched "uhm" in overlap with the final syllable of N's assessment.

This overt contest with both the "oh" receipt and the intervention it projects contrasts with the immediately subsequent development of the talk, in (49), in which only the post-"oh" continuation undergoes competition.

(49)   [Her:I:11:3]

```
   I: d-Tessa w'z mated um (0.3) oh about three weeks
      ago:.
1→ N: hhOh:.┌( )
2→ I:       └A n d (.) Kizzy w'z mated about two weeks
      ago┌:.
3→ N:     └Oh my goodness you do as┌:k for i┌t,
   I:                              └eh-h e h┘
```

Here N's appropriate "oh" receipt of the detailing of the puppy situation is permitted in the clear by I (arrow 1) whereas N's attempted continuation of the turn is cut off by I's overlapping continuation (arrow 2) of the detailing. Thus it is only after both dogs' matings have been detailed that N is permitted an ("oh"-plus-assessment) utterance in the clear (arrow 3). Example (48), in which both the "oh" and the utterance it projects undergo competition, suggests that the "oh" is being competed with in an attempt to forestall any subsequent turn components – an attempt that is unsuccessful in this case and results in further overlap competitive activity. In short, the "oh" is being competed with for what it projects. This then is a first sense in which an "oh" receipt to a hearably incomplete response to an itemized news inquiry may be inappropriate.

However, second, an "oh" receipt may be undesired and competed with for what it proposes in its own right and regardless of what it projects. Section 3 noted that an "oh" receipt of a possibly complete answer to a question may treat the answer as in fact complete – a satisfactory filling of a gap in information.

A return to a sequence such as (26) shows that the apparently un-problematic fact that the question cites an information gap that is subse-quently filled is in fact the product of fine-grained sequential negotia-tion.

(26)   [HG:II:25 (detail)]

```
N: ='hhh D'z he 'av 'iz own apa:rt┌mint?┐
H:                                 └'hhhh┘ Yea:h,=
N: =Oh:,
   (1.0)
N: How didju git 'iz number,
```

In this sequence, the "oh"-carried now-informed proposal instructs the informant that a gap in information has now been filled and that the informant may lawfully withhold from further talk.

By contrast, in (50), a hearably complete answer to a question that could have been referring to a similar information gap is continuation-receipted, and the question is thereby retrospectively formulated by the questioner as a topic-generative itemized news inquiry for which further detailing by the informant is appropriate.

(50)   [W:PC:1:MJ(1):11]

```
   J: When are you proposing setting off then.=
   M: ='t' Wuh we're t– we're leaving Su:nday
      mo:rnin:┌g
→  J:        └Ye:s.
   M: And we're ca:lling in Birmingham .....
```

In (26), an "oh" receipt is produced at the first point at which a hearably complete answer is produced and results in the curtailment of any fur-ther detailing in response to the question. In (50), by contrast, a con-tinuation receipt is produced at the first point at which a hearably com-plete answer is produced and, subsequent to this receipt, the informant (M) engages in further elaborate detailing of the planned trip.

Returning to (20) and (23), we can now suggest that more is being done than simply stifling the production of post-"oh" turn components.

(20)   [W:PC:1:(MJ)1:1]

```
J: When d'z Sus'n g┌o back.=
M:                  └'hhhh
```

```
J:    =(                         )
M:    =[u–She goes back on Satida:y=
J:    =Oₕh:.
M:     [A̱:n:' Stev'n w'z here (.) all la̱s'week .....
```

(23)   [Rah:B:2:JV(14):1]

```
J:    Oh:::. Have they'av yih visitiz gₒone then, ₁
V:                                     [They've go̱]:ne. Yes,
J:    Oh ₗ:ah
V:       [A::n:' they've gone to .....
```

In each of these cases, the questioner uses a now informed "oh" receipt to treat the prior answer as hearably complete while the answerer, with the production of an "oh"-intersecting continuation, treats the prior question as an itemized news inquiry generative of further topical elaboration. In each case, an in-the-course-of-being-produced "oh" is overlapped, not merely to stifle the production of further post-"oh" turn components, but also to preempt and, as far as possible, to delete the sequence curtailing implications of the now informed proposal accomplished by the use of a free-standing "oh" receipt.[21] In these cases, then, "oh" is being competed with for what it proposes in its own right and, through these cases, it can be seen that a questioner's choice between an "oh" and a continuation receipt is specifically consequential in proposing both how he viewed the initial question and how he is prepared to treat the answer that responds to it.

In sum, where new topics are being developed with the use of news announcements or itemized news inquiries, a free-standing "oh" receipt is a systematically inadequate response. In the context of news announcements, it is generally insufficient to promote continuation whereas, conversely, in the case of itemized news inquiries it may constitute a curtailing intervention into the informing sequence and, in turn, may be systematically competed with. In this latter context, a free-standing "oh" receipt may be produced by a questioner who began with a gap in information and who is unaware of, or unwilling to collaborate with, an answerer's desire to respond to the question in an elaborated or topic-generative fashion.

10. The production of free-standing "oh" as withholding

In the preceding sections of this chapter, it has been repeatedly noted that "oh" is regularly used as a turn component prefatory to additional turn components and that when it is produced in free-standing form it is regularly the "oh" producer who subsequently progresses the talk. These sequential projections are, as we have seen, understood and traded upon by "oh" recipients who display this understanding in withholding further talk, or producing competing talk, in the immediate environment of the particle's production.

In a number of cases, however, "oh" producers may refrain from the production of further talk in ways that are specifically identifiable by recipients as involving withholding. Thus the following sequence develops from a standard prerequest/pre-invitation object: "What are you doing?"

```
(51)   [NB:IV:9:1]

1  E:  Oh: I'm jis' sittin' here with Phil'n Martha'n
2      haa:eh fixin'm a drink they're goin' out tih
3      dinner:.
4      (.)
5  E:  H e's-
6  P:   Oh::::. Oh.
7  E:  Why: whiddiyih wa:nt.
8      (1.0)
9  P:  hhuhh Well?h I wanted .....
```

Here E's response (lines 1–3) details a current activity that potentially conflicts with what P might have in mind (either an extended telephone conversation or, as it turns out, an immediate visit). P's disappointed-sounding stretched "oh" receipt suggests that E's response does indeed pose some difficulty for her plans. However, rather than going on to detail these plans, P merely appends a shorter and terminally intoned "oh," thereby exhibiting a reluctance to elaborate. It is thus left to E (line 7) to inquire into the plan foreshadowed with the "pre-" object and depicted as frustrated with the stretched "oh." By this procedure, P manages the sequence so as begin her description of her prior intention (line 9) at the request of her recipient rather than on her own initiative.

A more extended instance of withholding through the production of a free-standing "oh" is the following.

```
(19)   [Campbell 4:1 (extended)]

1  A:      Well lis:ten, (.) tiz you tidju phone yer
2          vicar ye:t,
3          (0.3)
4  B:    ─  No I ain't.
5 (A):  (0.4) (˙hhh)
```

```
 6   A:        Oh:.
 7              (0.3)
 8 (A):        ˙hhhhh–
 9   A:        Ah::-::-⌈::
10   B:                  ⌊I w'z gonna wait .....
```

Here B indicates (line 4) that he has not fulfilled a previous undertaking
to phone his vicar but does not account for this failure. After this reply,
A permits a (0.4) gap to elapse before "oh"-receipting it and a further
(0.3) gap ensues after this receipt. Both gaps constitute opportunities for
the provision of the absent account and, after the second post-"oh" gap
(line 7), A's subsequent nonlexicalized utterance (line 9) exhibits a continuing reluctance to advance the sequence. B's subsequently initiated
account (line 10) can thus be seen to be elicited by the series of post-"oh"
withholdings by A, but without the account being requested or de-
manded as such. In these cases, then, "oh" producers successfully rely
upon the fact that the production of the particle routinely projects further talk as a means of inducing coparticipants to volunteer sequentially
relevant activities. By not producing, and hence overtly withholding
"oh"-projected talk that is "due" next, a speaker may induce a coparticipant to initiate or accomplish sequentially relevant activities that the
withholding speaker would rather not initiate or request.

11. Conclusion

Although it has been almost traditional to treat "oh" and related utterances (such as "yes," "uh huh," "mm hm," etc.) as an undifferentiated
collection of "back channels" or "signals of continued attention," the
observations presented in this chapter suggest that such treatments
seriously underestimate the diversity and complexity of the tasks that
these objects are used to accomplish. In both their variety and their
placement in a range of sequence types, these objects are used to achieve
a systematically differentiated range of objectives which, in turn, are
specifically consequential for the onward development of the sequences
in which they are employed. Within this collection, "oh" is unique in
making a change-of-state proposal which is most commonly used to
accept prior talk as informative. Such a proposal is, in certain of the
sequence types discussed here, strongly required and regularly used. In
others, the production of a free-standing "oh" may be disruptive of the
development of talk, competed with, or produced in the service of special
interactional objectives. All of these variations, however, testify to the

deeply structured and conventionalized character of the particle's production and interpretation in ordinary talk.

Unlike such objects as "yes" and "mm hm," "oh" in conversation is essentially backward looking and scarcely ever continuative. "Oh" appears to share this characteristic with other response cries discussed by Goffman (1981) and this characteristic is associated with the fact that, when it (and they) are uttered in ordinary talk, the utterer will commonly have more to say that is richer in content and more overtly directed to a recipient. In this regard, the routine use of "oh" in conversation can be viewed as instancing an exceptionally ritualized use of response crying which is nonetheless betrayed as such in the standard occurrence of additional conjoined or postpositioned turn components.

"Oh" occurs most densely perhaps in the environment of questions and their answers. Consideration of its placement in these sequences may contribute toward a broader line of inquiry and such inquiry suggests that the action of questioning is not only or fully accomplished within the span of a single utterance. Rather, if the observations of this chapter are correct, the action of questioning is, even in the simplest cases, the reciprocal achievement of two turns in a sequence having, at the minimum, a prototypical Q–A–"Oh" structure. Moreover, questions and answers are themselves the media through which a variety of activities are transacted in conversation, and choices among the (third-turn) receipt objects discussed in this chapter play a considerable role in the determination of what these activities have been, or will come to. Included within the scope of this determination will be whether a syntactically formed question was produced so as to accomplish questioning.

Finally, questions and answers are also the means by which other, nonconversational or quasiconversational, activities are accomplished. Medical consultations, news interviews, courtroom examinations, and classroom interaction all fall into these latter categories. All are marked by the absence of "oh" as a routine third-turn receipt object and, in certain cases, of other routine receipt objects as well. These absences may represent specific "identifying details" (Garfinkel forthcoming) that, in combination with others, are characteristic of the management of particular kinds of institutionalized interaction, such as a news interview or cross-examination. As such, they would necessarily contribute to the maintenance and reproduction *within the talk* that it is some special institutionalized activity which is in progress and, of course, to the pervasive sense within such contexts that something *other than* conversation is in progress.

In the *Philosophical Grammar* (1974:67), Wittgenstein observes:

> If we were asked about it, we would probably say "Oh!" is a sigh; we say, for instance, "Oh, it is raining again already" and similar things. In that way we would have described the use of the word. But now what corresponds to the calculus, to the complicated game which we play with other words? In the use of the words "oh" or "hurrah" or "hm" there is nothing comparable.

On the evidence in the present chapter, Wittgenstein's judgment would appear to be premature and indeed the uses of "oh" appear to be considerably more complicated than he suggests. For the particle participates in a wide variety of "language games": noticing; having one's attention drawn to something; remembering; being reminded, informed, or corrected; arriving at discoveries and realizations of various kinds, and many more. "Oh" is perhaps as deeply implicated in the behaviors of "coming to see something" as "Ouch" is in the domain of pain behaviors. In this way, then, the final word can perhaps remain with Wittgenstein. For it is the unreflecting, routine anchorage of "oh"'s in transparent and unproblematic contexts that permits their confident interpretation in ever more complex and reticulated contexts of use.

Notes

1. "Oh" is listed by the linguist Charles Fries among a collection of "signals of continued attention" which also includes "yes," "unh hunh," "yeah," "I see," "good," etc. (Fries 1952:49). Subsequently, "oh" is also listed as a member of a class of "noncommunicative" utterances including "wow," "zowie," "my God," and so on (ibid.). By contrast, Deborah James proposes that "oh"'s in both turn-initial position and in free-standing form ("oh$_2$") convey "definite semantic information and are appropriate in certain specific contexts" (James 1972:163). The present chapter, in arguing that "oh" makes a generic change-of-state proposal that is made relevant by, and particularized in, certain contexts, takes James's view of the matter.
2. Gail Jefferson (1978a:221–2) has cited the use of "oh" as a "disjunct marker" and notes that its use is associated with a "display of sudden remembering." She has also noted its use as a token of special interest (Jefferson 1972:313–4), its role in conjunction with "newsmarks" (Jefferson 1981a), and, in the context of repair, its use as a token of "prior trouble now resolved" (personal communication).
3. An intermediate case between a volunteered and a responsive production of "oh" is perhaps that in which the recipient of a telephone call recognizes the identity of the caller from a sample of the latter's voice. Such recognition is commonly asserted with "oh." See Schegloff (1979a) for a range of instances.
4. This sequence is treated in more detail in Drew (Chapter 6 herein).
5. See also the treatment of this sequence in Drew (Chapter 6 herein); Schegloff (1982) and Jefferson (1981b) have discussed the placement of continuations in extended talk by a single speaker.

6. See Button and Casey (forthcoming) for a characterization of hearably incomplete news announcements.
7. See Terasaki (1976) for a range of similar instances and a characterization of their sequential organization.
8. Sacks (1974), Terasaki (1976), and Jefferson (1978a) discuss aspects of these negotiations with reference to joke-telling, announcements, and storytelling respectively.
9. An "oh"-carried proposal that its producer was previously uninformed can, of course, be modified by additional turn components. In the following instance, F qualifies her "oh" proposal with additional turn components that refer to her prior information.

> [NB:I:2]

> F: ((f)) Wul when didju guys go:::.
> S: Ah: Saturday?hh
> → F: ((f)) Oh: fer, crying out loud. I thought it wz
>   the end'v th'mo:nth you were go:::i:n,

By these means, F asserts herself to have been previously misinformed rather than simply uninformed.

Similarly, in each of the next two cases, rejections of invitations are accompanied by candidate known-to-recipient accounts. In the first, the recipient of the account is specifically invited to "remember" the circumstances (the "two other kids") which are invoked to reject the invitation.

> [NB:I:5]

> F: 'hhh Oh: come o:n. ₁I could₁n' j's come down=
> T: [H m : ?]
> F: =the:re, hn 't'hh I got two other kids. Remember?
> → T: Oh:: that's ri₁:ght,₁
> F: [eYe::] ::::ah::

Here the recipient's ("oh" + "that's right") receipt accepts the prior account by treating its informing as a "just-now-recollected-as-relevant" remembering of previously and independently known information. And, in the following, a similar format is deployed and emphasized with an additional postpositioned "I FER ↑ GO:T. Com*letely*."

> [Frankel:TC:1:1:15–16]

> S: 'hhh So if you guys want a place tuh sta:y.
>   (0.3)
> G: 't'hhh Oh well thank you but you we ha- yihknow
>   Victor.
> → S: ↑OH that's ↑RI:GHT.=
> G: =That's why we were going ₁(we)
> → S: [I FER↑GO:T. Completely.

In various ways, then, recipients can qualify an "oh"-carried change-of-state proposal so as to formulate it as proposing misinformation or recollection rather than simply involving a prior lack of information. Moreover, just as a subsequently produced "that's right" may qualify a turn-initial "oh," so also a turn-initial "oh" qualifies the sense of "that's right" as involving a "just now" recollection of something known but not previously taken into account as relevant, rather than the sense of "independent confirmation" that "that's right," unprefaced by "oh," would otherwise convey.

10. For a characterization of how a reference to an expectably known-to-recipient event, by a party who asserts limited access to that event, solicits information from the recipient, see Pomerantz (1980a). Some discussion of source-cited reports as alternatively displaying limited access or sensitivity to the matters reported is presented in Pomerantz (1981, forthcoming).

11. The data also evidence the prospective readiness of questioners to assume this now informed status. A substantial number of "oh" receipts occur early, that is, in "latched" or slightly overlapped positions relative to the answers they receipt. Such receipts are rarely delayed longer than a micropause.

12. It may further be suggested that "oh" receipts, in proposing a questioner's now informed status, also implicate the questioner's acceptance of an answer as fact. In this context, informings of various kinds that are not "oh"-(or some equivalent) receipted (see note 13) are often subsequently contested. Moreover, in the environment of contested informings, those who seek to remain neutral may systematically avoid "oh" receipts. Thus Max Atkinson (1979b) has noted that arbitrators in British small claims courts, who question both plaintiff and defendent in the presence of the other, avoid the production of "oh" to receipt answers to their questions in favor of more neutral objects like "yes" and "certainly." In British news broadcasts, which are required by statute to exhibit balance and impartiality, interviewers entirely avoid such receipts. Here the avoidance of "oh" production serves both to sustain the interviewer's neutral posture and to maintain the interview as an event in which the "overhearing" audience, rather than the interviewer, is the target of the informing and in which the interviewer's role is restricted to eliciting such informings (see Heritage forthcoming). Finally, lay characterizations of talk also treat "oh" as routinely accepting what is asserted in the prior talk. Thus in *Northanger Abbey* (pp. 97–8 of the 1972 Penguin edition), Jane Austen depicts the following exchange:

> Soon after their reaching the bottom of the set, Catherine perceived herself to be earnestly regarded by a gentleman who stood among the lookers-on, immediately behind her partner . . . Confused by his notice, and blushing from the fear of its being excited by something wrong in her appearance, she turned away her head. But while she did so, the gentleman retreated, and her partner coming nearer, said, "I see that you guess what I have just been asked. That gentleman knows your name, and you have a right to know his. It is General Tilney, my father."
>
> Catherine's answer was only "Oh!" – but it was an "Oh!" expressing everything needful; attention to his words and perfect reliance on their truth.

In the following report from *The Times* (of London), a bride tells of her reaction to the discovery that her serviceman husband will have to depart for a war zone immediately after the wedding reception. The bride's gloss is a similar one: "As we left the church I whispered: 'When have you got to go?' He simply replied 'Tonight.' I said 'Oh' and accepted it."

13. In this connection, a strong distinction is to be maintained between free-standing "oh" that centrally functions as a backward-looking information receipt and a variety of assertions of ritualized disbelief, e.g., "yer kidding," "really?" "did you," etc., that treat a prior utterance as news for recipient.

The latter systematically advance the sequences in which they participate by inviting prior speakers to, at minimum, reconfirm the substance of the prior turn's talk. Commonly, speakers in receipt of such objects reconfirm the prior *and* advance the informing as in (a) and (b).

    (a) [NB:II:2:12]

    N: An' Warden, had to physically remove 'im from 'iz
       office, 'hhhh
→ E: Really?
→ N: Yeh they'd had quite a scuffle, a:nd .....

    (b) [NB:II:4:10 (r)]

    N: But uh I didn't get home til' 'hhh two las'night
       I met a very,h very n:ni:ce gu:y.
→ D: Di(.)dju::::.
→ N: I: really did through the:se frie:nds .....

Jefferson (1981a:62–6) refers to these objects as "newsmarks," that is, objects that specifically treat a prior turn's talk as news for the recipient rather than merely informative. In this regard, all newsmarks project further talk by the news deliverer/newsmark recipient by reference to the news but, Jefferson reports, different newsmarks project different trajectories for such talk. Any newsmark may be prefixed by "oh" and, in many cases, the presence or absence of such a prefix plays a role in projecting different trajectories.

Jefferson notes, for example, that "oh really?" regularly occurs in sequences that run as follows: (1) news announcement, (2) "oh really?" (3) reconfirmation, and (4) assessment (which is generally terminal or topic-curtailing). This sequence type is instanced in (c) and (d).

    (c) [NB:IV:7:5–6]

    M: How many cigarettes yih had.
       (0.8)
1→ E: NO:NE.
2→ M: Oh really?
3→ E: No:.
4→ M: Very good.

    (d) [NB:II:2:3]

    E: Hey that was the same spot we took off for
1→ Honolulu. (0.4) Where they put him on, (1.0)
     at that chartered place,
2→ N: Oh really?
3→ E: y::Yea::h.
4→ N: Oh::? for heaven sakes.

By contrast, Jefferson proposes, newsmarks formed as "partial repeats" and produced in a format "Oh"-plus-partial repeat regularly occur in sequences "*within* which further talk by reference to the 'news' is done" and, she continues: "That talk is either volunteered by the news-deliverer/ newsmark recipient in Slot (3), accompanying the 'confirmation' component . . . or is solicited by the news recipient/newsmark deliverer in Slot (4), thus replacing the sequence-terminal 'assessment' component with pursuit of further talk vis-à-vis the news" (ibid.:63–4). These alternative possibilities are displayed in (e) and (f).

(e)   [TCI(a):14:2]

1→ A: We're havin a h–buncha people over too :.
2→ B: ⌊Oh are yih?
       (.)
3→ A: Yeh it sort'v .....

(f)   [NB:I:1:17]

1→ E: They charge too much Guy,
2→ G: Oh do they?
3→ E: Yeh I think so,
4→ G: What do they cha:rge.

In sum, while free-standing "oh" functions as an information receipt, "oh"-plus-newsmark regularly functions as a news receipt, with different newsmark types standardly projecting different sequential outcomes for the onward course of talk by reference to the news.

Finally Jefferson notes that free-standing (i.e., not prefixed by "oh") partial repeat newsmarks regularly engender sequences such as the following:

(g)   [NB:IV:3:1]

1⌈→ L: I'm gonna take them up to Anthony's and dye them
 ⌊→   because they dye uhb– uhb, the– perfect ma:tch.
2→ E: Do they,
3→ L: Yeah,
4→ E: Ah hah,
5→ L: I mean sometimes you buy them at these places .....

Here the slot (4) "is occupied by an acknowledgment token, in contrast to () terminal assessments . . . and () solicitations of further talk. . . And (such objects) tend to be followed by a 'voluntary' production of more talk by reference to the news, now in Slot (5)" (ibid., p. 65). It may be concluded from these observations that "oh"-plus-partial repeat more strongly projects recipient commitment to further talk by reference to the news than either a free-standing "oh" or a free-standing partial repeat.

These considerations can be taken a further step by comparing two alternative syntactic designs of partial repeats – those that are *syntactically* formed as questions (e.g., "did you?") and those that are not (e.g., "you did?"). The latter form of free-standing partial repeat regularly engenders the kind of topic curtailment already observed in the case of "oh really?" Thus in (h) and (i), it can be observed that after such a newsmark, the news deliverer/newsmark recipient merely reconfirms (slot 3) the prior turn's talk and subsequently the news recipient/ newsmark deliverer produces a (slot 4) sequence curtailing assessment.

(h)   [TC II(a):14:15]

   ⌈→ C: Th'reason they're vacant is becuz they got'm
   ⌊→   all torn up.
1 ⌊   (0.6)
   ⌊→ C: Replumbing the whole place.

```
2→ E: You are?
3→ C: Yeah.
4→ E: Wul goo::d.h
```

    (i)   [Adeto:2:15–16]

```
1→ J: Think we're gonna get a rai:se, first of next
       month.
2→ G: You are?
       ((pause))
3→ S: We are,
4→ G: Congratulations.
```

In (j), after a similar free-standing newsmark, the news recipient/newsmark deliverer curtails elaboration of the prior turn's talk by re-issuing a prior query in the slot 4 position.

    (j)   [NB:I:1:5]

```
   G: Think he'd like ⌜to go?
1⌈ E:                 ⌊Played golf with 'im yes:terday
 ⌊     at San Clemente.
2→ G: Yuh did.
3→ E: Uh huh,
4→ G: Think he'd like tuh go?
```

Additionally, however, this form of free-standing partial repeat may project a further sequence type that is unique to it: *disagreement*. Thus in each of the following cases, after a free-standing partial repeat newsmark, the news recipient/newsmark deliverer moves to contradict the prior (slot 1) assertion and its subsequent (slot 3) reconfirmation.

    (k)   [Rah:B:1:1DJ(12):2]

```
  ⌈ I: Well she's gone to m: eh: eh: Chester:.
1⌊     (0.9)
  ⌊ I: Ja⌈nie:,
2→ J:    ⌊↑Janie has.
3→ I: ↑Ey?
4→ J: No she hasn't?
```

    (1)   [Earthquake Broom:1]

```
1⌈ T: That broom you lookin' for is on the s-
 ⌊     landing a'the stairs.
       (0.3)
2→ J: It i:s?
       (0.2)
3→ T: Yea⌈:h
4→ J:    ⌊I don't see any broom there,
```

    (m)   [TG:1]

```
1→ B: Why wh:at'sa matter with y-Yih sou⌈nd HA:PPY,hh
   A:                                    ⌊Nothing.
```

```
2→ A: I sound ha:p py?
3→ B:          Ye:uh
        (0.3)
4→ A: No:,
```

(n) [TG:3]

```
1→ A: ... You sound very far away.
        (0.7)
2→ B: I do?
3→ A: Meahm.
4→ B: mNo? I'm no:t,
```

In the following case, an initial assertion that gets a similar free-standing partial repeat is guardedly moderated in slot 3.

(o) [Travel Agency:10:ST]

```
1→ A: Derek we have no hea::t.
2→ D: Yih have no hea:t?
3→ A: We, can't feel any.=
```

Subsequent disagreement by a newsmark producer is, in the data to hand, uniquely associated with free-standing partial repeats that are not *syntactically* produced as queries. Where such partial repeats *are* syntactically produced as queries, subsequent disagreement does not occur. Thus a freestanding partial repeat that is not syntactically produced as a query alternatively projects either (1) sequence curtailment (as in [h]–[j]), or (2) disagreement (as in [k]–[o]); see also Pomerantz (Chapter 4 herein).

By contrast, cases in which a syntactically nonquery-formed partial repeat is prefixed by "oh" run similarly to "oh"-plus-query-formed-partial-repeats (see cases [e] and [f]); either slot (3) volunteered continuations develop (e.g., [p]) or such continuation is solicited by the news recipient/newsmark deliverer in slot 4 (as in [q]).

(p) [Rah:1:8]

```
     V: Oh I met Jani:e, eh:::m yesterday an'
1       she'd had a fo:rm from the Age Concern
        about that jo:b. h=
2→ J: =Oh she has?
3→ V: So: eh she w'z sending .....
```

(q) [NB:IV:14:1]

```
1→ E: Well, we just got do:wn,hh
2→ L: Oh you di: d?
3→ E:           Yea:uh.
4→ L: Oh how co:me,
```

In sum, whereas "oh you did?" appears effectively equivalent in sequential terms to "oh did you?" a parallel equivalence does not hold between "you did?" and "did you?" Whereas "you did?" may project disagreement and, in projecting disagreement, may license "paranoid" responses as in (o), "did you?" does not project the possibility of upcoming disagreement.

Two conclusions may be drawn from these observations. (1) Whereas a free-standing "oh" rarely promotes the onward course of an informing sequence, it is instrumental in combination with most newsmarks (except "really?") in promoting substantial further talk to the news receipted with the "oh"-plus-newsmark combination. "Oh" thus generally strengthens a newsmark's proposal of commitment to the materials it receipts as a potential topic for further talk. (2) Whereas a free-standing syntactically nonquery-formed partial repeat may project disagreement, an "oh" prefix to this form of newsmark entirely eliminates this possibility and constitutes further indirect evidence for the possibility that "oh" functions as an information receipt that is used to accept the information receipted as fact (see also note 12).

Finally, it may be noted that where a free-standing "oh" is itself query-intoned, it may function as a newsmark that promotes further talk to the news it marks. Such a use of "oh" is rare in the data to hand, and no attempt is made here to characterize its functioning.

14. In this context, answers to exam questions (Searle 1969:66–7) are never receipted with "oh," but with some version of confirmation/ disconfirmation (see McHoul 1978, Mehan 1979, for a range of instances). By this means, among others, the pedagogical frame of classroom interaction is continuously sustained *within the talk*.

15. None of these conclusions should be taken as implying that, in turns responsive to counterinformings, an "oh" preface *invariably* projects acceptance of the counterinforming by the counterinformed party. In the following case, involving conflicting identifications of bird song, Ben's "Oh yeh?" challenges Bill's counterproposal that the birds are quail, and Ben subsequently follows it with a reassertion of his initial identification that they are "pigeons."

```
          [JS:II:219–20]

  Ben:    Lissena pigeons.
          (0.7)
  Ellen: ⌈Coo-coo:::coo:::
  Bill:  ⌊Q u a i l, I think.
→ Ben:    Oh yeh?
          (1.5)
  Ben:    No that's not quail, that's a pigeon,
```

In the small number of cases to hand, "oh"-prefaced challenges to counterinformings are invariably question-intoned, but no further observations as to their character can be offered at the present.

16. On the types of repair and their initiation, see Schegloff, Jefferson, and Sacks (1977).

17. In the extended repair sequences of (35) and (36), more than "oh" receipts are provided for the finally successful repair event, e.g., "oh yeah" and "oh okay."

18. The major alternative means of achieving exit from a repair sequence involves simple continuation of the sequence in progress prior to the repair. This is illustrated in the sequence below.

```
          [Frankel:TC:1:1:2–3]

  S:      ='hhh Uh:m, 'tch'hhhh Who w'yih ↑ta:lking to.
          (0.6)
  G:      Jis' no:w?
```

```
S:      ˙hhhh No I called be-like between ele ven en'
→ G:                                       ⌐I: wasn'=
        =talking to a:nybody .....
```

Here G initiates repair on S's prior question. Following S's provision of the repair, G proceeds immediately to answer the now repaired question and hence accomplishes an exit to the repair sequence that she initiated.

19. For a discussion of overlap competition, see Jefferson and Schegloff (1975).
20. Gail Jefferson (1981b) has distinguished between "mm hm" as projecting "passive recipiency" and "yeah" as implying that its producer may shortly assume "active speakership."
21. In the case of (23) J's "Oh:ah" is sympathetically intoned and seems to treat the unexpectedly early departure of V's visitors as a source of disappointment to V. Here V's overlapped talk may be designed to stifle any further such expression and to delete such sympathy as is carried in the intonation of J's "oh." V's overlapped talk may, in sum, be designed to avoid or curtail any treatment of the visitors' departure as a source of disappointment for which sympathy might be appropriate. Later in the call, V again refers to the visitors' early departure but again discourages her coparticipant from treating the matter as a complaint or as a subject for sympathetic affiliation.

14. On the organization of laughter in talk about troubles

GAIL JEFFERSON
University of Manchester

In the course of an examination of conversations in which people talk about their troubles, a recurrent phenomenon was found: A troubles-teller produces an utterance and then laughs, and the troubles-recipient does not laugh, but produces a recognizably serious response. For example:

(1) [Frankel:TC:1:4:SO]

```
    G: You don't want to go through all the ha:ssle?
    S: 'hhhh I don't know Geri,
       (.)
 →  S: I've I've stopped crying uhheh-heh-heh-heh-heh,
 →  G: Wuh were you cry::ing?
```

(2) [NB:II:4:3:SO]

```
    E: It's bleeding just a tiny tiny bit hastuh be
       dre:ssed, bu t uh
                      [
    N:                  Oh::::: ::::.
 →  E:                           [
                                  Go:d it was he:ll. uh hahh!
       'hhh hhh
           [
 →  N:      What a sha::me.
```

(3) [Lerner:SF:I:2:SO]

```
    M: How you doing.
    J: Oh: pretty goo:d¹
       (0.8)
    M: 'hhhhhh ( )
              [
 →  J:         This week, hhhhhhehh heh heh
       'hhh
       [
 →  M:  'tlk Oh this week?
```

This is an SSRC-funded project based at the University of Manchester.

346

(4)   [NB:IV:4:4:SO]

E: You ought to see me broken out to<u>day</u> God I t(hh)ook
   a ba:th, and I'm just a ma:ss of b- little
→   p(h)imp(h)les:: heh heh ⌜˙hhh
→ L: ⌊Oh <u>that's</u> from uh:: n-nerves.

(5)   [Frankel:HB:II:9:SO]

J: about a month ago I said (.) you know what do we
   have to look <u>forward</u> to. We have our <u>hou</u>:se and
   everything I <u>said</u> I just˙hhh I was feeling empty.you
→   knhho(h)⌜o(h)w⌜˙hhh!
→ P: ⌊˙hhh ⌊<u>Y e a</u>⌋: h.

(6)   [NB:II:4:6-7:SO]

E: Then he gives you those (0.2) <u>c</u>odiene tablets and
   you're ⌜like on LS⌐D, and I was ⌜<u>vo</u>:mi⌐ti:ng, and
N: ⌊Yeah mm hm⌋   ⌊Yeah,⌋
   (.)
E. ˙tch⌜˙hhhh
·N: ⌊Oh::::⌐::˙go::sh (   )
E: ⌊So everybody's been nice in the **apartment**
→ just like with <u>my</u> le:g <u>ihh</u>⌜<u>hh</u> heh heh <u>huh</u>⌝
→ N: ⌊<u>Yee</u>:::a:::uh:,⌋

(7)   [Rahman:II:13:SO]

G: And (.) I <u>couldn't</u> go typ<u>i</u>ng on Thurs:day n<u>i</u>:gh⌐t:.
M: ⌊Mh
G: ˙t˙hh eh: because:- (But) I thought well I can't
   leave h<u>i</u>m here for <u>two</u> hours on his <u>ow</u>:n if he's
   been up <u>that</u> upset <u>and</u> I wasn't <u>out</u> <u>an</u> hour.=
→G: =hhu⌜h–<u>huh</u>⌐hhehh h⌐eh–⌐˙hhhh⌝}=
→M: ⌊<u>N o</u>⌊n o : ⌊n o⌊: : ,⌋
→G: =ehh ˙hhh=
→M: =<u>N̄</u>⌐o:.
G: ⌊<u>Anyway</u>: eh:m (.) So that's it I'll have to pack
   <u>that in</u>

(8)   [TCI(b):7:1:SO]

C: We:ll I::, <u>heard</u> about your accident I'm sorry to
   hear that.
L: <u>O̱h</u>:::: tha:nk you it's <u>s</u>ure been the most <u>painful</u>
   (.) of <u>all</u> my li:fe put <u>together</u> a:ll my: pain does
→ not comp<u>a</u>:re to <u>this</u> <u>foo</u>:t˙⌜eh heh–heh,⌝
→ C: ⌊C a n ˉyou⌋=
→ L: =ha⌐(ha)
→ C: ⌊Can you <u>wa</u>:lk good now?

(9)   [Rahman:II:14:SO]

```
G: Well you see it's different for me:. eh for (.) the
   other boy:s be cause they always had each othe:r.
M:                 [Yeh
M: E:xactly. Where Tho mas-        ]
G:           [(But)      [Ye:s,    ]
   (.)
M:    Well    h e ]
G: [[Well there's o]nly Na:then and they fight like the
   devil=
M: =Well thi s is i:t. ]
→ G:        [ehhhhh hh ]h h heh heh ]
→ M:                   [E [x [act ]ly, yes.
```

This recurrent phenomenon seems to run directly counter to a procedure whereby a recipient displays affiliation with a prior speaker. The gross shape of this procedure appears in the following excerpt from a newspaper report (Los Angeles *Times*, January 15, 1970) of a hearing in which Charles Manson and some of his followers were involved.

> Manson blinked repeatedly as he stared at Judge Dell while the latter was speaking. But, when he was speaking himself, Manson frequently made remarks he apparently intended to be humorous.
>
> *Laughing when he laughed* were four young women who once were members of Manson's hippie group – Diana Bluestein, Nancy Pittman, Lynn Fromme and Sandra Good, who held a small baby boy. They are not charged in connection with the murders. (Italics added)

What is implicit here is that Manson's followers were not even independent minded enough to decide, upon the occurrence of one of his "remarks," that it was "humorous" or not, but waited upon his laughter to signal to them what sort of response to produce. But it turns out that recipient laughter by reference to prior speaker's laughter is a recurrent phenomenon in ordinary conversation.

This phenomenon, and others in which the negotiation and sequentially constructed aspect of laughter is apparent, has been considered in some detail elsewhere; see, for example, Jefferson (1979) and Jefferson, Sacks, and Schegloff (forthcoming). For the purposes of this report it will simply be noted that laughing together is a valued occurrence which can be the product of methodic, coordinated activities, and that it is recurrently achieved via a recipient laughing by reference to a prior speaker's laughter. Following are several instances of that phenomenon.

(10)   [Rose:Fairmount]

D: I thought that was pretty outta sight didju hear

```
    me say are you a junkie.
    (0.5̄)
→ D: hheh heh=
→ E: =hhheh-heh-heh
```

    (11) [MC:I:2]
```
L: Cause she was off in the bushes with somebody, tch!
    (0.7)
→ L: ehh ┌hhhhhhh!
→ P:    └Oh(h)h hah huh!
```

    (12) [Schenkein:I:28]
```
E: He said well he said I am cheap he said, 'hh about
   the big things' he says but not the little things,=
→ E: =hhhhHA HA ┌HA HA HA
→ B:          └heh heh heh
```

    (13) [Rahman:II:21:SO]
```
M: Well (.) I (.) try to do a little bit e:very da:y,
   you ┌kno:w,┐
G:   └Y e ::┘s,
→ M: eh Not the floo:r one ehh:: h ┌euh he ┌h-heh-he ┌h
→ G:                            └e h h̄ └h e̱ : h̄ └he̱:h
```

    (14) [Rahman:I:6:SO]
```
→ G: it was a little bit sau:cy, hhh::::: ┌h e h  heh┐
L:                                     └Oh was it.┘
→ L: ehh hehh heh hah hah hah
```

    (15) [Schenkein:II:84]

```
B: Did you watch by any chance Miss International
   Showcase last night?
E: n:No I didn't ┌I was reading my-
B:             └You missed a really great
→   pro(h) ┌gram.
→E:       └O(hh)h i(h)t wa(hh)s? ehh heh heh heh!
```

This is not to say that recipients do not decline to laugh when the prior speaker laughs. They do. A dramatic instance is the following, in which a speaker makes a joke that is followed by over three seconds of silence. In a technique similar to that seen after a much shorter silence in fragments (10) and (11), the prior speaker begins to laugh. Whereas in those two fragments the prior speaker is joined by the recipient, in the following, the prior speaker laughs and laughs and laughs and laughs all by himself.

(16) [Adato:4:7:SO]

J: Hell`the horses <u>shit</u> in the streets, I mean why can't
   you uh (1.1) why can't human be<u>ings</u> use the same
   facilities.
   (3.2)
→ J: Ha ha ha! ah!ah!ah!ah! `hhhh! heh heh–uh ri(hh)ght?
   eh!ah!ah!ah!ah!ah! `hhhh! hoh! uh! uh huh huh
   ⌈huh `ehhhhhh
→ G: ⌊(   )
   J: Ohhhhh uh::::. Well I don't think, horses should
→   have (h)mh–mo(hh)re rights than human beings?
   `mhhhhh! `uh! `uh! `uh! <u>huh</u>–huh–huh–huh–huh–huh!
   `hmmmm!
→ G: <u>You</u> can have the right, to do that around your
   house all day <u>long</u>.

In this instance we see, in gross form and over two rounds, the standard shape of a "declining to laugh": A recipient does not laugh by
reference to the prior utterance; the prior speaker initiates laughter, and
the recipient breaks his silence, not by joining the laughter, but by
talking to the prior utterance. Recurrently, this series of events occurs on
a much finer scale. For example:

(17) [JG:II:2:17:SO]   ((Gene and Maggie occasionally
                          "see" each other))
   G: I thought (.) God dammit I thought I got in <u>love</u>
      with this broad`<u>you</u> know,
   M: Yahm,
→ G: So that shook the old (h)hou(h)se(h)hold up for
      a(h)wh(h)ile huh⌈h
→ M: ⌊Oh <u>yes</u> I can ima:gi⌈ne.
   G: ⌊You know, a:nd
      uh: I think Rae's (0.3) <u>re</u>alized that <u>hell</u> maybe
      it's good for me to go <u>ou</u>:t

(18) [NB:V:1–2:SO]   ((Angie's last name is "Friday"))

   E: he <u>got</u> a little po:wer tool Fri<u>:</u>day and I says you
      better take it do:wn t–Friday to th–t–Friday's and
      he⌈says Oh⌉:=
   A: ⌊°whhew°⌋
→ E: =I will Sa(h)turday<u>:</u> hhunh ⌈unh– u⌈nh–uh⌉
→ A: ⌊`hhhhh⌊w:<u>We</u>:⌋ll, it was
      <u>j</u>ust one of tho:se things

And in relatively gross or rather fine form, this is the configuration
which turns up again and again in troubles-talk. The troubles-teller
laughs, and the troubles-recipient declines to laugh by talking to the
prior utterance and thus by talking to the trouble (see fragments 1–9).

Now, it seems to be quite a different matter to decline to exhibit amusement at, for example, an occasional boyfriend's other romantic involvements, as in fragment (17), or at what must be a tired joke about one's name, as in fragment (18), and to decline to exhibit amusement at a coparticipant's trouble, as in fragments (1)–(9). It appears that in troubles-talk, a laughing troubles-teller is doing a recognizable sort of job. He is exhibiting that, although there is this trouble, it is not getting the better of him; he is managing; he is in good spirits and in a position to take the trouble lightly. He is exhibiting what we might call "troubles-resistance." But this does not mean that, as in fragments (10)–(18), a recipient is invited to join in the merriment, to also find the thing laughable, to affiliate with a prior speaker's exhibited position on it. In troubles-talk, it appears to be a recipient's job to be taking the trouble seriously; to exhibit what we might call "troubles-receptiveness."

Given the foregoing considerations, it becomes interesting that, on occasion, a troubles-recipient can be found to join a troubles-teller's laughter. It turns out that recurrently in troubles-talk the phenomenon of both parties laughing is associated with a distinctive feature of such talk; a time-out for pleasantries which we are calling a "buffer topic." Two such segments are shown.

(19) [Frankel:HB:II:4:SO]

```
J: I mean immediately when he to:ld me I was- I went
   cra:zy, and then- 'hh first thing I thought of was
   the animals.  As soon as he said the do:gs are okay
   somehow I could handle the whole thing.
      ⌜(You know?)
P: ⌞The whole thing yeah.
J: And even:, then I felt bad about Arle:ne, but (0.2)
   hh but somehow the dogs an:d Miao was the:re, and
   then when Brad found Miao this morning I just 'hhh
   her- her whiskers are all sin:ged bu⌜t
P:                                       ⌞'hhh O:h but
   she's ohhkhhay.=
J: =Y(h)ea(h)h.=
P: =hhY(h)ea(h)h? 'hh⌜hh
J:                   ⌞You know she wasn't meant to
   have whisk(h)ers'uh⌜hh!
P:                     ⌞Yihh!=
J: =(The) dog pulled out o:ne,⌜ihhh
P:                            ⌞ihh Yeah(h)right.=
P:    'hhhh
J: [[ So now she's got singed whisk(h)ers, 'hh But she
   m:uh Miao is sleepin:g, quietly in be:d'ehh
      ⌜hu-hu⌝
P: ⌞O k a⌟y.Th⌜at's good.⌝
J:           ⌞'hhhhhhhh!⌟
```

```
    (.)
J:  So we'll be staying here at my mother's ...

    (20)  [NB:IV:14:1-2:SO]
L:  Hello:,
E:  Aloha:·h
L:  Hi::. How are you.
    (.)
E:  I-did I wake you up?²
L:  No:. Huh-uh. Gee I been awake for a lo:ng time.
    ---(0.3)--- ((Possible tape break))
L:  Yeah.
E:  Oh: I- We:ll we just got do:wn·h
L:  Oh you di:┌d?
E:          └Yea:uh.
L:  Oh how co:me.
┌E: ·hhhh Oh we had to go to something last night at
│   Buena Vista Country Club I won a bottle of liquor
│   ehh::huh agai:n ehh hh┌uh
│                         └Go┐:d y┌ou:'re lu:cky:.┐
L:                         └huh huh huh huh┘huh
E:
L:  [┌Oh:::::::::::::,
E:   ·hh·hh·hh┘ └Almost everybody won something but,
└L: Uhh!  ┌huh-hu:h hu┐:h;
E:       └·hhhhhhhhhh┘
    (.)
E:  Ah::: I been to the do:ctor, hhhhhh
```

Buffer topics can consist of jokes and anecdotes associated with the trouble, or quite unrelated matters. They are recurrently initiated by the troubles-teller. That such talk is not introduced by a troubles-recipient appears to be one of the ways in which a coparticipant specifically aligns him/herself as a troubles-recipient. That is, in other materials, if someone has a joke, pleasantry, anecdote, story to offer, and it is relevant to, or can be seen to be occasioned by, the talk in progress, then one introduces it into the conversation.[3] That a coparticipant aligning as a troubles-recipient may refrain from introducing such talk is dramatically evident in the materials from which fragment (20) was extracted. Later in the conversation, it turns out that Lottie has also been to a party last night, and was awarded a trophy. Although these materials are deliverable-as-a-subsequent to Emma's talk, it appears that they are specifically withheld at this point in the conversation (and are delivered as buffer materials when Lottie takes over as troubles-teller).[4]

Even in the environment of a buffer topic, a participant aligned as a troubles-recipient may not immediately laugh, but can be seen to be brought to it via troubles-teller's activities. That feature seems to hold for fragments (19) and (20). While both these fragments require and reward a detailed analysis, for the purposes of this report, only fragment (19) will be closely considered.

The buffer topic here is the first of several in this conversation. It is edged into very delicately, with the troubles-recipient brought to laugh over a series of moves. It is initiated by the troubles-teller, who breaks off a potentially emotional narrative component, "and then when Brad found Miao this morning I just `hhh," deletes the report of her reaction to the discovery of the cat, and picks up again with an intrinsically cute description of the cat's condition, "her- her *whi*skers are all sin:ged."

```
J: And even:, then I felt bad about Arle:ne, but
   (0.2) hh but somehow the dogs an:d Miao was the:re,
   and then when Brad found Miao this morning I just
   `hhh her- her whiskers are all sin:ged but
```

That is, the report of what might well have been a tearful reunion, reference to which at this point might reoccasion tears, is replaced with a description biased toward less than serious treatment.[5]

Though biased toward nonserious treatment, the description is yet a component of the report in progress, and is potentially embedded into a continuing report with "but." That is, reference to the cat's whiskers can at this point turn out to have been a momentary, merely incidental bit of lightness in an ongoing, serious report. Alternatively, the "but" could introduce the humorous recounting of the fate of the cat's whiskers which in fact occurs a bit later. Syntactically and substantively the sentence-in-progress permits of such a continuation as "but you know she wasn't *m*eant to have whisk(*h*)ers" or the "but she's alright" that is subsequently supplied by the troubles-recipient. At this point, then, the teller has produced an object ("but") that does not discriminate between two relevant and competing directions (serious and nonserious), for an utterance that has yet to be completed and that can be completed with a move in either direction.

It is at just this point that the recipient produces a little inbreath, an object that recurrently announces the onset of speech. And at just this point, the teller stops talking.

```
J: her whiskers are all sin:ged bu┌t
P:                                  └`hhh
```

Whereas coparticipants to conversation can be sensitive to such a thing as a prespeech inbreath, and can and do cut off their own talk to permit the talk that the inbreath announces, they do not always do so, and in this conversation the troubles-teller does not always defer to the recipient's inbreaths, nor even to the onset of the recipient's speech. Throughout this conversation the troubles-teller can be found to be continuing across the recipient's talk. It may then be fair to say that this is a particularly sensitive moment in the interaction; one in which the teller has equivocally projected a serious or nonserious trajectory, where, now, discovering that the recipient is about to speak, the teller specifically leaves it up to the recipient to take the talk in one or another direction.[6] The recipient is in a position to provide the humorous alternative. In a subsequent time-out, it now having been established that such activities will be engaged in for this trouble, the teller now specifically formulates an upcoming item as a "laughable," and the recipient (1) moves immediately to laughter, just after the onset of the teller's laughter (cf. fragments 11, 13, and 15), and (2) elaborates on the laughable item, using materials from their shared biography.

```
(21)   [Frankel:HB:II:8:SO]

   J:   I just know things are gonna be al right now.
   P:                                     [·hhhh[ Yea]:h I-
   P:   That's uhhhh ·hhhh
   J:                 [It's gonna take ti:me it's like-
→        ·hhh·pt there's like some things that we laugh at we
         say are advantages no:w, y(h)ou know like the white
         rug that I hated, eh h h h h h h h
 →P:                           [Rihh(h)ght.'n]=
➤P:   =[[ that that Samb o did a job on a n y w a y.
   J:     [·hh-huhhh[( )!] [·hhhh]      [hheh Y(h)eah]=
   J:   =hnh-h nh
   P:         [Ye(h)ah right.
```

It may then be a sensitivity to the trouble rather than ignorance of the cat's whiskerless history that selects the materials with which the recipient completes teller's uncompleted utterance:

```
   J: her whiskers are all sin:ged bu t
→ P:                                 [·hhh Oh: but she's
      ohhkhhay.
```

The lexicon of "·hhh Oh: but she's ohhkhhay" is on track with the troubles-report. However, the last word is potentially moving toward laughter; that is, "ohhkhhay" is heavily breathy but not plosive. It is just on the edge; it has the sort of sounds that coparticipants can and do treat as an occasion to start laughing, but that they can and do treat as at best equivocal as to its status as a laugh (see, for example, fragment 14, in which a recipient with "hhh::::" to work with does not laugh, but with "*heh heh*" following the breath, does laugh). It also has the sort of sounds that can be expressing relief, compassion, and so on.

Thus, just as the teller has only potentially and equivocally provided an occasion for laughter, the recipient is only potentially and equivocally attending and taking up that possibility. And, just as the teller, with the last word of her utterance, leaves it to the recipient to select the direction the talk will take, so does the recipient, with her last word, provide the possibility for and/but leave it to the teller to decide upon the subsequent direction. And it is in the teller's confirmation of recipient's proposal about the cat that laughter unequivocally emerges.

```
   J: her whiskers are all sin:ged bu t
   P:                                  ['hhh Oh: but she's
      ohhkhhay.=
 → J: Y(h)ea(h)h,
```

It is possible that what we are looking at here is a troubles-teller's reluctance to proceed with available materials with which to make light of a trouble until the recipient indicates a willingness to participate in such an activity; that is, until the recipient warrants the appropriateness of such behavior and implicates herself in it (where it is certainly the case that although a troubles-teller can be overly upset by and receptive to his or her own troubles, the teller can as well be overly troubles-resistant, can be seen to be taking a trouble too well or too lightly, which can be assessed as a matter of irresponsibility or incompetence).

That, at this point, and indeed from the point at which the cat's whiskers were introduced, the teller is and has been cautiously working toward some particular materials can only be a matter of conjecture. The subsequent talk may perfectly well be spontaneously generated in and for this particular conversation. However, in materials in which a series of consecutive interactions have been recorded, we find items that occur in one introduced as if for the first time in a next. It is not unreasonable to suppose that when the cat's discovery was announced and when the current teller reacted however she reacted to that discovery, she and "Brad," at that time, went through a recounting of the history of the cat's unfortunate whiskers, finding in it some welcome comic relief. That, on its reoccurrence here, it is not marked as such, with, for example, "Like I said to Brad" or "Like Brad said to me" is standard enough, such marking routinely being reserved for situations in which the coparticipant to the initial interaction happens to be among those present in the current interaction.

Whether the teller is withholding further humorous materials until the recipient joins in the laughter and thus unequivocally aligns herself as a coparticipant in a time-out *from* troubles-talk rather than as she is so far operating; that is, as a recipient *of* troubles-talk (with, then, a possibly problematically cheerful troubles-teller), or whether the teller at this point has not yet discovered that there are further laughables to deliver, the fact remains that at this point in the interchange, with the "Y(h)ea(h)h," and no more, she has indicated that the report about the cat is possibly complete, the recipient's proposal that the cat is "okay" having been confirmed. That is, for a range of confirmables, including displays of understanding, two options recur. The prior speaker may provide a confirmation and no more, whereupon the recipient exhibits an understanding that the business is completed with, for example, an assessment, as in the following fragment.

```
   (22)  [SBL:3:3:6]

   M: The- Your leg (got) alright huh,
 → K: Oh yeah.
 → M: Oh good.  Tell Keith Moon hello for me.
```

Or, the prior speaker may provide a confirmation plus a continuation:

```
   (23)  [SBL:IV:6:13]

   A: And he's still living and she die:d and she died
      of cancer.
   M: 'tch!
      (0.2)
   M:   ┌Uh hhu:h,
   A: [[(    ‾) she had an (a mastectomy).
      (0.6)
 → M: And he's doing. alri:ght huh,
 → A: Yah, ‾(0.2) but then it went through her body.
```

And we can find materials in which both options are taken; the recipient treating the confirmation as terminating the current business, the prior speaker opting to continue:

```
   (24)  [Rahman:II:2]
   M: Lorna's alri:ght is she:?=
   G: =Yes she's fine I popped do:wn last night.=
```

```
→ M:  =[[Oh: that's good·She's alri[ght,
→ G:    [[eh: (         )         [for awhile, Thomas
        came with me
```

Thus, at this point in the interaction, a sequentially appropriate next utterance by the recipient, given that the prior speaker has done a confirmation, is an assessment such as "Oh good." However, in this case, the recipient produces an object which (1) proposes that there may be more to be said on the current matter and invites the teller to produce it, and (2) unequivocally joins in the laughter.

```
    P:  ·hhh Oh: but she's ohhkhhay.=
    J:  =Y(h)ea(h)h,=
→   P:  =hhY(h)ea(h)h?
```

The recipient's "hhY(h)ea(h)h?" is cautious in a variety of ways. Although it does, now, unequivocally join in the laughter, it is, but for the slightly higher ending intonation (indicated by the question mark/comma), an echoing of the prior utterance. This recognizable echoing may constitute a display that the recipient is specifically laughing *with* the prior speaker, *because* the prior speaker is laughing, rather than that the recipient independently finds something laughable in the prior talk. The slightly higher ending intonation may indicate caution of another kind: an interrogating of what is, after all, no more than a "yeah" to her own formulation of the cat's condition; a request for a stronger commitment by the prior speaker to the status report they are co-constructing; for example, an affirmation (minimally, another "yeah," more elaborately, e.g., "Oh yeah, she's just fine") or, for example, the sort of report that does occur later and gets an assessment, that the cat is now "sleeping quietly in bed."

The troubles-teller opts first to take up the recipient's laughter. She proceeds to offer materials that are not in line with the narrative of the missing and rediscovered cat, but are unequivocally part of a time-out for comic relief, during which both participants engage in laughing together (see fragment 19). Thereafter, she returns to the report at the point where they left off, now adding what can stand as an affirmation of her interrogated confirmation of the recipient's proposal about/understanding of the cat's condition:

```
J:  So now she's got singed whisk(h)ers, ·hh But she
    m:uh Miao is sleepin:g, quietly in be:d.
    ehh[hu-hu]
P:      [O·k a]y. That's good.
```

Upon a recognizable return to the narrative of the missing cat, the recipient returns to her alignment as a troubles recipient, no longer treating the troubles-teller's laughter as constituting an occasion for her own laughter; producing the standard device for declining to laugh, that is, responding, not to the laughter, but to the prior utterance, as in fragments (1)–(9) and (16)–(18).

In summary, this segment at least permits, and perhaps requires, analysis in terms of a tremendous caution about and sensitivity to engaging in laughter in the course of a troubles-telling, on the part of both teller and recipient. That there is such caution may have to do with the fact that this is troubles talk, specifically not an occasion for getting together for some laughs, where, however, coparticipants do routinely engage in pleasantries, but where those pleasantries are attendant to, and shaped by, the fact that they occur in the environment of troubles-talk.

Two orderings of laughter in the environment of troubles-talk have been considered: *Teller laughs/ recipient does not laugh*, and *teller laughs/recipient laughs*. These orderings appear to have a range of features shaped by and oriented to the fact that troubles-talk is in progress; among them, that a teller can be exhibiting resistance to a trouble, while a recipient can be exhibiting receptiveness to that trouble. There is another ordering: *Teller does not laugh/recipient laughs*. Instances are rare in the current corpus, and there is only one conversation in which this phenomenon occurs on a large scale. That conversation appears to involve an enormously troubles-receptive teller confronted by an equally troubles-resistant recipient. The remainder of this report will be directed to a consideration of that interaction.

First, some background. This troubles-teller seems to have a talent for turning cheer to gloom. So, for example, a compliment to her coparticipant, "*B*y the way I *l*oved your Christmas card," leads to "I just couldn't get *m*ine off at *a*:ll," which leads to "Well I started ad*d*re:ssing them see . . . so we had for instance uh ((clears throat)) the *S*addlers who we kno:w, u*h*::, uh Missiz Saddler just die:d so we had to cha:nge tha(h)a::*t*," which leads, of course, to a description of the circumstances of Mrs. Saddler's death, which leads to "*A*nd then I:'ve heard of: a*n*other: woman now who's got emphysema so terribly that she she blacks *ou*:t," which leads to "*O*hh this emphysema thing is *t*errible . . . and it is so *p*revalent. And there are *a*ll sorts of people that have it. And a lot of people get it uh after:: uh: ˙tch a:sthema. Asthema and bronchitis." This talk leads to a reference to this speaker's own respiratory troubles, at which point the segment under consideration starts.

(25)   [SBL:IV:6:16-20:SO:S]

```
A:  it gets me worried the way I get, with a: husky
    throat and I th[ink it's ]=
M:               [hYheah. ]
A:  =the[s m o : : g .]( ).
M:      [Are you getting an]y better?
    (1.0)
A:  Well I did for a while and now you see I've gotten so
    tired.
    (0.3)
A:  [[`hhh I'[m ( )
M:  [[Ya:h,  [ti:red-  and then this weather pro[bably=
A:                                              [Yes,
M:  =too:,
A:  Yes the weather and I'm just ti[red and this
M:                                 [°Yhheah°
    (.)
A:  combination sorta brought it on again you see but eh
    what happened to me:, uh it started up at Christmas
    you know the sec[ond (              )
→M:                 [ehh heh heh `hhh heh[`hhhhh]
A:                                       [So  it]
    (.)
A:  couldn't be uh emphysema or anything like that or it
    wouldn't (do[a
M:              [°uhh°
M:  =`hhh[I wasn[`t lau:ghing at you[my kitty was `hmhh
A:       [uh   [heh                 [(That's alright)
A:  Aw::
M:  Uh my[kitty climbed up-
A:       [Is-
    (.)
M:  and was hitting me on the ba:ck like somebody
    ra:pping me  on[the ba::ck, hheh heh]
A:                 [OH(h)how  c u : t e,]
```

In the course of a troubles-telling, recipient produces a laugh which, it
turns out, was not responding to that talk, but to an outside event. That
it was responsive to an outside event does not, however, mean that it
was not addressed to this interaction; the laugh produced to be ex-
plained, the explanation providing an occasion for turning to cheerful
matters and away from troubles. In this case the introduction of an
outside event generates talk; the prior troubles-teller offering appreciations of her coparticipant's cat.

```
A:  OH(h)ow cu:te, he[h heh heh
M:                   [`huhh `hhhhh She climbed
```

```
     rup here and was:ˌtapping me on theˌback she=
A:   [°O h : : : :,°]¯            [hunhh
M:     rwas sorta looking
A:   =[Jan was telling me]how she eats pencils and
     everythi:nˌg
M:             [ihYhheh=
A:   =˙huh heˌh heh
M:           [Yeh she was eating pencils awhile ago and=
A:   ˌˌeh eh
M:   =[[then, now she just cli(h)i(h)mbed up and was
     ˌtappi(h)ng m(h)e o(h)n th(h)e sho(h)u(h)lde(h)er
```

But the movement away from troubles-talk is short lived. Although the prior troubles-teller does not return to her non-emphysema, a resource for gloom is found. The talk about her coparticipant's cat occasions talk about a cat she used to have but has no longer, and misses terribly. At the introduction of this matter, and in its course, we find the recipient laughing.

```
     M:   and was tappi(h)ng m(h)e o(h)n th(h)e
          sho(h)u(h)lde(h)r ˙hhhh I looˌked back there toˌ
 →  A:                          [We  miss  t h a t]
          °beautiful° that Gau:cho so:, mhhˌhhmh
 →  M:                                      [Ye::ehh hehh
     A:   Cla::rence,
          (.)
     M:   ˙uhhhˌhh  O h : : : : : : : : :
     A:        [mi:sses him so he says it's]terrible.*
     M:   Ye:::ˌ:ah,
     A:       [I'm sick I ever got rid of himˌI really am,
 →  M:                                      [ehh hah huh
```

```
*  This utterance produced in 'smile voice'
```

In this segment it appears that the recipient is exhibiting a discriminative troubles-receptiveness/resistance. That is, on the announcement that the speaker plus some unspecified other(s) have a trouble, the bit of appended laughter occasions laughter by the recipient (this in contrast to the procedure seen in fragments 1–9). But when the trouble is located by reference to a specific third party, a troubles-receptive, serious response is produced. When the teller proceeds to speak for and about herself, the recipient laughs. Roughly, then, the recipient may be discriminating in terms of whose trouble this is proposed to be; the teller's trouble taken lightly, a third party's trouble taken seriously.

When the recipient begins to contribute to the troubles-talk, it is with a strongly troubles-resistant proposal, that is, that all this unhappiness was unnecessary ("You could have kept him"). Whereas prior to this proposal, the teller has formulated herself as the responsible party, she now undertakes an elaborate explanation that implicates other members of the household.[7]

```
    A: I'm sick I ever got rid of him I really am.
    M:                                 [ehh hah huh 'ahhhh
       (0.2)
 →  M: You could have kept him=
    M:    [he was
 →  A: 'But the way the kids you know
       (0.6)
    A: threw him around you know he:::, [I don't know ]=
    M:                                  [Ye : a h.hh ]
    M: =[[He lived through-        ]
 →  A:  [[My  m o  t h e r         ]
       (0.2)
    A: kept after me so much that
    M: 't k
    A:   [that one Sunday afternoon I was just m:mad at her
       and I was mad at (1.0) just everything and she said
       I was uh: he was just ruining the whole pla:ce and
 →  so (1.2) and the 'hh do:gs and (0.5) you kno:w uh'hh
       we were always cleaning up after (the dogs)
    M:                                       [Ye:ah?
       (1.2)
    A: So I said no I'll just get rid of the whole me:ss.
```

With the blame redistributed, the jettisoning of the cat is rereferenced, now as one component of a clean sweep rather than the target of a focused decision. With the situation now in proper perspective, the proposal that it was unnecessary, initially offered by the recipient, is offered by teller. With the situation now in proper perspective, the recipient, who initially can have been accusing teller of unnecessarily getting rid of the cat, now exhibits understanding and accord. However, she also exhibits that she is taking the whole thing lightly.

```
    A: So I said no I'll just get rid of the whole me:ss.
 →  M: Ya:h. We(h)ll tha:t's ri(h)ght. ehh heh heh
       he h
    A:   [Now we coulda kept the ca:t'but=
 →  M: =Do it a:ll with one stro:ke, ehh hehh hhah
    A:       [(                    )
    M: 'uhhhh
    A: (But I            )
    M:       [Ye::ah.
    A: And I wish I hadn't. But the:y said that they got a
       good 'hh home for him
```

Having secured recipient's understanding of the situation, if not her acknowledgment that it is a trouble, the teller introduces another aspect, a worry which recipient does nothing to assuage. In fact, it appears that the recipient is indulging in just a bit of malice.

```
      A:  But the:y said that they got a good ˙hh home for him=
   →  M:   =[ [ ⌈I hhope th⌈ey di:d     ⌉
      A:       ⌊(       )-  ⌊(      )⌋=
   →  M:  =ehh(h)Oh(h)ho she's so ⌈cute ˙hhh
      A:                          ⌊I keep wondering if maybe
          they were ˙hh you kno::w uh:m (.) lying to me and
          (0.4)
   →  M:  ˙hhh ⌈I don't know⌉
      A:       ⌊really  just⌋did away with him,
          (0.2)
      M:  Uh hu⌈h
      A:       ⌊You know,
   →  M:  Maybe they thought they'd made you feel better,
          (0.3)
      A:  ˙mp I kno:w.
   →  M:  I don't know though⌈they could've been telling=
      A:                     ⌊(              )
   →  M:  =⌈°the truth°
      A:   ⌊But they said that the, (0.7) ˙p that this is a
          good time to bring him in because (0.3) they know of
          several- they knew of several people who were
          asking (0.4) o:f uh (0.6) for cats with (0.2) with
          big furry tai:ls.
      M:  ˙t Oh:::::.
          (0.3)
      A:  And heavy, coa:ts.
      M:  ⌈⌈Yhhe:ah.
      A:  ⌊⌊(        )- they said that they: would contact
          these people and see if they would take him.
   →  M:  hYeah well I hope he did get a⌈good ho:me,
      A:                               ⌊(              )=
   →  M:  =⌈⌈He ma:y have,
      A:   ⌊⌊(          ).
          (0.2)
      A:  He may have bu⌈t I don't know.
      M:                ⌊Ye:ah.
          (0.6)
      A:  That's (what I was told) anyway.
   →  M:  Yeh- ehh ˙hehh hheh heh ˙hh˙hhh OH::::: uh this
          one's so cute,
```

In almost every utterance, recipient exhibits either strong troubles-resistance or, when exhibiting troubles-receptiveness, does so in a way that can only be demoralizing.

Troubles-recipients routinely provide reassurances. We do find weak reassurances as the initial one in this segment ("I h*h*ope they di:d"). A weak reassurance can terminate the matter, as it appears to be designed to do in this case (followed here by a reference to her own cat, "ehh*(h)Oh*(h)o she's so cute," which reoffers the initial cheerful distraction from talk about troubles). For example, in the following fragment, a troubles-teller gets a weak reassurance and thereupon moves to close off the conversation.

```
(26)  [JG:I(S):X15:6:SO]  ((re  Pete's unemployment))
  P: 'hhh But I think it'll iron itself out,
→ M: I sure hope ⌜so.
  P:             ⌞I'll see you Tuesday.
```

But recurrently, troubles-recipients provide strong reassurances. These can be offered on rather dubious and problematic grounds, as in the following fragment, in which a man is trying to discover whether his wife has survived an earthquake.

```
(27)  [FD:IV:44:R7:SO]
  L: uh we have uh::::: a casualty list here and your
     wife's name isn't on it.
  H: °Oh: thank Christ.°
     (0.3)
→ L: So I'm uh::: sure that uh she's alright.
```

Strong reassurances can also be found to be offered on no grounds whatsoever, as in the following fragment, in which the troubles-recipient has never even heard of the disease (a case of psoriasis which has resulted in a toe operation, and which, over time, far from being "alright," becomes progressively more virulent).

```
(28)  [NB:II:4:4:SO]
  E: I had to have my foot up on a pillow for two days,
     you know ⌜and- 'hhhmhhh
  N:         ⌞Yah?
  E: But honey it's gonna be alright I'm sure,
→ N: Oh I'm sure it's gonna be alri:ght,
```

Given that troubles-recipients are wont to provide extravagantly optimistic reassurances on matters that, over time, will prove them to have been right or wrong, it becomes interesting that the recipient in this case, for a matter on which her opinions are unlikely to be tested, structures her talk in such a way as to reify teller's fears. Yet in no way can she be characterized as a hostile or antagonistic coparticipant. She is aligned as a troubles-recipient, seriously considering the matters being presented to her, and hoping for the best. But this display may tremendously enhance the demoralizing effect of her contributions. That is, the troubles-teller is not in a position to mobilize such resources as are available on the occurrence of outright antagonism. So, for example, in the following fragment, someone undergoing heckling both absorbs the jibes and defends his position.

```
(29)   [Frankel:US:II:6-9:SO]
M: Did you kill your cat Vi::c? Kill the cats yet?
   (0.6)
V: No the cat go:es.tomorrow morning.
M: How's he going.=
V: =A.S.P.C.A:'in the morning.
M:                [V i a -  h h]
M: Is he go(h)o(h)i(h)ng v(h)i(h)a the furnace?'hh
   or via(h)a the truck' hh'hh hh hnh heh!
V:                                 [V i : :a] the truck.
M: °'hh hmff°
   (1.8)
A: It's a cute little k itten.
V:                    [Yea::h somebody'll- ado:pt
   that one, because it's cute and it's re::d you know,
   (0.8)
V: But my mo ther's cat (there's no hope, c a u s e
M:         [Ma:n I tell you I would take[it b'what
V: = h e ' s,)
M: =[th'hell'm I]gonna do with three:. I got two and
   that's enough.
   (0.3)
M: I'll end up like a frickin, (0.2) I'll have a-
   I'll be running a cat house.
V: You know what it's gonna cost me three do:lla:rs,
   (0.2) to give them the cat.
   (1.6)
M: And you dese:rve that. It sh ould c o : s t , )
J:                            [Well what d'you ex]pect
   for three bucks,
M: It should cost you fifty.=
J: =a whitewashed head or a clear conscience.
   (0.4)
V: [ [Cle-ar consci ence.]  [That's why I'm doing it.
M: [ [Mmm:::[mm::::[mm:::] ::[:::.
J: So?
   (0.4)
```

```
 J: So tha t's::i: t.
 M:       [Mm:mm:. [
( ):             [khh!=
 V: =hnhhh, hhu h
 M:              [Clear conscience˙ when they kill
   (that thin:g,)
 V: [Tha:t's ri:ght,
 V: That's uh- right o:n.
   (0.4)
 V:   Uh huh?
 M: [[They kill it then it's on their head not you:rs
   ri:ght?
   (1.8)
 V: ehRight.
   (0.4)
 M: Cause you know they're gonna wipe it ou:t.
   (0.3)
 V: Uh n-uh n-not that cat. They'll wipe out my
   mother's probably the big ca:t˙ two three years
   o:ld.
   (0.3)
 V: This little cat's got a cha:nce. °Maybe.°
   (0.7)
 M:   How come-
 V: [[Cause I kno:w if- hh ˙hh you go to Huma:ne
   Society they have kittens there.
 M: How co me your mothe:r, who's a cat lover,˙
 V:      [And-
   (1.3)
 M: (sets up) letting her cat go. I don't understand
   that.
```

Whereas in fragment (29) the one getting rid of his cat can see that his coparticipants are attacking him, are making the worst of it, and thus that he need not take their talk into account, in fragment (25) the one who got rid of her cat may find that whatever hopes she might have had as to her blamelessness and the cat's survival have been deeply eroded by the recipient's observably attempting to be supportive and trying to make the best of it and *nevertheless* being unable to offer absolution or optimism.

The teller counters the recipient's offer of a cheerful distraction with an exacerbated version of the trouble.

```
 A: That's (what I was told) anyway.
 M: Yeh- ehh ˙hehh hheh heh ˙hh˙hhh OH:::::
     uh this one's so c ute,
 A: [I don't know but]
 A: I: still feel that I did the wrong thing. And I'm
   sick abou:t it,
```

```
→ M:      ┌ehhh
   A:  ⌈ ⌈⌊Sometimes I feel so (0.4) (        ) I really feel
          (0.2) so tired and sort of (0.3) alone and
          everything I can go into tears about it no
          (0.2)
   A:  n┌o kidd┌ing I feel real badly abo┐ut it
   M:   ⌊hh    ⌊Yeh  w e l l  that's tru-⌋
   M:  Ah hah you really do┌miss (        ).
   A:                      ⌊He was in our house a little
          friend and I gave him awa:y.
→ M:  Yeh- uhh hahh hahh┌hu- ˙uhhh
   A:                    ⌊And I feel SO badly about it
          simply aw::ful.
```

```
------------------- end recording -------------------
```

Given the troubles-teller's exhibited penchant for gloom, it is not unlikely that this version of the trouble would have been delivered, independent of the recipient's activities. But the recipient may be heavily
contributing to its emergence, with the combination of troubles-resistance and dubious hopefulness that seems designed to exacerbate the
teller's troubles.[8]

This segment of the troubles-telling is greeted with laughter; again,
however, with an interesting exception. Earlier it was noted that alternative response types seemed to be discriminative as to whose unhappiness was being reported: the teller's meeting resistance (being taken
lightly), a third party's meeting receptiveness (being taken seriously).
Here, both a dramatized reference ("And I'm sick about it") and a senti-
mentalized reference ("He was in our house a little friend and I gave him
awa:y") meet with resistance, but a description of something that happens (i.e., "I can go into tears about it") is met with receptiveness.
Similarly, the accusation that meets the teller's initial announcement of
her unhappiness, and the demoralizingly dubious hopes that meet the
teller's fears for the cat's welfare appear to locate drama and sentimen-
tality as their targets.

The materials here are not, then, to be dismissed as a matter of, say, a
pathologically troubles-resistant recipient. The resistance is not across-
the-board, but is selective. It appears that a discrimination is being made
between those components of a troubles-telling that can be characterized as, say, manipulated, as constituting, for example, excuses, bids
for sympathy, sentimentalizing, and dramatizing, and those components that can be characterized as possible straight facts (for example,
"Clarence . . . says it's terrible," and that the teller sometimes cries
about it). This laughing recipient's activities, then, while "improper,"
are systematic and principled.

Summary

Whereas a troubles-teller can, and perhaps should, laugh in the course of a troubles-telling, and thus exhibit that he or she is in a position to take it lightly, that is, exhibit that he is troubles-resistive, a properly aligned troubles-recipient does not treat the teller's laughter as an occasion to participate in a laughing together, but rather proceeds to exhibit troubles-receptiveness. There appears to be, however, a distinctive segment of a troubles-telling in which both teller and recipient do properly laugh together: the buffer topics or time-outs. Even then it seems that recipient must be brought to laughter over a series of moves in which it is established that the current talk does constitute a time-out and laughter by recipient is indeed appropriate.

Thus, it appears that a constant balancing between receptiveness and resistance is maintained, in alternating activities within a segment and/or in alternating segments within a troubles-telling. In the single contrasting case, in which the recipient produces solo laughter, this systematic balancing is achieved; it is merely that the vehicles are reversed.

Notes

1. A downgraded conventional response to inquiry turns out to be a recurrent and systematic component of troubles-talk, adumbrating but not yet announcing a trouble. See Jefferson (1980b).
2. The caller's "Did I wake you *up*?" may premonitor a troubles-telling. Harvey Sacks proposes that "stories are ranked in terms of, and express their status by . . . the placing of the story in the conversation and the placing of the conversation in the recipient's life"; that one can propose that something is "important" by telling it immediately in a conversation, and even more so by "calling to tell it when the other isn't available to hear it; i.e., in the middle of the night" (see "On doing 'being ordinary,'" Chapter 16 herein). In this instance, the caller, by proposing that recipient might have been awakened by the call, proposes that the call was made unusually early, and thus that it may be urgent. Likewise, the recipient's protestation, "No:. Huh-uh. Gee I been awake for a lo:ng time" can be trouble-premonitory, proposing that she has been up for some significant time prior to this "unusually early" call. It turns out that she, too, has a trouble to tell.

   Compare fragment (20) with the following, in which a similar inquiry elicits the fact that the call just missed awakening its recipient.

   |NB:IV:4:1:SO|

   ```
   L: Hello:,
→  E: Are you awa:ke?
→  L: YE:AH.  (.) I ⌈just got u:p.
   E:            ⌊I-
   E: Oh did you?
   ```

```
L: Yea┌h.
E:    └ˑhhh Well goo:ud. I'm alo:ne. (0.3) Guy
   left me last night.
```

In this case, the one who has slept undisturbed until just before this call does not deliver a trouble. What we seem to have in fragment (20) is a buffer topic for a trouble that has been premonitored but not yet explicated. And, indeed, the playful "Aloha:" with which the caller announces herself may be seen as a buffer for a trouble that is yet to be even hinted at. Again, compare the opening of fragment (20) with this case, noticing that while the former has a series of buffers preceding the announcement of the trouble, the latter has none; indeed, has the trouble premonitory "Are you awa:ke?" as the caller's very first utterance. In these two fragments we may be looking at rather delicate instances of stories expressing their status by their "placing in the conversation and . . . in [recipient's] life," the trouble of fragment (20) a bit less urgent than the trouble of this fragment.

3. Sacks's lectures abound with references to and considerations of the occasioning and relatedness-to-prior-talk of topics and stories. See, for example; winter 1967 (March 9), pp. 1–3; spring 1970, lecture 5; winter 1971 (February 19), pp. 13–15; and spring 1971 (April 9), pp. 6–8. See also Jefferson, "Sequential Aspects of Storytelling in Conversation," in *Studies in the Organization of Conversational Interaction*, ed. J. Schenkein (New York: Academic Press, 1978).

4. That troubles-recipients may specifically withhold materials about themselves that have been occasioned by a troubles-teller's talk may be relevant to what Sacks talks of as the "psychiatrist's problem" in spring 1970, lecture 5, pp. 28–32. Roughly, it seems that a standard complaint by professionals who interact with troubles-tellers is that they find themselves bored, perhaps because in such interaction professionals are prohibited from offering materials about themselves that have been occasioned by a troubles-teller's talk. Now, that lay troubles-recipients, without any official prohibitions, withhold such materials, may constitute the common-sense basis of the official procedures used by professionals. But a resource that has been denied professionals is the entitlement to become themselves troubles-tellers, in that interaction, and thus the opportunity to disgorge, not only their troubles, but, for example, that they, too, went to a party last night. Whether lay troubles-recipients, who do have access to such a resource, find themselves less, or more, bored by a troubles-telling in which they are only temporarily setting aside materials occasioned by it, and how such matters bear on the relative performance of lay versus professional recipients, remains to be seen.

5. In some circumstances the intrinsic bias of some words or phrasings toward taking it lightly can be problematic. For example:

The first four men ever to walk across the polar ice cap returned to solid land Monday [and reported a variety of dangers and difficulties they encountered] . . . The team's ill-tempered Husky dogs were another problem . . . Three of them killed each other in fights. But the explorers gave them comic names and Hedges said: "You can't get very angry with a dog called Bubbles." (Los Angeles *Times*, June 24, 1969)

Symbolic of the Army's plight is that at some bases the men are not even trusted to carry the weapons necessary to fight the war they have been sent to wage. Part of the education program is directed toward eliminating the use of the word "fragging" because the Army feels the term is flippant. It is difficult, however, to imagine that the Army will be successful in stopping the men from saying, "Let's frag the sarge." (Los Angeles *Times*, January 9, 1972)

6. The product here will be a collaborative utterance, a phenomenon that Harvey Sacks introduced (see, for example, lecture 1, fall 1965, pp. 2–7; lecture 4, fall 1967, pp. 9–15; lecture 5, fall 1968, pp. 1–9) and Gene Lerner is developing in a doctoral dissertation now in progress. Of particular interest here is Lerner's discussion of "formatted" collaboratives, in which a first speaker produces a standard first part and a next speaker produces the standard second part; for example, ["If X . . ."] ["then Y"], and ["X, but . . ."] ["Y"]. The materials from fragment (19) under consideration here may constitute a version of a standard format for a collaborative utterance.

7. At least one member of the household is not implicated in this redistribution of the blame, and that is the Clarence whose unhappiness has been well received. It is not inconceivable that Clarence comes up for his share of the blame, and is specifically bypassed for the purposes of this particular telling, in "*o*ne Sunday afternoon I was just m:*m*ad at *h*er and I was *m*ad at (1.0) just *e*veryth*i*ng." To attempt to implicate him when (1) he has been named as a sufferer (perhaps specifically in an attempt to elicit sympathy for a matter that has so far been treated as laughable) and (2) his suffering has been sympathized with, whereas (3) the teller's suffering has been resisted, could drastically undercut the teller's current project.

8. In general, a heightened description of a trouble appears to be a standard component of troubles-talk. But such particulars as where in that talk it is delivered, and how it is introduced into the talk, can be responsive to recipients' activities.

15. Public speaking and audience responses: some techniques for inviting applause

J. MAXWELL ATKINSON
University of Oxford

1. Public speaking and audience responses

Analyzing audience responses

This chapter reports some preliminary observations from a study of sequences in which audiences at public meetings produce a display of affiliation in response to something said by a speaker (e.g., by clapping, cheering, laughing, etc.).[1] The collection of audio and videotape recordings of such interactions was initially prompted by an interest in two related sorts of problem that appear to have considerable importance for the organization of interaction in courts and a range of other multiparty settings where one speaker speaks at a time. The first, which has been discussed in more detail elsewhere (Atkinson, 1979a, 1982; Atkinson and Drew, 1979), concerns how public speakers hold the attention of nonspeaking recipients, such as members of a jury, congregation, or audience. The second has to do with just what it is about so much of the talk that takes place in courts and many other public settings that makes it hearable as persuasive. The two issues are closely interdependent in that a speaker who fails to resolve the problem of sustaining the attentiveness of audience members is unlikely to succeed in persuading any of them to affiliate with the position being proposed and/or to disaffiliate from that of an opponent.

It is easy enough to get a sense, from the way a speech is produced, that certain features of it may be relevant for the solution of one or both of these problems. But it is less easy to identify how audiences react to

This essay is one of a series based on analyses of sequences from public speeches in response to which audiences produce immediate displays of affiliation (see also Atkinson, 1983, 1984, and forthcoming). For their detailed and helpful comments on earlier versions, I am particularly grateful to Paul Drew, John Heritage, Gail Jefferson, and Anita Pomerantz. I would also like to thank David Brazil for his comments on my treatment of intonation and other "prosodic" features. Needless to say, however, responsibility for the errors that remain is entirely mine.

370

such practices (and hence which ones have an immediate impact) with the same degree of confidence and precision that is sometimes possible in analyses of interactions where participants take turns to talk. In the study of courtroom interaction, for example, the prolonged absence of any immediate local response by jurors to what has just been said prevents the analyst from being able to examine utterances in which recipients display their response to some prior talk in the same way as can be done in studies of conversation and other types of interaction. However much a particular segment may appear to be built to elicit attention, an observer thus has no immediate access to the way it was treated by the jurors themselves.

But there are, of course, many other public settings where audiences can and do respond to some of the things said by a speaker, and which therefore provide a more promising data base for investigating the sorts of issues outlined above. Before considering such materials in more detail, we may note some preliminary points about the general character of audience reactions. The first is that audiences are restricted in what they may do in response to what a speaker says, and are for the most part confined to the production of gross displays of *affiliation* (such as applause, cheers, and laughter) or *disaffiliation* (such as boos, jeers, and heckles).[2] With the exception of heckling, these displays involve simultaneously coordinated activities by a group of people, and have as a design feature that they can readily be *done together*. Cheers, boos, and jeers, for example, are constituted by extended vowel sounds which can both accommodate the contributions of late starters, and gain in volume and effect from the addition of extra voices. Applause is similarly an activity that can only be done effectively by a number of people together: One person can clap his hands, but it only becomes applause when several do so simultaneously.

Were it not the case that audiences are largely restricted to producing gross displays of affiliation/disaffiliation that can be collectively done as a single activity, it is easy to imagine the sort of unmonitorable verbal chaos that might otherwise characterize public meetings. Indeed, given the amount of competitive overlapping talk that would presumably be involved, it is difficult to see how such meetings could take place at all, and it may be no coincidence that there are very few settings where conduct of this sort is a routine feature (one candidate instance being the sort of religious meeting where participants are "seized by tongues").

Of the available methods for producing collective displays of affiliation, applause appears to occupy a predominant position in terms of both the relative frequency of its occurrence and its capacity to drown out and/or take over from other types of response. Thus applause frequently occurs either just after or in overlap with some other display(s) of affiliation, such as whistles, laughter, or shouts of "Hear, hear," "Yeah," and "Hooray":

(1) [BAA:80]

```
Ford:         Mister ↑Kenneth: (.)↓Everett=
          →  =[[((whistle))|———(9.0)————————————————————————|
Audience:      [x-xxXXXXXXXXXXXXXXXXXXXXXXXXXXXXXXXXXXXXXXXxx-x]
```

(2) [GE:79:4B]

```
Steel:        ... against La↑bour's el↓even >and the
              Tories< ni::↓ne=
Audience:  →  =Heh ↓he⌐h heh|———(7.0)—————————————|
Audience:         [xxXXXXXXXXXXXXXXXXXXXXXXXXXxx]
```

(3) [GE:79:4B]

```
Heath:        THAT is ent↓ah:rly unac↓ceptable=
Audience:  →  =Hear ⌐hear|————(8.0)————————————————|
Audience:         [x-xxXXXXXXXXXXXXXXXXXXXXXXXXXXXxxx-xx]
```

(4) [GE:79:4B]

```
Murray:       We ↑nee:d ↓in↑dustr↓ial ↑con↓front↑ation like
              we n↑eed ↓a ↑hole >in the ↓head<=
Audience:  →  =Hear h⌐ear
Audience:  →        [Yea⌐h::|————(8.0)—————————————|
Audience:  →           [x-XXXXXXXXXXXXXXXXXXXXXXXXXxxx-x]
```

(5) [BAA:80]

```
Keene:        >SHIR:LEY↓RUSSE⌐LL FO⌐R ↓YANKS
Audience:  →                 [EH RA[Y::::::::::::::::::
Audience:  →                       [x-xx-XXXXXXXXXXX]=
```

In each of these instances, applause quickly takes over from the other affiliative responses, and one reason for this presumably has to do with the relative ease with which it can be sustained over an extended period. For clapping is an activity that, unlike whistles and vocal responses, is not substantially dependent on or constrained by breathing considerations.

Another feature of applause also appears to be closely related to its tendency to take over from other sorts of response, namely, the fact that

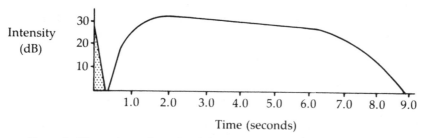

Figure 1. Electronic reading of applause intensity and duration for fragment (6). The shaded area shows the talk; the white area, the applause. (Taken from a PM 200 Pitch and Intensity Analyser manufactured by Voice Identification Inc., Somerville, New Jersey. I am grateful to R. A. W. Bladon, Director of the Oxford University Phonetics Laboratory, for his help in making this and other readings possible.)

it recurrently reaches maximum intensity soon after onset. Thus, whereas an isolated clap or two may be enough to get applause under way, a peak is quickly reached. This feature is illustrated in Figure (1), which is an electronic reading taken from just before applause onset in transcribed fragment (6).

(6)   [CPC:78:2A]

Speaker: ... I beg >to support the motion<=
              ⊢————————(8.0)————————⊣
Audience: =x–xxXXXXXXXXXXXXXXXXXXXXXXXXXxxxx–x

Within the first one and a half seconds after applause onset, its intensity rises steeply (from 0 to 30 decibels), after which it declines slightly over the next five seconds or so, before falling away more rapidly during the final one and a half seconds.

This pattern has been found to be massively recurrent across the corpus, though the electronically produced curve in Figure (1) differs somewhat from the pattern represented in the aurally produced transcripts in at least three respects (*cf.* Figure [2]). First, electronic readings

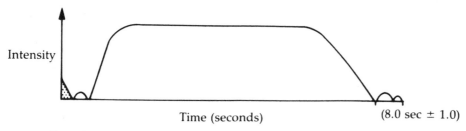

Figure 2. Freehand estimate of applause intensity and duration, based on transcription of fragment (6). The shaded area shows the talk; the white area, the applause.

appear to be less discriminating than the human ear in identifying an isolated clap (represented on the transcripts as "-x-"). This characteristic is because the electronic voice analyser continues to register the echo from a single clap beyond a point where it becomes inaudible to the human ear, thereby producing a curve with a smoother and more continuous beginning and ending than what can actually be heard. A second difference between electronic and aural readings is that the slow fall in intensity after a maximum level is reached (as shown by the former) sounds flatter, or more constant, to the human ear. This difference may again be the result of the voice analyser's capacity to register variations that the ear cannot detect. That the sharper rate of decrease at the end is somewhat less rapid than the initial increase in intensity is, however, hearable by nonelectronic means, and both the start and finish of the curve are thus interestingly consistent with the descriptive implications of various commonly used ways of referring to applause onset and termination, such as "a *burst* of applause," "the applause *died away*," "*subsided*," and so on. Third, the fact that the electronic voice analyser registers echo beyond a point at which it becomes inaudible to the human ear means that it regularly produces longer timings for the overall duration of applause; this feature is evident in the half-second difference between the transcribed and diagrammatic representations in Figures (1) and (2). As the concern of this chapter is very much with the way *participants themselves* elicit and produce such responses, electronically produced readings of applause duration and intensity have not been used (except where explicitly stated).

As far as the duration of applause is concerned, fragments (1)–(6) reveal a regularity that has been found to be remarkably recurrent in the data on public speeches studied to date. Except where they occur at the end of speeches, when there is much more variability, bursts of applause tend to last for seven, eight, or nine seconds (i.e., eight plus or minus one second). Nor is it just audience members who, by stopping clapping after about eight seconds, appear to be oriented to the production of that amount of applause as being in some sense adequate, or enough. For, as is evident in fragments (7) and (8), where the winners just announced have shown no sign of appearing on stage, the award-ceremony compère waits *eight* and *nine* seconds respectively before intervening to supply a solution to the problem posed by their being absent.

(7) [BAA:80]

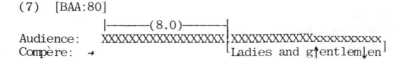

```
Audience:        =[[ XXXXXXXXX ]=
                     └──(1.2)──┘
Compère:         =Like >many film< actors Robert >Duval is
                 very busy at the mom↑ent he's ↑filming in
                 San Francis↓co:< ...
```

(8)   [BAA:80]

```
                 ├───────(9.0)────────┤
Audience:        x–xxXXXXXXXXXXXXXXXXXXXXXX│xxxxxxxxxx
Compère:    →                             └And↓re├─(1.4)─┤=
Compère:         =I'm afraid Ennio Morikonay ↑can't ↓be >with
                 us this: e:vening and ↓so I< ↑wonder >whether
                 we could ask< ↑you:: to re↑ceive the award
                 on his behalf?<
```

In neither of these instances, which were recorded from a televised show, was there any evidence that the compère timed her intervention with reference to a clock or watch; the timing suggests that she treated the period that had elapsed since applause onset as having lasted long enough for that point to be an appropriate place to propose termination.

To observe that a time span of eight (plus or minus one) seconds may be oriented to by participants as an appropriate period for applause to last is, of course, to suggest that there is something normative about it. Though it is a difficult point to demonstrate, there is at least some preliminary evidence (over and above one's own intuitive reactions to the materials) that more than nine seconds of applause may be noticeable and reportable as more than usual. In media news reports on public speeches, for example, an extract from a speech is sometimes quoted as having received the longest burst of applause, and in three such instances it has been possible to examine recordings of the original speeches. The applause in each case lasted for *ten, thirteen,* and *nineteen* seconds.[3] That this is so is clearly insufficient for showing conclusively that applause that extends beyond the upper limit of an eight (plus or minus one)-second norm will be noticed and reported as more than usual, nor does it say anything about the extent to which less than seven seconds may be noticeable as less than usual. But it is at least consistent with the above suggestions about response duration (as too is the fact that no instance has yet been found where applause lasting seven to nine seconds is reported as being noticeably extended).[4]

What and when to applaud: some preliminary observations

One of the most obviously noticeable features of affiliative audience responses is that *they do not just happen anywhere in the course of a speech, but do so in particular sequential positions.* There are at least two senses in which this can be seen to be the case, first in that they occur in response to sequences of talk that are recognizable as doing particular sorts of actions, and second in the timing of response onset and termination in relation to the preceding and subsequent talk.

In fragment (6), the first burst of applause occurs after the speaker *declares his support* for the motion at the end of his speech, and the second after the chairman *introduces* the next speaker in the debate (repeated references to previously cited fragments are numbered as for the originals, but without further reference to the data source).

(6)

```
Speaker:     ... I beg >to supp↓ort the m↓otion<=
             |————(8.0)————|
Audience:    =x-xxXXXXXXXXXXXXXxxxx-x
             (0.8)
Chairman:    Now it's my ↑pleasure to: (.) in↑vi:te
             Mister Michael >Hesel↑tī:ne the member or
             parliament< ↓for ↑Henley (0.2) >shadow
             ↑minister ↓of< the environment >to re↑ply to
             the de↓ba:te< (0.2) ↑Mist┌er Hes↓eltine┌=
Audience:                           └xx- xX - XXXX┘
             |————————(9.0)————————|
Audience:    =└XXXXXXXXXXXXXXXXXXXXXXXXXXXXXXXXXXxx-x
```

An affiliative response may also occur after a speaker *announces* the name of a prize winner (see fragments [5], [7], and [8]) and *congratulates* or *commends* someone (fragments [9] and [10]).

(9)   [BAA:80]

```
*Coppola:    Gra:julations=
*Duval:       =┌Thank you
Audience:      └x-xx-xxXXXXXXXXXXXXXXXXX ...
```

((*Speaking on film being screened to award ceremony
   audience))

(10) [CPC:80:V4]

```
Thatcher:    I am however (0.2) very ↓fortunate (0.4) in
             having (0.6) a ↑mar:vlous dep↓uty (0.4)
             who's wonderful ‾(.) in ↑all ↓places (0.2)
             at ↑all ↓times (0.2) in ↑all ↓things (0.2)
             Willie ↓Whitel┌aw┌————(8.0)————|
Audience:                  └xx│XXXXXXXXXXXXXXXXXXXx-x
Audience:                     └(ear eah)
```

During the course of speeches at political meetings, affiliative responses are commonly produced after a speaker *criticizes* or *insults* the opposition, *praises* or *boasts* about his or her own position, or does both at once, as in fragment (2).

(2)

```
Steel:      >Y'know when the< Guar:dian newspaper looked
            through  the manifestoes< la:st ↑week for
            ↓new id↑eas: (1ˉ.0) they awarded ↑us:ˉ: forty
            two: points (.) against La↑bour's el↓even and
            the Tories< ni::↓ne=
Audience:   =heh ↓he͵h heh
Audience:        ᴸxXXXXXXXXXXXXXXXXXXXXXXXXXXXXXXXXXXxx=
```

In the corpus of over a hundred such sequences examined thus far, audiences applaud at points where a speaker has just said something that is hearable as one or another of a relatively narrow range of actions. The overwhelming majority of these involve terminating declarations (e.g., of support or opposition to a motion, about future plans, intentions, prospects, etc.), commendations, congratulations, announcements of winners, opponent-directed criticisms or insults, and self-directed praises or boasts.[5]

Collective displays of affiliation by an audience, then, tend only to occur in response to a fairly limited range of actions by a public speaker. But there is also a second sense in which it may be said that affiliative responses are positioned in specific places during the course of a public speech, for there is a high degree of precision about their timing in relation to the prior talk. What is apparent in all the above examples, namely, that at least some audience members start to clap either *just before* or *immediately after* (i.e., with no gap) a possible completion point is massively recurrent across the corpus. Of these two positions, the earlier start is more commonly found, an observation that is consistent with others on the timing of affiliative responses in different interactional contexts (see, for example, Pomerantz 1975, and Chapter 4 herein; Davidson, Chapter 5 herein). In public settings, it is intuitively fairly obvious that an affiliative response that is already under way by the time the speaker reaches a completion point is likely to be noticeable and reportable as more enthusiastic/spontaneous than ones that start after even a slight delay.

Just as audiences produce affiliative responses close to possible termination or transition points in the talk, so also do speakers display an orientation to the occurrence of applause onset and completion. In none of the above instances does a speaker make any attempt to continue talking after the applause is under way. They also wait until the applause has finished before starting to speak or continuing with their speeches. With a few rare exceptions, examined in more detail elsewhere (Atkinson forthcoming b), these regularities in the way that speakers and audiences coordinate their activities apply across almost the entire collection of such sequences.

Taken together, the above observations about the timing of response onset and post-response continuation suggest that public speakers and audience members orient to the collaborative production of *one activity at a time*, the available options being either *talk* by a speaker or *response* by the audience. The turn-taking system used by participants in such settings, then, may be more similar to that for conversation (cf. Sacks, Schegloff, and Jefferson 1974) than might initially appear at first sight.

Such observations also have some important implications for the design and production of sequences of talk that precede affiliative audience responses. For if audience members are so regularly able to start cheering or clapping immediately after or just before a possible completion point in the talk, they must presumably be not only paying close attention to the ongoing talk, but also prospectively orienting to an upcoming transition relevance place *in advance of its occurrence*. Were this not so, one would expect to find either more frequent and/or longer pauses prior to applause onset, or more instances of applause starting in places other than at or just before possible completion points. Even a cursory inspection of such materials, however, reveals these to be relatively rare occurrences. The sequential positioning and timing of applause onset in relation to the prior talk, then, suggests that public speakers must be constructing that prior talk in such a way as to give audience members advance notice that and when a collective affiliative response will become a relevant activity for them to do. In other words, the fact that audiences may be said to come in on cue suggests that there must be recognizable cues (or instructions, techniques, devices, etc.) embedded in the prior talk. If audience members are able to identify these with the degree of precision implied by early response onset, then presumably they are also available for explication and description by analytic observers. The remainder of this chapter, then, is an attempt to make a start in that direction.

A brief remark may be in order about the reference to cues and devices in the plural, a usage that may seem to be going some way toward begging the question of how public speakers elicit affiliative audience responses. But, as will be seen from subsequent sections, evidence from the present research is consistent with that from an earlier study, where it was suggested that the use of a single procedure on its own may not be adequate for getting a simultaneously and collectively done activity under way (Atkinson 1979a; Atkinson and Drew 1979, chap. 3). An examination of how a speaker gets those present at an inquest to stand prior to the coroner's entry showed that there were several different ways in which participants could recognize what was being projected as the relevant next activity to be done. Were this not so, a speaker would have to rely on all those present being so equally alert or attentive that they would be able simultaneously to identify and act upon the sequential implicativeness of some single procedure. But the use of more than one way *in combination*, each of which projects the same action as relevant next, makes it more likely that most of those present will recognize at least one of them, and hence that a collectively done action may be initiated fairly immediately.

If collective displays of affiliation (such as applause and cheering) are particular instances of a more general class of actions which involve a group of individuals in the coordinated production of a simultaneous and immediate response, previous research suggests that the preceding action may typically feature the simultaneous use of *several* procedures to project some same action as the relevant next one to be done.

2. Some recurrently used response projection procedures

Namings

In commending, thanking, or introducing someone to an audience, speakers recurrently use a procedure that involves saying something about the person as a preliminary to naming him or her. The production of the name thereby provides a readily recognizable completion point such that the audience can begin to respond before the speaker has finished saying it:

(10)

```
Thatcher:    I am however (0.2) very ↓fortunate (0.4) in
             having (0.6) a ↑mar:vlous dep↓uty (0.4)
             who's wonderful (.) in ↑all ↓places (0.2)
             at ↑all ↓times (0.2) in ↑all ↓things
             (0.2)
          →  Willie ↓Whitel┌aw┤————————(8.0)————————┤
Audience:                  └xx XXXXXXXXXXXXXXXXXXXXXXXx-x
Audience:                    (ear eah)
```

Whereas in fragment (10) the person to be named is initially identified by using an alternative descriptor ("deputy"), this is sometimes done by referring to him by name, and then repeating it again at a later point:

(6)

```
Chairman:   Now it's my ↑pleasure to: (.) in↑vi:te
          → Mister Michael >Hesel↑tī:ne the member of
            parliament< ↓for ↑Henley (0.2) >shadow
            ↑minister ↓of< the environment >to re↑ply
            to the de↓ba:te<
            (0.2)
          → Mist er Hes↓eltine├────(9.0)────┤
Audience:        [x- X - XXXXXXXXXXXXXXXXXXXXXXXXXXxx-x
```

In both these sequences the speakers begin by indicating that what they are about to do will be something different from what was being done previously (via the disjunction markers "however" and "now"). They also indicate that what they are embarking on is something that is a source of personal good fortune or pleasure.

Insofar as speakers in such settings are regularly involved in talking as representatives of, or on behalf of, the audience, the marking of what is about to be said as something that has their *personal* approval may also be to propose the upcoming relevance of a display of *collective* approval. Fragment (10), for example, is an extract from the final speech on the last day of the 1980 Conservative Party Conference. Mrs. Thatcher's commendation of her/their deputy leader is thus readily hearable as something in response to which an audience of party members may (or should) be expected to produce a collective display of affiliation.

After projecting that they are moving on to something new and pleasurable, the speakers in fragments (10) and (6) locate what this is with reference to particular persons ("having a marvelous deputy," "to invite Mr. Michael Heseltine"). Additional descriptive information about the person just identified is then supplied, and it is noticeable that this information appears to be closely tied to what it is that, by this point, is recognizably in progress. Thus Mrs. Thatcher upgrades her initial assessment of her deputy as "marvelous," by elaborating on his virtues ("wonderful in all places," etc.). By contrast, the chairman in fragment (6) continues the chairman's job of introducing the next speaker with bland or factual descriptors that locate Mr. Heseltine's position in Parliament (M.P. for Henley) and the Conservative Party ("shadow minister of the environment"). That such preliminaries have been completed is then marked by a terminally intoned final beat and a pause, after which the person just described is named. And the name forms used, it may be noted, are ones that require several beats to deliver. Thus, while there are clearly other reasons for selecting "Willie Whitelaw" and "Mister Heseltine" rather than other possibilities like "Bill" or "Mike," shorter options such as these would be completed so quickly that a delay before response onset would be a likely outcome.[6]

Such sequences, then, are built up over their course in a way that informs the audience that what is in progress is something in response to which a collective display of affiliation would be a relevant next thing to do. They also project a clearly recognizable completion point (the name of the person talked about), and provide a monitor space (cf. Davidson, Chapter 5 herein) just prior to completion initiation. The procedure thus operates to make it possible for the audience to start a response *before* the speaker reaches the final point of completion (i.e., before the speaker has finished saying the name).

For such a procedure to work, the person being introduced does not necessarily have to be explicitly identified, as in the examples already considered, before being named. Thus, in fragment (1) the compère leaves the audience to find the precise identity of the person for themselves from the preliminary descriptive information provided. The stressed first name and the micropause between that and his surname may therefore serve to provide a slightly longer monitor space, during which they can anticipate a surname that would link "Kenneth" with the earlier clues about his identity.

(1)

```
Ford:      >↑Here to read the ↓nominations:i-is a m↑an<
           (0.7) >who ↑seems to ↓live anotheh a↑nother<
           life >on vid↓eo< a ↑lif:e (0.3) ↑So
           bi↓zarr:e and ↑way: ↓ou:t that if he ↑didn't
           ex↓ist (0.4) We >would↑n˙t know ↓how to
           in↓vent h↓im< (0.4) >↑Ladies an gentle↓men<
           (0.2)
        →  Mister ↑Kenneth: (.) ↓Everett=
Audience:  =[[((whistle))⌐─────────(9.0)──────────|
             ⌊x-xxXXXXXXXXXXXXXXXXXXXXXXXXXXXXXXXXxx-x
```

Though in this case enough details are supplied to enable anyone familiar with British television personalities to identify whose name is about to be announced, a procedure regularly used for announcing winners at award ceremonies provides the audience with several named possibilities, from which one will eventually be selected:

(11) [BAA:80]

```
Announcer:   The best supporting ↓actress: (0.4) the
             nominations ar:e (0.4) Lisa Ikeh↑orn: (0.4)
             for the Europeans: (0.6) Marriel Hemingw↑ay
             (0.4) for Manhatt↑n (0.6) Rachel Roberts::
             (0.4) for Y↑anks: (0.4) Meryl: Str↑eep:
             (0.4) for Manhatt↓n (1.4) an the winner:↓iz:s
             (1.4)
         → RACHEL ROBERTS  for Y↑ANKS|————(9.0)————|
Audience:                 [x–xxXXXXXXXXXXXXXXXXXXXXXXXXXXxxxx–x
```

(12) [BAA:80]

```
Announcer:   The best supporting act↑or (0.7) the
             nominations ar:e (0.5) Robert Duvah:l (0.4)
             for Apocalyps:: ↑Now: (0.8) Dennyem E↑liot:
             hh (0.4) for Saint J↑ack (0.8) John H↓urt:
             (0.8) for A:li↑en (0.8) Chris:topher Walcum
             (1.0) for the Deer ↓Hunter (1.8) The winner
             iz::
             (0.8)
         → Robert Duval:  :   (0.5) for A↑pocalypse N↓ow:  ]=
                         [x–xxxxxxxxxxxxxxxxxxxxxxxxxxx ]=
           =|————————(8.0)————————|
Audience:  =[XXXXXXXXXXXXXXXXXXXXXXXXXXXXXXXXXXXXXXXXXXX=
```

A noticeable feature of these sequences is that the pause before the person is named tends to be longer than in the introductions and commendations considered above. The longer pause is, of course, because the announcer has to open an envelope before being able to reveal the result. But, whereas in the previous examples the audiences know perfectly well whose name is being projected, this is not so in the award-ceremony announcements. Given that any of the four names might be inside the envelope, they are placed in the position of having to wait for the duration of the pause before responding. In other words, there is no doubt that a collective response will become relevant as soon as the news is out, even though the identity of the person shortly to be named remains a temporary mystery. A situation is thus established where the audience knows precisely that and when they should respond, but can do nothing about it for however long it takes for the announcer to open the envelope and read out the name. Viewed in these terms, then, this apparently simple procedure emerges as a particularly effective way of building up suspense.

It is also noticeable that, as in the previous naming sequences, the use of name forms that take several beats to deliver *after* the name has become identifiable enables the audience to produce an early response. The practice of repeating the name of the film after that of the winner provides even more time for the audience to get a response under way before the announcer reaches completion.

Sometimes, however, orderly transitions between turns by speaker and audience do not occur, and the following example underlines the organizational importance of the projection of a completion point that is recognizable by an audience in advance of its occurrence. After stating that three award results are to be declared, the announcer goes straight on to announce the first one without listing any nominees beforehand (even though this sequence comes after a long series of announcements like those in fragments [11] and [12]).

(13) [BAA:80]

```
Announcer:   ·hhh An thē A↑ca:de↓meh: ·hh ↑hon↓ours the
             m↑akers of ↑these pro:gr↓ah:ms ·hhh with
             th↑ree: (.) R↑eddif↓fusion Star aw↓ar:ds (.)
             The fl↑a:me of knowl↓edge aw↓ar:d for the
             best sch↑ools progr↓ahm (.) went to
             R↑ichard Ham↑ford ·h for How: We↓Use to L↓ive.
         →   (1.4)
             ·hhh Thē:  ┌H↑ar:↓lequ in: Awa↓r:d┤───(2.5)────┤=
Audience:               └x – xx – xxx – xx – xx – xxxxxxxxxx'
Announcer:   =┌(°Sorry°)├───────(5.0)────────┤
Audience:    └XXXXXXXXXXXXXXXXXXXXXXXXXXXXXXXXXXXX
```

After naming both the winner and the program, then, nothing happens for nearly one and a half seconds, whereupon the announcer responds to the absence of an audience response by starting to announce the second award. As he does this, the audience starts to applaud, and, by abandoning continuation, he defers to the audience response as having sequential priority over his next announcement. Once the applause is well under way, he can be heard apologizing to the compère, thereby acknowledging both that something had gone wrong, and that he had had something to do with it.

What happens in the continuation of this sequence, however, is that the audience soon comes to terms with the new projection procedure that has just been introduced into the proceedings:

(13) [continued]

```
Announcer:   =The ↑Har:le↓quin A↓war:d for the b↑est
             docu↑mentary-or-f↑ahctu↓al programm ·hh
             went to ↑ANN W↓ood and ↑IAN ↓Bolt for:: the
```

```
          B↑ook ↓Tower:=
          ├───────────(7.0)──────────┤
Audience: → =x-x-xxXXXXXXXXXXXXXXXXXXXXXXXXXXXXXXxx    =
Audience:    ┌-xx - x - xx - x-x┐
Announcer:  =└The H↑ahrle↓quin A┘war:d >for the< ↑best
            ↓dra↓ma: or light enter>↑tain↓ment
            prograh:m< ˙hh went to >↑ANna ↓Ho:me and
            ↑Roger ↑Single↓ton< ↓Tur:ner  ┌˙hh for  =
Audience:                                  └-x- x -

Announcer:   ┌Gra::nge ↓Hill ├───────(7.0)──────┤
Audience: → └xx - xxx - xxXXXXXXXXXXXXXXXXXXXXXXXXXxx
```

After the second winner is announced, the audience responds immediately on completion of the name of the program, and after the third at the same point as in the earlier film award sequences, namely, *before* the speaker has finished saying the name of the program/film. This example, then, suggests that the introduction of a new procedure for announcing winners without any prior warning may initially result in a disorderly transition between the completion of the announcement and response onset.[7] But it also shows that audience members are quickly able to identify the source of the trouble, to see how the procedure should have worked, and to coordinate the timing and production of subsequent displays of affiliation accordingly.[8]

These various examples illustrate procedures that can be used by public speakers to project that and when an affiliative response will become relevant in the environment of introductions, commendations, and announcements. They underline the organizational importance of *projecting* a clearly recognizable completion point in advance of its occurrence, and suggest that failure to do so can result in a delayed response that may be treated as noticeable and accountable (as in fragment [13]). Although it may be common for audiences to applaud on hearing the name of a person being introduced or commended, displays of affiliation obviously also occur after a speaker has made various other sorts of assertion. What some of these are and how they can be built to project the upcoming relevance of an audience response are therefore considered further in subsequent sections.

Lists

It was noted earlier that public speakers are frequently involved in speaking on behalf of the audience being addressed, and that affiliative responses recurrently occur after *self-directed* statements of praise or boasts and *opponent-directed* criticisms or insults (or in other words favor-

able assessments of "us," and unfavorable assessments of "them").
This is particularly so at political meetings, recordings of which provide
the main data base for the observations to be reported in the remainder
of this chapter.

Fragment (14) is another extract from Mrs. Thatcher's closing address
to the 1980 Conservative Party Annual Conference. "This week" is readily hearable as referring to the proceedings of the conference. That an
interpretation of the week's deliberations is about to be produced is
projected by "This week has demonstrated" and, as party leader addressing a gathering of the party faithful, she is, of course, highly unlikely to do anything other than to offer a praiseworthy assessment of
"us," with which the audience will be readily able to affiliate.

(14) [CPC:80:V4]

```
Thatcher:    This week ↓has ↑demonstrated (0.4) that we
             are a ↑party ↓un↑i͟:ted ↓in ↑pur:pose (0.4)
             ˙strategy (0.2) and res↓ol:ᵣve
Audience:                               ˡ(ear: ᵣear)ˌ=
Audience:                                    ˡxxXXˌ
             |——————————— (8.0) ———————————|
Audience:    =XXXXXXXXXXXXXXXXXXXXXXXXXXXXXXXXXXXXXXXXXxxx
```

After projecting an upcoming assessment of the week's proceedings,
Mrs. Thatcher pauses and then proceeds to assert comembership with
the audience (via the use of "we"), and identifies party unity as the
matter to be addressed. Even though she pauses for nearly half a second
after "united in purpose," no response occurs at that point. In terms of
our earlier analysis, it would appear that what might otherwise (e.g.,
syntactically) be regarded as a possibly completed boastful assertion
becomes recognizable as such at *too late* a point in the course of its
production for audience members to be able to produce an immediate or
early response. In other words, it is not until after "purpose" that the
possible completeness of the assertion becomes apparent. But the
chances of an immediate response occurring at that point are also reduced by the statement thus far being marked as nonterminal with an
upward shift in intonation. By thereby proposing to continue talking
beyond that point, Mrs. Thatcher informs the audience that it is not yet
time to respond. After the ensuing pause, it then becomes apparent that
what has been projected is a *list* of dimensions on which the party has
shown itself to be united, and an affiliative audience response gets under way just prior to the completion of what is projected in advance (by
"and") as the final item in the list.

That the last item is also the third item is of particular interest in the light of a study by Jefferson (forthcoming a) of the way speakers and recipients in conversational interaction orient to "three-partedness" in list construction. More specifically, the following observations would appear to have considerable relevance for understanding how such a procedure can also work to project the relevance of an audience response when used by a public speaker:

> List completion can constitute utterance completion; i.e., a point at which another can or should start talking. Crucially, *forthcoming completion is projectable from the point at which a list is recognizably under way;* i.e., given two items so far, a recipient can see that a third will occur, and that upon its occurrence utterance completion can have occurred whereupon it will be his turn to talk (Jefferson forthcoming a:13, my italics)

Although these remarks were based on an analysis of conversational interaction, it only requires the substitution of "respond collectively" for "talk" to make them equally applicable to interactions between public speakers and audiences. For the present research shows that three-part lists can also be used by speakers in producing a range of the different sorts of actions that recurrently elicit displays of affiliation by an audience.

In fragment (14), then, Mrs. Thatcher's *boast* about party unity is completed by the *third* item in a list, as was the *commendation* of her deputy considered earlier:

(10)

```
Thatcher:   I am however (0.2) very ↓fortunate (0.4) in
            having (0.6) a ↑mar:vlous dep↓uty (0.4)
            who's wonderful ⎺(.)
         ①→ in ↑all ↓places
            (0.2)
         ②→ at ↑all ↓times
            (0.2)
         ③→ in ↑all ↓things
            (0.2)
            Willie ↓Whitel⎡aw⎤────(8.0)────┤
Audience:               ⎣xx⎦XXXXXXXXXXXXXXXXXXXXXXXx-x
Audience:                  ⎣(ear eah)
```

In the following example, an *other-directed insult* is produced by declaring Soviet Marxism to be bankrupt on *three* counts:

(15) [CPC:80:V4]

```
Thatcher:   Soviet ↓mar:xism is
         ①→ ideol↑ogically
```

```
        ②→ ↓pol↑itically and
        ③→ ↑mor↓al↑ly bank↓ru⌐pt|————(9.0)————|
Audience:                        ⌊xxXXXXXXXXXXXXXXXXXXXXXXXXXXX
```

In this case, as in the commendation of her deputy (fragment [10]), the completion of the action in progress was projected not to occur, and does not occur, immediately on completion of the third item in the list (i.e., after "morally"). But the completion of the boast about party unity (fragment [14]) *did* coincide with completion of the third item, and was recognized to have done so by the audience members (who started to applaud just before the speaker finished saying "resolve"). In other words, three-part lists sometimes feature as *preliminary specifications* of a yet to be completed activity in progress, and sometimes as *expansions* of one that could have been completed after the first item. Both procedures, however, are constructed in such a way as to enable an audience to anticipate an upcoming point at which the activity will be complete, and hence to respond just before it is reached.

There is also some evidence to suggest that, in cases where a third list item and an action are completed simultaneously, the immediate sequential relevance of a collective response is so strongly established that one will be produced there and then, irrespective of whether the speaker has more to say. The following example (fragment [16]) is from a speech made at the 1980 Labour Party Conference by a member of the National Executive Committee to a fringe meeting organized by supporters of amendments to the party's constitution. His boast about a commendable decision becomes evident and could have been completed after the first item in the list. But, as with Mrs. Thatcher's boast about her party's unity (fragment [19]), continuation beyond that possible completion point is proposed by a nonterminal upward intonational shift during the first list item:

(16)   [LPC:80:DV10]

```
Heffer:    The national executive de↓ci:ded (0.8) that
           we ag↑reed in >↑PRINCIPLE< (0.8) that we
           ↑MUST-T ↓AG↑AIN TRY AND GET SOME
           CONSTI↑TUTIONAL >AMENDMENTS< (0.5)
        ①→ BE↑FOR:E YOU (0.2)
        ②→ AT CONFERENCE (0.2)
        ③→ THIS ↓WEEK ⌐SO ⌐>THAT YOU CAN STILL MAKE⌐
Audience:              ⌊xx ⌈-XXXXXXXXXXXXXXXXXXXXXXX⌉=
Audience:                  ⌊eh ::::::::::::::::::::::
Heffer:    ⌐⌐YER MINDS UP<
Audience:  =⌈-XXXXXXXXXXXXXXXXXXXXXXXXXXX⌐(edited cut)
Audience:   ⌊:::::::::::::::::::::::::::::⌋
```

It is noticeable in this case that, although the speaker does *not* project the upcoming third item as the last by inserting "and" after the second one, the audience nonetheless produces an immediate response which persists through and beyond the continued talk with which the clapping and cheering overlap (in contrast with fragment [17]).

In a similar sequence, where a third item completes the expansion of a boast by Mrs. Thatcher about her government's actions in relation to trade union law, some members of the audience produce a brief flutter of subdued applause which overlaps with her continuing to talk beyond that point:

(17)   [CPC:80:V4]

```
Thatcher:   As you know we've made the first crucial
            changes in trade union ↑law (0.4)
         ①→⌈to remove the worst abuses of the closed
           ⌊↑shop (0.2)
         ②→⌈to restrict picketing to the place of work
           ⌊of the parties in disp↑ute (0.2)
         ③→ and to encourage secret bal↓lots ˙hhh=
            ├─────────────────(2.5)──────────────────┤
Audience:    ⌈x-xxxxxxxxxxxxxxxxxxxxxxxxxxxxxxxxxxxxxxx⌉=
Thatcher:   =⌊Jim Prior has carried ↑all ↓these measures⌋
            =⌈↑thro⌉ugh ˙hhh with the support of the
Audience:    ⌊xxx-x⌋
Thatcher:   vast ma↓jority of trade ↓union
            ↓memb⌈ers┌────────────(10.0)───────────────┤
Audience:        ⌊xxx│xxxxxxxxxxxxxxxxxxxxxxxxxxxxxxxxxxxxxxxxxxxxxx-x
Audience:            ⌊(Yeah)
```

That only a few members of the audience appear to treat the third item in this list as a place to respond is evidence of potential relevance to the earlier suggestion that, in order to get a large group of people to produce a collectively done activity (such as applause), such an outcome may be more assured if a public speaker runs together several devices that project the same next action (see the section on "What and When to Applaud" above). Thus, in fragment (17) it looks as though some members of the audience treated the co-occurrence of list completion with possible activity completion as projecting the immediate relevance of a response, whereas others did not. There is some evidence that those who withheld at that point may have done so in response to the *competing* sequential implications of other devices that project *continuation* beyond this possible completion point, and that are being simultaneously used by the speaker.

Even before taking the inbreath after completing the third item, Mrs.

Thatcher had produced a shift of gaze direction that is noticeably different from that which she recurrently features at preresponse completion points in the course of her speeches. In all the other video-recorded instances examined thus far, she starts to move her head downward on the last one or two beats of the talk preceding response onset in such a way that, by the time completion is reached, her gaze has shifted from a position where she was facing the audience slightly to her left, down to the script on the lectern in front of her. At that point, she visibly closes her mouth (i.e., purses the lips) and audibly clears her throat, these latter components of the sequence occurring in that order, and usually in slight overlap with applause onset. In fragments (14) and (15), for example, her head begins the downward movement at the points indicated by the asterisks above "resolve" and "bankrupt":

(14)

Thatcher: ...↑<u>pur</u>:pose (0.4) strategy (0 2) and
           *
           res↓<u>ol</u>:ve

(15)

Thatcher: ... ideol↑<u>ogically</u> ↓pol↑<u>itically</u> and
                                        *
           ↑<u>mor</u>↓al↑ly <u>bank</u>↓rupt

But in the sequence followed by the flutter of applause (fragment [17]), she starts to look *up* from her text on the "b" of "ballots," and is facing the audience to the left of her by the time she takes the inbreath that immediately follows:

(17)
                               *
Thatcher: ... and to encourage secret <u>bal</u>↓lots ˙hhh

In other words, what Mrs. Thatcher does in this sequence is almost the *exact opposite* of what she recurrently does in the environment of other transitions between talk completion and response onset. By starting to look *up* at the audience on the penultimate beat before completion of the third item in the list, she can thus be seen to be proposing continuation beyond that point, a proposal that is then retrospectively confirmed by the immediately following inbreath, and by the further talk thereby projected. As was noted earlier, then, it appears that procedures with *competing* and *opposite* sequential implications are being simultaneously mobilized: The third item in a list is projected as the last by a preceding "and," list completion coincides with a response-relevant activity (i.e., a boast about her/their government's actions), and the third item in the list is completed with terminal intonation on the final beat of the last word ("ballots").

Viewed in these terms, the short flutter of applause would appear to have been produced by a section of the audience that recognized the devices projecting completion, but *not* those projecting continuation. Meanwhile, applause was withheld at that point by what sounds (on the tape) like a much larger group who, by so doing, can be heard to be responding to the sequential implications of the devices used by Mrs. Thatcher to propose continuation. Two and a half seconds into her subsequent talk, those producing the applause (which has failed to reach maximum intensity) stop clapping, and wait for her to reach another completion point. This in fact turns out to be a form of recompletion in that Mrs. Thatcher goes on to refer back to the government measures just boasted about:

(17)

```
Audience:    =⌈x-xxxxxxxxxxxxxxxxxxxxxxxxxxxxxxxxxxxxxxxxxxxx
Thatcher:     ⌊Jim Prior has carried ↑all ↓these measures
             ⌈↑thro⌉ugh ˙hhh with the support of the
Audience:    ⌊xxx-x⌋
Thatcher:    vast ma↓jority of trade ↓union
Audience:    ↓memb⌈ers⌈────────────(10.0)────────────|
             ⌊xxx⌊xxxxxxxxxxxxxxxxxxxxxxxxxxxxxxxxxxxx-x
Audience      ⌊(Yeah)
```

It is noticeable here that the recompletion involves a commendation of the minister who carried through the measures just boasted about and the elaboration of a further dimension to the boast and commendation (i.e., the claim that he and the government's actions had widespread support among trade unionists). Several response-relevant activiites are thus implicated in Mrs. Thatcher's continuation beyond the start of the short flutter of applause, and it is also the case that upcoming termination is projected by a falling intonational contour that extends over several beats of the last five words. In other words, what she goes on to say involves the use of a number of devices, all of which project the relevance of an affiliative response at the next possible transition point. It is therefore perhaps not surprising that the audience is able to respond concertedly and promptly: The applause starts just before completion (after which a shout of agreement is also to be heard), it quickly reaches a level of maximum intensity, and lasts somewhat longer than usual. In short, it is hearable as a *burst* of applause by the whole audience, rather than as a *flutter* by a few.

In this section, then, an attempt has been made to show how speakers can use lists to build response-relevant activities, and to project a completion point that an audience is able to recognize in advance of its occurrence. But it is not, of course, the only way in which this can be done. Though lists are fairly regularly produced prior to an audience response, they are by no means the most recurrent verbal construction found in such sequential environments.

Contrasts

In the collection of instances where applause occurs during the course of speeches by politicians, making a point in the form of a contrast is by far and away the most commonly used preresponse verbal construction. On present evidence, contrasts feature in about one-third of such cases.[9] Contrastive devices can be used by a speaker to do several sorts of things, including boasts about one's own side (fragment [18]), insults aimed at an opponent or opponents (fragments [19] and [20]), and to boast about "us" and insult "them" simultaneously (fragments [21] and [2]);

(18) [GE:79:1B]

```
Callaghan: I can s↑ay to ↓you: Mister Ch↓air↑man: (0.5)
            ⌐that in this: el↓ec↑shun I d↑on't int↓end
      ①▸ ⌊(0.8) to ma̅ke the most ↓promises (0.8)
            ⌐I intend that the next Labour government ( . )
      ②▸ | shall ↑KE̅E:P ( . )
            ⌊↦↓the most promises<=
Audience:   =⌐°hear hear°
Audience:   ⌊x–X–XXXXXXXXXXXXXXXXXXXXXXXXXX ((edited cut
            after 6.0 secs.))
```

(19) [GE:79:4B]

```
Heath:      ⌐°Neow° the la:bour:: (0.4) prime minist↑er
            | und ↓his coll̅↑ea:gues ↓are b↑oasting >in
      ①▸ | this election cam↑paign< (0.7) that they
            | have brought infla:tion de↑own from the
            ⌊disah:strous level of twenty six per ↓cent
            ⌐(1.4̅) But we are: ent↓itled to inqu↑ah:re
      ②▸ | (0.4)
            | Who put it ↑up ( . )
            ⌊↓tuh  twenty six per ↓cent=
```

```
Audience:    =hehh┌eh
Audience:         └x-xxXXXXXXXXXXXXXX ...
```

(20) [GE:79:4B]

```
Steel:       >THE ↑TRUTH IS: BEGINNING TO ↑DAW:N ON OUR
             ↓PEOPLE THAT THERE ARE ↑TWO: CON↓SERVATIVE
             ↓PAR:TIES ↓IN ↓THIS ↓ELECTION< (0.6)
          ┌->↑ONE IS ↓OFFERING THE CONTIN:UATION OF THE
      ①-┤ POLICIES ↓WE'VE ↓HAD ↓FOR THE ↓LAST< FIVE
          └↑YEARZ:
          ┌-AND THE OTHER IS ↓OFFERING A RE↓TURN TO THE
      ②-┤ ↓POLICIES ↓OF FORTY YEARS =
          └=┌AG↓O:
Audience:      └eh-he┐h-heh|————————(8.0)————————|
Audience:            └X-xXXXXXXXXXXXXXXXXXXXXXXXXXXXXXxxx-
```

(21) [G:79:4B]

```
Thatcher:    >Because it is that< cha:nging (.) ↓nature
             (.) >which'as ma:de< so many former 1↑a:b↓our
             >↓cabinet minis↑ters< ↑lea:ve ↓the labour
             party 'h and we're proud to have >some of
             them with ↓us< because they find their
             ↑former ↓aspir↓ations are ↑now better
             repres↓ented
          ①-┌ 'hh by the ↑modern day con↑SER:va↓tive party
          ②-┌ 'hh than by ↓the >modern ↓day lab↓our
             └par↓┌ty<
Audience:        └(eear eer)|————————(9.0)————————|
Audience:        └xx-X-XXXXXXXXXXXXXXXXXXXXXXXXXXXXXXXXXxx- x
```

(2)

```
Steel:       >Y'know when the< Guar:dian newspaper looked
             through >the manifestoes < la:st ↑week for
          ①-┌↓new id↑eas: (1.0) they awarded ↑us::˙ forty
             └two: points (.)
          ②-┌against La↑bour's el↓even and the Tories<
             └ni::↓ne=
Audience     =heh ↓he┌h heh|————————(7.0)————————|
Audience:            └xXXXXXXXXXXXXXXXXXXXXXXXXXXXXXXXXXxx=
```

Given the adversarial character of political debate, it may be that the juxtaposition of two contrasting items is particularly adaptable for making political points. Certainly it is the case that the method of "verbal antithesis" in such environments has a long history, and was well enough known in classical rhetoric and oratory to be formally classified as one of the main "artistic figures." Moreover, students of that tradition appear to have had a sense for how such constructions work to project an upcoming completion point in the course of a speech:

> Closely connected with the desire for a periodic style is the tendency to frequent use of verbal antithesis, an artistic figure which provides a happy means of completing the period and the sense. It is useful because the second part of the antithesis supplies the reader or hearer with something he is already expecting. (Dobson, 1919:27–8)

One suggestion here, then, is that antitheses or contrasts provide a way of accomplishing completion. Another is that they may work to project a second part that the reader or hearer is already expecting. Although it would indeed appear that the identification of what is being said as the first part of a contrast may provide a basis for recognizing what it will take to reach completion, it is not clear whether or not Dobson is also suggesting that a first part enables hearers to "expect" the second of two contrastive parts. In other words, this passage could also be read as proposing that recipients of the first part of a contrast can anticipate the detailed contents of an upcoming second part.

On this issue, the data from contemporary public speeches suggest that the contrastive devices that occur prior to an affiliative response recurrently involve a punchline, or an element of surprise, and that second parts are only fairly rarely expectable or predictable in detail. Thus, of the above examples, the contrast in fragment (21) is perhaps the only one where the content of the second part ("than by the modern day labour party") can be readily anticipated. But the others involve a "puzzle-solution" format, which may either be set up in the first part of the contrast and resolved in the second (e.g., fragments [18] and [19]), or posed before the first part of a contrast becomes identifiable, and in such a way that its solution is provided by *both* parts of the contrast (e.g., fragment [20]). But whether the details of the second part of a contrast are expected or not, the device would appear to work in much the same way as far as projecting a recognizable completion point is concerned. For, if members of an audience can recognize something being said by a speaker as the first part of a two-part contrast, they are then in a position to analyze and identify what it will take to complete the second part.

Closer examination of such sequences shows that, as with those involving the projection of names and final list items, the last few beats of the talk tend to be produced in such a way as to provide a monitor space during which audience members can anticipate that completion is imminent, and hence be ready to produce an early or immediate response. In fragment (18) for example, Mr. Callaghan marks the word that con-

trastively distinguishes the second part with the first ("keep") by producing it with an upward shift in intonation and an increase in volume
and emphasis. He then pauses briefly before completing the second
part:

(18)

```
Callaghan:  ... I d↑on't int↓end (0.8) to make the most
            promises
            (0.8)
            I intend that the next Labour government
         →  (.) shall ↑KEEP (.)
            >↑the most promises<=
```

An almost identical form of construction and delivery is also used by
Mr. Heath in fragment (19):

(19)

```
Heath:      ... that they have brought infla:tion de↑own
            from the disah:strous level of twenty six
            per ↓cent
            (1.4)
            But we are: ent↓itled to inqu↓ah:re
         →  (0.4) who put it ↑up
            (.)
            ↓tuh ↓twenty six per ↓cent
```

In these and the other examples already cited, the second part of the
contrast is produced by repeating much of the first, and changing at
least one element, and so thereby marks it as recognizably different from
the first. In most instances, the new material is sandwiched between
repeated components, as in the case of "labour" in fragment (21):

(21)

```
Thatcher:   ... by the ↑modern day con↑SER:va↓tive party
            ·hh than by ↓the >modern ↓day lab↓our par↓ty<
```

Such sequences are thus constructed in such a way that the second
part of the contrast is readily recognizable as being similar and closely
related to the first. The repeat of elements from the first *after* the contrastive implications have become evident then provides a monitor
space within which the audience is able to anticipate imminent completion and to produce an immediate or early response.

In the relatively rare instances where a delayed response occurs after the completion of a contrast, the design and production of the preceding talk exhibit marked differences from the above sequences. Thus in the examples considered so far, both parts of the contrast were fairly brief, were of a similar length, and shared a number of common constructional units. Accordingly, fragment (22) starts in a way that appears to be projecting a contrastive second part that will be of similar structure and duration. But this is not what subsequently happens:

(22) [GE:79:4B]

```
Shore:   ①⌐ ⌐An'you know it's ↑one thing to ↓sell to
           └ ⌐›sitt↓ing ↓tenants‹ ̄(0.7) an'its ↑quite
          ⌐an↓other (0.2) to kee:p hou:s↑es ↓empty (0.4)
        ②│ while they're ↑HAW:KED ›ar↓ound‹ (0.2) to
          │ find ↑some PURCHa↓ser (0.2) who could ↑just
          └ as well ↓buy (0.7) in the open ↓market (0.2)
           ›like any ↓other (0.2) owner ↓occupier ↓does:
           (1.0)
           |─────────(5.0)─────────|
Audience: -x- (0.2) -x-xx-xxxxxxxxxxxxxxx -xx
```

As it unfolds, then, the second part of the contrast is produced over the course of several further bursts of talk after the completion of the first part. If it is difficult for readers to keep track of the connection between the two parts, the audience also may have had similar problems, in that they remain silent for a whole second after completion, and then start to applaud more hesitantly, quietly, and briefly than usual.

Fragment (22), then, is one of several in the corpus that suggest that, for a contrast to work effectively in eliciting an immediate or early audience response, the second part should closely resemble the first in the details of its construction and duration. Otherwise, the audience appears to be faced with two sorts of problem. The first is that the absence of a close constructional similarity between the two contrasting parts makes it difficult for them to anticipate a projected completion point, and hence to respond on or before its occurrence. And the second is that, in monitoring the detailed elaborations involved in the production of an extended second part, audience members may find their attention being distracted away from the contents of the first. Thus, by the time completion is finally reached, the contrastive connections between the two parts may have become opaque (if not actually forgotten). Given that an understanding and appreciation of the point being made presumably depends on audience members being able to recognize the *link* between *both* parts of a contrast, a speaker who dwells too long on the second part may run the risk that the point being made by juxtaposing the two may not be immediately grasped, or perhaps even missed altogether.[10]

If the use of an extended second part of a contrast is unlikely to assure an immediate response, brief contrasts produced close to a completion point also appear to have a similar outcome. In fragment (23), for example, the speaker announces that he is about to make an important point about his party's electoral program. On starting the projected segment, he raises his voice, and moves toward completion with several downward shifts in intonation. That a contrast is about to be produced, however, is not projected until fairly late (at "better"), and its substance does not become evident until the last four words ("not working than working"):

(23) [GE:79:3B]

```
Pardoe:    >an'which will< ↑GUARAN↓TEE: (0.5) >what is
           perhaps< the ↑most im↑portant thing that can
           >be ↓°guaran↓teed°< (1.0) That >↑NO ONE IN
           ↓BRITAIN CAN ↓EV↑ER AG↓AI:N BE
①②→ BETTER OFF BY ↑NOT WORKING THAN ↓WORK↓ING<
           (0.7)
           >THAT'S THE ↑FIrst ↓thing to guaran↓tee<
           ├──────────(5.0)──────────┤
Audience:  -x-xx-xxxxxxxxxxxxxxxxxxxxxxxxxxxx-x
```

That the audience has still not responded more than half a second after completion is consistent with earlier suggestions about the importance of providing a monitor space within which an audience can anticipate when to respond. For an upcoming contrast is projected much closer to completion by Pardoe than was done by the speakers in fragments (18)–(21). It is then rapidly completed with a second part that begins and ends during the final three beats. In other words, it would appear that the audience has hardly any time to recognize that a completion point is about to be reached, let alone to get a response under way. Faced with a post-completion silence, Mr. Pardoe does not merely wait for the audience to start clapping, as was done by Mr. Shore in fragment (22), but uses a much more active and exposed method of pursuing a response. This involves *recompletion*, with the point just made being referred back to and reiterated in summary form.

In the following example, an identical procedure is used by Mr. Heath after a silence follows the completion of an elaborated second part of a contrast similar to that produced by Mr. Shore in fragment (22).

(24) [GE:79:4B]

```
Heath:      ┌In ↑my: view it ↓is ↑right >that the
          ①→│ government should consider ↓these matt↑ers<
            └and take them into account (1.0) What is
            ┌entah:rly unaccepta↓ble (0.8) is the view::
            │that pah:rliament ↑never ↓can (0.6) and
          ②→│never should (0.6) appro:ve any >legisl↓ation<
            │(0.8) nor should a government pursue ↑any
            │↓policy (0.8) unless ↑first of ↓aw:l >the
            └trade unions them↓selves (.) approve ↓of it<
             (0.5)
             THAT is ent↓ah:rly unac↓ceptable=
Audience:   =Hear ┌hear├────────(8.0)────────┤
Audience:        └x-xx XXXXXXXXXXXXXXXXXXXXXXXXXXXXxx-x
```

By recompleting a just completed point, the speaker continues to focus on that, rather than proceeding with other possible options (such as going on to expand on it, to make a related one, or to talk about something else). The point is thus marked as being sufficiently important for it to be worth inviting the audience to pay further attention to it. Such a procedure, then, can be heard to be informing audience members that the speaker does not propose to continue until they have supplied some evidence that they understood and appreciated the point just made as a noticeable and important one. Insofar as no instances have yet been found where the audience fails to produce a prompt display of affiliation after a recompletion of this sort, it appears to be an extremely effective way of eliciting a response that had previously been withheld.

Occasionally, speakers use this form of recompletion in a somewhat different sequential environment, namely, *after* the audience has already begun to respond. Given the speed with which audience responses attain maximum intensity (see Section 1), such continuations are likely to be rendered inaudible by the clapping and cheering, as happens in the following example, where the audience has started to respond just prior to the completion of the second part of a contrast:

(25) [V6:RI:81]

```
Foot:     ①- ┌THERE'S NO::: (0.3) DESPAI:R (0.3) IN THIS:::
             └(.) GREAT (.) DEMONSTRATION: (.)
          ②- ┌THERE IS A DETERMINATION TO DESTROY: THEM
             └AN'THEIR POLI┌CIES┐├────(0.2)────┤
Audience:                   └Yeh:│:::::::::::::::│=
Audience:                        └x-xxXXXXXXXXXX─┘
```

```
Foot:          ┌(THAT'S WHAT WE'RE HERE FOR*)
Audience:    = │::::::::::::::::::::::::::::::::::::::::::...
Audience:      └XXXXXXXXXXXXXXXXXXXXXXXXXXXXXXXXXXXXXXX...
```

(*Talk drowned by cheering and applause - retrieved by
   lip-reading from video-tape)

Mr. Foot's production of "THAT'S WHAT WE'RE HERE FOR" after the
audience responses have got under way can be heard to be proposing
that his point was not fully completed when the end of the contrastive
second part was reached, and hence also that the audience had responded prematurely.[11] Insofar as early response onset is hearable as a
display of greater than usual enthusiasm for what the speaker is saying,
the use of such post-response pursuits may have considerable advan-
tages for an orator. Thus it provides a way of transforming what was
already a slightly early response into a very early one, such that it may
even drown out the recompletion (as occurs in fragment [25]).

   Given that such pursuits are also effective devices for eliciting a response where none has yet begun (as in fragments [23] and [24]), it
would appear that such devices can be safely written into speeches at
places where displays of affiliation are desired. For this form of recompletion has, on present evidence, a "can't lose" character, in that it
will work either to elicit a response where none has started, or to make
one already in progress hearable as more than usually early and enthusi-
astic.[12] But this is not, of course, to suggest that there is an equivalence
between each of these two possibilities, as the former risks being heard
as rather "lame" in the way it draws attention to the absence of a
response where one had been expected and/or ineffectively projected.

   The discussion of how certain sorts of verbal constructions work to
enable an audience to anticipate that and when a collective display of
affiliation will become relevant suggests that an immediate or early audience response is made possible by the use of different devices that
have a common design feature: Once they are recognizably under way,
namings, lists, and contrasts project a recognizable completion point
that can be anticipated by audience members some time before completion is finally reached.

3. Some preliminary observations on prosodic and non-vocal phenomena

Prosodic features

In relation to some of the sequences discussed above, various references
have been made to shifts in volume, intonation, emphasis (i.e., prosodic

features) and nonvocal activities, and the way these appeared on occasions to be closely coordinated with the verbal constructions used in response-elicitation sequences. Although such phenomena have yet to be subjected to detailed analysis, it is nonetheless possible to note some grossly observable regularities that suggest that prosodic and nonvocal activities may be recurrently implicated in the way audiences are informed that and when an affiliative response will become relevant.[13]

That prosodic shifts are somehow involved in projecting the upcoming relevance of a display of affiliation is perhaps most vividly demonstrated by listening to speeches made in languages one does not understand. Such an exercise, with extracts from speeches by Hitler, Mussolini, and Castro, suggested (to the author and three others) that it is possible for hearers to anticipate that and (approximately) when an affiliative audience response is likely to occur, even without understanding what a public speaker is actually saying. The impression gained from this exercise is that, at some point before response onset, speakers can be heard (and seen) to "change gear," as it were, and to launch into a sequence that is marked as being noticeably different from the talk that had just preceded it. This appears to be manifested in such details as changes in gestural activity, an increase in the volume at which the talk is produced, and its subsequent production with a more emphatic beat or rhythm. Then, as an elicitation sequence approaches completion, there tends to be a slight increase in the pace of the talk, with termination being preceded by one or more downward shifts in intonation.

Although such phenomena are notoriously difficult to discriminate, represent, and read in transcribed form, some or all of them are hearably present in most of the extracts examined thus far. As an example, fragment (5) is of some interest, in that *all* the prosodic features mentioned above are involved. Thus after opening the envelope, the announcer raises her voice (an increase in volume being indicated by capital letters), speaks more quickly (indicated by > . . . <), and with a more emphatic beat than before (stressed components being indicated by underlining). The announcement of the name of the winner and winning film is also produced with two downward intonational shifts (indicated by ↓ just

(5)

```
Announcer:  a:n:d the ↑winne↓ri::z:s
            (3.2)
            >SHIR:LEY ↓RUSSE⌐LL FO⌐R ↓YANKS<
Audience:             ⌊EH RA⌈Y:::::::::::::::::
Audience:                   ⌊x–xx–XXXXXXXXXXX...
```

before the shift occurs), the second of which coincides with the final stressed beat of the announcement.

These observations suggest that prosodic shifts may be involved in marking various stages in the production of a response-elicitation sequence. The increase in volume, for example, may be implicated in projecting that what is upcoming is to be heard as more noteworthy than what went before. Then, insofar as speakers can be seen to be putting more effort into what they are saying (by sustaining the new level of amplitude, and talking with greater rhythmic emphasis), they may thereby display to the audience that what is in progress is something to which closer attention should be paid. As well as contributing toward making less attentive members of the audience more alert, such shifts are also available to be analyzed and treated by hearers as evidence that a response-relevant assertion is now in progress and/or nearing completion. A downward intonational shift that coincides with an assertion that is approaching termination may by then be hearable as projecting an imminent completion point.

Although it was suggested that prosodic features alone can be used by hearers unfamiliar with the language in which a speech is being made to anticipate approximately when an audience response will occur, this is not to propose that they are so powerful that they will work *independently of* other procedures to assure the actual production of a response by copresent audience members who *do* understand the same language. Thus, in fragment (23), where the contrast only became apparent just prior to completion (and no immediate response followed), the talk had been produced with all the response-relevant prosodic features referred to above. After projecting what is upcoming as an important point, Mr. Pardoe raises his voice, speaks more quickly, and proceeds toward completion with several downward shifts in intonation:

(23)

Pardoe: ... that >↑NO ONE IN ↓BRITAIN CAN ↓EV↑ER
AG↓AI :N BE
→ BETTER OFF BY ↓NOT WORKING THAN ↓WORK↑ING
(0.7)
>THAT"S THE ↑FIRrst ↓thing to guaran↓tee<

This example suggests that, for a prompt response to ensue, prosodic shifts may have to be mobilized *in conjunction with* other response-relevant features in the talk's construction and delivery. Thus, in the earlier discussion of fragment (18) it was noted that the word that establishes the second assertion as contrastive with the first ("keep") is produced with an increase in volume and an upward shift in intonation:

(18)

```
Callaghan:  ... I d↑on't int↓end (0.8) to make the most
            promises
            (0.8)
            I intend that the next Labour government
         →  (.) shall ↑KEEP (.)
            >↓the most promises<=
```

There is also a slight pause before and after the punchline of the point being made becomes evident. The second part of the assertion, however, remains incomplete until the repeat of the phrase previously used to complete the first assertion ("the most promises"). This repeat is produced at a slightly quicker pace and with a fall in intonation.

Another punchline is prosodically marked in a similar way in fragment (19):

(19)

```
Heath:      ... that they have brought infla:tion de↑own
            from the disah:strous level of twenty six
            per ↓cent
            (1.4)
            But we are: ent↓itled to inqu↓ah:re
         →  (0.4) who put it ↑up
            (.)
            ↓tuh ↓twenty six per ↓cent
```

In fragment (15), the identification of Mrs. Thatcher's critical target is completed with "marxism," which is stressed, stretched, and downwardly intoned. Each of the three items in the list is then marked with stresses and intonational shifts that give the talk a rhythmic beat. As is fairly common in the production of lists, the early (nonterminal) items are completed with rising intonation, whereas the last one is completed with a downward shift.[14]

(15)

```
Thatcher:   Soviet ↓mar:xism is ideol↑ogically
            ↓pol↑itically and ↑mor↓ally bank↓rupt
```

These preliminary observations, then, suggest that prosodic features are more finely coordinated with the verbal constructions used in the production of response-elicitation sequences than can be detected from speeches made in languages that are foreign to an observer. Eventually, therefore, it may be possible to show in greater detail how they are implicated in the way public speakers display that they are launching into such a sequence, locate key elements in the point being made, and project an upcoming completion point.

Nonvocal activities

Whereas most of the research done thus far has relied on audio recordings preliminary observations of video recordings suggest that nonvocal activities may be closely involved with prosodic and other features in the production of response-elicitation sequences. It was, for example, noted earlier that the direction and timing of Mrs. Thatcher's head movements appeared to be relevant to whether she was proposing completion or continuation.

Fragment (25) provides further evidence of the way nonvocal activities can be finely coordinated with prosodic and verbal constructions in the production of a response-elicitation sequence. At the start of the first part of the contrast (at "THERE'S"), Mr. Foot raises his right arm to a point where the flat palm of his hand is facing toward the crowd from a position level with his head. He then "pats the air" with short forward movements, which come to a temporary halt at the points marked by asterisks during the first part of the contrast. These patting movements appear to be closely coordinated with the rhythmic beat of the talk, in that they reach completion points simultaneously with stressed words, or stressed parts of words, and start again (i.e., the hand moves back to its original vertical position) just after short pauses.[15]

(25)

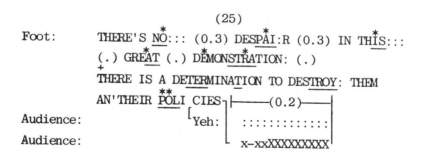

At the point marked with a cross at the beginning of the second part of the contrast, Mr. Foot returns his hand to the position from which the patting movement begins, and holds it there making no further movements until the stressed beat of the last word in the second part of the contrast. He then stabs it rapidly downward all the way to below his waist (at the point marked by double asterisks).

In the light of the earlier suggestion that public speakers can be seen and heard to change gear as they launch into a response-elicitation sequence, this example suggests that such a shift may be displayed and recognized in a change in the type and amount of gestural activity that accompanies the talk. It also shows that hand and arm movements involved may be closely coordinated both with the rhythm of the talk and with specific features of its sequential construction: The beginning of each part of the contrast is gesturally marked by the raising of a hand; each part is distinguished by the use of different gestures during the course of its production; and completion of the second part is projected one beat before its occurrence by a swoop of the arm that is much faster and more extended than any of the preceding movements. That this swoop also occurs just as the assertion is reaching possible completion can be seen as projecting the imminent relevance of a response. The response is then produced at the point where the hand swoop reaches its destination, so that in this example it looks as though the audience is being "conducted" by the speaker to "come in on time."

In spite of their preliminary nature, these observations on the occurrence of various prosodic features and nonvocal activities in preresponse sequences suggest that they are strongly implicated, together with other procedures reported on earlier, in providing an audience with advance notice that and when a collective display of affiliation will become relevant. Insofar as they also appear to be used to focus the attention of audience members on what is being said (and details thereof), prosodic shifts and nonvocal activities may work in similar ways for participants in large-scale public settings as they do in conversational interaction. In other words, the present observations would seem to be consistent with studies that report an increase or shift in prosodic and gestural activity where an interactant has grounds for supposing that a recipient is not displaying attentiveness (see, for example, C. Goodwin 1981a). For, as was noted much earlier (in Section 1), public settings are environments where a major problem for speakers is that of holding the attention of their audiences.

Finally, the close coordination of prosodic and gestural shifts with other recurrent features in the production of such sequences is generally supportive of the proposal that the work of response elicitation may involve a speaker in the simultaneous mobilization of a range of procedures, each of which projects the upcoming relevance of a collective display of affiliation and/or a sequential position. It seems likely, therefore, that a more adequate understanding of how these processes work will involve the identification of what procedures have such sequential implications, and the ways in which they may be combined and coordinated to elicit an immediate or early affiliative response.

4. Concluding remarks

The present research was initially undertaken in response to difficulties associated with obtaining analytic access to the ways in which audiences analyze and respond to sequences of talk by public speakers in settings like courtrooms, where gross displays of attentiveness and affiliation do not routinely occur. Observations made thus far suggest a range of identifiable techniques or procedures that are recurrently used by speakers in the production of sequences that precede collective displays of affiliation (cheers, applause, etc.). These techniques include particular verbal constructions, as well as prosodic and nonvocal activities, which may be mobilized in a variety of combinations. It has been suggested that such procedures work by providing audience members with a basis for analyzing and interpreting what is being said as something that projects both the upcoming relevance of an affiliative response, and a clearly recognizable completion point at (or before) which such a response may begin.

Although a more detailed description of how these techniques work must await further research, on the basis of present evidence, where several of them are coordinatedly mobilized, the talk can be heard and treated as constituting an invitation to the audience to respond affiliatively and immediately when (or before) completion is reached. The research also suggests that such techniques can be mismanaged in systematically describable ways.

More generally, evidence is beginning to accumulate to the effect that contrastive devices are massively recurrent across a range of environments, both interactional and textual, where persuading or convincing an audience is a central practical concern (Atkinson 1981b, 1983, 1984). It may also be the case that the present research on response-elicitation sequences has reached a point where it will become possible to begin to describe just what it is about the way some *individual* orators perform that results in their achieving reputations as outstandingly effective (or ineffective) public speakers (Atkinson 1984 and forthcoming). Whether or not such studies will eventually have specific practical implications for the training of practitioners (and/or warning their audiences), of course, remains to be seen. If they do, however, it would presumably strengthen the case for applying a similar approach to the analysis of interaction in other multiparty settings like courtrooms, classrooms, and lecture theaters, where the operational dynamics of public speaking are clearly important, but are still only vaguely understood in their details. As has been hinted at in parts of the present chapter, research of this sort may have some implications for intriguing and difficult questions like how particular extracts from political speeches come to be noticed, selected, replayed, quoted, and discussed in the news media.

Although the idea of applause and other collectively produced displays of affiliation as invited rather than spontaneous or audience-initiated phenomena may nowadays be a relatively unfamiliar one, there appears to have been a more explicit appreciation of its elicited character in earlier periods of history. In the first century A.D., for example, Quintillian's *Institutes of Oratory* included a discussion of the issue, and recommended that applause should not "be too eagerly sought" (ed. Watson 1856, vol. II:246).[16] This work also contains a fairly extended consideration of "the power of exciting laughter in an audience" (ibid., vol. I:430–56).[17] Much more recently, there was apparently sufficient awareness of the phenomenon of invited applause for there to be a special word in the English language for referring to talk that works with such an effect. Thus, the *Shorter Oxford English Dictionary* (1973 edition:344) dates the origin of "claptrap" at 1727, and defines it as "a *trick, device,* or *language designed to catch applause.*" Insofar as this definition comes close to summarizing the procedures described here, there might initially seem to be a case for seeking to revive its use as a technical term. One reason for not doing so, however, is that in everyday usage the pejorative connotations of "claptrap" have come to predominate over the technical (to an even greater extent than is the case with "rhetoric"). And another is that the dictionary also informs us that the word has no plural which, in the light of the observations reported in this chapter, seems curiously lacking in descriptive adequacy.

Notes

1. The data base consists of recordings from the 1979 British General Election (referenced as GE), Annual Conferences of the Conservative Party (CPC) and the Labour Party (LPC), and the 1980 Awards Ceremony of the British Academy of Film and Television Arts (BAA). A guide to the way applause has been transcribed is provided in the Transcript Notation at the beginning of the book.

   Previous versions of parts of this chapter have been presented at meetings of the British Sociological Association Sociology of Language Study Group, Cambridge (1980) and Aberystwyth (1981), the U.S. Law and Society Association, Amherst (1981), and the Colloquium on Connectedness in Sentence, Text, and Discourse, Tilburg (1982).
2. Throughout the chapter, activities such as clapping and cheering are referred to as "displays of affiliation," or "affiliative responses." But in particular local instances more precise implications may be involved. Applause may, for example, be a way of welcoming, thanking, or congratulating some

identified person, or it may be done as a display of agreement with some decision, proposal, or a particular point being made by a speaker. Although subsequent research may show that such differences are systematically related to the way applause and other responses are produced, little evidence to this effect has been noted so far. Accordingly they are grossly characterized here as *affiliative*, which is an implication that appears to be common to *all* the actions listed above.

3. It is possible that observations of this sort may eventually be shown to have some intriguing implications for the way particular extracts from speeches are selected for quotation and discussion in the media. In pursuit of such interests, a corpus of relevant data from televised speeches and news programs featuring extracts from them is being collected and studied in collaboration with John Heritage.

4. A perhaps farfetched explanation of the eight-second phenomenon can be inferred from some recent work on short-term memory (as reported in a recent BBC "Horizon" science documentary). It suggests that, for certain sorts of tasks, eight seconds may be a crucial cutoff point. This observation raises the possibility that the tendency for applause to stop after a similar duration may result from audience members forgetting what it was they were applauding.

5. A distribution is shown in Table (1), which shows that opponent-directed criticisms/insults and self-directed praises/boasts were present in various combinations in 86 percent of the cases (i.e., [a]–[d]). Given that commendations almost always involve strong elements of "us"-directed praise, it would not be stretching the point too far to add the 9 percent to the 86 percent, thereby giving a total of 95 percent. Even allowing for sampling and coding problems, then, phrases like "overwhelming majority" and "massively recurrent" would seem to be reasonably justifiable in the face of such figures. An unexpected bonus from this exercise was that the five cases coded as "other" may provide an interesting collection for further study.

Table 1. *Distribution of actions hearably produced by speakers just prior to applause onset during political speeches*

Actions	Number (N = 100)
(a) Opponent-directed criticism/insult	34
(b) Self/us-directed praise/boast	40
(c) Combined insult and boast	10
(d) Combined boast/commendation	2
(e) Commendation	9
(f) Other	5

6. That these forms are preferred to alternatives like "Will" or "Mike" is, of course, also consistent with recipient design considerations for some particular occasion of use. For a detailed discussion of such issues see, for example, Sacks and Schegloff (1979).

7. Another possible source of trouble in fragment (13) may have to do with the fact that *several* announcements are being projected simultaneously. Thus

there is some evidence that difficulties may be more likely to occur when more than one person is being announced or commended. In this context, the following example is relevant, and is also of interest because it is the only one found so far in which a speaker explicitly proposes that there may be a "proper" place to applaud (i.e., not "too early"). It may also be noted that the provision of preliminary information of the sort featured in earlier examples is depicted as something that the allegedly premature applause has prevented.

[CPC:80:DV10]

```
Prior:       An that is to: say (0.2) how much I value
             the support (0.4) and the ad↓vice that I've
             had (0.2) from Gay Gowrie Jim Lester and
             Patrick May↓hew (.) who are sitting on my
             right ↓here=
             ├────────(5.0)────────┤
Audience:    =x-xx-xxxxxxxxxxxxx-x⌈x
                                  ⌊Yes >I don't want you to
             clap too early because I want just to say
             another word about ↑each of ↓them.<
```

8. A similar example from another public setting is the following fragment, where the congregation at a Church of England service is presented with the problem of identifying the completion point of each prayer:

[CE:ES:1]   (Remembrance Sunday)

```
Vicar:       ... and will you after (.) each prayer (.)
             make the response, (1.0) Hear us Holy Lord.
             (1.0) Hear us Holy Lord. (2.0) Oh God the
             Father of all Righteousness (0.5) Make us
             (.) a righteous (.) nation.
             (1.5)
Vicar:       Hea⌈r us:: Holy Lord⌉
Congregation:    ⌊ear us Holy Lord⌋
```

After the first prayer, the vicar can be heard to "prompt" the congregation, but in the next two responses, his voice cannot be heard at all. That the congregation is so quickly able to produce the response on their own presumably results from their having successfully identified the structure of the first prayer, and its repetition in the second and third (the links between Righteousness-righteous, Redeemer-redeemed, and Holiness-Holy presumably being crucial). The prayers are also built with a monitor space *after* the words "righteous," "redeemed," and "Holy":

[Continued]

```
Vicar:       Oh God the Son, Redeemer of all mankind,
             (0.5) make us a redeemed people
             (0.5)
Congreg: →   Hear us Holy Lord
Vicar:       Oh God the Spirit (0.5) Lord of all
             Holiness (0.5) make us a Holy Church
             (0.5)
Congreg: →   Hear us Holy Lord
```

For more extended discussions of the way the ongoing interactions in a setting provide participants with data that can be analyzed to facilitate their competent participation in the proceedings, see Pollner (1979), and Atkinson (1979a).

9. This is a preliminary estimate derived from a work in progress on "The Televised Behaviour of Public Figures" supported by the (British) SSRC grant number HR 8576; research director is John Heritage. It is based on video tapes of some 450 political speeches lasting a total of approximately 30 hours, and including some 2,000 applause events. An initial search through these materials by David Greatbatch suggests that namings, contrasts and lists, together with six other verbal projection devices not described here, may be involved in as many as 70 percent of all such events. I am grateful to Heritage and Greatbatch for permission to publish these estimates in this volume.

10. In the light of earlier remarks on short-term memory (see note 4), it may have at least some curiosity value to note here that the "long-winded" second parts of the contrasts in fragments (22) and (24), both of which are followed by a delayed response, take *more than* eight seconds to produce (twelve and fifteen seconds respectively from the end of the first part to completion of the second). In *all* the cases where a prompt or early response occurs after a contrast, however, the time taken to produce the second part is much less than eight seconds (cf. note 4).

11. This procedure closely parallels that described for conversation by Jefferson (1981a) as "post-response pursuit of response," one class of which is made up of *recompletions*. In relation to these she notes that, by recompleting an utterance *after* a recipient has already started to respond, a speaker can provide materials out of which a retrospective reinterpretation of his utterance can be constructed. It may, for example, display what was just said as having not been adequately built for a response at the point where it was initially invited and initiated (ibid:50).

12. There is in fact some evidence that fragment (25) was indeed regarded as a particularly effective or impressive sequence of speaker–audience interaction, in that it was used to conclude a televised party political broadcast produced by and on behalf of the Labour Party. It ended with a printed invitation to join the party being superimposed and read out over film of the demonstrators cheering and applauding this particular extract.

13. Though the point is not developed here, the prosodic and nonvocal activities found in public speaking appear in some ways to differ from the way they feature in everyday conversational interaction. Pauses, for example, tend to be longer and more frequent, and some of the possible reasons for this have been discussed in a preliminary fashion elsewhere (Atkinson and Drew 1979:205–99; Atkinson, 1982:108–9). But insofar as they appear to have relevance for resolving the problem of attracting, sustaining, and/or upgrading the attentiveness of audience members, prosodic and nonvocal activities in public settings may eventually be shown to work in ways that closely parallel (in a perhaps exaggerated fashion) their operation in smaller-scale everyday interactions. In this respect, recent research by C. Goodwin (e.g., 1982), Heath (Chapter 11 herein), and Schegloff (Chapter 12 herein) is suggestive of many interesting lines of comparative analysis.

14. The observation that lists recurrently exhibit these intonational features derives from research on listing by Jefferson (forthcoming a).

15. That the gestures featured in fragment (25) coincide with stressed beats in the talk is consistent with observations of other videotaped fragments in the

present corpus, and with research conducted with reference to data from quite different settings (see, for example, Bull 1981).

16. I am grateful to William Twining for drawing this and other classical works on oratory to my attention.

17. "Invited laughter" thus appears to be another phenomenon that was known to classical writers on oratory, and that has also been subjected to detailed empirical study by conversation analysts (see, for example, Jefferson 1979, and Chapter 14 herein; Jefferson, Schegloff, and Sacks, forthcoming). And, while the present research on applause elicitation owes much to this more recent work on laughter, neither project was motivated by a knowledge of the concerns of classical rhetoric and oratory.

PART VI
Everyday activities
as sociological phenomena

As part of his introduction to an earlier collection of research reports, George Psathas commented on the widespread impact of Harvey Sacks's unpublished lectures in the following terms:

> Sacks was a co-worker par excellence. He shared his data and his observations freely and generously. His lectures, transcribed and mimeographed since the mid-1960's, have been read by large numbers of persons over the years as citations to his unpublished work will attest. This unpublished corpus has achieved national and international circulation . . . This book is evidence of the influence and importance of his work. (Psathas 1979:3–4)

Several years later, these remarks apply with at least equal (if not greater) force to the contents of the present book. Although most of the studies reported here have been carried out since 1975, when Sacks died in a car accident, many of them take as their starting points themes and issues that were originally explored or suggested in the lectures. Sacks's work can now be seen to have had an even wider *instructional* impact than was evident at the time when Psathas was writing his introduction to *Everyday Language*. More than half the contributors to the present book learned about and became committed to conversation analysis at a distance of six thousand miles from the University of California campuses where Sacks and his colleagues were based. As the unpublished lectures were so important in making this learning possible, it seemed appropriate to conclude this collection with an edited example of the sort of material that might suddenly arrive as the latest installment in what will be remembered by its recipients as the most inspiring correspondence course they ever took.

This final chapter may also serve as a reminder of the sociological origins, interests, and implications of conversation analysis. Sacks did his graduate studies with Erving Goffman and Harold Garfinkel in the early 1960s. If his mentors had already succeeded in identifying so-

411

ciology's serious and long-standing neglect of the study of naturally oganized everyday activities, his own work was marked by a determination to find ways of cutting into the problem that would establish the viability of such a research program beyond doubt. In order to do that it was necessary not just to articulate an analytic approach to the phenomena of everyday life, but to do so in such a way that it could be learned, applied, and expanded on by others. Conversation analysis has certainly developed in recent years, and one particularly noticeable feature of recent work is that it has tended to become more detailed and more technical. Research reports typically concentrate on the identification and explication of particular interactional devices and practices, and less attention is given to discussions of the sociological rationale for doing such studies, or of the broader implications their findings may have. In part, of course, this approach is responsive to the problems of excessive length and repetition that would otherwise be involved. More importantly, however, the sustained focus on the details of interaction is sensitive to the fact that participants themselves observe and analyze each other's actions in extraordinarily detailed and systematic ways. Minimally, then, any empirically adequate approach to research into social interaction must presumably seek to come to terms with the phenomena in a no less detailed fashion than is routinely done by participants themselves.

Such a focus does not therefore mean that conversation analysts have somehow lost sight of or become less committed to the originating aims of the research tradition within which they are working, even though they may not be rehearsed by every author of every single paper that is ever written. Were this to be done, however, it is likely that one theme that would continually recur would be the claim contained in the following chapter by Sacks – namely, that it is through the deployment of techniques and practices of the sort described in this book (and elsewhere in the literature of conversation analysis) that everyday activities are produced, recognized, and treated as orderly phenomena. In other words, devices, techniques, machineries, and the like are viewed as analytically interesting only insofar as and to the extent that they can be shown to be usable and used by real-world people for the living of real-world lives.

16. On doing "being ordinary"

HARVEY SACKS

Late of the University of California, Irvine

Usually I start the course by doing what I do in the course, without any programmatic statements and without any indication of why it should be of any interest to anybody. Now – and this may be unfair – the course will turn out to be much more severely technical than most of you could possibly be interested in, and some good percentage of people will drop out, and usually that has the consequence that they get nothing out of the class. So I decided to spend the first session telling people something that I take it could hardly *not* be of interest to them. Then, when they drop out, they would at least have heard what I figure would be worth the price of the course. I guess I should say that if this is not absorbing to you, you could hardly imagine how unabsorbing the rest will be.

Now, in this course I will be taking stories offered in conversation and subjecting them to a type of analysis that is concerned, roughly, to see whether it is possible to subject the details of actual events to formal investigation, informatively. The gross aim of the work I am doing is to see how finely the details of actual, naturally occurring conversation can be subjected to analysis that will yield the technology of conversation.

The idea is to take singular sequences of conversation and tear them apart in such a way as to find rules, techniques, procedures, methods, maxims (a collection of terms that more or less relate to each other and that I use somewhat interchangeably) that can be used to generate the orderly features we find in the conversations we examine. The point is, then, to come back to the singular things we observe in a singular sequence, with some rules that handle those singular features, and also, necessarily, handle lots of other events.

So, what we are dealing with is the technology of conversation. We

This chapter was compiled by Gail Jefferson, and is an edited transcript of lecture 1, spring 1970; with additional materials from lecture 2, winter 1970; lecture 4, spring 1970; and lecture 1, spring 1971.

413

are trying to *find* this technology out of actual fragments of conversation, so that we can impose as a constraint that the technology actually deals with singular events and singular sequences of events – a reasonably strong constraint on some set of rules.

The way I will proceed today is, in many ways, nothing like the way I will proceed throughout the rest of the course. In this lecture I will not be attempting to prove anything, and I will not be studying the technology of telling stories in conversation. I will be saying some things about why the study of storytelling should be of interest to anybody. And the loosest message is that the world you live in is much more finely organized than you would imagine. Now the pileup of evidence about that would only serve to give a great deal of flesh to that assertion, and you do not have to stay around after today to have caught that message, and to have been armed with some materials that would permit you to wander around noticing things that you might not have noticed, and find them ghastly.

A good deal of what I will say has its obscure intellectual source in a novel called *Between Life and Death* (trans. Maria Jolas, 1970) by Nathalie Sarraute. (I say obscure because if you were to read the book it is not likely that you will find that it says what I say, but with some consideration you might see how it is that I owe what I am saying to this source.) The book is absolutely not assigned reading. I am just citing a debt.

A kind of remarkable thing is how, in ordinary conversation, people, in reporting on some event, report what we might see to be, not what happened, but the ordinariness of what happened. The reports do not so much give attributes of the scene, activity, participants, but announce the event's ordinariness, its usualness. And if you think of literature or poetry you can perfectly well know that out of any such event as is passed off as, for example, "It was a nice evening; we sat around and talked," really elaborated characterizations are often presented.

This brings me to the central sorts of assertions I want to make. Whatever you may think about what it is to be an ordinary person in the world, an initial shift is not think of "an ordinary person" as some person, but as somebody having as one's job, as one's constant preoccupation, doing "being ordinary." It is not that somebody *is* ordinary; it is perhaps that that is what one's business is, and it takes work, as any other business does. If you just extend the analogy of what you obviously think of as work – as whatever it is that takes analytic, intellectual, emotional energy – then you will be able to see that all sorts of nominalized things, for example, personal characteristics and the like, are jobs that are done, that took some kind of effort, training, and so on.

So I am not going to be talking about an ordinary person as this or that person, or as some average; that is, as a nonexceptional person on some statistical basis, but as something that is the way somebody constitutes oneself, and, in effect, a job that persons and the people around them may be coordinatively engaged in, to achieve that each of them, together, are ordinary persons.

A core question is, how do people go about doing "being an ordinary person"? In the first instance, the answer is easy. Among the ways you go about doing "being an ordinary person" is to spend your time in usual ways, having usual thoughts, usual interests, so that all you have to do to be an ordinary person in the evening is turn on the TV set. Now, the trick is to see that it is not that it *happens* that you are doing what lots of ordinary people are doing, but that you know that the way to do "having a usual evening," for anybody, is to do that. It is not that you happen to decide, gee, I'll watch TV tonight, but that you are making a job of, and finding an answer to, how to do "being ordinary" tonight. (And some people, as a matter of kicks, could say, "Let's do 'being ordinary' tonight. We'll watch TV, eat popcorn," etc. Something they know is being done at the same time by millions of others around.)

So one part of the job is that you have to know what anybody/ everybody is doing; doing ordinarily. Further, you have to have that available to do. There are people who do not have that available to do, and who specifically cannot be ordinary.

If, for example, you are in prison, in a room with no facilities at all; say, it has a bench and a hole in the floor and a spigot; then you find yourself doing things like systematically exploring the cracks in the wall from floor to ceiling, over the years, and you come to have information about the wall in that room which ordinary people do not have about their bedroom wall. (And it may be that prison walls are more interesting than other walls, since among other things prisoners are occupied with is leaving information on the wall that they have been there, so there are things to read on the walls.) But it is not a usual thing to say, well, this evening I am going to examine that corner of the ceiling.

Of course it is perfectly available to anybody to spend an afternoon looking at a wall. You could choose to do that. If you take drugs, you are permitted to do that. But unless you take drugs you would not find yourself allowed to do it, though nobody is around. That is to say, being an ordinary person that is not a thing you could allow yourself to spend the day doing. And there is an infinite collection of possibilities, of things to do, that you could not bring yourself to do. In the midst of the most utterly boring afternoon or evening you would rather live through the boredom in the usual way – whatever that is – than see whether it would be less or more boring to examine the wall or to look in some detail at the tree outside the window.

There are, of course, people whose job it is to make such observations. If you were to pick up the notebooks of writers, poets, novelists, you would be likely to find elaborated studies of small, real objects. For example, in the notebooks of the poet Gerard Manley Hopkins, there are extended naturalistic observations of a detailed sort, of cloud formations, or what a leaf looks like, looking up at it under varying types of light, and so on. And some novelists' notebooks have extended and detailed observations of character and appearance.

Now, there is a place in Freud's writings where he says, "With regard to matters of chemistry or physics or things like that, laymen would not venture an opinion. With regard to psychology, it is quite different. Anybody feels free to make psychological remarks." Part of the business he thought he was engaged in was changing that around; that is, co-jointly to develop psychology and educate laymen, so that laymen would know that they do not know anything about it and that there are people who do, so that they would leave such matters to the experts, as they learned to leave chemical and physical matters to the experts.

My notion is that as it is for chemistry and physics, so it is for making distinctive observations about the world and its persons. It is just a thing that, in being ordinary, you do not do. For whole ranges of things that you might figure to be kind of exciting, something like the following talk will be offered (this is not made up, but is actual). Somebody talking about a man she met the night before says:

> He's just a real, dear, nice guy. Just a real, real nice guy. So we were really talking up a storm, and having a real good time, had a few drinks and so forth, and he's real easygoing. He's intelligent, and he's uh, not handsome, but he's nice looking, and uh, just real real nice, personable, very personable, very sweet.

You do not get, from somebody doing "being ordinary," a report of the play of light on the liquor glasses, or the set of his eyebrows, or timbre of his voice.

I think it is not that you might make such observations but not include them in the story, but it is that the cast of mind of doing "being ordinary" is essentially that your business in life is only to see and report the usual aspects of any possibly usual scene. That is to say, what you *look* for is to see how any scene you are in can be made an ordinary scene, a usual scene, and that is what that scene is.

Now you can plainly see that that could be a job; that it could be work.

The scene does not in the first instance simply present itself, define itself, as insufferably usual, nothing to be said about it. It is a matter of how you are going to attack it. What are you going to see in it? People are regularly monitoring scenes for their storyable possibilities. I give you a gruesome instance of it, from a book called *An Ordinary Camp* (1958) by Micheline Maurel. She reports the first day in a concentration camp. The first hours are horrifying. Then there is a lull. "Little by little conversation sprang up from bunk to bunk. The rumors were already beginning to circulate. Luckily, the news is good. We'll be home soon. We'll have an unusual experience to talk about." A way in which this event was dealt with while it was taking place was that in the end it will turn out to have been a good story. An experience that might leave one utterly without hope you can see as wonderfully relevant for being able to survive it. And plainly enough, you have experienced being in scenes the virtue of which was that, as you were in them, you could see what it was you could later tell people had transpired.

There are presumably lots of things that, at least at some point in people's lives, are done just for that; that is, it seems fair to suppose that there is a time, when kids do "kissing and telling," that they are doing the kissing in order to have something to tell, and not that they happen to do kissing and happen to do telling, or that they want to do kissing and happen to do telling, but that a way to get them to like the kissing is via the fact that they like the telling.

So it seems plain enough that people monitor the scenes they are in for their storyable characteristics. And yet the awesome, overwhelming fact is that they come away with *no* storyable characteristics. Presumably, any of us with any wit could make of this half-hour, or of the next, a rather large array of things to say. But there is the job of being an ordinary person, and that job includes attending the world, yourself, others, objects, so as to see how it is that it is a usual scene. And when offering what transpired, you present it in its usual fashion: "Nothing much," and whatever variants of banal characterizations you might happen to use; that is, there is no particular difference between saying "Nothing much" and "It was outta sight."

I suppose you have all heard the usual characterizations of "our Protestant society," or "our Puritan background," which involve that ordinary people/Americans/Europeans are built in such a way that they are constrained from doing lots of experiences that they might do, were they not repressed. We think of the kinds of repressions that people have that are sociologically based; that is, the Puritan Ethic involves spending most of your time working, holding off pleasure, which we think of as definitively what it means to be a usual person in Western Civilization. Though that is manifestly important, it misses an essential part of the thing, which is, whether you were to have illegitimate experiences or not, the characteristic of being an ordinary person is that, having the illegitimate experiences that you should not have, they come off in just the usual way that they come off for anybody doing such an illegitimate experience.

When you have an affair, take drugs, commit a crime, and so on, you find that it has been the usual experience that others who have done it have had. So we could perfectly well remove the Puritan constraint, as people report it is being removed, and the ordinary cast of mind would nonetheless be there to preserve the way we go about doing "being ordinary." Reports of the most seemingly outrageous experiences, for which you would figure one would be at a loss for words, or would have available extraordinary details of what happened, turn out to present them in a fashion that has them come off as utterly unexceptional.

My guess is that you could now take that point with you, and, watching yourself live in the world – or watching somebody else, if that is more pleasant – you could see them working at finding how to make it ordinary. Presumably, it would be from such a sort of perceived awareness of, for example, the ease with which, after practice, you see only the most usual characterizations of the people passing (that is a married couple and that is a black guy and that is an old lady) or what a sunset looks like, or what an afternoon with your girlfriend or boyfriend consists of, that you can begin to appreciate that there is some immensely powerful kind of mechanism operating in handling your perceptions and thoughts, other than the known and immensely powerful things like the chemistry of vision, and so on.

Those sorts of things would not explain how it is that you end up seeing that, for example, nothing much happened; that you can come home day after day and, asked what happened, report, without concealing, that nothing happened. And, if you are concealing, what you are concealing, if it were reported, would turn out to be nothing much. And, as it happens with you, so it happens with those you know. And, further, that ventures outside of being ordinary have unknown virtues and unknown costs. That is, if you come home and report what the grass looked like along the freeway; that there were four noticeable shades of green, some of which just appeared yesterday because of the rain, then there may well be some tightening up on the part of your recipient. And if you were to do it routinely, then people might figure that there is something odd about you; that you are pretentious. You might find them jealous of you. You might lose friends. That is to say, you might want to check out the costs of venturing into making your life an epic.

Now, it is also the case that there are people who are entitled to have their lives be an epic. We have assigned a series of storyable people, places, and objects, and they stand as something different from us. It may be that in pretty much every circle there is a somebody who is the subject of all neat observations, as there are, for society in general, a collection of people about whom detailed reports are made that not merely would never be ventured about others, but would never be thought of about others. The way in which Elizabeth Taylor turned around is something noticeable and reportable. The way in which your mother turned around is something unseeable, much less tellable.

The point is that it is almost everybody's business to be occupationally ordinary; that people take on the job of keeping everything utterly mundane; that no matter what happens, pretty much everybody is engaged in finding only how it is that what is going on is usual, with every effort possible. And it is really remarkable to see people's efforts to achieve the "nothing happened" sense of really catastrophic events. I have been collecting fragments out of newspapers, of hijackings, and what the airplane passengers think when a hijacking takes place. The latest one I happened to find goes something like this.

> I was walking up towards the front of the airplane and I saw the stewardess standing facing the cabin and a fellow standing with a gun in her back. And my first thought is he's showing her the gun, and then I realized that couldn't be, and then it turned out he was hijacking the plane.

Another, about the hijacking of a Polish plane, goes like this. The plane is now in the midst of being hijacked, and the guy reports, "I thought to myself, we just had a Polish hijacking a month ago and they're already making a movie of it." A classically dramatic instance is, almost universally, that the initial report of the assassination of President Kennedy was of having heard backfires.

Just imagine rewriting the monumental events of the Old Testament with ordinary people having gone through them. What would they have heard and seen, for example, when voices called out to them, when it started to rain, and so on. Indeed there is one place in the Old Testament where we find such an occurrence. Lot is warned of the burning of Sodom and Gomorrah, and is permitted to bring his daughters and sons-in-law out. "And Lot went out, and spake unto his sons in law, which married his daughters, and said, 'Up, get you out of this place;

for the Lord will destroy this city.' But he seemed as one that mocked
unto his sons in law." And they stayed behind.

Let us turn, now, to some fragments of conversation, from tape-recorded telephone calls, in which events that are dramatic, in their way,
are being reported. Looking at these reports, we can begin to pick out
some of the work involved in doing "being ordinary."

```
Jean:     Hello,
              (0.4)
Ellen:    Jean.
Jean:     Yeah,
              (0.4)
Ellen:    Well I just thought I'd re-better report to you
          what's happened at Cromwell's toda:y=
Jean:     =What in the world's ha:ppened. ⌈hhh
Ellen:                                     ⌊Did you have
          the day o:ff?
Jean:     Ya:h?
              (0:3)
Ellen:    Well I: got out to my car at fi:ve thirty I: drove
          arou:nd and of course I had to go by the front of
          the sto:re,=
Jean:     =Yeah?=
Ellen:    And there were two (0.2) police cars across the
          street and leh-e colored lady wanted to go in
          the main entrance there where the si:lver is and
          all the⌈(    ),⌉(things).
Jean:           ⌊Y e a h,⌋
              (0.4)
Ellen:    A:nd, they wouldn't let her go i:n, and he, had
          a gu::n,
              (0.2)
Ellen:    He was holding a gun in his hand a great big
          lo:ng gu::n?
Jean:     Yea:h?
Ellen:    And then over on the other si:de, I mean to the
          right.of there, where the (0.2) employees come
          ou:t, there was a who:le, oh:: must have been ten
          uh eight or ten employees standing there, because
          there must have been a:, it seemed like they had
          every entrance ba:rred. I don't know what was
          goin⌈g o:n ⌉
Jean:         ⌊Oh my⌋Go:d,
```

Let's look at the materials keeping the events in mind, thinking out
what was happening, and playing around with the talk by reference to
some way of considering what was happening. I have in mind something like this. When this lady interprets the events, she interprets them

so as to find how the police being there involves that they were legitimately there.

We can notice, at least nowadays, that the legitimate presence of the police has become a kind of distributional phenomenon; that is, whereas this lady is able to use the presence of the police to find what was going on, taking it that the police belonged there, others might see the same scene with the same parties taking it that the police were doing something that they had no business doing. That is, if this action took place in a black neighborhood, watched by black people, then "the very same scene" would perhaps turn into, for the perception of the parties, an altogether different phenomenon.

There are places where the police can count on the presence of two of their cars to provide for their visible, legitimate presence, such that others will then search the scene to find what the police might be doing that they should be doing, and, for example, pick up on that someone is trying to get into the entrance where the silver is. Whereas there are others who will not at all see the events in that way, but, seeing two police cars on the scene, may now look to see what kind of bother the police, by being on the scene, are producing, as compared to what kind of bother they are properly responding to.

That sort of differential organization of the sheer perceiving of an event is of considerable importance for the way in which the fact of the police on the scene tells people that although there is a trouble, things are okay. For example, that this lady can drive right by the scene knowing that things are more or less well in hand, that something is happening but that the police will take care of it, rather than that something is happening and the police are making it happen.

That sort of phenomenon has become a markedly distributional one, and you ought to learn to appreciate the difficulty involved in groups talking to each other where each of them figures that all they did was to see what was happening. That is, the notion of distributional issues involved is unavailable to either group by virtue of the fact that all they are doing is scanning a scene to see what is happening. They are not arguing anything, they are not imagining anything. They are seeing the scene in some organization. And to tell them that they are imagining it, or that they are making a case, since you perfectly well know what was there to be seen by virtue of what *you* saw, is to put them in a position where they could not really come to understand what you are talking about.

That turns on the fact that each group is specifically committed to a trust of vision, without any conception of what they understand by "vision." We can move from here to a discussion of the sorts of utter puzzlement that people have about the kinds of claims that others make about, for example, the police and what they are doing, when each group figures that all they are doing is reporting what they saw and not making a case for anything, being perfectly willing to be fair. This lady is not designing a right-wing report. All she is doing is reporting what she saw. To tell her that it is not what happened is to attack a kind of trust that she has, and should have, in what she simply sees; to propose a situation that would be quite uncomfortable for her to live with; to undermine something that an enormous mass of, in some ways Western, ideology has led her to believe she should, in fact, trust.

The point is, roughly, that it is a culturally and temporally distributional thing that people do or do not trust their eyes. Even such people as those academics who figure that they are attuned to "the ideological foundations of perception" may not use that sort of attuning to come to appreciate the distrust of vision that some cultures have. The academics see it as a kind of anti-empiricism, where it may not at all be anti-empiricism, but that, in the light of the kinds of troubles that people get into when they take a culturally ordered orientation to vision seriously, a focus on other senses might seem to pay off better. The fact that people systematically distrust what they see might well not be approached as, "How in the world do they survive with that magical view of things?" but as a perfectly empirical position.

Another thing – again getting into these kinds of tender problematic areas – this lady is perfectly comfortable as a witness to the scene. And yet you can perfectly well imagine how she would not see herself as a witness at all. In her report there is, for example, no hint of any interest in stopping and helping out, or of getting worried about what is going to happen.

More importantly, there is no hint that she had any fear that somehow, for example, that policeman was about to turn to her and ask her what she was doing there. The massive comfort in her innocence, and in the legitimate audience status that she has, is something that we should give real attention to, in at least this way. It is the kind of thing that we know can be readily shaken. There are times and places where someone would not feel all that comfortable passing such a scene, and – you can readily imagine it – would figure, "Oh my God, here I am, the first thing that happens is they're going to figure I'm involved."

That never dawns on our lady. And until it dawns on her, she can have no sense of an empathy with, for example, a kid in the ghetto. And nonetheless I suppose you could bring her to see that; that is, you could show her how her whole sense of innocence affects the whole way she sees the scene. There is no fear on her part at all that anybody is going to mistake her for a party to the scene, though she is perfectly willing to assign others a nonwitness, party-to-the-scene status.*

Again, there is no feeling on her part that she ought to do anything, and nobody would pretty much figure that she ought to feel that she should do anything. That sort of trust in the ability of the police who are there to handle whatever needs to be handled, and that they will handle it well, is another aspect of the way in which, being a witness, she can sheerly be a witness. One might consider, when one is doing "being a witness to a scene," the conditions under which your witness status could be transformed in a series of different ways, one of them being into someone who could be seen by others, for example, the lady in the car next to yours, or the man across the street, not as a witness, but possibly as "a car moving away from the scene"; as "the escaped robber." Or, not that you are a witness to a scene that is being ably handled, but that you are somebody who is callously passing it by.

I raise these possibilities because if you read the story you can feel utterly sure that no such issues crossed her mind, and you can then think of scenes in which you have been involved, or others have been involved, in which you see whether or not such issues do emerge, and then focus on what the conditions are that would lead somebody like this lady here to at least have it cross her mind that when the policeman turns around with his gun he is going to shoot her, or tell her to halt; or that somebody else might see her and wonder what in the world she is doing there.

Let us turn, now, to the second fragment. This one occurs at some distance into a telephone call.

---

*That the "colored lady" who "wanted to go in . . . where the silver is" was herself a bystander, comes out in a subsequent conversation, between the recipient of the report and someone who was there [GJ].

```
Jean:    We:ll she said that there was some woman that the-
         that they were: b-uhh ha:d he:ld up in the front
         the:re that they were pointing the gun at and
         everythi:ng, (0.2) a k-nigro woman,
              (0.6)
Penny:   ·hhh No::::: ↓no::.
Jean:    What.
Penny:   That was one of the employee⌈s.
Jean:                                  ⌊Oh.=
Penny:   =He ran up to her and she just ran up to him and
         says what's happened what's aa- well the kids were
         all lau::ghing about it.
```

Madge: Say did you see anything in the paper last night
          or hear anything on the local radio, ·hh Ruth
          Henderson and I drove down, to, Ventura yesterday.
Bea: Mm hm,
Madge: And on the way home we saw thē -- most gosh awful
          wreck.
Bea: Oh:::
Madge: we have ev- I've ever seen. I've never seen a car
          smashed into sm- such a small space.
Bea: Oh:::
Madge: It was smashed, -- ·hh from the front and the back
          both. It must have been in- caught in, between two
          car::s,
Bea: [Mm hm, uh huh
Madge: [[Must have run into a car and then another car
          smashed into it and there were people laid out and
          covered over on the pavement,
Bea: Mm
Madge: We were s-parked there for quite a while. But I
          was going to, listen to the local r-news and
          haven't done it.
Bea: No I haven't had my radio on either.
Madge: Well I had my television on, but I was listening
          to uh the blast off, you know.
Bea: Mm hm,
Madge: The uh ah-[astronauts.
Bea: [Yeah.
Bea: Yeah,
Madge: And I, I didn't ever get any local news
Bea: Uh huh,
Madge: And I wondered.
Bea: Uh huh, no, I haven't had it on . . .

Earlier, I was talking about the constraints set on experiences by "the
ordinary cast of mind." I want now to focus on entitlement to have
experiences. I want to suggest that, in having witnessed this event, and
having suffered it as well, in some way (for instance, having had to stop
on the freeway in a traffic jam by virtue of it), she has become entitled to
an experience. That she is entitled to an experience is something different from what her recipient is entitled to, or what someone who otherwise comes across this story is entitled to.

In part, I am saying that it is a fact that entitlement to experiences are
differentially available. If I say it as "entitlement," you may think of it as
not having rights to it, but that is only part of it. It is also not coming to
feel it at all, as compared to feeling it and feeling that you do not have
rights to it. The idea is that in encountering an event, and encountering
it as a witness or someone who in part suffered by it, one is entitled to an
experience, whereas the sheer fact of having access to things in the

world, for example, getting the story from another, is quite a different thing.

A way to see the matter is to ask the question, what happens to stories like this once they are told? Do stories like this become the property of the recipient as they are the property of the teller? That is, the teller owns rights to tell this story, and they give their credentials for their rights to tell the story by offering such things as that they saw it, and that they suffered by it. Now the question is, does a recipient of a story come to own it in the way that the teller has owned it; that is, can the recipient tell it to another, or feel for it as the teller can feel for those events?

For example, you might, on seeing an automobile accident and people lying there, feel awful, cry, have the rest of your day ruined. The question is, is the recipient of this story entitled to feel as you do? I think the facts are, plainly, no. That is to say, if you call up a friend of yours, unaffiliated with the event you are reporting, that is, someone who does not turn out to be the cousin of, the aunt of, the person who was killed in the accident, but just a somebody you call up and tell about an awful experience, then, if the recipient becomes as disturbed as you, or more, something peculiar is going on, and you might even feel wronged – although that might seem to be an odd thing to feel.

Now one reason I raise this whole business, and a way that it is important, is that we could at least imagine a society in which those having experienced something, having seen and felt for it, could preserve not merely the knowledge of it, but the feeling for it, by telling others. That is, if they could feel for it, then anybody they could tell it to could feel for it. Then, plainly, that stock of experiences that others happened to have would not turn on the events that they happened to have encountered, but could turn on the events that anybody who ever talked to them happened to encounter – as we think of a stock of knowledge that we have.

That is to say, if I tell you something that you come to think is so, you are entitled to have it. And you take it that the stock of knowledge that you have is something that you can get wherever you get it, and it is yours to keep. But the stock of experiences is an altogether differently constructed thing. As I say, in order to see that that is so, we can just, for example, differentiate how we deal with a piece of knowledge and how we deal with someone else's experience, and then come to see that experiences then get isolated, rather than that they are themselves as productive as are pieces of knowledge.

Now that fact obviously matters a good deal, in all sorts of ways.

Among the ways it comes to matter is that if having an experience is a basis for being aroused to do something about the sorts of things it is an instance of; for example, the state of the freeways, the state of automobiles, the state of whatever else, then plainly the basis for getting things done is radically weakened where those who receive your story cannot feel as you are entitled to feel.

Of course there is no reason to restrict the matter to misery. Plainly, it holds for joy, as well. Plainly it is specifically an attendable problem that joy is not productive, but that those having such an experience as entitled them to be joyful, telling it to others, they can feel "good for you" but there are rather sharp limits on how good they can feel for themselves for it, and also, even sharper limits on the good feeling that they can give to a third party with the story.

Again, if we think about it, we can perhaps just see that limited entitlement is not intrinsic to the organization of the world, but is a way we somehow come to perceive and feel about experience, or the way we were taught to do that, which is altogether different from the ways we think about knowledge. I presume, if one wanted, one could develop some historical discussion in which, somehow, knowledge was able to achieve a status for itself that is different from experience, though one could presumably find bases for attempts to do that for experience, which have failed. Obvious instances are, for example, attempts at universal religion, which are attempts to preserve a kind of feeling that somebody once had, encountering something or somebody, and where the whole history that we have is that it has not worked. It is extremely difficult to spread joy. It is extremely easy to spread information.

Now that is one order of thing – the distributional character of experience and the import of its distributional character for, say, troubles and joys in the world, in, say, sharp contrast to knowledge and its distributional character. You might figure it would be a severe enough kind of fact with regard to people's rights/abilities to have experiences, if they were restricted to those events that they took part in or witnessed, but that is not yet the full story of the kinds of constraints that are set on the possibility of having an experience.

The second sort of constraint is that if you are going to have an entitled experience, then you will have to have the experience that you are entitled to. You could figure that, having severe restrictions on your chances to have experiences, which turn on, for example, something, in some fashion important, happening to cross your path, or your happening to cross its path, that having happened, well, then you are home free. Once you got it you could do with it as you pleased. No. You have to form it up as the thing that it ordinarily is, and then mesh your experience with that.

That is to say, the rights to have an experience by virtue of, say, encountering something like an accident, are only the rights to have seen "another accident," and to perhaps have felt for it, but not, for example, to have seen God in it. You cannot have a nervous breakdown because you happened to see an automobile accident. You cannot make much more of it than what anybody would make of it. So we can think of the way that you are entitled to an experience as: you borrow for a while that experience which is available, as compared to you now invent the experience that you might be entitled to.

But since you are so sharply restricted with regard to the occasions of having an experience, then presumably people are happy enough to take them as they come. That is, you are not going to get many surprising new feelings, or whatever, out of this experience, but it is the only experience that you have any chance legitimately to have, so you might as well have it. You might as well form up this automobile-wreck story as an ordinary wreck story rather than attempt to make it into something that would occasion that you are really reaching for experiences. Of course, people are readily seen to be reaching for experience with something that anybody knows is "just a wreck," "just a something," and that they make into a life's work.

In that regard, there are a whole bunch of ways that the teller of this story relays to us how she went about bounding this experience. That is to say, what she made of it is not just told in the story, but is told in other ways.

Among the ways that she goes about locating the kind of experience this event was is that she does not tell it right off in the conversation (and that is not available to you in the excerpt) but she tells it somewhere into the conversation. You will find that stories are specifically differentiated in terms of their importance to the teller by reference to where the teller places them in a conversation.

So, for example, among the ways a teller can make out a story as really important, is to tell it right off. And a way to make it even more important than that is to call to tell it when you figure the other is not available to hear it, for example, to call them up in the middle of the night. Stories are ranked in terms of, and express their status by, your calling somebody up and saying, "I know you were sleeping, but . . . ," where it is not that they happen to be sleeping, but you call them when they are sleeping, in that if you do not call them then, if you call them when they get up, you have already told them something about the story; that is, it is not so important as you might otherwise want to make it out. So the placing of the story in the conversation and the placing of the conversation in the recipient's life are ways that you go about locating the importance of the story.

Then, of course, she also tells aspects of the story's importance in the telling itself. For example, while it was an important enough experience for her to say to herself, I am going to listen to the radio, other things got in the way of that. She is not embarrassed to say that, instead of that, she watched the astronauts, an action that obviously for some other story would be altogether perverse. For this story it is perfectly okay, and is a way to locate how the events matter, that is, to produce it while indicating that if it came down to trying to find out more, or watching the astronauts, she watched the astronauts.

Aside from that, she could go home and go about her business, as compared to, for example, she went home and went to bed, or, she had nightmares all night, or that it in other ways interfered with the life that she was engaged in when this happened. She was coming home, there was the accident, she was stopped for a while, and then she went home and watched the astronauts. That is plainly a way to locate how the story matters, and is plainly an appropriate way for this story. Had she said, it ruined the rest of my day, I was shaking all over, I went to the doctor, I had nightmares, then her friend could say, well, you're just oversensitive. So this business of the character of the experience fitting the conventional status of the event is something that is dealt with in the telling of the story.

At least the initially blandest kind of formulation we might make is that, although lots of people figure that experience is a great thing, and apparently at least some people are eager to have experiences, they are extraordinarily carefully regulated sorts of things. The occasions of entitlement to have them are carefully regulated, and then the experience you are entitled to have on an occasion that you are entitled to have one is further carefully regulated. Insofar as part of the experience involves telling about it, then the telling of it constitutes one way in which what you might privately make of it is subject to the control of an open presentation, even to what you thought was a friend.

That is to say, your friends are not going to help you out, by and large, when you tell them some story, unless you tell them a story in the way anybody should tell it to anybody. Then they will be appropriately amused or sorrowed. Otherwise you will find that they are watching you to see that, for example, you are making something big out of something that you are not entitled to make big, or something small that should have been bigger, or missed seeing something that you should have seen, all of which could be deduced by virtue of the way you requiredly formed the thing up.

Now, I am not by any means saying let us do away with the ways in which we go about being ordinary, but, rather, that we want to know what importance it has. At least one tack we can take is to treat the overwhelming banality of the stories we encounter – in my data, in your own experiences – as not so much something that allows, for example, for statistical analysis of variation, or that makes them therefore uninteresting to study, but as a specific feature that turns on a kind of attitude; say, an attitude of working at being usual, which is perhaps central to the way our world is organized.

References

Anderson, R. J., and Sharrock, W. W. Forthcoming. Aspects of the distribution of work tasks in medical encounters. In Schenkein (forthcoming).

Argyle, M., and Cook, M. 1965. Eye contact, distance and affiliation. *Sociometry*, 28:289–304.

Argyle, M., and Cook, M. 1976. *Gaze and Mutual Gaze*. Cambridge: Cambridge University Press.

Atkinson, J. M. 1979a. Sequencing and shared attentiveness to court proceedings. In Psathas (1979:257–86).

Atkinson, J. M. 1979b. Displaying neutrality. Paper presented at the Conference on the Possibilities and Limitations of Pragmatics, Urbino, Italy.

Atkinson, J. M. 1981a. Ethnomethodological approaches to socio-legal studies. In A. Podgorecki and C. J. Whelan (eds.), *Sociological Approaches to Law*, pp. 201–23. London: Croom Helm.

Atkinson, J. M. 1981b. Persuasive devices in political and legal oratory. Paper presented at the Annual Meeting of the U.S. Law and Society Association, Amherst, Mass.

Atkinson, J. M. 1982. Understanding formality: notes on the categorization and production of "formal" interaction. *British Journal of Sociology*, 33:86–117.

Atkinson, J. M. 1983. Two devices for generating audience approval: a comparative study of public discourse and texts. In K. Ehlich et al. (eds.), *Connectedness in Sentence, Text and Discourse*, pp. 199–236. Tilburg, Netherlands: Tilburg Papers in Linguistics.

Atkinson, J. M. 1984. *Our Masters' Voices: The Language and Body Language of Politics*. London: Methuen.

Atkinson, J. M. Forthcoming. Refusing invited applause: preliminary observations from a case study in charismatic oratory. In Van Dijk (forthcoming).

Atkinson, J. M., and Drew, P. 1979. *Order in Court: The Organisation of Verbal Interaction in Judicial Settings*. London: Macmillan.

Austin, J. L. 1962. *How to Do Things with Words*. Oxford: Oxford University Press.

Bauman, R. (Ed.). 1977. *Verbal Art as Performance*. Rowley, Mass.: Newbury House.

Bergmann, J. R. 1979. Aspects of psychiatric intake interviews. Paper presented at the Social Science Research Council/British Sociological Association Conference on Practical Reasoning and Discourse Processes, St. Hugh's College, Oxford.

Birdwhistell, R. 1971. *Kinesics and Context: Essays in Body Communication*. Harmondsworth: Penguin.

Bloomfield, L. 1933. *Language*. New York: Holt Rinehart and Winston.

Brown, P., and Levinson, S. C. 1978. Universals in language usage: politeness phenomena. In E. Goody (ed.). *Questions and Politeness: Strategies in Social Interaction*, pp. 56–310. Cambridge: Cambridge University Press.

Bull, P. E. 1981. The social functions of speech-related body movement. End of Grant Report (HR 6404/2) to the Social Science Research Council, London, mimeo.

Button, G. 1979. No close closings. Paper presented at the Social Science Research Council/British Sociological Association Conference on Practical Reasoning and Discourse Processes, St. Hugh's College, Oxford.

Button, G. Forthcoming a. Moving out of closings. In Schenkein (forthcoming).

Button, G. Forthcoming b. Varieties of closings. In Psathas and Frankel (forthcoming).

Button, G. and Casey, N. Forthcoming. Topic nomination and topic pursuit. *Human Studies*.

Casey, N. 1981. The social organization of topic in natural conversation: beginning a topic. Ph.D. dissertation, Plymouth Polytechnic.

Chomsky, N. 1965. *Aspects of the Theory of Syntax*. Cambridge, Mass.: MIT Press.

Condon, W. A. and Ogston, W. D. 1966 Sound film analysis of normal and pathological behaviour patterns. *Journal of Nervous and Mental Disease*, 143:338–47.

Condon, W. A., and Ogston, W. D. 1967. A segmentation of behaviour. *Journal of Psychiatric Research*, 5:221–35.

Coulter, J. 1971. Decontextualized meanings: current approaches to *verstehende* investigations. *Sociological Review*, 19:301–23.

Coulter, J. 1973. Language and the conceptualization of meaning. *Sociology*, 7:173–89.

Davidson, J. A. 1978a. An instance of negotiation in a call closing. *Sociology*, 12:123–33.

Davidson, J. A. 1978b. Some findings of a detailed analysis of schizophrenic talk. Paper presented at Yale Psychiatric Institute.

Davidson, J. A. Forthcoming. Modifications of invitations, offers and rejections. In Psathas and Frankel (forthcoming).

Dobson, J. F. 1919. *The Greek Orators*. London: Methuen.

Drew, P. 1981. Adults' corrections of children's mistakes. In P. French and M. Maclure (eds.), *Adult-Child Conversation: Studies in Structure and Process*, pp. 244–67. London: Croom Helm.

Drew, P. Forthcoming. Analyzing the use of language in courtroom interaction. In van Dijk (forthcoming).

Duncan, S. 1972. Some signals and rules for taking speaking turns in conversation. *Journal of Personality and Social Psychology*, 23:283–92.

Duncan, S., and Fiske, D. W. 1977. *Face to Face Interaction: Research, Methods and Theory*. Hillsdale, N.J.: Lawrence Erlbaum Associates.

Dunstan, R. 1980. Contexts for coercion: analyzing properties of courtroom "questions." *British Journal of Law and Society*, 6:61–77.

Efron, D. 1941. *Gesture, Race and Culture*. New York: Kings Crown Press. (Reprinted as Approaches to Semiotics No. 9, ed. T. A. Sebeok. The Hague: Mouton.)

Eglin, P., and Wideman, D. 1983. Inequality in service encounters: professional power versus interactional organisation in calls to the police. Mimeo. Wilfrid Laurier University.

Ekman, P., and Friesen, W. 1969. The repertoire of nonverbal behavior: Categories, origins, usage and coding. *Semiotica*, 1:49–98.

Ekman, P., and Friesen, W. 1972. Hand movements. *Journal of Communication*, 22:353–74.

Ervin-Tripp, S. 1979. Children's verbal turn-taking. In Ochs and Schieffelin (1979:391–414).

Ervin-Tripp, S., and Mitchell-Kernan, C. (Eds.). 1977. *Child Discourse.* New York: Academic Press.

Frankel, R. 1980. Analyzing doctor–patient interaction. Paper presented at the First Anglo-German Colloquium on Ethnomethodology and Conversation Analysis, Konstanz, West Germany.

Frankel, R. Forthcoming. Interviews. In van Dijk (forthcoming).

Freedman, N. 1972. The analysis of movement behaviour during clinical interviews. In A. Siegman and B. Pope (eds.), *Studies in Dyadic Communication,* pp. 153–75. Elmsford, N.Y.: Pergamon Press.

Fries, C. 1952. *The structure of English.* London: Longman.

Fromkin, V. A. 1971. The non-anomalous nature of anomalous utterances. *Language,* 47:27–52.

Fromkin, V. A. (Ed.). 1973. *Speech Errors as Linguistic Evidence.* The Hague: Mouton.

Fromkin, V. A. (Ed.). 1980. *Errors in Linguistic Performance: Slips of the Tongue, Ear, Pen, and Hand.* New York: Academic Press.

Garfinkel, H. 1967. *Studies in Ethnomethodology.* Englewood Cliffs, N.J.: Prentice Hall.

Garfinkel, H. Forthcoming. *A Manual for the Study of Naturally Organized Ordinary Activities* (3 volumes). London: Routledge and Kegan Paul.

Garfinkel, H., and Sacks, H. 1970. On formal structures of practical actions. In J. C. McKinney and E. A. Tiryakian (eds.), *Theoretical Sociology,* pp. 338–66. New York: Appleton-Century-Crofts.

Givon, T. (Ed.). 1979. *Syntax and Semantics 12: Discourse and Syntax.* New York: Academic Press.

Goffman, E. 1955. On face work. *Psychiatry,* 18:213–31.

Goffman, E. 1963. *Behaviour in Public Places.* New York: Free Press.

Goffman, E. 1964. The neglected situation. *American Anthropologist,* 66:no. 6, pt. 2:133–6.

Goffman, E. 1971. *Relations in Public.* New York: Basic Books.

Goffman, E. 1974. *Frame Analysis.* New York: Harper and Row.

Goffman, E. 1976. Replies and responses. *Language in Society,* 5:257–313. Reprinted in Goffman (1981:5–77).

Goffman, E. 1981. *Forms of Talk.* Oxford: Basil Blackwell.

Goodwin, C. 1977. Some aspects of the interaction of speaker and hearer in the construction of the turn at talk in natural conversation. Ph.D. dissertation, University of Pennsylvania.

Goodwin, C. 1979a. The interactive construction of a sentence in natural conversation. In Psathas (1979:97–121).

Goodwin, C. 1979b. Review of S. Duncan, Jr., and D. W. Fiske, *Face to Face Interaction: Research, Methods and Theory. Language in Society,* 5:439–44.

Goodwin, C. 1979c. Unilateral departure. Paper presented at the 74th Annual Meeting of the American Sociological Association, Boston, Mass.

Goodwin, C. 1980. Restarts, pauses and the achievement of a state of mutual gaze at turn beginning. *Sociological Inquiry,* 50:272–302.

Goodwin, C. 1981a. *Conversational Organization: Interaction between Speakers and Hearers.* New York: Academic Press.

Goodwin, C. 1981b. Shifting focus. Paper presented at the 76th Annual Meeting of the American Sociological Association, Toronto, Canada.

Goodwin, C. 1982. Participation status. Paper presented at the 10th World Congress of Sociology, Mexico City.

Goodwin, C. Forthcoming. Gesture as a resource for the organization of mutual orientation. *Semiotica*.

Goodwin, C., and Goodwin, M. H. 1982. Concurrent operations on talk: notes on the interactive organization of assessments. Paper presented at the 77th Annual Meeting of the American Sociological Association, San Francisco, Calif.

Goodwin, M. H. 1980. Some aspects of processes of mutual monitoring implicated in the production of description sequences. *Sociological Inquiry*, 50:303–17.

Goodwin, M. H. 1982a. Processes of dispute management among urban black children. *American Ethnologist*, 9:76–96.

Goodwin, M. H. 1982b. "Instigating": storytelling as social process. *American Ethnologist*, 9:799–819.

Goodwin, M. H., and Goodwin, C. Forthcoming. Gesture and co-participation in the activity of searching for a word. *Semiotica*.

Gordon, D., and Lakoff, G. 1971. Conversational postulates. *Papers from the Seventh Regional Meeting of the Chicago Linguistic Society*, 63–84.

Greatbatch, D. L. 1982. The turn-taking system for news interview interaction. Paper, University of Warwick.

Grice, H. P. 1975. Logic and conversation. In P. Cole and J. L. Morgan (eds.), *Syntax and Semantics 3: Speech Acts*, pp. 41–58. New York: Academic Press.

Harris, R. 1979. The concept of a rational speaker. Paper presented at the Social Science Research Council/British Sociological Association Conference on Practical Reasoning and Discourse Processes, St. Hugh's College, Oxford.

Heath, C. C. 1981. The opening sequence in doctor-patient interaction. In P. Atkinson and C. C. Heath (eds.), *Medical Work: Realities and Routines*, pp. 71–90. Farnborough: Gower.

Heath, C. C. 1982a. The display of recipiency: an instance of a sequential relationship between speech and body movement. *Semiotica*, 42, no. 2/4.

Heath, C. C. 1982b. Preserving the consultation: medical record cards and professional conduct. *Journal of the Sociology of Health and Illness*, 4:56–74.

Heath, C. C. Forthcoming. Interactional participation: the coordination of gesture, speech and gaze. In P. Leonardi and V. D'Urso (eds.), *Proceedings of the Symposium on Natural Rhetoric and Discourse Processes*. Padua: University of Padua.

Heath, C. C. In prep. *The Partnership: Essays in the Social Organisation of Speech and Body Movement in the Medical Consultation*. Cambridge: Cambridge University Press.

Heringer, J. T. 1977. Pre-sequences and indirect speech acts. In E. O. Keenan and T. L. Bennett (eds.), *Discourse across Time and Space*, pp. 169–80. Southern California Occasional Papers in Linguistics 5, University of Southern California.

Heritage, J. C. 1978. Aspects of the flexibilities of natural language use. *Sociology*, 12:79–103.

Heritage, J. C. 1980. The availability of context. Mimeo. University of Warwick.

Heritage, J. C. Forthcoming. Analyzing news interviews: aspects of the production of talk for an overhearing audience. In van Dijk (forthcoming).

Heritage, J. C., and Atkinson, J. M. 1983. Context maintenance in institutional interaction. Paper presented at the Second International Conference on Social Psychology and Language, Bristol, England.

Heritage, J. C., and Watson, D. R. 1980. Aspects of the properties of formulations in natural conversations: some instances analyzed. *Semiotica*, 30:245–62.

James, D. 1972. Some aspects of the syntax and semantics of interjections. In *Papers from the Eighth Regional Meeting of the Chicago Linguistic Society*, pp. 162–72.

James, W. 1950. *Principles of Psychology*. New York: Dover.

Jefferson, G. 1972. Side sequences. In Sudnow (1972:294–338).

Jefferson, G. 1973a. A case of precision timing in ordinary conversation: overlapped tag-positioned address terms in closing sequences. *Semiotica*, 9:47–96.

Jefferson, G. 1973b. A consideration of stories told in conversation as conversation artifacts. Paper presented at Seminars in Ethnomethodology, Graduate Center, City University of New York.

Jefferson, G. 1974a. Error correction as an interactional resource. *Language in Society*, 2:181–99.

Jefferson, G. 1974b. Notes on the sequential organization of laughter in conversation: onset sensitivity in invitations to laugh. Paper presented at the 73d Annual Meeting of the American Anthropological Association, Mexico City.

Jefferson, G. 1977. The poetics of ordinary talk. Paper presented at the Second International Institute on Ethnomethodology and Conversation Analysis, Boston University.

Jefferson, G. 1978a. Sequential aspects of story telling in conversation. In Schenkein (1978:219–48).

Jefferson, G. 1978b. What's in a "nyem"? *Sociology*, 12:135–9.

Jefferson, G. 1978c. At first I thought . . . Lecture, University of California, Los Angeles.

Jefferson, G. 1979. A technique for inviting laughter and its subsequent acceptance/declination. In Psathas (1979:79–96).

Jefferson, G. 1980a. End of Grant Report on conversations in which "troubles" or "anxieties" are expressed (HR 4805/2). London: Social Science Research Council. Mimeo.

Jefferson, G. 1980b. On "trouble-premonitory" response to inquiry. *Sociological Inquiry*, 50:153–85.

Jefferson, G. 1981a. The abominable "Ne?": a working paper exploring the phenomenon of post-response pursuit of response. University of Manchester, Department of Sociology, Occasional Paper No. 6. A shortened version is to appear in P. Schroder (ed.), *Sprache der Gegenwart*. Mannheim, in press.

Jefferson, G. 1981b. "Caveat speaker": a preliminary exploration of shift implicative recipiency in the articulation of topic. End of Grant Report. London: Social Science Research Council. Mimeo.

Jefferson, G. Forthcoming a. List construction as a task and interactional resource. In Psathas and Frankel (forthcoming).

Jefferson, G. Forthcoming b. On exposed and embedded correction in conversation. *Studium Linguistik*.

Jefferson, G. Forthcoming c. An exercise in the transcription and analysis of laughter. In van Dijk (forthcoming).

Jefferson, G. Forthcoming d. Notes on some orderlinesses of overlap onset. In G. Jefferson, *Two Explorations of the Organisation of Overlapping Talk in Conversation*. Tilburg, Netherlands: Tilburg Papers in Language and Literature no. 28.

Jefferson, G. Forthcoming e. On a failed hypothesis: 'conjunctionals' as overlap vulnerable. In G. Jefferson, *Two Explorations of the Organisation of Overlapping Talk in Conversation*. Tilburg, Netherlands: Tilburg Papers in Language and Literature, no. 28.

Jefferson, G. Forthcoming f. On the interactional unpackaging of a "gloss." Tilburg, Netherlands: Tilburg Papers in Language and Literature, no. 29.

Jefferson, G. Forthcoming g. "Caveat speaker": preliminary notes on recipient topic-shift implicature. Tilburg, Netherlands: Tilburg Papers in Language and Literature, no. 30.

Jefferson, G. Forthcoming h. Notes on a systematic deployment of the acknowledgement tokens "yeah" and "mm hm." Tilburg, Netherlands: Tilburg Papers in Language and Literature, no. 30.

Jefferson, G. Forthcoming i. The pseudonym problem: on changing names to protect the identity of participants in conversational data. Tilburg, Netherlands: Tilburg Papers in Language and Linguistics, no. 31.

Jefferson, G. Forthcoming j. Caricature versus detail: on capturing the particulars of pronunciation in transcripts of conversational data. Tilburg, Netherlands: Tilburg Papers in Language and Literature, no. 31.

Jefferson, G., and Lee, J. R. E. 1981. The rejection of advice: managing the problematic convergence of a "troubles-telling" and a "service encounter." *Journal of Pragmatics*, 5:399–422.

Jefferson, G., Sacks, H., and Schegloff, E. Forthcoming. Notes on laughter in pursuit of intimacy. In Schenkein (forthcoming).

Jefferson, G., and Schegloff, E. 1975. Sketch: some orderly aspects of overlap in natural conversation. Paper presented at the Meetings of the American Anthropological Association. Mimeo.

Jefferson, G., and Schenkein, J. 1977. Some sequential negoatiations in conversation: unexpanded and expanded versions of projected action sequences. *Sociology*, 11:87–103. (Reprinted in Schenkein [1978:155–72].)

Karcevskij, S. 1964. Du dualism asymétrique du signe linguistique. In J. Vachek (ed.), *A Prague School Reader in Linguistics*, pp. 81–7. Bloomington: Indiana University Press.

Kendon, A. 1972. Some relationships between body motion and speech. In A. Seigman and B. Pope (eds.), *Studies in Dyadic Communication*, pp. 177–210. Elmsford, N.Y.: Pergamon Press.

Kendon, A. 1977. *Studies in the Behaviour of Social Interaction*. Bloomington: Indiana University Press.

Kendon, A. 1979a. Some theoretical and methodological aspects of the use of film in the study of social interaction. In G. P. Ginsburg (ed.), *Emerging Strategies in Social Psychological Research*, pp. 67–91. New York: Wiley.

Kendon, A. 1979b. Gesture and speech: two aspects of the process of utterance. In M. R. Key (ed.), *Nonverbal Communication and Language*, pp. 207–27. The Hague: Mouton.

Levinson, S. C. 1979. Activity types and language. *Linguistics*, 17:356–99.

Levinson, S. C. 1981a. The essential inadequacies of speech act models of dialogue. In H. Parret, M. Sbisa and J. Verschueren (eds.), *Possibilities and Limitations of Pragmatics: Proceedings of the Conference on Pragmatics at Urbino, July 8–14, 1979*, pp. 473–92. Amsterdam: Benjamins.

Levinson, S. C. 1981b. Some pre-observations on the modelling of dialogue. *Discourse Processes*, 4:93–110.

Levinson, S. C. 1983. *Pragmatics*. Cambridge: Cambridge University Press.

Lynch, M. Forthcoming. Closure and disclosure in pre-trial argument. In Psathas and Frankel (forthcoming).

McHoul, A. 1978. The organization of turns at formal talk in the classroom. *Language in Society*, 7:183–213.

McHoul, A. Forthcoming. Notes on the organization of repair in classroom talk. In Schenkein (forthcoming).

Maynard, D. 1982. Aspects of sequential organization in plea bargaining discourse. *Human Studies*, 5:319–44.

Maynard, D. 1983. Social order and plea bargaining in the courtroom. *Sociological Quarterly*, 24:233–52.

Maynard, D. Forthcoming. *Inside Plea Bargaining: The Language of Negotiation.* New York: Plenum.

Mehan, H. 1978. Structuring school structure. *Harvard Educational Review*, 45:311–38.

Mehan, H. 1979. *Learning Lessons: Social Organization in the Classroom.* Cambridge, Mass.: Harvard University Press.

Mehan, H. Forthcoming. The structure of classroom discourse. In van Dijk (forthcoming).

Miller, G. A. 1978. Practical and lexical knowledge. In E. Rosch and B. B. Lloyd (eds.), *Cognition and Categorization*, pp. 305–19. Hillsdale, N.J.: Erlbaum.

Nida, E. A. 1964. *Towards a Science of Translating.* New York: E. J. Brill.

Ochs, E. 1979. Transcription as theory. In Ochs and Schieffelin (1979:43–72).

Ochs, E., and Schieffelin, B. 1979. *Developmental Pragmatics.* New York: Academic Press.

Parsons, T. 1937. *The Structure of Social Action.* Glencoe: Free Press.

Pike, Kenneth L. 1966. Etic and emic standpoints for the description of behavior. In A. G. Smith (ed.), *Communication and Culture*, pp. 152–63. New York: Holt, Rinehart and Winston.

Pollner, M. 1979. Explicative transactions: making and managing meaning in traffic court. In Psathas (1979:227–53).

Pomerantz, A. M. 1975. Second assessments: a study of some features of agreements/disagreements. Ph.D. dissertation, University of California, Irvine.

Pomerantz, A. M. 1978a. Compliment responses: notes on the co-operation of multiple constraints. In Schenkein (1978:79–112).

Pomerantz, A. M. 1978b. Attributions of responsibility: blamings. *Sociology*, 12:115–21.

Pomerantz, A. M. 1978c. A sequential analysis of interpreting absences. Mimeo.

Pomerantz, A. M. 1980a. Telling my side: "limited access" as a "fishing" device. *Sociological Inquiry*, 50:186–98.

Pomerantz, A. M. 1980b. Investigating reported absences: catching truants. Paper presented at the First Anglo-German Colloquium on Ethnomethodology and Conversation Analysis, Konstanz, West Germany.

Pomerantz, A. M. 1981. Speakers' claims as a feature of describing: a study of "presenting the evidence for." Paper presented to the 76th Annual Meeting of the American Sociological Association, Toronto, Canada.

Pomerantz, A. M. Forthcoming. Giving a source or basis: the practice in conversation of telling "what I know." *Journal of Pragmatics*, 8:4.

Pomerantz, A. M., and Atkinson, J. M. Forthcoming. Ethnomethodology, conversation analysis and the study of courtroom interaction. In D. J. Muller, D. E. Blackman, and A. J. Chapman (eds.), *Topics in Psychology and Law.* Chichester: Wiley.

Psathas, G. (Ed.). 1979. *Everyday Language: Studies in Ethnomethodology.* New York: Irvington.

Psathas, G., and Frankel, R. (Eds.). Forthcoming. *Interactional Competence.* Norwood, N.J.: Ablex.

Quintillian 1856. *Institutes of Oratory.* Edited and translated by J. S. Watson. London: Bohn.

Robinson, J. A. 1981. Personal narratives reconsidered. *Journal of American Folklore*, 94:58–85.

Rosch, E. 1977. Human categorization. In N. Warren (ed.), *Advances in Cross-Cultural Psychology*, pp. 1–49. New York: Academic Press.

Rosch, E., and Mervis, C. B. 1975. Family resemblances: studies in the internal structure of categories. *Conitive Psychology*, 7:573–605.

Rosch, E., Mervis, C. B., Gray, W., Johnson, D., and Boyes-Braem, P. 1976. Basic objects in natural categories. *Cognitive Psychology*, 8:382–439.

Rosch, E., Simpson, C., and Miller, R. J. 1976. Structural bases of typicality effects. *Journal of Experimental Psychology: Human Perception and Performance*, 2:491–502.

Sacks, H. 1964–72. Unpublished transcribed lectures, University of California, Irvine. (Transcribed and indexed by G. Jefferson.)

Sacks, H. 1972a. An initial investigation of the usability of conversational data for doing sociology. In Sudnow (1972:31–74).

Sacks, H. 1972b. On the analyzability of stories by children. In J. J. Gumperz and D. Hymes (eds.), *Directions in Sociolinguistics*, pp. 325–45. New York: Holt, Rinehart and Winston.

Sacks, H. 1973a. On some puns with some intimations. In R. W. Shuy (ed.), *Report of the 23d Annual Round Table Meeting on Linguistics and Language Studies*, pp. 135–44. Washington D.C.: Georgetown University Press.

Sacks, H. 1973b. Lectures at the Linguistic Institute. Ann Arbor, Mich.

Sacks, H. 1973c. The preference for agreement in natural conversation. Paper presented at the Linguistic Institute. Ann Arbor, Mich.

Sacks, H. 1974. An analysis of the course of a joke's telling in conversation. In R. Bauman and J. Sherzer (eds.), *Explorations in the Ethnography of Speaking*, pp. 337–53. Cambridge: Cambridge University Press.

Sacks, H. 1975. Everyone has to lie. In B. Blount and M. Sanches (eds.), *Sociocultural Dimensions of Language Use*, pp. 57–80. New York: Academic Press.

Sacks, H. 1978. Some technical considerations of a dirty joke. In Schenkein (1978:249–270). (Edited by G. Jefferson from unpublished lectures: fall 1971, lectures 9–12.)

Sacks, H. 1979. Hotrodder: a revolutionary category. In Psathas (1979:7–14). (Edited by G. Jefferson from unpublished lectures: lecture 18, spring 1966.)

Sacks, H. 1980. Button button who's got the button? *Sociological Inquiry*, 50:318–27. (Edited by G. Jefferson from unpublished lectures: lecture 13, spring 1966.)

Sacks, H. Forthcoming a. You want to find out if anybody really does care. In Schenkein (forthcoming). (Edited by G. Jefferson from unpublished lectures: fall 1964[R], tape 4.)

Sacks, H. Forthcoming b. Some considerations of a story told in ordinary conversation. *Poetics* (special issue: Narrative Analysis: An Interdisciplinary Dialogue, ed. U. Quasthoff and E. Gulich). (Edited by G. Jefferson from unpublished lectures: lectures 1 and 2, winter 1970.)

Sacks, H. Forthcoming c. On members' measurement systems. In Psathas and Frankel (forthcoming). (Edited by G. Jefferson from unpublished lectures: 1966, 1967, and 1970.)

Sacks, H. Forthcoming d. The inference-making machine: notes on observability. In van Dijk (forthcoming). (Edited by G. Jefferson from unpublished lectures: winter 1964–65.)

Sacks, H., and Schegloff, E. 1979. Two preferences in the organization of reference to persons in conversation and their interaction. In Psathas (1979:15–21).

Sacks, H., Schegloff, E. A., and Jefferson, G. 1974. A simplest systematics for the organization of turn-taking for conversation. *Language*, 50:696–735. (Variant version published as Sacks, Schegloff, and Jefferson 1978.)

Sacks, H., Schegloff, E. A., and Jefferson, G. 1978. A simplest systematics for the organization of turn-taking in conversation. In Schenkein (1978:7–55).

Sapir, E. 1921. *Language: An Introduction to the Study of Speech*. New York: Harcourt Brace and World.

Schegloff, E. A. 1968. Sequencing in conversational openings. *American Anthropologist*, 70:1075–95. (Reprinted in J. J. Gumperz and D. Hymes [eds.], *Directions in Sociolinguistics*, pp. 346–380. New York: Holt, Rinehart and Winston, 1972.)

Schegloff, E. A. 1972. Notes on conversational practice: formulating place. In Sudnow (1972:75–119). (Reprinted in P. P. Giglioli [ed.], *Language and Social Context*, pp. 95–135. Harmondsworth: Penguin, 1972.)

Schegloff, E. A. 1973. Recycled turn beginnings: a precise repair mechanism in conversation's turn-taking organization. Paper presented at the Linguistic Institute. Ann Arbor, Mich. Mimeo.

Schegloff, E. A. 1977. Unpublished lectures: adjacency pairs as base sequences. Second International Institute on Ethnomethodology and Conversation Analysis, Boston University.

Schegloff, E. A. 1979a. Identification and recognition in telephone conversation openings. In Psathas (1979:23–78). (A shortened version previously appeared in I. DeSola Pool [ed.], *The Social Impact of the Telephone*. Cambridge: MIT Press.)

Schegloff, E. A. 1979b. The relevance of repair to syntax-for-conversation. In Givon (1979:261–288).

Schegloff, E. A. 1979c. Repair after next turn. Paper presented at the Social Science Research Council/British Sociological Association Conference on Practical Reasoning and Discourse Processes, St. Hugh's College, Oxford.

Schegloff, E. A. 1980. Preliminaries to preliminaries: "can I ask you a question?" *Sociological Inquiry*, 50:104–52.

Schegloff, E. A. 1982. Discourse as an interactional achievement: some uses of "uh huh" and other things that come between sentences. In D. Tannen (ed.), *Georgetown University Roundtable on Languages and Linguistics*, pp. 71–93. Washington D.C.: Georgetown University Press.

Schegloff, E. A., Jefferson, G., and Sacks, H. 1977. The preference for self-correction in the organization of repair in conversation. *Language*. 53:361–82.

Schegloff, E. A., and Sacks, H. 1973. Opening up closings. *Semiotica*, 7:289–327. (Reprinted in R. Turner [ed.], *Ethnomethodology*, pp. 233–64. Harmondsworth: Penguin.)

Schegloff, E. A., Sacks, H., and Roberts, B. 1975. Home position in body behaviour. Paper delivered at the American Anthropological Association Meetings, San Francisco.

Schenkein, J. N. 1972. Towards an analysis of natural conversation and the sense of *heheh. Semiotica*, 6:344–77.

Schenkein, J. N. (Ed.). 1978. *Studies in the Organization of Conversational Interaction*. New York: Academic Press.

Schenkein, J. N. 1978a. Identity negotiations in conversation. In Schenkein (1978:57–78).

Schenkein, J. N. 1979. The radio raiders story. In Psathas (1979:187–202).

Schenkein, J. N. 1980. A taxonomy for repeating action sequences in natural conversation. In B. Butterworth (ed.), *Language Production*. Volume 1, *Speech and Talk*, pp. 21–47. London: Academic Press.

Schenkein, J. N. (Ed.). Forthcoming. *Studies in the Organization of Conversational Interaction*. Volume 2. New York: Academic Press.

Searle, J. R. 1969. *Speech Acts*. Cambridge: Cambridge University Press.

Searle, J. R. 1975. Indirect speech acts. In P. Cole and J. L. Morgan (eds.), *Syntax and Semantics*. Volume 3, *Speech Acts*, pp. 59–82. New York: Academic Press.

Searle, J. R. 1979. Literal meaning. In J. R. Searle, *Expression and Meaning*, pp. 117–36. Cambridge: Cambridge University Press.

Searle, J. R. 1980. The background of meaning. In J. R. Searle, F. Kiefer, and M. Bierwisch (eds.), *Speech Act Theory and Pragmatics*, pp. 221–32. Dordrecht: Reidel.

Simmel, G. 1920. The sociology of the senses: visual interaction. In R. E. Park and E. W. Burgess (eds.), *Introduction to the Science of Sociology*, pp. 356–61. Chicago: Chicago University Press.

Smith, Alfred G. (ed.). 1966. *Communication and Culture: Readings in the Codes of Human Interaction*. New York: Holt, Rinehart and Winston.

Snow, C. E., and Ferguson, C. A. (Eds.). 1977. *Talking to Children*. Cambridge: Cambridge University Press.

Sociological Inquiry. 1980. Special issue on "language and social interaction," 50, no. 3/4.

Sociology 1980. Special issue on "language and practical reasoning," 12, no. 1.

Sudnow, D. 1972. *Studies in Social Interaction*. New York: Free Press.

Taylor, T. J. 1981. A Wittgensteinian perspective in linguistics. *Language and Communication*, 1:263–74.

Terasaki, A. 1976. Pre-announcement sequences in conversation. *Social Sciences Working Paper No. 99*. Irvine: University of California.

Thompson, F. 1973. *Lark Rise to Candleford*. Harmondsworth: Penguin.

Turner, R. 1970. Words, utterances and activities. In J. Douglas (ed.), *Understanding Everyday Life*, pp. 169–87. London: Routledge and Kegan Paul.

Turner, R. 1972. Some formal properties of therapy talk. In Sudnow (1972:367–96).

Turner, R. 1976. Utterance positioning as an interactional resource. *Semiotica*, 17:233–54.

van Dijk, T. A. 1977. *Text and Context*. London: Longman.

van Dijk, T. A. (Ed). Forthcoming. *A Handbook of Discourse Analysis*, Volume 3, *Genres of Discourse*. London: Academic Press.

Watson, D. R. 1975. Tying down misunderstandings and other interactional uses of pro-terms. Department of Sociology, University of Manchester. Mimeo.

Watson, D. R. 1978. Categorization, authorization and blame negotiation in conversation. *Sociology*, 12:105–13.

Watson, D. R. 1981. Conversational and organisational uses of proper names: an aspect of counseller-client interaction. In P. Atkinson and C. C. Heath (eds.), *Medical Work: Realities and Routines*, pp. 91–106. Farnborough: Gower.

Watson, D. R. Forthcoming a. Some features of the elicitation of confessions in murder interrogations. In Psathas and Frankel (forthcoming).

Watson, D. R. Forthcoming b. The presentation of victim and motive in discourse: the case of police interrogations and interviews. *Victimology*, Special issue: Proceedings of the First World Congress of Victimology, Syracuse, Sicily.

Weber, M. 1968. *Economy and Society* (ed. G. Roth and C. Wittich). Totowa N.J.: Bedminster Press.

Weinreich, U. 1963. On the semantic structure of language. In J. Greenberg (ed.), *Universals of Language*, pp. 142–216. Cambridge, Mass.: MIT Press.

Weitz, S. (Ed.). 1974. *Nonverbal Communication*. New York: Oxford University Press.

Werner, H. 1956. Microgenesis and aphasia. *Journal of Abnormal and Social Psychology*, 52:347–53.

Wittgenstein, L. 1974. *Philosophical Grammar* (ed. R. Rhees, trans. A. J. P. Kenny). Oxford: Blackwell.

Wootton, A. 1981a. The management of grantings and rejections by parents in request sequences. *Semiotica*, 37:59–89.

Wootton, A. 1981b. Childrens' use of address terms. In P. French and M. Maclure (eds.), *Adult–Child Conversation: Studies in Structure and Process*, pp. 142–58. London: Croom Helm.

Wootton, A. 1981c. Two request forms of four year olds. *Journal of Pragmatics*, 5:511–23.

Yates, F. 1966. *The Art of Memory*. London: Routledge and Kegan Paul.

Zimmerman, D., and West, C. 1975. Sex roles, interruptions and silences in conversation. In B. Thorne and N. Henley (eds.), *Language and Sex: Difference and Dominance*, pp. 105–29. Rowley Mass.: Newbury House.

Index of names

441

Subject index